THE ORIGINS
OF PROSLAVERY
CHRISTIANITY

THE ORIGINS

OF PROSLAVERY

CHRISTIANITY

White and Black Evangelicals in Colonial and Antebellum Virginia

BY CHARLES F. IRONS

The University of
North Carolina Press
Chapel Hill

© 2008
The University of
North Carolina Press
All rights reserved

Designed by Jacquline Johnson
Set in Monticello
by Keystone Typesetting, Inc.
Manufactured in the
United States of America

The paper in this book meets the guidelines for
permanence and durability of the Committee on
Production Guidelines for Book Longevity of the
Council on Library Resources.

Library of Congress Cataloging-in-Publication Data
Irons, Charles F. (Charles Frederick)
   The origins of proslavery Christianity : white and
black evangelicals in colonial and antebellum
Virginia / by Charles F. Irons.
      p. cm.
   Includes bibliographical references and index.
ISBN 978-0-8078-3194-6 (cloth: alk. paper)
ISBN 978-0-8078-5877-6 (pbk.: alk. paper)
   1. Slavery and the church—Virginia—History.
2. Slavery and the church—Southern States—
History. 3. Slaves—Religious life—Virginia.
4. African Americans—Virginia—Religion.
5. Slaves—Religious life—Southern States.
6. African Americans—Southern States—Religion.
7. Turner, Nat, 1800?–1831—Influence.
8. Evangelicalism—Political aspects—Southern
States—History. I. Title.
E445.V8.I76   2008
241′.67509755—dc22
2007044530

cloth   12 11 10 09 08   5 4 3 2 1
paper   12 11 10 09 08   5 4 3 2 1

CONTENTS

MAPS, TABLES, AND ILLUSTRATIONS

Maps

Tables

Illustrations

ACKNOWLEDGMENTS

In 1915, Katharine Du Pre Lumpkin was a precocious nineteen-year-old college graduate. She had grown up in Georgia and South Carolina and knew well the racial mores of the American South. Lumpkin found these mores challenged when she attended a leadership conference sponsored by the YWCA late that year. Her YWCA leader encouraged Lumpkin to consider the parable of the Good Samaritan when deciding whether or not to allow an African American woman to address their group. The force of the parable overwhelmed Lumpkin's segregationist upbringing and launched her on a career in which she championed equal justice for all.[1]

I have often wondered why more white southerners in the colonial and antebellum periods did not have such conversion experiences. If the command to love one's neighbor made Lumpkin realize in 1915 that segregation was wrong, why did so few white southerners realize that race-based slavery was wrong? By all accounts, white southerners in the nineteenth century were among the most devoted Christians in the Western world, but their faith seems only to have strengthened their determination to hold another people in bondage. This book represents my attempt to understand this staggering moral failure—to understand why the parable of the Good Samaritan fell on deaf ears for so many generations. Both whites and blacks are the protagonists, for southern whites were the ones who taught themselves not to hear the parable's lesson, but African Americans were the ones who kept telling it.

While the subject matter of this book has often left me discouraged, the people whom I have met in the course of its creation have provided abundant inspiration and wise counsel. I first entered the world of nineteenth-century evangelicals at the University of Virginia, amid an extraordinary cohort of young historians that included Brian Schoen, Watson Jennison, Susanna Lee, Aaron Sheehan-Dean, John Riedl, Andrew Witmer, Johann

Neem, and Wayne Hsieh. Faculty members who left a particularly deep intellectual footprint include Joseph Kett, Joseph Miller, Heather Warren, and Grace Hale. Peter Onuf was an early influence, too, and he has become an increasingly valuable role model. He does not allow his own prodigious scholarship to detract from his careful mentoring of young scholars.

Archivists at several institutions have gone far beyond the call of duty to bring this project to fruition. The staff at the Albert and Shirley Smalls Special Collections Library at the University of Virginia has been incredible. Margaret Hrabe, Heather Riser, Regina Rush, Bradley Daigle, and Edward Gaynor have been especially generous with their time. Fred Anderson and Darlene Herod have always made me feel welcome at the Virginia Baptist Historical Society. Representatives of the other denominational collections in Virginia have been equally supportive. For their courtesy and professionalism, I am grateful to Laurie Preston of Randolph Macon (Methodist), Paula Skreslet of Union Theological Seminary (Presbyterian), and Julia Randle of Virginia Theological Seminary (Episcopal). Nelson Lankford, Lee Shephard, Frances Pollard, John McClure, and Paul Levengood have helped make the Virginia Historical Society my favorite place to work. A Mellon Fellowship in 2006 facilitated a particularly fruitful visit to that institution. I make frequent trips to Wilson Library at the University of North Carolina, where I have never met an unhelpful person, and to Duke University, where Elizabeth Dunn has worked occasional miracles.

At my own institution, Elon University, I have received course releases from the dean, department, and faculty that have made it possible to forge ahead on this research. Lynn Melchor, our interlibrary loan officer, and I are good friends now. Elon students Andrew Redman, Zachary Usher, Sean Barry, and—especially—Stephanie Murr checked citations. Most of all, I have appreciated the fellowship of my remarkably collegial department and the mentorship of Mary Jo Festle, Clyde Ellis, and Jim Bissett.

Much to my surprise, the "giants" in the field of southern history are quite accessible, and I have many colleagues to thank for their thoughtful suggestions. Mitchell Snay, Beth Schweiger, Vernon Burton, Jewel Spangler, Clarence Walker, Bill Link, Janet Lindman, Eric Burin, and Bob Calhoon all read early versions of one chapter or another and offered profound advice. Peter Wallenstein and Bertram Wyatt-Brown selected a very early version of Chapter 6 for inclusion in the edited volume *Virginia's Civil War* and offered helpful suggestions for how to develop the ideas further. Scot French, Jason Phillips, Randall Stephens, Luke Harlow, Ralph Luker, Seth Dowland, Greg Kimball, and many others answered questions and encouraged me with their interest in the project. Paul Harvey and an anonymous reader for the University of North Carolina Press read the most carefully and shaped most decisively the final product. They engaged the ideas in the manuscript at every level and forced me to clarify my thinking on several key issues. At the press, Katy O'Brien, Charles Grench, and Stephanie Wenzel have been patient and courteous. They make it a real privilege to publish with Chapel Hill.

Edward Ayers is the towering figure in my intellectual biography. His star has risen fast and far since I have known him, but he has always made time to discuss my work or my career. Not a day goes by in which I do not discover some new scholarly debt that I owe to him, and I hope that he recognizes in this book my attempt to follow in his footsteps.

My family has sustained me in this, as in every, endeavor. In addition to the myriad talents with which I was already familiar, I have learned that my mother happens to be a brilliant copyeditor. She, my father, and my two brothers have provided every form of emotional and logistical support imaginable. I am grateful.

My wife, Dana, has been living with this book for our entire married life. It is her support that has been the most essential, and her companionship that has been the sweetest. This book is dedicated to our daughter, Caroline Frances, in the hopes that she—like her namesake from Assisi—will understand the parable.

THE ORIGINS
OF PROSLAVERY
CHRISTIANITY

THE CHIEF CORNERSTONE

Wherefore also it is contained in the scripture, Behold, I lay in Sion a chief corner stone, elect, precious: and he that believeth on him shall not be confounded. Unto you therefore which believe he is precious: but unto them which be disobedient, the stone . . . [is] a stone of stumbling, and a rock of offence.—1 Peter 2:6–8

Black and white abolitionists in the nineteenth century identified churches, in the words of James G. Birney, as "the bulwarks of American slavery." While these critics of slavery did not spare northern congregations for their complicity in perpetuating the peculiar institution, they singled out southern churches for particular condemnation. Henry "Box" Brown, a fugitive from slavery in Virginia, asserted in 1849 that "there is not a particle of religion in their slaveholding churches. The great end to which religion is there made to minister, is to keep the slaves in a docile and submissive frame of mind." Birney and Brown lashed out at southern churches because they saw the enormous practical and ideological work that white southern Christians were doing to protect slavery. The region's white Christians penned compelling defenses of slavery for the secular and denominational presses, guarded against insurrection by policing worship meetings in the quarters, gave regional apologists grounds for boasting by converting thousands of slaves to their faith, and enabled those skeptical of slavery's justice to subvert their concerns through mission work among the enslaved. It is for good reason, then, that historians of slavery and of the sectional conflict have endorsed abolitionists' contention that the South's white Christians contributed decisive ideological support to an evil institution.[1]

At the same time, in Virginia and in other slaveholding states, white Christians shared many religious beliefs and experiences with the men and women of African descent whose enslavement they justified by faith and defended through their churches. For starters, most white and black Virginians who attended church—roughly 88 percent of them by 1850—identified themselves as evangelicals.[2] White and black evangelical Protestants agreed that they were all sinners, that Jesus Christ had died for their sins, and that God had called them into community with one another. Sunday morning only became the most segregated time of the week after the Civil War. Before emancipation, black and white evangelicals typically prayed, sang, and worshipped together. Though men claimed formal leadership of these congregations, and though whites typically relegated blacks to sweaty balconies or back-row pews, evangelical churches nonetheless contained a broader cross section of Virginians than did any other institution. Black and white, rich and poor, male and female—souls from every demographic background—found a place in the Lord's House.[3]

This book is about the interactions between those antebellum black and white Virginians who identified themselves across vast chasms of power as evangelical Protestants. It seeks to connect the two aforementioned truths: that it was evangelical whites who built the strongest defense of slavery, and that whites and blacks interacted constantly within evangelical communities. The central thesis is that white evangelicals forged their policies on slavery in response to the spiritual initiatives of black evangelicals. When whites theorized about their moral responsibilities toward slaves, in other words, they thought first of their relationship with bondmen and -women in their own religious communities. Moreover, African American Virginians were active players in this process of ideological negotiation; through their ecclesiastical choices, they largely determined the timing and nature of decisions that white evangelicals made about race and slavery. An appreciation of black agency within evangelical communities is therefore critical to understanding the evolution of the proslavery argument.

The emphasis here is on process and not outcome. This study confirms the basic narrative of evangelical participation in southern culture, a story, as one scholar has put it, of evangelicals' journey "from dissent to dominance."[4] But in charting evangelicals' rise from the margins of southern society in the colonial period into the mainstream by the nineteenth century, it offers new insights into the ways in which black southerners inadvertently helped to shape the proslavery argument through their individual and corporate actions. It also shows that nonslaveholding whites learned some of their most important lessons about proslavery in their churches. In evangelical congregations, whites from different economic backgrounds built a shared consensus on slaveowning by jointly receiving black converts into fellowship, helping to discipline black members, debating the relative duties of slaves and slaveowners, and seeking new strategies to attract black converts.[5]

To a large extent, this argument that black southerners strongly influenced the proslavery argument is the southern corollary to some of the best work on the origins of radical abolitionism in the North. James Huston showed that some abolitionists developed their hatred of slavery by witnessing its most brutal features, and John Ashworth argued that widespread black resistance to slavery was an essential precondition for both moral and political antislavery in the North.[6] Building on these observations, Paul Goodman, Richard Newman, John Stauffer, and others went on to demonstrate how central interracial relationships were to the antislavery movement. They found that white antislavery activists in the North learned immediate abolitionism from African Americans.[7] White, evangelical proslavery activists also had regular contact with African Americans. While these interracial relationships were predictably less egalitarian or cooperative in spirit than those in abolitionist circles, they were just as important in shaping whites' arguments about slavery.

Evangelicals were those Protestants who set themselves apart from Catholics, Anglicans, Congregationalists, and other Christians by their emphasis on a personal, saving experience of faith and their sense of mission. A brilliant cohort of transatlantic divines—including George Whitefield, John Wesley, and Jonathan Edwards—launched the evangelical movement in the mid-eighteenth century when they preached the importance of a "Second Birth," a conscious, emotional conversion experience. They rejected some of the forms and rituals of traditional Christianity in favor of less structured services so that, they hoped, worshippers could experience the presence of God rather than hide from saving faith behind ritual. In a postwar reminiscence, former Virginia slave Charlotte Brooks exemplified the evangelical attitude toward liturgy in her description of Louisiana Catholicism. "I never wanted them beads I saw others have," she explained, "for I just thought we would pray without any thing, and that God only wanted the heart."[8] Significantly, evangelicalism was a subset of Protestantism and not synonymous with it. Some Presbyterians and some Baptists, for example, resisted identification as evangelicals because they considered their Calvinism inconsistent with the direct personal appeals to conversion made by ministers of evangelical "heart religion," and some high church Episcopalians protested the movement within their denomination toward less formal services.[9]

A majority of white Virginians regularly attended an evangelical church by 1850. In that year, roughly 121,000 white Virginians claimed full membership in an evangelical Methodist, Baptist, Presbyterian, or Episcopal church. While at first blush this figure seems a small fraction of the state's 894,800 white residents, the distinction between full members and adherents reveals the scope of evangelical ascendancy. Nineteenth-century churchmen distinguished between those who enjoyed full fellowship and the much larger number who simply attended services. Prospective members had to give a public profession of faith before appearing on the rolls, which excluded most minors from membership. Moreover, church members set the bar high for new converts, and many adults attended church for years without having a conversion experience or growing confident enough in their faith to make a public profession. Historians have not yet worked out a reliable way to translate the very restrictive official membership lists into numbers of total adherents—into an accurate count of bodies in the pews. This task is difficult in part because the ratio of adherents to members appears to have changed over time and to have varied by denomination. It became easier to move from adherent to member during the course of the nineteenth century, for instance, and the membership rolls of Presbyterians and Episcopalians were consistently more restrictive than those of Baptists or Methodists. But even using the extremely conservative ratios that Henry Carroll calculated in 1890, the year for which there is the best available data, slightly more than one-half of white Virginians routinely attended evangelical services by mid-century, most of those in Baptist or Methodist churches. If anything, this figure understates the number of evangelicals and their cultural power in the late antebellum period, for it includes only the relatively committed believers and excludes occasional visitors.[10]

A similarly high proportion of black Virginians attended an evangelical church by 1850. Church statistics indicate that there were approximately 46,000 black Baptists in that year, 9,963 black Methodists, and roughly 400 African American Presbyterians and Episcopalians in full membership. There are potential problems using the same methodology to calculate the proportion of adherents in the commonwealth's back population, just as there are some problems with using the same term, "evangelical," to denominate black and white members of the same churches. The exigencies of slavery may have altered the ratio of adherents to members for African Americans in a variety of ways. Slaveowners may have restricted the movement of some would-be adherents and prevented them from attending church at all, for example, or white clerks may have practiced less precision in reporting black membership and blurred the line between member and adherent in the statistics. But these pressures tug the numbers both ways, and no multiplier takes into account those enslaved persons who listened to evangelical white itinerants but did not physically attend church on a consistent basis. Again using Carroll's ratios, roughly 40 percent of all black

Virginians (slave and free, and including a few Presbyterians and Episcopalians) regularly worshipped in an evangelical church.[11]

These prodigious numbers were the fruit of decades of work by white and black evangelists. As a table of the membership of the two largest evangelical denominations in 1790 and 1850 demonstrates, evangelicals reaped tens of thousands of converts between 1790 and 1850, and their numbers grew at a rate far exceeding that of the state's population. Methodists had the most success among white Virginians; Baptists, among black Virginians. Relative geographic areas of denominational strength contributed to the disparate racial makeup of the Baptist and Methodist churches. Much of the Methodists' strength in 1850 came from across the Alleghenies, where there were relatively few slaves or free blacks. Virginia residents in the Western Virginia and Holston conferences of the Methodist Episcopal Church, South, and in the Western Virginia, Pittsburgh, and Ohio conferences of the Methodist Episcopal Church contributed 24,892 whites and 1,515 blacks to official state membership totals. In contrast, Baptists were strongest in the Tidewater and Piedmont, where most of the state's African Americans lived, though there were also pockets of Baptist influence in the predominantly white counties of the west and southwest. Since this book focuses on the interactions between black and white evangelicals, congregations in the Tidewater and the Piedmont where these interactions were the most frequent receive the most attention.

Black churchmen, like other evangelicals, believed in the necessity of an emotional conversion experience, but there were distinctive features of African American faith and practice. Only a minority of enslaved men and women could read, for example, making literacy a less common if a still privileged part of black devotional practice. Black evangelicals also placed special emphasis on the role of the spirit and accommodated an African cosmology to a Christian God. Moreover, many who were enslaved gravitated with expectation to Old Testament stories of emancipation rather than to New Testament stories of redemption. Others have dealt insightfully with these and other important variations in African American religious experience.[12]

Even though there may have been differences in faith and practice, sometimes substantial, between black and white evangelicals, the fact remains that some black Christians chose to affiliate with a biracial evangelical church while other black Christians did not. Church membership was voluntary, even for slaves, so those who chose to unite with a body of white evangelicals were agreeing to share fellowship across racial lines. Because of

Table 1. Evangelical Baptists and Methodists in Virginia, 1790 and 1850

	Church members	Estimated total of members and adherents[a]	Members and adherents as a percentage of all Virginians (by race)
1790			
Whites	28,383	105,497	23.9
Baptists	15,391	60,025	13.6
Methodists	12,992	45,472	10.3
Blacks	9,353	35,106	11.5
Baptists	5,926	23,111	7.6
Methodists	3,427	11,995	3.9
Total	37,736	140,603	18.8
1850[b]			
Whites	110,452	403,533	45.1
Baptists	42,377	165,271	18.5
Methodists	68,075	238,263	26.6
Blacks	54,795	209,715	39.8
Baptists	44,832	174,844	33.2
Methodists	9,963	34,871	6.6
Total	165,247	613,248	43.1

Sources: U.S. Bureau of the Census, *First Census, 1790*, 48–50, and *Seventh Census, 1850*, 242–57; Asplund, *Universal Register*, 50, 89; Gardner, "Virginia Baptists and Slavery," pt. 2, 1259; *Minutes of the Methodist Conferences*; *Minutes of the Virginia Baptist Anniversaries* (1849), 61; *Minutes of the Virginia Baptist Anniversaries* (1851), 66; *Minutes of the Accomac, Albemarle, Columbia, Concord, Dan River, Dover, Goshen, James River, Middle District, Portsmouth, Rappahannock, Roanoke, Salem Union, Shiloh, Strawberry Baptist Associations* (1850); *Minutes of the Columbia and Goshen Associations* (1853); *Minutes of the Annual Conferences of the Methodist Episcopal Church, South*, and *Minutes of the Annual Conferences of the Methodist Episcopal Church* (1850–51). Please see Appendix A for more detail.

[a]Based on Henry Carroll's adherence ratios of 2.9 adherents per member for Baptists (including children) and 2.5 adherents (including children) per member for Methodists. These ratios are almost certainly low, because Carroll calculated them in 1890. Antebellum churches were both more rigorous in their examination of new members and more demanding in their discipline of existing members.

[b]Includes Virginia Baptists affiliated with the Baptist General Association of Virginia and Virginia Methodists affiliated with the ME Church, South, or ME Church.

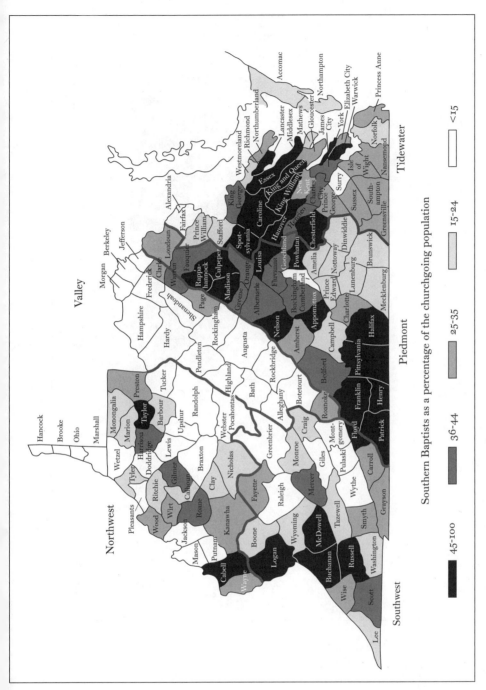

Map 1. Distribution of Virginia Baptists by County, 1860

Southern Baptists as a percentage of the churchgoing population

45–100   36–44   25–35   15–24   <15

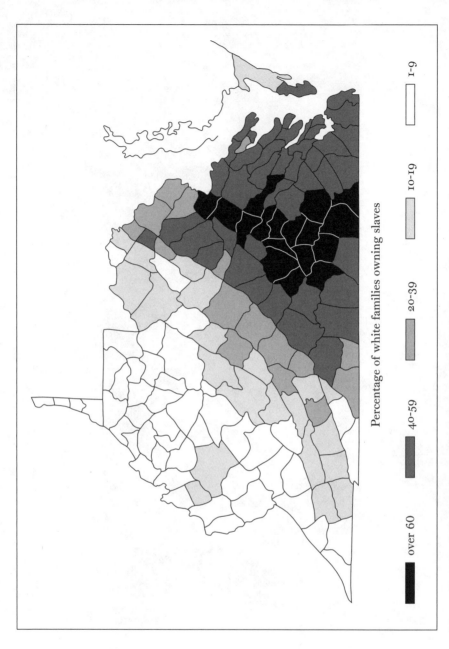

Map 2. Slaves and Slaveowning in Virginia, 1860 (from Link, *Roots of Secession*, 40)

Percentage of white families owning slaves

over 60 | 40-59 | 20-39 | 10-19 | 1-9

their physical proximity to white evangelicals and the mutual obligations that devolved upon them as members of the same spiritual communities, these churchgoers may be labeled evangelicals with some confidence. They were in a unique position to influence white evangelicals' thoughts and feelings about slavery.

The use of the term "evangelical" to describe African American Christians in the so-called invisible church of hush arbors and secret prayer meetings is more problematic. On one hand, there are good reasons to use the term for this population as well. Enslaved members of the visible and invisible churches worshipped together on many occasions; members of the invisible church learned the Gospel from evangelicals and accepted the necessity of conversion; and most whites saw continuity in black religious beliefs across the visible and invisible churches. On the other hand, there are compelling reasons to exclude members of the invisible church from the ranks of evangelicals. Most persuasively, these men and women openly denied white evangelicals' spiritual authority. Some black Virginians so forcefully rejected white evangelicals' version of Christianity that it is difficult to conceive of them as part of the same spiritual community. Furthermore, members of the invisible church more often accommodated African practices—conjure, for instance—and accepted heterodox versions of Christianity. Fields Cook learned in his childhood that he needed physically to visit heaven and hell before he could accept Jesus, an example of the kind of folk belief that persisted in the invisible church.[13] In light of these difficulties, the term "evangelical" in this text when applied to African Americans always refers to members of the visible church and, depending on the situation, may or may not include members of the invisible church as well. When necessary to distinguish between the two, alternative language, usually "Christians" or "members of the invisible church," denominates those who avoided biracial evangelicalism.

Virginia's numerically dominant white evangelicals not only worshipped alongside the state's African American evangelicals, but they also exercised a leadership role in defending their enslavement. Adherents to other religious traditions—including several thousand Quakers, Lutherans, Catholics, members of the Christian Church, and Jews—and tens of thousands of unchurched Virginians largely deferred to white evangelicals when it came to the central political and moral issue of the age. Even those outside the evangelical fold realized that the two most dangerous opponents of slavery, abolitionists and would-be insurrectionists, both drew on evangelicalism to add moral force to their positions. They therefore allowed white evangelicals, who had rehearsed proslavery arguments in response to the assertiveness of their black brethren or to the criticism of whites within their faith tradition, to take the lead in defending their state and region from slavery's critics. In this manner, evangelicalism—as negotiated by black and white Virginians—became the chief cornerstone of Virginia's slave society.

But this book is only incidentally about how white evangelicals' beliefs about slavery became politically salient or about the evangelical contribution to Confederate nationalism. Too much anticipation of the telos of the political narrative—fratricidal war and emancipation—distorts our understanding of southern religious history, for it tends to reduce religious commitment to a proxy for sectional or racial interests.[14] In many accounts, white evangelicals appear more focused on rebutting abolitionist accusations of wrongdoing and girding their region for war than on the salvation of souls, and blacks are committed to their faith only insofar as it offers them bodily or psychological liberation. I have attempted to treat religious commitment as an analytical category akin to that of race, class, or gender and not as simply another theater in which white southerners played out their struggle for sectional and racial supremacy. This attempt altered the work in two important ways: First, it provided a framework for understanding those actions by white evangelicals that worked against their individual or corporate interests in protecting slavery. Faith alone prevented evangelical whites from embracing polygenesis, for example, or from cutting off slaves from religious worship, even though both courses promised to increase their personal safety and regional honor. Second, it justified the inclusion of topics like evangelical unionism and conflict among black evangelicals, topics that only subtly influenced the proslavery argument. A broader view of nineteenth-century evangelicalism leads to an important secondary theme, that white southerners' religious commitment was never completely prostituted to the slave power; it sometimes abetted and sometimes inhibited slaveholders' political ambitions.

Though proslavery evangelicalism eventually became a regionwide phenomenon, the Virginia context of this study is meaningful. Not only was Virginia the largest and most populous of the slave states, but it was also the hearth of the evangelical movement in its southern manifestation. Already in 1790, Virginia claimed more Baptists than did any other state and roughly one in five of the nation's Methodists. Presbyterian and Episcopalian evangelicals, too, claimed important Virginia origins. The 1740s missionary work of Samuel Davies in Hanover County, a revival at Lexington's Liberty Hall Academy, and the reasoned defenses of evangelicalism penned by Virginian John Holt Rice showed Presbyterians that they could emphasize the Second Birth without abandoning their Reformed theological heritage entirely. Virginia's Episcopal bishops Richard Channing Moore and William Meade for a time in the early nineteenth century represented the *only* evangelicals in the Episcopal Church's national councils, though the trends that they initiated within their church gained widespread regional, even national, acceptance.

Black Virginians were also pioneers in the introduction of their version of evangelicalism to the South. By the late eighteenth century, after nearly six decades of natural population growth and a cessation of the African trade in 1778, Virginia's black residents were almost all native-born and generations removed from intact African religions. Though many still practiced African traditions dissociated from fully articulated belief systems (some of which they would ultimately incorporate into their practice of Christianity), enslaved opponents of evangelicalism had increasingly fragile cultural resources with which to resist conversion by the time of the Revolution. Mechal Sobel has artfully documented the process, which happened early in Virginia, through which African-based peoples synthesized West African and European religious traditions to forge an "Afro-Baptist Faith."[15] So many black Virginians became evangelicals in the late eighteenth century that Sylvia Frey and Betty Wood have identified the commonwealth as "the geographic source of the emerging black leadership."[16] These scholars named Virginia the "source" because African Americans from the commonwealth participated in a massive outmigration from 1790 through the beginning of the Civil War, taking their belief systems with them. In the 1830s alone, well over 100,000 African American slaves left Virginia, out of an overall slave population of about 450,000. Virginia was the wellspring both of ideas and, for states in the West, of settlers; white and black expatriates made the commonwealth the religious and cultural center of the antebellum South.[17]

Even if Virginia did not occupy such a central position in ecclesiastical and African American history, the exercise in confining the study to a particular location would nonetheless be profitable. Holding the geographic variable constant makes it easier to see white evangelicals' movement over time through successive varieties of proslavery.[18] When they began their colonial ministry in the mid-eighteenth century, neither evangelicals nor the Anglican churchmen with whom they competed saw any problem with African slavery, consonant as it appeared to be with the Old Testament permission to hold "heathen," whom they understood to be those outside God's covenant, in bondage. When black men and women of their own initiative joined evangelical churches in numbers that far surpassed white evangelicals' expectations, white evangelicals realized the irrelevance of the

Old Testament model of slavery and searched for new ways to understand a master-slave relationship in which both parties belonged to the community of faithful. White evangelicals thus embraced paternalism, the idea that master and slave owed each other reciprocal duties. From the perspective of evangelical whites, one of those responsibilities was "civilizing" people of African descent. Some white evangelicals followed the logic of their paternalist mission in the early national period to the idea that they were preparing slaves and free blacks for self-governance. They therefore tolerated black evangelicals' persistent attempts to exercise spiritual leadership and strongly supported—indeed, they led—the colonization movement.

Nat Turner abruptly brought an end in 1831 to this tolerance of black assertiveness. With his militant revolt against slaveholder authority, he precipitated a spiritual crisis over how much access whites should allow the enslaved to the Gospel. Whites' resolution of this crisis involved a determination to expand blacks' access to evangelicalism but to curtail autonomous black religious expression. In the resulting mission to the slaves, white evangelicals tried to defuse the liberating power of black Christianity by bringing as many enslaved and free black Virginians under their supervision as possible. The nature of whites' interactions with believers of color changed; whites cared more about bringing black bodies into their buildings than they did about preparing their African American coreligionists for colonization. This depersonalization of the terms of their exchange did not signal a lack of white responsiveness to black spiritual initiatives, however. In order to attract black Virginians into their churches, white evangelicals bent laws, built new spaces, wrote new catechisms, and otherwise labored to meet the expressed spiritual needs of black Virginians. White evangelicals encountered just enough resistance to their mission work from more secular proslavery whites to convince themselves that they were doing real good for their state's black residents, in contrast to northern abolitionists who were offering to black southerners only divisive moralizing. Disagreements between northern and southern evangelicals over the mission to the slaves contributed to the schisms of the Presbyterian, Baptist, and Methodist denominations in the 1830s and 1840s. In short, white evangelicals moved from one variety of proslavery to another as black evangelicals continually altered whites' perception of the peculiar institution.

Though it is tempting to reduce this series of complex shifts to one grand movement from antislavery to proslavery, this simplistic interpretation caricatures the complexity of white evangelicalism and overstates the antislavery credentials of eighteenth-century believers. Scholars who reduce their treatment of evangelicalism to an examination of the shift from antislavery to proslavery Christianity generally stress the materialist basis of proslavery evangelicalism. They argue that white southerners opportunistically turned to religion either to gain slaveholding members or to repel attacks by abolitionist activists. "The proslavery argument—horrible in its purpose of enforcing perpetual bondage upon a whole race of people—was yet an impressive example of how gymnastic, how muscular, how imaginative and driven the human mind can be under pressure," marveled Joel Williamson, for one.[19] Others have generally agreed with Williamson that, like southern politicians, southern divines invented ingenious new ways to justify their ownership of black men and women after encountering the scathing criticism of Garrisonian abolitionists in the 1830s. When southern whites cast about for some novel and decisive rebuttal of the antislavery assault, Anne Loveland suggests that "they found it in the Bible."[20] Evangelical leaders appear in this model as mere functionaries of the slaveholding elite, offering their rhetorical and organizational gifts to protect the property and persons of their most wealthy neighbors.

Those historians who write most empathetically about the faith commitments of white southerners have also stressed white evangelicals' decisive turn from egalitarianism to authoritarianism, for they are eager to create a usable Christian past by demonstrating ideological distance between "authentic" evangelicalism and its proslavery successor. These scholars describe the apostasy of white southern evangelicals from an egalitarian faith in the eighteenth century to a materialist one at some point in the nineteenth. Donald Mathews, perhaps the most influential student of southern religion and among the most theologically astute, wrote that white evangelicals regressed from the egalitarian and "morally halcyon days of the eighteenth century" to cultural captivity in the 1850s, by which time they were "so fettered by racism and social rank as to deprive [their religion] of the dynamic and celebratory mood which salvation in Christ theoretically should have conferred."[21] But there was no single moment of surrender, no crisp transition from authenticity to exploitation. The eighteenth century was not as glorious as these scholars imagine, nor was the nineteenth as morally bankrupt. While there were a very few eighteenth-century Jeremiahs, white evangelicals in the South never seriously threatened slavery. "For eighteen centuries," as E. Boyden of Albemarle County explained in 1860, "men understood the Scriptures to teach that slavery is an allowable institution, not a hideous sin, or any sin at all, however undesirable as an institution of the State."[22] White evangelicals' conviction that scripture supported their position and the tangible benefits they believed they were conferring on their black brethren also insulated the vast majority of them from the feelings of guilt that some historians have posited they must have harbored.[23]

All this is to say that white evangelicals forged their support for slavery in the context of their relations with enslaved men and women. They did not self-consciously prostitute themselves to their region's political interests, nor—except in the rarest instances—did they demonstrate any awareness of hypocrisy. There were doubtless some slaveowners as depraved as Frederick Douglass's onetime "master" Thomas Auld, who "found religious sanction and support for his slaveholding cruelty" and "made the greatest pretensions to piety."[24] Precisely how many, like Auld, claimed divine sanction for atrocious behavior only with a knowing wink of their lascivious or sadistic eyes, historians will never be able to discern with any precision. But historians can judge with confidence that for so many nonslaveholding evangelicals to endorse a biblical defense of slavery—and, more importantly, for so many hundreds of thousands of black Americans willingly to enter religious fellowship with slaveholders—the matrix of faith and self-interest that animated white evangelicalism must have been much more complicated than Douglass indicated.

Whereas Mathews, Christine Heyrman, and others have found in their study of white, southern evangelicalism interest-driven discontinuity, Eugene D. Genovese and Elizabeth Fox-Genovese have emphasized the steady unfolding of an increasingly rigorous proslavery argument from the foundational assumption of "religiously legitimated social cohesion."[25] Always attuned to the relationship of ideas to the means of production, they have suggested that northern evangelicals, caught up in the economic possibilities of the market revolution, began to prioritize liberation of the individual conscience over social order, whereas agrarian southerners maintained a household-based worldview long into the nineteenth century. In the Genoveses' interpretation, northerners were the theological innovators, discarding traditional Christian teachings on hierarchy and threatening atomization of communities by an embrace of wage labor. White southerners, in the Genoveses' view, responded aggressively to abolitionists not because northerners threatened slaveowners' property in persons, but because they threatened heresy and anarchy. The South's white evangelicals earnestly believed that all labor should be "contained within the household, in which it was supported and governed according to the principles of dependence. Labor that escaped household governance could plausibly be viewed as anomalous and disruptive."[26]

Black southerners play a relatively minor role in the Genoveses' account of proslavery Christianity. This is disappointing, given the couple's brilliant earlier work that demonstrated the rewards of incorporating the actions of black and white southerners in the same analytical framework.[27] Other scholars have demonstrated how profoundly enslaved persons shaped the ways in which whites thought about everything from family life to politics. Several have worked directly on the commonwealth. Anthony Iaccarino, for instance, showed how African American Virginians put enough pressure on their owners to shape the development of the first party system, and William Link placed enslaved persons at the center of his account of secession in Virginia. In some ways, this book is an ecclesiastical version of Iaccarino's and Link's political analyses; while they argue that Virginia slaves altered the political process, in this work I argue that slaves altered the ecclesiastical processes through which white Virginians forged a politically relevant proslavery argument.[28]

Though this book tries to restore some agency to black Virginians, that agency did not always take the shape of resistance to oppression. Church records—like all records accurately documenting life in a regime that depended on force for its survival—do contain hidden transcripts of struggle.[29] But resistance was not the sole defining factor of black Christianity; slaves and free blacks were interested in worshipping God as much as plotting rebellion or building racial consciousness. Moreover, black Christianity itself was not unitary; African American evangelicals sometimes clashed both with unchurched blacks and with one another. The number of disciplinary cases that black churchgoers initiated against one another that resulted in expulsion is sufficient evidence that black believers were not all part of the same quest for racial uplift. The model for this study, then, is not a Hegelian one of black action and white reaction. Virginians of African and European descent sometimes cooperated rather than collided, and sometimes they responded together to new social realities, like creolization or massive outmigration. Scholars such as Mechal Sobel, Sylvia Frey, Betty Wood, Paul Harvey, Vernon Burton, and Erskine Clarke, who have studied the reciprocal influence of black and white evangelicals on one another, have pioneered such an approach. In their own work, they have successfully captured how quotidian interactions could be opportunities for the exchange of ideas between racial groups.[30]

The focus here on the experiential origins of proslavery Christianity not only demands the inclusion of more black voices, but it also involves a different cast of characters than those in traditional accounts of antebellum evangelicals. Very often, despite the small proportion of Presbyterians in the southern population (and minuscule proportion of black, southern Presbyterians), a few Presbyterian divines stand in for all southern evangelicals, none more prominently than South Carolina's James Henley Thornwell. Michael O'Brien put it this way: "On the whole, intellectual sophistication was in inverse proportion to popularity. In numbers of adherents, the sequence from high to low ran Baptists, Methodists, Presbyterians, and Episcopalians. But, from most to least complex in dogma, it probably ran Presbyterian, Episcopalian, Methodist, and Baptist. So, an intellectual history might best be served by a look at the Presbyterians and Episcopalians. James Henley Thornwell was certainly the former's most sophisticated thinker and prominent conservative."[31] The contention in this book that actual contact between races was a precondition for ideological change leads in precisely the opposite direction; those environments in which slave and free interacted the most were the most significant.

Since evangelicals so privileged the authority of scripture, historians have appropriately devoted some energy to studying not only how white, southern evangelicals came to terms with slavery, but also how they came to terms with slavery in the Bible. The question of how white evangelicals who otherwise valued equality before the Lord could find scriptural justification for a practice so abominable as chattel slavery has inspired a lively debate. The Genoveses once again have emerged as the leading light on one side of the issue, arguing for the soundness of white southerners' use of the Bible. In their words, "To this day, the southern theologians' scriptural defense of slavery as a system of social relations—not black slavery but slavery per se— has gone unanswered, although some recent efforts deserve respectful consideration." Mark Noll has launched the most thoughtful of those recent efforts. He has argued that white Americans in the nineteenth century applied a faulty scriptural hermeneutic because of their assumptions about the nature of racial difference. In Noll's view, "It was the acceptance of black racial inferiority that supplied the missing term to many of the arguments that defended American slavery by appeal to scripture."[32] This book fits squarely with Noll's position and demonstrates the relational pathways that white evangelicals followed to their faulty hermeneutic. White evangelicals did not constantly adjust their defense of slavery because they discovered new passages in the Bible or developed new modes of interpretation, but because the terms of their relationships with black evangelicals changed.

In order to show how the sustained interaction between black and white Virginians shaped the development of Virginians' proslavery ideas and practices, I have prioritized the use of material authored by Virginians themselves. Sources external to the state appear only when recently expatriated Virginians generated them or when there is positive testimony that

Virginians read and valued those texts. The records of denominational organizations—of Baptist associations, Methodist conferences, Presbyterian synods, and Episcopal conventions—proved to be especially rich windows into the religious lives of African American evangelicals. These bodies were venues in which whites—and, very occasionally, blacks—debated ecclesiastical policies and to which individual congregations submitted invaluable reports about local events. Since a narrow majority of Virginia evangelicals (but the vast majority of black believers) were Baptists, it was important to move beyond the aggregate level to look at individual Baptist congregations. Minute books from the commonwealth's Baptist churches give an even more intimate view of interracial interactions than do the association records. Autonomous or semiautonomous black churches left some written material, but little other than folklore, shards of evidence from the narratives, or anthropological evidence survives for the equally important but more informal invisible church.[33]

Virginia evangelicals left other rich resources beyond these records of day-to-day events. Some among them published denominational newspapers, for example. The first of any duration, the Baptist *Religious Herald*, began publication in 1822. Particularly for the later chapters, these weekly papers have been an invaluable resource for showing how leading white clerics depicted their thoughts on slavery for a wide audience.[34] Still other white evangelicals published catechisms explicitly for the use of enslaved men and women, sermons or pamphlets on the peculiar institution, or manuals on how most effectively to minister to bondmen. Black Virginians, too, left their mark in the documentary record, most often in the form of narratives published after their escape from slavery. Black and white Virginians, the nation's most active participants in the colonization movement, together received ample press in the literature of the American Colonization Society, another useful published source. And, of course, since many evangelicals were also statesmen, politicians' speeches or editorials on slavery constitute an additional pool of information. Whenever possible, both in an effort to secure a lay perspective and to show the domestic context of so many of the interracial interactions, I have supplemented the public record by drawing upon private sources, primarily the unpublished letters and diaries of those Virginians who self-identified as evangelicals.

The range of these sources and the inclusion of information from black Virginians such as Lott Cary and Francis Fedric, who were fortunate enough to find a way out of slavery, does not, of course, compensate for the relative paucity of African American sources. It is a painful irony that a work insistent on the role of black evangelicals is able to bring so few, muffled voices to the fore. This lacuna is largely a function of the lack of sources, for Virginia's strict antiliteracy laws post-1831 effectively silenced a generation of believers.[35] But some of the weight on sources created by whites may come, in part, from my initial research into the topic of evangelical proslavery. In order to answer questions about the ideology of white slaveholders and their allies, I first turned to the works left behind by white proslavery apologists, as have all previous writers on the topic. From those sources, however, I learned that much of the story lay elsewhere, in the black community and with a scarcer paper trail. Hopefully, by documenting white preoccupation with the actions of black evangelicals I have advanced the case for black agency, even where it was impossible to capture those agents' own words.

The first chapter deals with the origins of evangelical churches in Virginia and the conversion of the first significant numbers of people of African descent. From the beginning, evangelicalism was a biracial enterprise. Early evangelical challengers to the established Anglican Church solicited African American membership and allowed a few blacks to share their ministry, albeit usually unequally. While the numbers of black converts were small before the Revolution, evangelical whites were nonetheless sensitive to criticism that they were upsetting the social order. They therefore explained that—far from destabilizing slavery—evangelical conversion changed the heart and made better slaves, a seminal moment in the evolution of proslavery. Many more black men and women joined evangelical churches after independence, particularly during the "Great Revival" of 1785–92. This cohort guaranteed a permanent African American presence within evangelicalism and gave early evangelicals' racially inclusive rhetoric a basis in empirical fact. By 1792, all observers knew that to be evangelical meant to share spiritual experiences across racial lines.

Chapter 2 discusses the reactions of whites and blacks to the Great Revival. Black evangelicals tried to push their new brethren to accept ideas of racial equality, at the same time that white evangelicals confronted the Revolutionary legacy of antislavery and adjusted to the loss of their status as religious outsiders. The potential dangers facing white evangelicals as they sought to resist black insubordination and affirm slavery's justice were myriad. Black evangelicals, who demonstrated their spiritual independence by aligning with antislavery clerics such as James O'Kelly, threatened to disrupt the growing evangelical movement if whites came down too decisively in slavery's favor. Rather than offend their black coreligionists or quarrel too much with one another, Virginia whites decided not to make any statements on slavery per se and to leave the issue in the hands of the civil government.

Even though Virginia evangelicals agreed to tolerate disagreement within their ranks on the justice of slavery, they also agreed that mass conversions meant that they could no longer treat their slaves as distant, "heathen" others. Out of this realization and the need to acknowledge their shared humanity with black believers came a more paternalist ideology of slaveholding.

From the end of the War of 1812 through 1831, as recorded in Chapter 3, southerners participated, albeit a bit less enthusiastically than did their northern counterparts, in building benevolent organizations. Among the new initiatives endorsed by both northern and southern evangelicals was the American Colonization Society, conceived largely by white Virginia evangelicals. Before experience revealed its awful limitations, even African American evangelicals in the commonwealth—but not in the North—supported colonization as a biblical response to slavery. Virginia blacks actually worked alongside whites to equip and to send the first colonists. Indeed, unity was the watchword of this period. Even as black and white evangelicals cooperated, Presbyterians and Episcopalians united with Baptists and Methodists to form what one scholar called an "evangelical united front" in the 1820s. White evangelicals conscious of the political divisiveness of slavery and committed to maintaining neutrality on the issue imagined a greater role for colonization than was, in fact, possible. Many taught their slaves to read and write; a few hundred manumitted slaves and funded their passage to Liberia; and all tolerated considerable independent black religious activity—for they assumed that such activity was consistent with true paternalism and a process of gradual preparation for freedom.

Nat Turner, identified by some as a Baptist preacher and prophet, provoked a severe spiritual as well as political crisis, explicated in Chapter 4. He and his followers killed nearly sixty whites, and white Virginians perceived the event as a spiritual calamity as well as a public safety emergency. Across the state, white evangelicals responded to the August 1831 insurrection by reexamining their attitude of stewardship toward black churchmen. Their belief in the necessity of sharing the Gospel made whites unwilling to eliminate black worship after the insurrection, although some anxious whites urged that that was the surest way to protect the public safety. Since many white evangelicals derived (or hoped to derive) their economic welfare from black labor, they were unwilling to eliminate slavery, either. The middle course that Virginia whites chose, a massive state-sanctioned and privately funded effort to organize enslaved evangelicals into faith communities where they could be supervised by whites, largely replaced colonization. In simpler terms, control replaced stewardship. Turner thus failed to free the state's blacks, but he successfully chained whites—at least white evangelicals—to a program of slave missions and to the conviction that slaveowning mandated a constant posture of spiritual oversight.

White evangelicals soon learned that oversight was not enough to bring Virginia blacks into their churches, especially on the restricted terms allowed by the state legislature after the Southampton Insurrection. Chapter 5 details how white evangelicals consulted across state and denominational lines about the best way to reach black Virginians. Ultimately, African American Virginians indicated to whites that they were most likely to join quasi-independent churches composed entirely of black evangelicals. Whites accordingly allocated money and personnel to build separate houses of worship or to facilitate separate worship services in the same buildings. This physical separation, especially evident in urban congregations, symbolized the growing emotional separation between white and black evangelicals. Whites were more responsive to black evangelicals than ever, but their motivation was conditioned less by interpersonal relationships and more by a desire to bring blacks into the safety of the visible church.

Northern evangelicals were skeptical of the mission to the slaves, and many insisted that southern whites emancipate their enslaved brethren instead of pursing their conversion. White Virginia evangelicals led southerners out of national denominational organizations as a result of this conflict over how best to care for black members. In the increasingly rancorous sectional conflict, the quasi-independent churches that black Virginians had formed in the state's towns and cities became rhetorical treasures for white Virginians, who began to regard these thriving congregations as normative of slave religion. Whites attributed to clerics associated with these missions considerable spiritual and political influence. The thriving churches were the best evidence white southerners could offer to prove that God approved of slavery.

Black Virginians take a lower profile in Chapter 6, which explores how white Virginia evangelicals, who had led the mission to the slaves and the charge for ecclesiastical secession in the 1830s and 1840s, somewhat incongruously acted as convinced unionists during the political crisis of the late 1850s and in the secession winter of 1860–61. The key contribution of the section is that white evangelicals' support for slavery, which was very firmly established by the late 1850s, did not necessarily lead evangelicals to support disunion; politics and religion followed divergent—not reinforcing —trajectories in the Upper South. This chapter therefore validates the preceding ones by showing that proslavery evangelicals did not forge their proslavery arguments only in order to advance a sectionalist agenda, but through a more complex process of racial interaction. Virginia ministers counseled their flocks that secession was sinful until all contractual means for the resolution of conflict over slavery had been exhausted. Once Lincoln's call for troops signaled to them the North's abandonment of constitutional processes in favor of the force of arms, though, white Virginians no longer felt any moral scruples against secession. Their reluctance to secede for overtly materialist reasons gave white Virginia evangelicals the perception that they possessed the moral high ground when they finally departed the union, and they threw themselves into the service of the Confederacy with self-righteous passion.

Black evangelicals, meanwhile, seized the opportunities that war afforded them to flee from white churches and from white supervision of their spiritual lives. With astounding celerity during and immediately following the Civil War, African American Virginians established their own, fully independent congregations. In so doing, black churchgoers offered a powerful and enduring critique of the proslavery Christianity to which white evangelicals had introduced them.

Chapter One

FISHERS OF MEN, 1680–1792

And he saith unto them, "Follow me, and I will make you fishers of men."
—Matthew 4:19

Anglo-Virginians and African Virginians had a long history of interaction in the Old Dominion before some of them became evangelicals in the 1730s. Despite fluidity in the colony's early years about the legal status of people of African descent, that history was generally a one-sided story of exploitation.[1] This was true in an ecclesiastical as well as an economic and personal sense. Just as English colonists coerced labor from African bodies and offered precious little in return, so too they suppressed African belief systems but did not invite Africans into their Anglican churches. Until the very end of the eighteenth century, as one scholar put it, "most of the slaves lived and died strangers to Christianity."[2]

Sympathetic reformers within the Anglican Church blasted Virginia divines for their unwillingness to pursue the souls of black Virginians (or of Indian peoples, for that matter). Failure to do so, they argued, eroded Anglicans' claim to be the spiritual shepherds of all Virginians and was in open defiance of the ministers' early charge to preach to the "salvage people which doe or shall adjoine unto them, or border unto them."[3] Both an evangelical faction within the Anglican Church and a number of ministers from dissenting sects took up this critique of "Virginia's Mother Church" when they arrived in Virginia in the 1730s and after. They hoped to distinguish themselves from traditional Anglicans through their attention to black Virginians. Africans and African Americans, for their part, helped to expose the limits of the Anglican Church's spiritual reach by responding only haltingly to Anglicans' late and desultory efforts to convert them. They were much more receptive to dissenting evangelical ministers, especially in the post-Revolutionary period. Black Virginians' decision to listen to dissenters simultaneously helped to destroy the Anglican Church and to cement evangelicalism's biracial character. Furthermore, Virginia's African American converts repeatedly asserted that liberation should accompany conversion and thereby forced both Anglicans and evangelicals to explain the relationship between slavery and Christianity in new ways.

Anglo-Virginians and African Virginians in the seventeenth century were not as far apart doctrinally as Anglo-Virginians may have assumed. Some of the Africans who disembarked a Dutch man-of-war onto Virginia soil in 1619 bore Portuguese names, evidence that they had received baptism into the Catholic Church. There are few records of precisely how the commonwealth's Anglican churches accommodated these Catholic interlopers, though the shared Christian heritage of Atlantic creoles and Virginia's English settlers may have been one of the reasons that Anglo-Virginians in the colony's first decades did not automatically assume that all men and women of African descent would be slaves for life. The names of free blacks living in Virginia in the 1640s, such as Emanuel Driggous, Bashaw Ferdinando, and John Francisco, illustrate the success that some people of color who arrived in Virginia as baptized Christians had in escaping slavery. Others who converted while living in Virginia also pressed the connection between Christianity and freedom. Several men and women of African descent sued in court for their freedom in the colony's first decades on grounds that it was unlawful for Christians to hold one another in bondage.[4]

The demographic composition of the African arrivals and the occasional flexibility of Virginia's laws had changed by 1705. Anglo-Virginians had been importing bonded laborers directly from Africa for more than a generation when, in that year, members of the colony's elected assembly, the House of Burgesses, passed a comprehensive slave code. A few of the forced migrants who flooded into the commonwealth from Africa had knowledge of Christianity, and others practiced Islam; but the vast majority practiced African traditions foreign to Anglo-Virginians.[5] White Virginians who wanted to preserve their access to bonded labor and who perceived a growing cultural distance between themselves and these new arrivals described Africans as "savages" or "heathens" and used this definition to justify their perpetual enslavement.[6] Whites at the same time increased their financial commitment to African labor and intensified this sense of cultural difference by purchasing new slaves at a furious rate over the next several decades, roughly 1,000 persons per year between 1700 and 1740. This figure often surpassed the annual totals for voluntary European immigrants, and by 1760, more than 40 percent of Virginia's population was African-based.[7] In the context of such a tremendous influx of non-Anglican peoples, white authorities gave less weight to individual conversions and emphasized instead the unchurched status of the group. Since most African arrivals were not Christian, Anglicans felt justified in enslaving them.

Anglo-Virginians found in their King James Bible a description of Hebraic slavery that seemed to correspond perfectly to the labor patterns that emerged in the commonwealth during the late seventeenth century. English indentured servants, most of whom were baptized while infants into the Anglican Church, were the equivalent of the biblical *ered ivri* (Hebrew slaves), while men and women of African descent fit the description of *ered canaani* (non-Hebrew slaves). By law, the Israelites could not keep Hebrew slaves in bondage beyond a jubilee every seven years, roughly the terms of an indenture. They could, however, place those outside their covenant relationship with God into perpetual, hereditary slavery. As the summary of the Hebraic slave code in Leviticus indicates,

> Both thy bondmen, and thy bondmaids, which thou shalt have, shall be of the heathen that are round about you; of them shall ye buy bondmen and bondmaids. Moreover of the children of the strangers that do sojourn among you, of them shall ye buy, and of their families that are with you, which they begat in your land: and they shall be your possession. And ye shall take them as an inheritance for your children after you, to inherit them for a possession; they shall be your bondmen for ever: but over your brethren the children Israel, ye shall not rule one over another with rigour.[8]

Some seventeenth-century Anglicans did believe that the Curse of Ham in Genesis 9 justified the enslavement of Africans, but most did not need to appeal to this mythology in the light of such a clear scriptural distinction between the servitude of Christians and non-Christians.[9]

Anglicans in Virginia who accepted this religious distinction between slave and free could not make the imaginative leap of including people of color in the body of Christ. They cited myriad difficulties in ministering to slaves, especially the linguistic and cultural differences between African arrivals and Englishmen. Many whites felt that such a gulf, in terms of both language and customs, made either conversion or true communion impossible. When Governor Francis Nicholson sought legislation in 1699 to spur the conversion of Indians and Africans, the burgesses protested that he was asking too much. People of African descent, the burgesses explained, were extremely unlikely converts, owing to the "Gros Barbarity and rudeness of their Manners, the variety and Strangeness of their Language and the weakness and shallowness of their Minds."[10] Anglo-Virginians complained of these obstacles into the eighteenth century, despite contemporary evidence that the difficulty of communicating the fundamentals of their faith might not have been so insurmountable, after all. Also in the seventeenth century, Portuguese settlers in South America routinely overcame the language barrier between them and their chattel by using a small corps of African Christians—mostly Kongolese—to catechize victims of the Atlantic slave trade. Protestant Englishmen only lacked access to a ready cadre of African catechists because they failed to recruit one following importation.[11] Moreover, Anglican clergymen readily devised means to communicate with illiterate Englishmen and Algonquin-speaking Indians. New Englander John Eliot translated the Bible into Massachusett in 1663, and the challenge for southern divines of learning African dialects should not have differed by degree.

Slaves themselves made swift religious assimilation impossible, for Africans carried with them across the middle passage their own, durable belief systems. Men and women of African descent indicated a strong preference for remembered African traditions, for Islam, or, in the case of the Kongolese, a form of Catholicism. Though wars within Africa, the transatlantic voyage, and the auction block had a way of separating slaves with similar ethnic and theological origins, most Virginia slaves nonetheless retained some beliefs from their parents. There is considerable evidence for the vitality of these African traditions. In some cases, slaves from different West African ethnicities cobbled together a synthetic African religion, labeled by subsequent observers as "conjure" or "voodoo." In others, ethnic enclaves enabled some men and women to keep ancestral traditions alive into the nineteenth century.[12] As a result either of their adherence to African or African-based religions, of their contempt for the beliefs of their enslavers, or of the profound difficulty of communicating on a substantive theological level with white Anglicans, Virginia's African slaves spurned the Church of England from the time of their arrival throughout the colonial period.

Africans, along with Indians and dissenters who also remained outside the Anglican Church, forced Anglicans to adopt a more limited understanding of the nature of their religious establishment. At the beginning of their sojourn in Virginia, English settlers had believed that their colonial church should encompass all of the colony's residents, and their initial treatment of Indians reflected this understanding. In the relatively peaceful year of 1617, the colonists' enthusiasm for inclusion of Indians within the Anglican Church peaked. Flushed with the triumph of Pocahontas's Anglican baptism and subsequent journey to England, Anglo-Virginians planned a system of schools for Indians—hoping to facilitate similar cultural and religious transformations. One generous English donor to the proposed schools suggested that Indian children might be trained until the age of twenty-one, then given the same liberties as Englishmen. Opechancanough, powerful heir to the Powhatan Confederacy and kinsman of Pocahontas, brought all such dreams abruptly to an end when he led a devastating uprising against the Virginia English in 1622. His warriors killed 347 people, roughly one-quarter of the colony's white residents. Colonialists then defined even geographically proximate Indians as outside and antagonistic to their community—and therefore excepted from the obligation of attending Anglican worship.[13] Anglo-Virginians who still expressed a desire to convert and acculturate the Powhatans after this point generally restricted their proselytization to the native peoples whom they held in slavery. White Virginians from the 1620s through the 1670s thus conceived of Indian slavery as a way to facilitate conversion but recognized most Powhatans as beyond their reach.[14]

The absence of Africans from the established church was more theologically problematic than was that of the Powhatans. Anglo-Virginians could cultivate the fiction that Indians belonged outside the geographic bounds of their settlements, but they invited Africans into their most intimate spaces to perform their domestic and agricultural labor.[15] Virginia blacks were thus undeniably parishioners of the colonial establishment, even if, as John Nelson explained, "few among them would have considered themselves as such" or "few, if any, of the dominant white inhabitants would have been willing to acknowledge it."[16] Rather than compel bonded African immigrants or the Scotch-Irish immigrants who came voluntarily into the commonwealth in the 1730s to join their churches or adopt their beliefs, Anglican Virginians simply abandoned the hope of a spiritually homogenous state. Enslaved Africans, by remaining outside Anglican worship, had demolished the establishment's claim to universality. "What was left," in one historian's analysis, "was the derivative understanding of establishment: official confirmation and recognition, tax support, governmental surveillance, and special benefits and immunities" for a specific denomination.[17] These special benefits were not enough to enable the Church of England to reach all Virginians, but they were burdensome enough that dissenters from the Anglican Church deeply resented its establishment.[18]

Despite whites' decision not to introduce slaves to Anglicanism and thereby to jeopardize the correspondence between "slave" and "heathen," some slaves expressed a persistent desire for admission into Virginia churches. Anglicans thus needed to clarify whether or not conversion affected a slave's civil status. Many rightly feared that bondmen and -women might expect conversion to lead to emancipation, much as it had for Muslim and African slaves in medieval Europe. Legally savvy blacks such as Elizabeth Key, who won her freedom in 1656, and Fernando, who found his suit for liberty denied only because the judges could not (or would not) translate his Portuguese baptismal certificate, hastened a pronouncement from ecclesiastical and civil authorities by bringing the conflict between conversion and slavery to a head.[19] In late 1667, Virginia's General Assembly, which created the laws governing the establishment of religion, passed a statute denying that baptism implied manumission and closing such a route to freedom. Black Christians, even at this early stage, were already forcing whites to explain how Christianity and slavery were compatible.

Within the text of the statute, the burgesses offered a novel explanation for why they accepted the enslavement of their fellow Christians. It was important for converted Africans to remain in slavery, they argued, because the liberation of those such as Elizabeth Key created a powerful disincentive for planters to allow their slaves access to the Gospel. With this neat rationalization, the burgesses tried to recapture the moral high ground from the enslaved men and women who were calling on Anglo-Virginians to recognize their shared humanity. The burgesses framed themselves as the compassionate ones, suggesting in the statute "that diverse masters, ffreed from this doubt, may more carefuly endeavour the propagation of christianity by permitting children, though slaves, or those of greater growth if capable, to be admitted to that sacrament."[20] The law did not immediately bear fruit, and few if any slaveowners undertook new efforts to convert their slaves after the passage of the law. This lack of missionary activity allowed Anglo-Virginians' association between "African" and "heathen" to remain intact for a few more decades. But the law created the theoretical possibility that Virginia slavery could continue even if that association somehow disappeared. It was thus a critical step in the transition of Virginia slavery into a system based on arbitrary racial differences rather than religious distinctions.

Morgan Godwyn, a passionate Anglican minister who was in Virginia when the burgesses passed the 1667 statute, was distraught that so many slaveholders were neglecting African souls. He recognized that failure to include blacks in the Anglican communion represented a departure from Anglican ideals and tried in vain to call his fellow churchmen to task for their sins of omission. Arriving in Virginia in 1665 or 1666, Godwyn perceived immediately the failure of whites to reach out spiritually to slaves and began chastising his parishioners for it. He continued to rebuke them after the passage of the law, which theoretically should have removed their objections to slave conversions. The minister was so strident in his advocacy for African Virginians that he soon wore out his welcome among Anglo-Virginians. He left the commonwealth in disgrace in 1670 but continued his crusade from afar, broadening his critique to include English treatment of slaves in Barbados as well.[21]

In a 1680 pamphlet titled *The Negro's & Indians Advocate, Suing for their Admission into the Church: or a Persuasive to the Instructing and Baptizing of the Negro's and Indians in our Plantations*, Godwyn identified white Barbadians' and Virginians' failure to incorporate slaves into the Anglican Church as "no less than a manifest Apostacy from the Christian Faith." Accurately forecasting strategies that dissenters would use to criticize the established church, Godwyn warned that Anglicans' inattention to blacks exposed Anglicans to legitimate charges of inconsistency. Indeed, he warned, Quakers were already making such accusations. "For shame cease to call your selves *Christ's Ministers*," he quoted one Quaker critic of the church as saying, "unless you will be contented to work in Christ's *Vineyard*, to preach his Doctrine truly, and to exhort and edifie *the poor of his Flock*, as he commanded you; and to testifie both to small and great, *bond and free*, (as his Apostles and Ministers did)." Godwyn adopted the Friends' line of attack against his own codenominationalists and insinuated that whites unwilling to invite blacks into their congregations should not even call themselves Christians, much less pretend to a lively establishment.[22]

At the same time that Godwyn demanded that blacks be included within the Church of England, he inadvertently helped engender a powerful pro-slavery argument. In seeking to overturn whites' objections to black participation in parish life, he not only cited the 1667 statute that conversion would not lead to emancipation, but he went much further and assembled a list of reasons why slaves' conversion was in slaveowners' best interest. In prioritizing the goal of bringing all ethnicities under the care of the church, Godwyn was apparently willing to leave intact the hierarchical relationship between masters and slaves. To this end, he argued too forcefully against owners' reservations about slave conversion and insisted that access to Anglican teaching would make enslaved men and women more efficient and less insubordinate: "So that this *Authority* of the *Master* is so far from being hereby diminished," he insisted, "that it is rather confirmed, and a stricter observance for that cause charged upon the Servants *Conscience*." The minister's own words elsewhere in his most famous pamphlet suggest strongly that Godwyn made such claims only for rhetorical effect and that he was actually opposed outright to chattel slavery. But his audience heeded the prophetic minister's concessions to slaveowners more than they did his criticism of slavery.[23] White Virginians in the late seventeenth century still did not take any substantive steps to expose their slaves to Anglicanism, but they gained from Godwyn the conviction that when bondmen or bond-women did find their way into a church, conversion would only reinforce whites' claims to mastery.

In the half-century following Godwyn's diatribe, Virginia Anglicans continued to ignore the tens of thousands of unconverted slaves among them, even as they embraced the idea that conversion did not threaten slavery. They drew additional confirmation of this idea from William Fleetwood's 1705 *The Relative Duties of Parents and Children, Husbands and Wives, Masters and Servants*, in which the author taught that God had ordered the world in a series of overlapping hierarchies—and that baptism left those hierarchies intact.[24] Like Godwyn, Fleetwood also advocated recruitment of slaves into the church, so much so that he helped organize in 1701 the Society for the Propagation of the Gospel in Foreign Parts (SPG) to promote the Christianization of American Indians, slaves, and others unreached by the Gospel. The SPG sent out dozens of missionaries to the American colonies, but none to Virginia. The decision by SPG officials to bypass the commonwealth indicated, on one hand, the relative strength of the Anglican Church in Virginia. On the other hand, it indicated that white Virginians did not consider the proselytization of their slaves a high enough priority to ask for assistance from the SPG.[25] The bishop of London tried to address lingering reluctance to include Africans in Anglican worship in a 1727 letter heavily influenced by Godwyn and Fleetwood. He blessed the burgesses' legal and theological innovation of 1667 and assured Chesapeake slave-holders that conversion would not change slaves' civil status. "And so far is Christianity from discharging Men from the Duties of the Station and Condition in which it found them," he explained, "that it lays them under stronger Obligations to perform those Duties with the greatest Diligence and Fidelity."[26]

Virginia Anglicans in the early eighteenth century were still more willing to invest in the conversion of Indians than Africans. Even when they acknowledged the general theological problem of living in close proximity to unconverted "heathen," they tended to make specific plans only to minister to Indians. In the context of white Virginians' decision—unthinking or not—to replace indentured servants with enslaved Africans, the commonwealth's Anglicans with missionary zeal channeled their energy at native peoples. Thus, officials in Williamsburg passed the first comprehensive slave code in 1705 while at the same time inviting more Indians to attend William and Mary for education and acculturation. And thus Governor Alexander Spotswood in 1711 called the dearth of Indian and black converts "no small reproach both to our Religion and Politicks after above a whole Century that the English hath been . . . here." He then attempted to create an additional school for Virginia Indians but gave no attention to slaves.[27]

It was not until 1724 that roughly one-third of Virginia's Anglican clergymen, as measured by a questionnaire sent out by the bishop of London, were finally willing to admit in principle the desirability of ministering to Africans and African Americans. The bishop asked seventeen questions of the colonial clergy over whom he had oversight, including, "Are there any Infidels, bond or free, within your Parish; and what means are used for their conversion?" Eleven of the twenty-eight respondents noted that they were interested in obtaining slave conversions, and the uniquely enterprising minister from Accomack Parish even claimed to have baptized about 200. That a relatively large fraction of clergymen expressed a desire to bring blacks into the Anglican fold, several even claiming that they "had exhorted Masters to send their slaves to church," represented an important shift toward inclusion.[28] However, even these boosters complained that few masters ever responded to such exhortations. Furthermore, almost two-thirds of the divines continued to ignore slaves entirely, a few with open hostility to their conversion. The cleric from St. Mary's Parish wrote only, "Particular means discouraged," and the rector from Wilmington acknowledged that "the Negroes generally live and die without the Christian religion." Perhaps most revealing of all, not even the eleven clerics most aggressive in evangelizing slaves included black men or women in their official tally of communicants or families in their parish—or in their estimation of what proportion of their parishioners attended weekly services.[29] Some Anglicans may have professed a desire to convert slaves to Christianity, but, in practice, they still considered people of color invisible in an ecclesiastical sense.

While white Anglicans took the first, halfhearted steps to include slaves in their churches between 1680 and 1730, black Virginians who converted continued to insist that slavery and Christianity were incompatible. White Virginians ultimately learned that they could not keep the 1667 statute in abeyance until a particular African or African American convert demanded his or her freedom. Instead, blacks' efforts to link conversion with liberation were so widespread that whites needed to make an apology for slavery a part of their presentation of the Gospel to black Virginians. Whites still had not learned to communicate to prospective converts the compatibility of slavery and Christianity forcefully enough by 1730, when baptized slaves rose up to seize the liberty they believed was their due in the Chesapeake Rebellion of 1730.[30]

In an irony that demonstrated both black Virginians' spiritual independence and white Anglicans' enduring lack of interest in black Christianity, baptized slaves planned their insurrection for Sunday morning, when whites would be at church without them. It is an arresting image: whites meeting serenely to read through Morning Prayer and perhaps to hear a sermon or to receive the sacrament, totally uninterested in the spiritual lives of their bondmen—who even at that moment were acting on their own faith and leaving their chains behind. These Africans, among whom probably ranked some Kongolese Christians, erroneously believed that George II had declared all baptized slaves free but that Virginia's officials had suppressed that mandate. Between 200 and 300 slaves selected leaders, "commit[ted] many outrages against the *Christians*," and fled into the swamps of Norfolk and Princess Anne counties. Vengeful whites and their Indian allies apprehended the group fairly quickly and killed at least 29 of them. James Blair, the Anglican commissary in Virginia, reported on the event in a 1731 letter to England, indicating that "there was a general rumor among them that they were to be set free. And when they saw nothing came of it they grew angry and saucy, and met in the night time in great numbers."[31] This episode confirms that Elizabeth Key and Fernando were not the only black Virginians who equated spiritual and civil freedom—or who acted on that equation in a manner sure to gain white attention. It also helps explain why those whites most outwardly concerned with the welfare of enslaved men and women, Godwyn and his successors, felt the need publicly to affirm the practice of slaveholding.

Many of the participants in the 1730 rebellion were African-born. Anglican priests who completed their bishop's 1724 survey had despaired at the prospect of catechizing first-generation slaves like these, even though some of these men and women had prior exposure to Christianity. A few ministers expressed the hope that enslaved men and women born in America might be more open than were their forebearers to conversion without liberation. The ministers from Elizabeth City, Blisland, Petsworth, Middlesex, and Overwharton each identified generational differences among Virginia slaves and speculated that the younger generation would be more tractable. "The owners are generally careful to instruct those that are capable of instruction and to bring them to baptism," came word from Elizabeth City, "but it is impossible to instruct those that are grown up before they are carried from their own country." An Anglican divine on leave from labors in Virginia at the time of the survey, Hugh Jones, published from London an account of religion in Virginia in which he also cited strong generational differences. "But as for baptizing wild Indians and new Negroes," he shuddered, "I question whether Baptism of such (till they be a little weaned of their savage

Barbarity) be not a Prostitution of a Thing so sacred. . . . But as for the Children of Negroes and Indians, that are to live among Christians, undoubtedly they ought all to be baptized."[32] Jones's language not only suggested that creolization might change patterns of racial and ecclesiastical interaction, but it also indicated how thoroughly Virginia Anglicans had accepted the link between whiteness and Christianity, and between darker skin tones and savagery.

These clerics were closely attuned to changes in the demographic makeup of the Old Dominion, for they were writing at the same time that the enslaved population was beginning to grow by natural increase and the proportion of American-born slaves was rising. Chesapeake slaves enjoyed more balanced gender ratios and a lower mortality rate than did those men and women consigned to the Caribbean, but even so, the birth rate for Virginia slaves did not surpass the death rate until about 1710. By the 1730s, the number of children born into Virginia slavery exceeded the number carried into it through the Atlantic trade.[33] Overall, the trend was toward creolization and creation of an African American identity, but there were important subregional variations. Slaves in the more established Tidewater area experienced natural population growth first, but those in the fast-growing Piedmont remained largely foreign-born until just a few years before the Revolution.[34] By the imperial crisis, though, natural increase accounted for almost 90 percent of the slaves added to the colony. In 1778, confident that they had a fecund enough domestic source of perpetually unfree laborers, planters in the General Assembly cut off the international slave trade. They thereby ensured that native-born African Americans would form a higher proportion of the commonwealth's enslaved population every year.[35] By 1800, at least four of five Virginia slaves, and probably closer to nine of ten, had been born in the commonwealth.[36]

Evangelicals, and not traditional Anglicans, successfully exploited this demographic transformation. Some early evangelicals, of course, were Anglican, most notably George Whitefield, the "Divine Dramatist." Whitefield was the most important member of a transatlantic cohort of divines who helped initiate the so-called First Great Awakening.[37] He was an ordained Anglican minister and a forebearer of the Methodist faction within the Church of England. He and his Methodist successors tried to inspire in their auditors an emotional conversion, in which the converts recognized their dependence on divine grace and experienced a powerful change of heart. Methodists initially believed that it was possible to have this change without abandoning the forms of Anglican worship and remained for many years within the Anglican fold.[38] Other evangelicals, notably Baptists and

Presbyterians, operated outside the Anglican tradition. Baptists' and Presbyterians' ecclesiology accommodated the evangelical insistence on a second birth more readily, because Baptists and Presbyterians limited their membership to those who had already had a conversion experience. By law, Anglicans in colonial Virginia determined parish membership primarily based on geographic location.

Evangelical Methodists, Presbyterians, and Baptists, from their first experiences in the American South, fixed themselves firmly in the tradition of Morgan Godwyn. Like the earlier Anglican reformer, they called whites to account for their failure to minister to the enslaved. By consistently and sometimes provocatively upbraiding traditional Anglicans for their lack of interest in the enslaved, evangelicals intended to communicate to white and black Virginians two things: that the Anglican Church had failed in its duty to provide for the spiritual welfare of all its parishioners and that everyone, from the highest to the lowest in society, needed a saving relationship with God.[39]

George Whitefield himself spent little time in Virginia but nonetheless modeled for subsequent evangelicals how they could make concern for slaves an integral part of their ministry. Whitefield passed very briefly through the commonwealth on his first visit to British North America and preached in Williamsburg at the invitation of Commissary James Blair in December 1739.[40] This foray into the religious life of the Old Dominion did little to upset the status quo; unlike in Georgia or in South Carolina, there were neither confrontations with the commissary over itineration nor any subsequent schisms. Soon after the visit, however, Whitefield published from Philadelphia an open letter that scandalized white Virginia Anglicans, addressed "to the Inhabitants of *Maryland*, *Virginia*, *North* and *South-Carolina*, concerning their Negroes."

In his letter Whitefield made advocacy on behalf of the enslaved the foundation of his campaign for spiritual renewal in the South. "I have lately passed through your Provinces in my Way hither," he wrote only five weeks after leaving Williamsburg, and "I was sensible touched with a Fellow-feeling of the Miseries of the poor Negroes." With a powerful prophetic voice, he went on to proclaim that "God has a Quarrel with you for your Abuse of and Cruelty to the poor Negroes." Except for Whitefield's canny refusal to condemn slavery outright—"I shall not take it upon me to determine" whether or not slaveholding itself be a sin, he noted evasively—much of the brief letter read as an abolitionist tract more forthright than any from the 1850s. The minister even suggested that slaves might be justified in revolting, arguing that "should such a Thing be permitted by Providence, all good Men must acknowledge the Judgment would be just."[41] Whitefield was using dangerous language.

Whenever Whitefield spent time in the South, he elaborated on the nature of his concern for the enslaved. It became clear that he was not quite an insurrectionary but that he did want to link the spiritual destinies of southern blacks and evangelical southern whites. Allan Gallay and Harvey Jackson have documented Whitefield's work in South Carolina and Georgia, and how evangelicals there were so sympathetic to slaves that they ran afoul of white authorities. The legal difficulties of Whitefield's followers became most acute in February 1742 when Hugh Bryan, a particularly enthusiastic convert, prophesied in writing to Charleston authorities that reports of slave meetings in the backcountry were signs of a pending insurrection. He predicted that God was planning to use "African Hosts" to destroy the city. To say the least, this was a severely miscalculated effort to urge Charlestonians to repent and believe in the Gospel of Christ. Members of the Bryan family, under Whitefield's personal guidance, were usually more circumspect. They supported his school for black children in Georgia and tried to show benevolent care to the enslaved persons on their plantations. So consumed by concern for blacks were white evangelicals that Gallay concluded "the most important reform undertaken by Evangelicals concerned the institution of slavery."[42]

Ultimately, Whitefield turned his and the Bryans' assault on slavery not into a call for emancipation but into a plea for black and white southerners to look beyond the forms of religion and to embrace a personal relationship with God. More than freedom, Whitefield wanted enslaved men and women to hear the Gospel "preach'd with Power amongst them, that many will be brought effectually home to God." The reluctance of white Anglicans to preach with such power—or to preach at all to blacks—was a sure indicator that they themselves had not been saved, according to the grand itinerant. "But I know all Arguments to prove the Necessity of taking Care of your Negroes Souls, though never so conclusive," he explained, "will prove ineffectual, till you are convinced of the Necessity of securing the Salvation of your own. That you yourselves are not effectually convinced of this, I think is too notorious to want Evidence."[43] As would later evangelicals, Whitefield thus made the startling assertion that participation in ministry to slaves was evidence of salvation.

Evangelical ministers from dissenting traditions answered Whitefield's call to minister to black Virginians. Virtually every well-known dissenter who preached or stationed himself in Virginia before 1770—among them Presbyterians Samuel Davies and John Todd and Baptists Shubal Stearns and Daniel Marshall—attracted scores of black Virginians to his ministry. Anglicans found slaves' participation in dissenting worship unnerving, both because it signaled a threat to their establishment and because dissenters were offering privileges to African American worshippers that threatened racial hierarchies. Many bonded men and women were learning to read from the dissenters or were assembling in vast numbers to listen to dissenters' sermons. Evangelicals did not know at first how to decouple the good news of the Gospel from their Protestant devotional practices, which included public preaching and training in literacy. While they struggled to find a way to minister to African Virginians within the legal and social constraints of a slaveholding society, dissenting whites defended their ministry to slaves against Anglican critics who worried about their property in persons. In defense of their activities, dissenters reiterated more forcefully than ever the compatibility of slavery and Christianity and effectively translated Godwyn's concession that conversion made better slaves into a straightforward proslavery argument.

Two streams of Presbyterians entered the commonwealth in the late 1730s and 1740s, one markedly more evangelical than the other. By situation and inclination, the more evangelical Presbyterians were the ones who engaged enslaved Virginians most directly. Under the leadership of Samuel Davies, they made an aggressive campaign of proselytization and education of black Virginians the basis of their critique of the established church. The Scotch-Irish Presbyterians who migrated into Virginia through the Shenandoah Valley were less evangelical. They settled in relatively insular communities and generally accommodated themselves to Anglican hegemony rather than challenging it. Moreover, they did not initially purchase many slaves, making ministry to those of African descent a nonissue in their communities.[44] In contrast, New Light Presbyterians such as Davies and his colleague John Todd set up their ministries in the heart of Virginia, Hanover County, and had higher ambitions than to deliver a Gospel message to those who were already Presbyterian. As some of the commonwealth's first identifiable evangelicals, they repeatedly called for spiritual renewal and intimated that neither black nor white Virginians were receiving adequate spiritual instruction through the Anglican Church.

Davies, who arrived in Virginia in 1747 and settled permanently in Hanover County in 1748, crafted his ministry to the lowliest Virginians as an implicit critique of the establishment. As a dissenter ministering at the suffrage of the colonial government, the missionary had to be careful not to offend Anglicans too directly lest he lose the privilege of preaching. Thus, he delivered much of his criticism of the Anglican Church by implication rather than frontal assault. In an early letter to correspondents in England that he either planned or allowed to be published, for example, Davies courteously and obliquely accused Anglicans of spectacular failure. "My design," he demurred, "is not to boast of Proselytes, or to asperse the church of *England* here established, but I hope I may observe, without the umbrage of calumny, what glares with irresistible evidence, that Religion has been, and in most parts of the colony still is in a very low state." He went on, in many subsequent letters, to document an outreach to unchurched slaves that, by definition, also condemned the Anglican establishment. Again and again, he called attention to the irony of "neglected *Heathen Slaves* in this Christian colony."[45]

Davies succeeded in attracting hundreds of enslaved Virginians to his call in large part because he was so responsive to their demands. By 1755, he was able to report that about 300 slaves attended his services regularly and, what's more, that about 100 of those had studied the catechism, modeled a Christian life, and received adult baptism. The following year, he estimated that there were "more than a *thousand* Negroes" who regularly attended services with him. It was no coincidence that the number of Africans and African Americans in attendance tripled during this period; Davies and his Presbyterian colleagues had just begun to deliver books to slaves, to train them in literacy, and to worship using an updated "evangelical" psalmody. The London-based Society for Promoting Religious Knowledge among the Poor, which Davies had lobbied while in England from 1753 to 1755, supplied the books. In grateful letters to benefactors in the society, Davies testified that slaves liked best the psalms and hymnals and requested hundreds of additional copies. The music books, he explained, "enabled them to gratify their peculiar taste for *Psalmody*." Davies was not appealing to the racial essentialism of Thomas Jefferson's generation and caricaturing African American spirituality by its performative components.[46] Rather, he was responding to the requests of black Virginians in an early example of how enslaved church members altered evangelical practices. One of the ways that African American Virginians let their requests be made known was by serenading Davies at all hours. "Sundry of them have lodged all night in my kitchen," he wrote, "and, sometimes, when I have awaked about two or three a clock in the morning, a torrent of sacred harmony poured into my chamber, and carried my mind away to Heaven."[47]

Other Virginia Presbyterian clergy, notably Todd and John Wright, also catered to slaves' devotional preferences. Wright, in Cumberland, set up two or three schools for slaves and taught literacy on Sunday, when most found release from their labors. Todd, Davies's "most intimate Friend, and an honest-hearted Assistant," also set up schools for reading, distributed free books, and tried to make worship accessible to newcomers to the faith. In 1762, he successfully argued before the Hanover Presbytery for permission to use more "evangelical" music in his services. He was concerned that worshippers might not understand the language of older translations of the psalms and, because of their formal settings, might not actually experience joy in the singing of them. Todd referred explicitly to slaves when he made his plea for rousing music that all could understand. Unless the presbytery adopted Watts's more accessible version of the psalms, he asked, "How can our common hearers, our servants, or even ourselves, stand forth and sing, with propriety, or understanding?"[48]

White Virginians could not be so responsive to black Virginians without cultivating personal relationships with them. These relationships may not have been the warmest, nor were they free from white perceptions of racial superiority. However, they were informal and outside the context of coerced labor. Davies and his fellow ministers had to try to win the affections of enslaved men and women in order to accomplish their spiritual goals, and this meant behaving in a winsome manner toward them. Robert Henry's quick laugh, "vehement manner, and vein of humor" made him "peculiarly acceptable to the African race," who built a community under his superintendence at Cub Creek. Whites who gained access to the private lives of the enslaved witnessed scenes that shaped their subsequent ministries. Davies, for example, championed slave literacy because he had observed firsthand that people of African descent were capable of learning to read and that some would apply their learning to Christian discipleship. He watched one of his own slaves, though beginning at forty years old and with an imperfect grasp of English, learn to read the Bible.[49]

Anglicans not convinced of the necessity or propriety of including slaves within their churches were confident that such intimacy between whites and blacks was dangerous. Davies reported being treated fairly well while in the commonwealth, but he received some extraordinarily harsh volleys upon his departure.[50] After Davies left the colony in 1758 to become the president of the College of New Jersey, one Col. Edwin Conway described Davies's ministry as seditious. Conway was either citing a document now lost to history or, more likely, was projecting insurrectionary intent onto Davies's biracial ministry. In a letter to Anglican authorities, he fumed that the Presbyterian minister "hath sent among our Negroes a Small Pamphlet . . . wherein you may Perceive Mr. Davies hath much Reproached Virginia. And informs the Negroes they are Stronger than the Whites, being Equal in Number then, & having an Annual addition of thousands."[51] Speaking more broadly about "new life" evangelicals in general, Anglican planter Landon Carter voiced similar concerns in 1766, professing his belief that "it is from some inculcated doctrine of those rascals that the slaves in this colony are grown so much worse."[52] In many quarters, whites did not yet accept biracial Christianity as practiced by evangelicals.

Davies's departure in 1758 roughly coincided with the arrival in Virginia of two distinct groups of Baptists, the "Regulars" and the "Separates." Each would challenge Anglican authority even more directly than had the path-breaking Presbyterian. Members of the Philadelphia Association of Regular Baptists, led by John Garrard, carried a creed-oriented, liturgical brand of worship from Pennsylvania to the Northern Neck in 1753, settling at Mill Creek Church in Berkeley County. Determinedly Calvinist, the Regulars accepted the Philadelphia Association's Confession of Faith as their own in 1756.[53] In 1754, the more charismatic Separate Baptists entered Virginia from the opposite point on the compass. Representatives from Shubal Stearns's Sandy Creek Association ventured into Virginia from North Carolina. Stearns and the Separates spurned formal creeds or liturgies, indeed formality in almost any guise. Separate preachers delivered heartfelt appeals for conversion, expected emotional responses from their congregants, and occasionally allowed women to serve as deaconesses or elderesses; these departures from traditional order so disgusted Regular Baptists that they refused to participate in the ordination of preachers for congregations Stearns established in Virginia in 1755. The Regulars protested that Separates "encouraged noise and confusion in their meetings."[54] These two groups were unified in their beliefs that only adults cognizant of their spiritual choices could legitimately seek baptism, that converts had to submit to being immersed completely underwater for their baptisms to be valid, and that the state had no right to control religious practice.

In their attitudes toward African Americans, the two factions also had much in common. Following the pattern pioneered by Whitefield and the New Light Presbyterians, the first Baptist ministers in the commonwealth rebuked the Church of England by reaching out to those to whom Anglicans would not, African Americans. For Baptists, this work began within their households. In 1771, John Williams took the initiative to include in family worship his fifteen slaves; "I had all my family given up to the Lord by prayer, the children black & white, particularly, by laying on of hands," he boasted.[55] The Dodson family, cofounders of the Broad Run Baptist Church, in 1764 initiated three of their own slaves into the congregation as full members, "Negro Dick," "Negro Sarah," and "Negro Adam."[56] The charter members of Upper King and Queen Baptist Church encouraged their slaves to join with them, and at least seven of the first twelve black members were slaves in their households.[57] The black members of these pioneer churches were not always bound to white members; Linville Creek Baptist in Rockingham County welcomed in June 1765 two new members, Joseph Thomas and an unrelated "Negro called Joe."[58] Among these early Baptists, interest in slaves and their salvation was a badge of honor. His eulogist praised the labors of Lewis Lunsford, who began his ministry in 1774, because "to win one soul to Christ, if eve a decrepit old negro slave, was a pearl of greater price to him, 'Than the rich gems of polish'd gold / The sons of Aaron wore.'"[59] Although the total number of black converts remained low in the Baptists' early years—only an estimated 5 percent of the commonwealth's 2,000 or so Baptists in 1770 were African American—Baptists were actively seeking black conversion and were earning a reputation for treating slaves as spiritual equals.[60]

One hundred black Baptists in 1770 may not have been an impressive record, but Baptists did not have to attract many African Americans to full membership to shame the Anglicans. The decisions of these first enslaved and free black converts confirmed Baptists' widespread interest (and modest success) in ministering to the slaves. Virginia's burgesses worried that Baptist dissenters, who were already flouting state authority by preaching without licenses, were also eroding slaveowner control.[61] To prevent Baptists from passing some of their insubordinate spirit on to the slaves, the lawmakers debated—but did not pass—legislation in 1772 to "guard against the Corruption of our Slaves" by more carefully regulating dissenting preachers.[62] Such a law would have been largely superfluous because Baptist ministers were already vulnerable to prosecution for their failure to seek licensure; its near-passage reveals how discomfiting nonevangelicals found biracial worship. Some of those concerned remonstrated publicly against the Baptists, prompting David Thomas in a 1774 pamphlet to rebut charges that his "noisy religion ha[d] set whole families at odds." According to critics, Baptists had "not only divided good neighbors, but slaves and their masters; children and their parents; yea, wives and their husbands." Though he reassured readers that Baptists believed "servants and slaves [should] be in subjection to their masters," Thomas insisted that slaves, even if they rejected the evangelicals' call to conversion, were entitled to hear it more clearly than they did from the representatives of the established church. "The elect slaves must be redeemed," he chided Anglican readers, "though others choose to hug their chains and even curse their best friends, who offer to set them [spiritually] free."[63]

Anglicans, somewhat chastened by the attentiveness of dissenters to Africans and African Americans, modestly increased their attention to the most dispossessed in the decade and a half before the Revolution.[64] Anglican clergy in most communities began to baptize African American newborns, to the point that by the mid-1760s some white observers concluded that "it is a pretty general Practice all over Virginia for Negro Parents to have their Children christened, where they live tolerably convenient to the Church."[65] To this minimal, initial exposure to Anglicanism, some divines tried to add ongoing programs specifically for black Virginians. The Associates of Dr. Bray, an international Anglican missionary organization similar to the SPG and established in 1723, helped to fund a school in Williamsburg for the capital city's black population in 1760. The school ran for fourteen years under the patronage of several of the city's leading lights, including William Hunter, the editor of the *Virginia Gazette*, and Thomas Dawson, rector of Bruton Church and president of William and Mary. No more than 30 children attended at any time, a relatively small portion of the town's estimated 700 enslaved blacks. The Williamsburg academy, itself a clear echo of Davies's earlier, more informal schools, served as a model for a handful of other, similarly short-lived enterprises. Anglicans in Fredericksburg ran a school from 1765 to 1770, and at least two ministers, Jonathan Boucher of Hanover County and James Marye of Orange County, imitated Davies in another particular by distributing devotional literature to slaves.[66] That Boucher and Marye were ministers in the very communities from which the influential Presbyterian had just departed likely influenced their decision to buck white opinion and offer slaves literacy. Blacks in those areas had enough experience in the religious marketplace to demand that literacy be a part of their spiritual training.

The Anglicans most interested in black Virginians were evangelical reformers within the denomination, "Methodists," who believed that they could bring themselves into a more fulfilling, authentic relationship with God by applying method to their pursuit of holiness. Though the exact date of their first arrival is contested, by 1772 Methodists had established a firm foothold in Virginia and were preaching the Gospel to slave and free alike.[67] The first Methodists deferred to clerical authority in Virginia and carried out their evangelism from within the Anglican Church. At the first annual conference of American Methodists, held in Philadelphia in June 1773, the ten ministers present, including two from Virginia, agreed: "All the people among whom we labour to be earnestly exhorted to attend the [Anglican] church, and to receive the ordinances there; but in a particular manner, to press the people in Maryland and Virginia, to the observance of this minute."[68] Notwithstanding their strong theoretical adherence to Anglicanism, though, early Virginia Methodists acted like a denomination long before they became one in 1784 by holding separate religious exercises or class meetings. As described by Virginian Thomas Lyell, Methodists within a congregation met "weekly together not only to hear a sermon and unite in acts of public worship but afterwards, as members of the society to receive such private instruction, such Godly admonition, and advice, as the preacher might *find time*, and *profess the ability*, to *impart*. By this means, together with the concluding acts of devotion, singing and prayer, their Class meetings, in process of time, became schools of correction, and instruction of incalculable importance and of the greatest advantage."[69]

Methodists encouraged black Virginians who were not always welcome at normal parish meetings to attend these smaller class meetings and the more infrequent conference meetings. As Jesse Lee, a Virginia native and the first Methodist historian, remembered, he and his colleagues always planned their quarterly conference meetings around the work routines of enslaved Virginians. They scheduled these sessions on a Saturday and Sunday, according to his account, because "many of the slaves could not attend these meetings, except on the Lord's day."[70] According to Dinwiddie County's Devereux Jarratt, an Anglican minister deeply sympathetic to the Methodist movement, blacks perceived their welcome in the Methodist movement and participated widely in the early revivals. When Jarratt preached before one Methodist meeting in 1776, he observed that "the chapel was full of white and black, and many were without that could not get in. Look wherever we would, we saw nothing but streaming eyes, and faces bathed in tears."[71] Because Methodists did not distinguish between whites and blacks in their official records until 1786, it is difficult to tell the early ratio of black and white auditors. In 1786, there were 890 black Methodists in the United States and 18,271 white members of the society. The proportion of black Methodists was higher in Virginia, with roughly 370 black and 3,814 white members.[72] Even so, African Americans made up less than 10 percent of early Methodist societies.

The lopsided ratio of black to white, even after intentional attempts by evangelical dissenters to recruit black members, underscores the rhetorical quality of the early ministry to the slaves. Evangelicals did believe that all men, regardless of ethnic background, deserved to hear of Christ's sacrifice for them. But their outreach to black Virginians was as much a part of the fashioning of an identity in the context of a hierarchical, Anglican society as it was an expression of interracial concern. By spending time with slaves, the lowest on Virginia's social ladder, evangelicals could claim that they, like Christ, identified with the poor and downtrodden of the world, while the apostate Anglicans catered to the rich and the proud.[73] Despite the willingness of twentieth-century scholars to accept such claims at face value, eighteenth-century evangelicals meant them less as a declaration of sociological fact than as a spiritual critique of the established church. Presbyterians, Baptists, and Methodists did evince a concern for the spiritual welfare of the lowest in their society, slaves, but they also courted wealthy and powerful members. None of these groups could have developed as successful movements without the active support of elite Virginians.[74]

The small proportion of early African American evangelicals, especially relative to the intensity of white calls for their conversion, is significant in other ways as well. First, it shows the fragility of evangelicalism's early biracial character. With so few black coreligionists, whites could have easily jettisoned the practice (if not the theory) of interracial ministry once they did not need blacks' symbolic presence to compete with an established church. Second, the relatively low number of black conversions muted the ideological conflict among whites about the justice of slavery. Since the vast majority of Virginia's enslaved men and women remained outside the Christian tradition, even if a few joined evangelical churches and a few more received a pro forma baptism as infants in the Anglican Church, the correspondence between slave and "heathen" remained close in white minds. The theological question for whites thus remained whether or not conversion should mean freedom for an exceptional few, rather than whether or not the wholesale enslavement of their fellow Christians was morally objectionable.

In their process of defending their search for a few black converts, white Presbyterians, Baptists, and Methodists further strengthened the fledgling proslavery arguments of Godwyn and Fleetwood by insisting that conversion made slaves more faithful servants. They thus prepared a way for subsequent generations of evangelicals to conceive of slavery as a part of God's plan. Even Samuel Davies, the foremost apostle to the enslaved in Virginia's early history, distanced himself publicly from the idea of emancipation in order to secure his ministry against accusations that he was subverting the social order. He justified slavery as one of many hierarchical relationships approved by God in a 1757 sermon, *The Duty of Masters to Their Servants*. In what would become the most important plank of the proslavery argument, he taught that "the appointments of Providence, and the order of the world, not only admit, but require, that there should be civil distinctions among mankind; that some should rule, and some be subject; that some should be Masters, and some Servants. And Christianity does not blend or destroy these distinctions, but establishes and regulates them, and enjoines every man to conduct himself according to them."[75] In sum, on the eve of the

Revolution, evangelical dissenters in the commonwealth were making an aggressive case against the established Anglican Church by seeking to convert those whom Anglicans would not, enslaved Africans. At the same time, they were reinforcing rather than challenging the practice of slaveholding.

White evangelical dissenters courted black Virginians in order to weaken the Anglican Church until 1775, but with the eruption of imperial tensions, white evangelicals suddenly had more effective avenues available through which to assail Anglican hegemony. Dissenters successfully associated the Anglican Church with the abuses of the Crown and allied with secular leaders to convince their fellow citizens that an established church had no place in a republican society. Baptists led the fight for disestablishment, seconded strongly by the Presbyterians and, after 1784, the Methodists.[76] The Virginia Assembly responded to dissenters' many petitions and ceased making payments to Anglican ministers in 1776, repealed religious taxes in 1779, and disbanded the vestries in 1782. By late 1785, emboldened by a massive petition campaign, the legislators were ready to make even more far-reaching changes. Though Thomas Jefferson was then in France, they unearthed and passed the Statute for Religious Freedom that he had drafted in 1779 and closed the door to any reestablishment.[77] By linking their own cause with that of the patriots, dissenters eviscerated the religious establishment.

Black Virginians found that the Revolutionary years brought them new opportunities as well. About 5,500 men and women of a total slave population estimated at 225,000 slipped their bonds and fled to British lines during the war. Though this figure represents a smaller total than historians long believed, it is nonetheless high enough that most slaves would have known someone who had earned his or her freedom—or died trying—by fleeing to the British army. Lord Dunmore invited this sort of flight in a November 1775 proclamation in which he promised freedom to those able-bodied slaves who would fight for him against the rebellious colonists. Though smallpox or dysentery claimed most of the 800 or so men who immediately accepted his offer, black Virginians expressed a continued willingness throughout the Revolution to risk death and disease rather than endure slavery. Benedict Arnold, on his 1781 romp through the commonwealth, accepted approximately 2,000 fugitives into his lines, including 23 of then-governor Jefferson's own slaves. Many of these 2,000 fugitives traveled from a significant distance to make their escape, fifty miles in the case of Thomas Jefferson's Robin, Barnaby, Harry, and Will, indicating just how passionately black Virginians wanted their freedom.[78]

Most of the African American men and women who had cast their lot with Britain and, against long odds, had survived smallpox epidemics and the hardships of war escaped from the commonwealth with the British. Most ultimately found freedom in Nova Scotia or elsewhere within the British Empire.[79] Others who remained in Virginia also gained their liberty. The Virginia legislature passed in 1782 a statute that made manumission easier by empowering owners to free their slaves without first seeking approval from the state. Even if, as Eva Wolf has suggested, many manumitters freed certain slaves as a part of a broader strategy of slave management and not because they were seeking to divest themselves of slave property, the net result of the statute was still an expanded free black population. Prominent Virginians such as George Washington and Robert Carter freed significant numbers of slaves, and the free black population in the commonwealth rose from an estimated 2,000 in 1760 to more than 30,000 by 1810.[80] Enslaved Virginians in the 1780s could thus count on a growing cohort of free black allies and could draw upon inspiring memories of friends or acquaintances who had gambled successfully for freedom during the Revolution. These changes empowered African Americans within evangelical churches and elsewhere to display much more initiative.

One of the most basic ways that black men and women displayed spiritual initiative was by affiliating with the denominations of their choice. Historians have often asserted that African Americans joined Baptist and Methodist churches because they found in those communities more fulfilling outlets for innate spiritual needs: an expressive worship style, for example, or the ritual of baptism by immersion. However, what begins as a thoughtful analysis of continuities across African and Christian theologies often becomes in effect a form of racial essentialism.[81] Black Virginians joined Baptist or Methodist denominations not primarily because elements of the Baptist or Methodist tradition corresponded to remembered fragments of African belief, but because white and black evangelicals recruited them to those denominations. In Virginia, Baptists ultimately allocated the most resources to spreading the Gospel among black Virginians and accordingly reaped the largest percentage of black converts. In other states, notably South Carolina and Georgia, Methodists took in a far higher proportion of African Americans. In places like Liberty County, Georgia, or Hanover County, Virginia, where Presbyterians sought black converts, black Presbyterianism thrived. The several thousand African Virginians who belonged to Baptist and Methodist churches by 1792 had consciously selected those denominations over others.[82]

One thing that may have attracted black men and women to Baptist and Methodist churches during and after the Revolution was the growing number of black evangelists within these denominations. Tantalizing details in the official histories of many churches indicate that African Americans during this period undertook a variety of autonomous and near-autonomous efforts to bring in new slave members. At Buck Marsh Baptist Church, for example, whites noticed in October 1791 that several of their black coreligionists had taken it "upon them to be teachers & preachers of funerals." Significantly, whites did not try to halt the practice, only to require that blacks not preach "without first obtaining liberty or license from the church."[83] Henry Toler, a white Baptist minister, found signs of black mission work at several of his preaching appointments. When, in October 1786, he preached at one Brother Boone's, Toler discovered a group of eleven black Virginians waiting to relate their religious experiences to him and to join the Baptist Church. In his journal, Toler noted that some of the testimonies he heard that day "were particularly clear." More to the point, he intimated that one of their number had been instrumental in converting the others, recording that the "chief of them converted several years back."[84] African American Virginians did not limit their evangelical efforts to within the Baptist tradition. Harry Hosier, a black Methodist, traveled with Francis Asbury and preached to black audiences while his colleague preached to whites. One of the secrets of Cub Creek Presbyterian Church's success was the "two or three leading men among them" whom white officials allowed to serve as "a sort of overseers or superintendents of the rest."[85]

Indeed, to the surprise of many whites, sometimes blacks exercised spiritual authority over members of both races. In the Baptist church at Allen's Creek, for example, slaves who were "preachers of talents" baptized both whites and blacks in the late 1780s.[86] Sometime after 1790, Robert Semple reported that the biracial congregation at Gloucester "at length did what it would hardly have been supposed would have been done by Virginians; they chose for their pastor William Lemon, a man of color. He, though not white as to his natural complexion, had been washed in the laver of regeneration; he had been purified and made white in a better sense."[87] No one ordained Samuel Templeman's unnamed slave, but Isaac Backus noted during his 1789 journey through Virginia the man's decisive influence over Templeman and other whites. The enslaved man complained that Templeman sold liquor on the Sabbath, prompting Templeman to get "a stick next morning with an intent to scourge him for it; but as soon as the negro saw his master come into the stable where he was, he very humbly asked liberty to speak, which being obtained, he gave a relation of his experiences, which was followed with such an exhortation to his master, as not only made him forget his cruel design, but also proved a means of his conversion." Templeman subsequently became a Baptist minister.[88]

In their zeal to become active members of Baptist churches, African American Virginians like Templeman's unnamed slave obligated white Baptists to reevaluate their ideas about religion and racial hierarchy. Eager converts in Isle of Wight County put white Baptists in a bind when they sought admission to the racially mixed Mill Swamp Baptist Church without their owners' permission. Congregants wondered in June 1777, "What shall a Church do with her Minister if he will not Baptise a servant until his or her master or mistress be willing?"[89] Once black men and women were members, the churches had to decide their place within the church polity. With some exceptions, most churches allowed them to attend, but not to vote at, all congregational meetings. Linville Creek Baptist Church seems to have been surprisingly accommodating of black members, perhaps because slaves comprised only 10.4 percent of Rockingham County's population, and there were no free blacks. In "the case of black members or slaves; it was considered whether they should be admitted to a seat among us on days of business—resolved that they should." In Nansemond County, where slaves and free blacks made up 47.7 percent of the population, whites in South Quay Baptist Church were more careful with the distribution of ecclesiastical privileges. They resolved in 1778 that it was the "duty for our black Brethren to attend conferences when convenient," though "for instruction" and not for decision making.[90]

Some of the most prominent black Baptists were enslaved, a fact that confirms that the increase in black evangelical activity during the Revolutionary era was not confined exclusively to free blacks. Richard Dozier reported in May 1782 that he had heard Lewis, a slave from Essex County, preach to a biracial audience in the Northern Neck.[91] While it is unknown whether Lewis was so fortunate, several black preachers in the post-Revolutionary era were compelling enough that their white coreligionists purchased their freedom. In 1792, whites and blacks in both the Portsmouth Baptist Church and the Roanoke Baptist Association collaborated to purchase the freedom of especially effective slave preachers Josiah Bishop and Simon. At least a few of this first generation of dynamic slave preachers hailed directly from Africa, a sign that acculturation alone did not account for the flurry of black evangelical activity. "Uncle Jack," an African living in Nottoway County, also impressed his white coreligionists enough in 1792 that they purchased his freedom and urged him to continue preaching.[92]

African Americans who were not preachers also made their presence known within Baptist churches. In the South Quay Baptist Church, a slave named Nero used the church to challenge the authority of his master, John Lawrence. In August 1780, each complained to the church that the other was acting in an un-Christian manner. The master's word did not immediately triumph over the slave's, and white male voting members expelled both men for a cooling-off period. Lawrence brought his servant up on charges of disobedience twice more in 1782 and again in 1786, but Nero evidently had strong allies in the church, for he never suffered more than a few weeks' excommunication. Nero did not permanently damage the status of blacks within the church by his willingness to stand up for himself, for whites at South Quay eventually grew to respect the spiritual judgment of their black brethren and to recognize their comparative advantage in ministering to others of African descent. In 1788, they resolved "that in order to know the state of our black brethren in Gates County from time to time; that some one of them be appointed to frequently see them, hold prayer with & among them, admonish & stir them up to holy duties, & if need require to give any information to the Church that may be necessary." A "Bro. Jack of Benton" accepted the appointment to look into the spiritual lives of black members who lived over the state line in North Carolina.[93]

When slaves wanted to leave a church voluntarily, white members were usually happy to provide them with formal letters of dismission from one church to another. White members of Baptist churches wrote at least 100 such letters before 1790 and many tens of thousands more in subsequent decades on behalf of African Americans.[94] White members sometimes consulted with black members in search of specific information about the character of the person seeking the transfer. At Buck Marsh in 1789, for example, before writing letters for Dick, James, Grace, and Esther, the church decided to appoint "Br. Tho. Berry to inquire (of the Black Brethren who are acquainted with their conduct) of their orderly walks."[95]

The greatest indication of black spiritual initiative in the early national period was the formation of autonomous black Baptist churches. Some black Virginians who were not content to worship alongside whites dared reprisals by worshipping on their own—not in hush arbors, but in public congregations of believers. In the most exhaustive but still incomplete survey of such congregations, Mechal Sobel found that black Virginians had established autonomous or semiautonomous churches in Lunenburg, Williamsburg, King and Queen County, Nottoway County, Portsmouth, and Gloucester County by 1800. To put this modest tally of six congregations in perspective, she found only five other black Baptist churches anywhere else in the nation at the turn of the century, a clear illustration of the primacy of the pioneering role of black Virginians.[96] Williamsburg blacks, in a drama that would unfold elsewhere, literally bled for the right to praise God on their own. Moses and his better-known successor, free black Gowan Pamphlet, founded what became Williamsburg's African Church, with an all-black congregation. Possibly because zealous whites responded violently to the novel sight of a black man reading publicly, Moses endured regular whippings for his efforts to gather the initial core of believers during the 1780s.[97]

Black Methodists also took the pulpit with some regularity, though, unlike Baptists, they did not form any independent congregations in the South. In addition to licensing black Methodists such as Richard Allen to preach in northern cities, white Methodists recognized the preference that enslaved men and women in the South expressed for black preachers and tried to accommodate them. Most often, this occurred through unofficial channels, and white Methodists permitted black worshippers to exhort one another more or less extemporaneously. Robert Ayres's description of a 1788 meeting is instructive: "The first thing I saw Remarkable was a Negro woman," he wrote, "standing (as I think) on one of the seats, and began to Cry and Tremble, and presently fall backwards, which together with the alarm of the Exhortation set the Whole Congregation in an uprore."[98]

At other times, enslaved or free black ministers within the Methodist Church received more formal support. A bondman in Hanover County, John Charleson, converted at a Sunday school run by Methodists around 1790 and began a preaching career that lasted over four decades.[99] Henry Evans, born a free black in Virginia, emigrated to Fayetteville, North Carolina, where he established a biracial Methodist church.[100] In his final recorded words, Evans expressed the intensity of conviction with which his generation of black Virginians attempted to spread the Gospel. "I have come to say my last word to you," he reported to his followers while leaning on the altar rail. "It is this: None but Christ."[101] Along with Harry Hosier, Charleson, Evans, and other black ministers played a critical role in bringing African Americans into the Methodist Church.

Evidence from fugitive slave advertisements also reveals the late eighteenth century to have been a time of rich African American evangelical activity. These advertisements are particularly useful sources, because they corroborate denominational records in which white evangelicals may have had an interest in exaggerating the number of African American conversions. Evangelical slaveowners had no interest in linking their religion with slave resistance and so would have been unlikely to include this information in advertisements for fugitive slaves gratuitously. What is more, Anglican or agnostic slaveowners would only have identified slaves as participants in Baptist and Methodist churches if they thought that characteristic was important enough to assist in the individual's recapture. The advertisements' numerous examples of slave preaching and religious expression thus offer important confirmation of the story of black agency seen in the church minutes.

In the 1770s, a few owners identified fugitive slaves as religious, but more did so in the 1780s and early 1790s. James Govan, for example, advertised that his former slave, Sam Cooper, who fled over Christmas in 1790, was "sensible and artful in his conversation, reads well, and frequently assumes the character of a Baptist preacher." Guy, an Amherst County slave who fled in 1792, "professeth to be a baptist, and talks much on religion." With the exception of his denomination, Guy's description resembled that of Ben, who fled at the holidays in that year and "has been a Methodist for several years, and sometimes preaches publicly." Spotsylvania County's irrepress-ible Titus, who was "uncommon sensible and artful for a negro, fond of preaching and exhorting, being, as he says, of the Baptist persuasion," ran away twice, in 1793 and 1795. Stepney, a "Methodist Preacher," escaped in 1794. The waterways, urban retreats, and swamps in which these fugitives sometimes hid must never have lacked for evangelical preaching.[102]

Virginia Baptists and Methodists of color were participating in a hemisphere-wide process, one in which hundreds of thousands of expatriate Africans found in evangelical Protestantism a new basis for community organization. In 1785, two black women, Mary Alley and Sophia Campbell, brought Methodism to Antigua, converting hundreds before the arrival of the first official (white and male) missionary. White Methodists in the United States responded to this dramatic news and sent one of their own to organize the converts into an affiliated branch of the Methodist Church. The missionary could scarcely process the huge number of converts whom he encountered and listed the large but indefinite number of 1,000 black Anti-guans as Methodists in the 1786 *Minutes*.[103] Rebecca Protten, an enslaved woman who converted under the tutelage of German Moravians on St. Thomas, wrought a similar transformation on that island. Protten recast the Moravians' message to fit the needs of slaves and was instrumental in the conversion of hundreds of enslaved men and women.[104]

Black Virginians were among those who played a role in the spread of evangelical Protestantism in the Caribbean. George Liele, born a Virginia slave, preached in Silver Bluff, Georgia, for a time before migrating as a free man to Jamaica in 1782. There he established that nation's first Baptist church. Liele's childhood Virginia friend, David George, took advantage of the presence of British troops during the Revolution to gain his freedom and went first to Nova Scotia, then to Sierra Leone. George established pioneering black Baptist churches in both locations. Another intimate of Liele's, Andrew Bryan, remained in slavery in the United States after his mentor's departure. Bryan, like Williamsburg's Moses before him, endured beatings and public humiliation in the process of founding (or, in this case, re-planting) a church, the First African Baptist Church of Savannah.[105] Occasionally the process even worked in the reverse; in 1788, Israel Decoudry, a free black of Caribbean birth, founded the Davenport Baptist Church in Petersburg.[106]

At times, black religious leaders turned their thoughts and their correspondence to the topic of resistance to slavery. Just as white Baptists and Methodists had linked their cause to the American Revolution, some black evangelicals also combined evangelicalism and liberation. Gowan Pamphlet, Moses' successor as head of Williamsburg's First African Church, personified the relationship between black religious expression and opposition to slavery. Pamphlet's sympathies for black civil and spiritual liberation were familiar enough to white authorities that they linked his name to "a letter addressed to the 'Secret Keeper, Norfolk,' from the 'Secret Keeper, Richmond,'" which they found in the streets of Yorktown in 1793. The letter promised a broad insurrection that would involve slaves from Virginia to South Carolina, with possible reinforcements from Toussaint L'Overture in Haiti. The arrival in Norfolk of refugee planters and their slaves from war-torn Hispaniola in July 1793 may have inspired this scheme; Norfolk city authorities noted that the city's slaves became "extremely insolent & troublesome" following their association with "French Negroes from St. Domingo (with whom the place is also overrun)."[107]

George Liele's letters from Jamaica give further, extraordinary evidence of the interconnectedness of black religious expression in the late eighteenth century, though without insurrectionary overtones. The Virginia expatriate, in correspondence with American Baptist officials in 1790, demonstrated remarkable knowledge of the achievements of his black coreligionists in locations across the Western Hemisphere. Eight years removed from his last mainland home, Savannah, he nonetheless knew that "Brother Andrew Bryan, a black minister at Savannah, has TWO HUNDRED MEMBERS, in full fellowship and had certificates from their owners of ONE HUNDRED MORE, who had given in their experiences and were ready to be baptized." Moreover, Liele reported that he had "received accounts from Nova Scotia of a black Baptist preacher, brother David George," and that he had also heard from "Brother Amos," in Providence, Rhode Island, and "Brother Jessy Gaulsing, another black minister, [who] preaches near Augusta, in South

Carolina, at a place where I used to preach."[108] Through such men as these, more of whom had their origins in Virginia than anywhere else, black evangelical Protestantism was becoming a hemisphere-wide phenomenon.

There was little Presbyterian flavor to this upsurge in black evangelical activity, ironically, either in Virginia or elsewhere. Though Samuel Davies had been the most active and visible advocate of missions to the slaves in the 1740s and 1750s, after the Revolution Presbyterians chiefly targeted white converts and did not welcome black participation in their denomination as warmly. Baptists and Methodists far more aggressively ministered to slaves and successfully convinced black Virginians that their denominations were the most hospitable to people of color. For a time, the Presbyterian Virginia Synod continued to send pastors to predominantly black congregations at Cub Creek, Briery, and Bethesda (a church that grew out of Cub Creek). White Presbyterians after the turn of the century were barely able to keep the Cub Creek church alive, however, and witnessed a string of secessions in their other churches. One Presbyterian minister explained that his codenominationalists could not compete with the Baptists or Methodists, who more willingly gave black men leadership positions; "in many instances," he complained, those black Virginians "who had been brought into the Presbyterian church were swept off by one or the other of these sects."[109]

The refusal of black Virginians to join Presbyterian churches serves as a reminder of the voluntary nature of their religious activity in the 1780s and early 1790s. Slaveowners did not require conversion of their bondmen and bondwomen, nor could an owner demand his or her slave be made a member of a church without that person first giving a profession of faith. Africans and African Americans actively chose to join Baptist and Methodist churches, with two important consequences for ensuing generations of evangelicals. First, they prevented white evangelicals from abandoning their ministry to slaves once disestablishment obviated the need for white evangelicals to set themselves apart from Anglicans by demonstrating concern for slaves. Second, they guaranteed that evangelicalism would remain a biracial movement and created in biracial churches key sites of interracial interaction.

The complexion of evangelicalism darkened in the early national period as slaves and free blacks joined evangelical churches at a much faster rate than did whites. This was especially true during the period of most dramatic church growth, the Great Revival of 1785 to 1792. In the span of those seven years, Virginia Baptists more than tripled their prewar membership. A leading minister during the revivals, John Leland, recorded more than 6,000 adult baptisms of new members between 1785 and 1789 alone.[110]

Another contemporary, John Asplund, counted 22,900 Virginians as members of the swelling denomination in 1792, a number that excluded at least 66,000 adherents.[111] The proportional increase in the number of new African American members was even more impressive than the aggregate figures. Using extant congregational records, Robert Gardner retraced Asplund's investigations and calculated the numbers of black members in both 1780 and 1790. In 1780, 776 of Virginia's 7,208 Baptists—roughly 11 percent—were people of color; by 1790, 5,926 black Virginians belonged to a Baptist church, making up 28 percent of the total membership of 21,317 and reflecting almost an eightfold decennial increase.[112] Black Baptist ministers had succeeded in just a few years of active ministry in making their denomination markedly and permanently biracial.

Black Virginians also made Methodism truly biracial by joining at a similarly astonishing rate. In 1786, 3,965 white and 379 black Virginians belonged to the Methodist Church. But, over the next six years, the efforts of black and white missionaries began to bear fruit. In the words of Methodist minister and historian Jesse Lee, "Such a time for the awakening and conversion of sinners was never seen before among the Methodists in America. The greatest revival was in the south parts of Virginia." By 1792, at least 12,857 white and 3,494 black Methodists resided in the commonwealth. Like the Baptists, the total of 16,351 represented more than a threefold increase in just six years. And, again like the Baptists, the proportion of black members leaped significantly, from just less than 10 percent to 21 percent.[113] Put another way, the number of white Methodists tripled during the Great Revival, but there was a ninefold increase in the number of black Methodists.

Thanks to the efforts of scores of black ministers and thousands of black laypeople, evangelical churches were thoroughly integrated by 1792, even though the whites with whom blacks entered into fellowship had never promised to slaves or free blacks civic equality. African Americans of faith had forced white evangelicals to live up to their rhetoric from colonial times, when the Old Dominion's first evangelicals had cited the Anglican Church's failure to welcome blacks as evidence of Anglicans' spiritual bankruptcy.

A handful of antislavery whites may have made evangelicalism look attractive to enslaved Virginians. Most white evangelicals, though, still accepted the argument that Godwyn, Fleetwood, and Davies had first laid out to defend evangelization: that conversion actually made better slaves.[114] This was certainly the message in Henry Pattillo's *Plain Planter's Assistant*, which he published in 1787. Pattillo trained under Davies and Todd in Virginia before moving to Orange County, North Carolina. He repeated for a new generation of Virginians and North Carolinians in 1787 his mentor's contention that allowing enslaved men and women to convert did not jeopardize an owner's investment in chattel slavery. In a catechism that he penned for the instruction of those euphemistically identified as "servants," Pattillo answered the question, "When negroes become religious, how must they behave to their masters?" He explained, "The scriptures in many places command them, to be honest, diligent and faithful in all things, and not to give saucy answers; and even when they are whipt for doing well, to take it patiently, and look to God for their reward."[115]

The evangelicals' victories in Virginia during the Great Revival from 1785 to 1792 had important repercussions across the nation. The role of Virginians in forging American conceptions of religious liberty is well known; the principles hammered out by Jefferson and the Baptists have informed American jurisprudence on church-state issues for more than two centuries. But the role of Virginians in developing a racially integrated church was also important. As the largest slave state and the state with the most Baptists and Methodists in 1792, early national Virginia modeled the possibility of fellowship without freedom in addition to the promise of statutory religious liberty. The tremendous black presence within evangelical ranks, to say nothing of the efforts of energetic black ministers, did, though, demolish the background assumption behind the proslavery defenses of early evangelicals—that most slaves were "heathen" and most whites Christian. Dealing with this changed theological reality would be one of the greatest challenges faced by evangelicals in the years following the Great Revival.

Chapter Two

GROWING PAINS, 1792–1815

For ye are yet carnal: for whereas there is among you envying, and strife, and divisions, are ye not carnal, and walk as men?—1 Corinthians 3:3

Baptist Reuben Pickett of the Roanoke Association spoke for the majority of Virginia's evangelical churchmen when he reported in a 1797 letter to Isaac Backus, "Religion is rather at a low ebb with us, and I suppose it to be generally the case, at least as far as I can hear. Iniquity generally abounds and the love of many hath waxen cold, so that the times are truly lamentable."[1] Pickett's complaint was no empty jeremiad; the Great Revival had come to an end, and Virginia's evangelicals had indeed entered a "wintry season." Presbyterians had not experienced the same kind of explosive growth as had Baptists and Methodists during the revival and saw only a small slowdown in church growth. The downturn was much more jarring for the commonwealth's two largest denominations, which witnessed a sharp decline in new conversions and, in some years between 1792 and the War of 1812, actually lost members. Baptists began counting new additions by the tens or hundreds, not the thousands, and increased their rolls from 22,900 in 1792 only up to about 30,000 by 1810.[2] Methodists suffered even more. Their Virginia membership dipped from 16,351 in 1792 to 13,211 in 1797 and did not rebound to Great Revival levels until 1804. The number of black Methodists did not reach 1792 levels until 1806.[3]

Virginia's evangelicals faltered in part because they found it difficult to recalibrate their rhetorical posture from that of dissenters to that of insiders. As ecclesiastical outsiders, white evangelicals had very publicly reached out to black Virginians as part of their protest against Anglican authority. True, they universally disavowed antislavery ambitions, but they nonetheless earned a reputation as the loudest advocates for those in chains. This stance fit their role as reformers of a corrupt establishment but became problematic once they gained legal recognition and a larger membership. White evangelicals risked earning an inaccurate and potentially damaging reputation among Virginia slaveholders as abolitionists if they did not define their existing beliefs with more precision.

But when denominational leaders moved in the late 1780s and 1790s to codify a conservative position on slavery, they encountered surprisingly strong internal opposition. The strongest opposition came from black evangelicals who had joined in the revivals and now worshipped with whites, if not alongside them, then in special sections of the sanctuary behind or above them. These men and women formed a numerically significant and often vocal internal lobby that made it impossible for white evangelicals glibly to dismiss emancipation. White evangelicals could only go so far in their affirmation of slavery without undermining the relationships that they had forged with their black coreligionists. A small minority of antislavery whites formed a second internal constituency that confronted the white, proslavery majority within the commonwealth's evangelical churches. These prophetic few, most of whom were strongly influenced by the natural rights ideology of the American Revolution, spoke against slavery loudly and persistently enough to create significant debate within evangelicals' councils. In alliance with black Virginians, they held at bay the strongest ecclesiastical advocates of slaveholding.[4]

In the late 1780s and early 1790s, white evangelicals who affirmed the justice of slavery were thus in a difficult, or at least an awkward, position. They needed to maintain good relations with antislavery factions within their churches and with slaves themselves, while at the same time convincing slaveholders unfamiliar with their historic proslavery position that they were not threatening their property in persons. Denominational authorities managed to accomplish both of these tasks through creative inaction; they sidestepped rather than resolved conflicts with these internal constituencies. Instead of casting their lot with the antislavery reformers or the strongest advocates of chattel slavery, white evangelicals stated emphatically that slavery was a civil, and not a spiritual, affair. In so doing, they elaborated upon the principle contained in the 1667 statute that conversion did not alter the civil status of the enslaved and insisted that only civic bodies were competent to legislate on slavery.

Most antislavery whites within the evangelical fold accepted this decision, especially since they could, at this juncture at least, still promote emancipation in their capacity as private citizens without risking spiritual censure from their home churches. Most black members, too, accepted the noncommittal stance on slavery, most likely because white evangelicals softened it with ecclesiastical regulations designed to ameliorate the harshest aspects of bondage. Men and women who remained in denominations that ultimately affirmed the justice of their servitude compelled their white brethren to make numerous informal concessions to them short of advocating emancipation. Whites drew on ideas already present in the writing of Godwyn, Fleetwood, Whitefield, and Davies and acknowledged much more openly the mutual obligations that believing masters and slaves owed to one another.[5] In this way, white evangelicals bound by their own faith commitments to interact daily with black Virginians adopted the ethic that historians have labeled paternalism.

Historians have oversimplified this complex series of negotiations between black and white evangelicals as an evangelical capitulation to slaveholder interests. Since most scholars have caricatured the early evangelicals as lower-class challengers to elite, slaveholding Anglicans, they have therefore depicted the ecclesiastical wrangling of the 1780s and 1790s as the death struggle of an egalitarian impulse within evangelicalism. This approach is problematic for several reasons, among them that it ignores the demonstrable presence of slaveowners in the first generations of evangelicals, it exaggerates the antislavery tendencies of colonial evangelicals, and it incorrectly places the Great Revival *after*, not *before*, the denominational debates on slavery.[6] Post-Revolutionary evangelical leaders did not arrest any religious momentum for abolition because no real momentum ever existed. In continuity with the colonial practice, white evangelicals did not give justice to their enslaved brethren in the early national period. Historians who have focused too much on the moral failure of white evangelicals to act against slavery at that time have overshadowed the story of black evangelicals seeking and winning smaller victories within the church.

White evangelicals took the first step toward a reevaluation of their position on slavery during the War for Independence when they stopped criticizing Anglicans for their neglect of people of African descent. When Virginia's patriot leadership destroyed the legal foundations of the Anglican establishment early in the Revolution, the commonwealth's Baptists, Methodists, and Presbyterians realized quite sensibly that calling attention to the Church of England's failure to care for black souls was no longer a useful rhetorical strategy to attract members. White evangelicals therefore began to emphasize their compatibility with republican society more than their concern for black souls in the early 1780s.[7] That this change did not stanch the tremendous influx of black converts is an eloquent testimony to the work of black evangelicals, who continued to recruit slaves and free blacks to join them in evangelical churches.

While black evangelicals were making certain that evangelicalism remained biracial even after whites muted their calls for slave converts, white evangelicals were busily identifying their respective denominations with the Revolution. In a state where disestablishment of the Anglican Church had been an important part of the Revolutionary experience, such a task came easily to those who had protested the loudest against Anglican hegemony.[8] Baptist John Leland, who originally hailed from Massachusetts but was in Virginia for the bulk of the Great Revival, was one of many evangelicals who cited the natural resonance between his denomination's prewar values and those of the fledgling nation. "It is not to be wondered at that the Baptists so heartily and uniformly engaged in the cause of the country against the king," he quipped. "The change suited their political principles, promised religious liberty, and a freedom from ministerial tax."[9]

Virginia Methodists had the furthest to go in their efforts to associate themselves with the Revolution, for they had aligned themselves with Britain and the Anglicans as late as 1776.[10] During the course of the war, however, Virginia Methodists had begun to renounce loyalism and to turn against the Anglican Church, much more so than did their northern coreligionists. In 1779, a group of Virginia Methodists meeting in Fluvanna County ordained one another and started celebrating communion without the supervision of an Anglican cleric. Francis Asbury talked the Virginians out of their popular but defiant ecclesiastical position in April 1782. Virginians' conciliatory actions at their meeting with the Methodist superintendent left them eager to act at the Baltimore Christmas Conference in 1784. There, Virginia Methodists led their coreligionists from across the nation in declaring absolute ecclesiastical independence from the Anglican Church and, ultimately, even from John Wesley and the British Methodists.[11] By early 1785, then, Methodists had realigned themselves with the successful patriot cause. Following Yorktown, they also recognized that getting right with the Revolution was a more effective strategy for achieving church growth than demonstrating concern for black souls.

But evangelical whites could not ignore questions about slavery's justice, both because they faced bondmen within their congregations and because emancipation became part of the very Revolutionary legacy with which they were associating themselves. Mechal Sobel has stressed that it was the experience of biracial fellowship that led some whites to question slavery, maintaining that "it was not ideology but the reality of contact and shared spiritual lives that brought whites to this changed perception."[12] Unquestionably, this was true in some cases. Early evangelical churches were intimate places, and after the influx of black members in the Great Revival, many whites had worshipped alongside an African American Christian for the first time. Blacks and whites extended to one another the right hand of fellowship, heard one another's conversion narratives, sang with one another, and disciplined one another. This intimacy gave way to empathy in some cases.

But the Revolutionary legacy was at least as important as daily contact with the enslaved men and women in building antislavery sentiment among evangelicals. Whites across the nation, not just those in meaningful spiritual contact with slaves, began in the early 1770s to perceive inconsistencies between their republican political sympathies and their acceptance of slavery. For some, the congruence between the colonial complaint against Great Britain and the slaves' case against their owners was too perfect to ignore. "If we would but consider for a moment, the origin of the contest between Great Britain and ourselves," wrote one anonymous pamphleteer in 1785, "and would but condescend to compare their situation with respect to us, to our then situation with respect to what was at that time called the Mother Country, we shall be able to discover the injustice of our conduct toward the Africans."[13] In states above the Mason and Dixon line where the proportion of slaveholders was low, these idealists managed to destroy the practice of slaveholding altogether—or at least to set it on the road to extinction. Between 1777 and 1784, statesmen in Vermont, Pennsylvania, Massachusetts, Rhode Island, and Connecticut ended slavery. The mechanisms differed from state to state—judicial action rendered slavery illegal in Massachusetts in 1783, and Pennsylvanians legislated in 1780 to end the practice gradually—but everywhere signified that local citizens had identified an incompatibility between slavery and republican freedom.[14]

Of enormous significance for the development of the intersectional slavery debate, northern statesmen by their prompt, post-Revolutionary action against slavery forestalled the need for northern evangelicals to wrestle with the issue on their own. Few northern evangelicals discussed slavery in an ecclesiastical context until the 1820s and 1830s, for civic bodies had obviated the need for religious action by ending the practice. In stark contrast, southern statesmen of the Revolutionary era espoused theoretical opposition to slavery but did not take substantive action against it. The General Assembly voted to end Virginia's participation in the Atlantic slave trade in 1778 and passed in 1782 a bill to remove legal obstacles to manumission. But these ambivalent acts kept the question of slavery's future in the public eye instead of resolving it, and Virginia evangelicals thus had to generate their own positions on the issue.[15] Rather than sparing southern evangelicals internal conflict over slavery, their politicians thrust it upon them.

Thomas Jefferson, the towering figure in early national Virginia, epitomized the tendency of politicians from the Upper South to create moral conflict over slavery without taking tangible steps to end it. He publicly labeled slavery "a great political and moral evil" but kept more than 600 African Americans in bondage during the course of his life and only freed a handful, most of whom were his children by Sally Hemings.[16] St. George Tucker, a friend of Jefferson's and by 1788 a professor of law and policy at the College of William and Mary, wrote more voluminously against human bondage. In his 1796 *Dissertation on Slavery, with a Proposal for the Gradual Abolition of It*, Tucker very clearly identified the Revolutionary, as opposed to the evangelical, roots of his convictions. The essay originated as a lecture titled "An Enquiry into the Rights of Persons, as Citizens of the United States of America," not as a venture in moral philosophy. "Whilst America hath been the land of promise to Europeans, and their descendants, it hath been the vale of death to millions of the wretched sons of Africa," he taught, adding that "the genial light of liberty, which hath here shone with unrivalled lustre on the former, hath yielded no comfort to the latter." Like Jefferson, Tucker did not implement this beatific vision; two days after submitting his published *Proposal* to the Virginia General Assembly, he wrote to a Petersburg slave trader about the possibility of selling four women whom he regarded as chattel.[17]

The passion with which men such as Jefferson and Tucker denounced slavery must not obscure white Virginians' overwhelming commitment to the institution. Even more than the inconsistent actions of these Revolutionary luminaries, which themselves betrayed the limits of Revolutionary antislavery, the extraordinary number of Virginians who retained slaves after the passage of the 1782 act liberalizing manumission showed that few whites felt bound to divest themselves of that species of property. Statewide, about four in ten whites lived in a slaveholding household in 1783. If anything, this statistic understates the degree of slaveholder dominance in most of the state, for included in the aggregate ratio are hundreds of households in western counties where slaves were fewer and farther between. Scotch-Irish immigrants into the Shenandoah Valley had not brought slaves with them when they immigrated from Pennsylvania or Ireland at midcentury, and though many would eventually purchase slaves, few had done so by the immediate post-Revolutionary period. Only 8.5 percent of Shenandoah County's 1,310 households contained slaves in 1783, for example, pulling down the state average considerably. In the Piedmont and Tidewater, however, whites had long relied on slave labor, and in several counties a majority of households contained slaves. Powhatan County, just west of the new capital of Richmond, was at the high end of the spectrum; slaveholders headed 80 percent of that county's 271 households. In all, more than 200,000 of 442,117 white Virginians literally lived with slavery in 1790.[18]

White evangelicals constituted their share of these slaveholding households. There were differences by denomination, Baptists and Presbyterians being most likely to own slaves and Methodists the least likely, but no branch of evangelicalism was free from chattel slavery. A comparison of available census records and membership rolls has revealed that Baptists were precisely as likely as their unchurched neighbors to own slaves.[19] The minutes of individual churches provide ample evidence to support this conclusion. When Theodorick Noel baptized fifty souls into Upper King and Queen Baptist Church on 24 February 1788, for example, the seventeen slaves included in that group were the legal property of the new white initiates.[20] Despite the fact that so many Presbyterians lived in the western counties and did not yet participate fully in the state's slave economy, prominent Presbyterians, too, owned slaves. In the tradition of Samuel Davies, denominational spokesman William Graham of Liberty Hall Academy owned human chattel, and individual congregations even bought and sold slaves to support their ministers. Presbyterian churches in Bedford and Cumberland counties were among those that invested in human property.[21] Methodist ministers were the least likely to be slaveowners, though plenty of the Methodist rank and file claimed property in persons. James O'Kelly, eventually destined to leave the Methodist Church to found a new branch of American Christianity, was among the antislavery Methodist ministers who acknowledged, to his disappointment, that many of his connection owned slaves. "And what still serves to augment my pain," he mourned when criticizing slavery, "my beloved Methodist brethren approve of it."[22]

White evangelicals like O'Kelly who questioned slavery may have been persuaded by the natural rights ideas articulated by Jefferson and Tucker, but they had additional, theological reasons to reconsider the justice of slaveholding in the 1780s and 1790s. Black Virginians during the previous decade had broken the correspondence between heathen and African that had supported North American slavery for almost two centuries. As long as the vast majority of slaves had "lived and died strangers to Christianity" in colonial days, keeping the occasional convert enslaved had not caused white evangelicals many scruples. When tens of thousands of people of African descent were clamoring for admission to evangelical churches following the Revolution, however, and were starting their own churches when whites were too slow or unwilling to facilitate the admission of blacks to white congregations, it became impossible for whites to maintain the illusion that religious commitment provided a meaningful distinction between them and their slaves. Most whites simply latched on to the arguments that men like Godwyn, Fleetwood, Whitefield, and Davies had articulated in defense of slave missions before the Revolution—that conversion made individuals better suited for the station into which they were born—and never doubted slavery's scriptural basis. A vocal minority of white evangelicals, perhaps as many as one-third in some congregations, could not ignore the contradiction as easily and demanded discussion of the issue in their churches.

Whites' discovery of the changed theological calculus of slavery after the Great Revival may only have been one of many factors leading to a fresh examination of the nature of slavery and racial difference in the early republic, but it was a factor of particular salience to spiritually committed whites and therefore deserves more attention from historians. Scholars such as Winthrop Jordan and David Brion Davis have skillfully chronicled the evolution of antiblack racism and have rightly identified other reasons why whites questioned the justice of slavery and meaning of race in the age of Revolution, including the increased valuation of individual worth that came with evangelicalism, the acculturation of American-born slaves, and the rise of natural rights philosophy. The recovery of mass black conversion as an additional rationale for white evangelicals' debates over slavery, though, is important. It alone helps to explain why evangelicals who had not worried one whit about slavery's righteousness before the Revolution suddenly began to consider it a theological problem in the war's aftermath. Furthermore, it helps to explain why some evangelicals wanted to discuss slavery with their pastors rather than their elected representatives, for some initially conceived of human bondage as a moral and theological problem rather than a civic issue.[23]

Evangelical visitors to the commonwealth from areas less committed to slavery catalyzed white evangelicals' consideration of the contradictions between African slavery and both the Revolution and the Gospel. For once, the cry of "outside agitator" partly rings true; in the two denominations in which whites engaged in the most protracted discussions about slavery, the Baptist and the Methodist, outsiders were the loudest voices for emancipation.[24] Massachusetts-born John Leland authored the Baptists' strongest denunciation of slavery and campaigned hardest for its extirpation, at least until his return to the Bay State in 1791. Interlopers from Great Britain paced the Virginia Methodists' debate over slavery. Bishop Thomas Coke traveled throughout the Old Dominion in 1785 in a desperate attempt to gain support for an ambitious antislavery position that he had helped to install in the national church's inaugural *Discipline* in December 1784. The first conversation Coke recorded in his diary with a Virginian on the topic, on 30 March 1785, was typical. "We now talked largely on the minutes concerning slavery," he wrote of his conversation with one Brother Seward, "but he would not be persuaded. The secret is, he has twenty-four slaves of his own: but I am afraid, he will do infinite hurt by his opposition to our rules." Not discouraged, Coke resolved on 1 April, "I now begin to venture to exhort our societies to emancipate their slaves," and he was consistent enough in his efforts to have gathered an angry crowd of his "principal friends" by 1 May.[25]

Some whites who responded favorably to the message of apostles of liberty like Leland and Coke considered a move toward antislavery a continuation of their ministry to slaves in colonial times. Before the Revolution, interest in the spiritual welfare of slaves had been enough to set evangelicals apart from Anglicans, who only belatedly became attentive to the spiritual lives of the enslaved. Once the established church gave way following the Revolution to rival sectarian factions, evangelicals interested in keeping their reputations as champions of the lowly did not find the pursuit of black members sufficient to demarcate themselves from one another.[26] All evangelicals shared the belief that both blacks and whites needed the Gospel, so those who would win the competition for the allegiance of slaves and the reputation as respecters of God and not of men needed to go further than demand blacks' inclusion in worship. Some went so far as to press for an end to slavery.

Virginia Quakers demonstrated to evangelicals the possibility of such radical action, for they were the only religious group in the commonwealth during the Revolution to adopt a rigorous antislavery position. Another outside agitator on the slavery question, New Jersey Friend John Woolman, began his work against human bondage following a 1746 journey through the South. He immediately committed to paper his despair at the existence of such an institution but did not publish his thoughts until 1754 as *Some Considerations on the Keeping of Negroes*.[27] Woolman's work, and that of Anthony Benezet, a like-minded Friend, reached fruition quickly in northern colonies, but Virginia Quakers did not decide until 1773 that they would "most earnestly recommend to all who continue to withhold from any their just right to freedom, as they prize their own present peace and future happiness, to clear their hands of this iniquity, by executing manumissions for all those held by them in slavery who are arrived at full age." The Friends followed through on this recommendation and systematically removed slaveholders from their connection, especially after the 1782 statute opened the manumission process.[28]

A very small minority of white evangelicals followed the Quakers' example and freed their slaves. These manumissions do not reveal a great deal about the intradenominational debates over slavery, other than showing that antislavery sentiment extended deeper into the Methodist ranks than it did among other denominations.[29] They do, however, help to illuminate the intellectual and emotional pathways that members of the commonwealth's antislavery vanguard followed to arrive at their positions. For one thing, as Eva Wolf has discovered in the most careful study yet of manumissions under the 1782 law, these pathways were not as well worn as historians have come to believe. Not only were there thousands fewer manumissions than previously thought—perhaps as few as 8,000—but those that did occur were not always antislavery acts. Most slaveholders who freed their bondmen and bondwomen between 1782 and the mid-1790s appear to have been authentic opponents of slavery; they typically freed all of their slaves and indicated strong antislavery sentiment in their deeds of manumission. In contrast, those who freed slaves from the mid-1790s through the repeal of the act in 1806, representing a majority of all manumissions, rarely freed all of their slaves and did not usually record antislavery motives. In other words, later manumitters used selective manumission as a means of increasing control over their slaves.[30]

Deeds of manumission for Surry County from the 1780s through the mid-1790s reveal the strong confluence of Revolutionary and evangelical ideas about human freedom among those who did decide to free their slaves. Manumitters recorded in the deeds their reasons for emancipating and rarely failed to mention both the natural rights ideology of the Revolution and the Gospel imperative to love their neighbors as themselves.[31] In the single most common formulation, repeated almost verbatim dozens of times, one of the first manumitters wrote on 22 August 1782,

> I Anselm Bailey of Surry County in Virginia being persuaded that freedom is the natural right of all mankind and that it is my duty to do unto others as I wou'd be done by in the like situation, having under my care Ne[g]ro Aaron (now in his minority) who I have heretofore held as a slave. I do for myself, my heirs, executors, and administrators relinquish all my right, title, interest, and claim, or pretention of claim whatsoever either to his person or to any estate he may acquire after he shall attain to the age of twenty one years, which will be nearly on the first day of the first month one thousand and seven hundred and eighty six, at which time the above named Negro to enjoy his full freedom without any interruption from me or any person claiming under me, yet I believe it right for me to act as Guardian over him untill he shall arrive to the age above said.[32]

So common was this preamble across several counties that there must have been some coordination or mutual support among emancipators.[33] Even in variant texts, the mutual reinforcement of secular and spiritual motivations is clear. George Gardner wrote in 1790 that "after a deliberate consideration of the practice of slavery I conclude it to be altogether contrary to the laws of nature, reason, and religion."[34] Bailey, Gardner, and other manumitters shared with many white Virginians in the late eighteenth century the belief that the Revolution had somehow unleashed a new epoch of human history and had moved mankind closer to the millennium. The political faiths of Jefferson and Madison converged on some level with the eschatological hopes of committed evangelicals, and the manumission papers convey the power of that synergy.[35]

The Surry County deeds also suggest that fellowship with black believers helped motivate antislavery manumitters. Black Methodism was particularly strong in the Tidewater area. Surry did not have its own circuit until 1790, when it reported 244 black and 677 white members. The nearby circuits of Portsmouth, Sussex, and Brunswick likely included Surry congregations before that date, and all reported large numbers of black members. By 1791, the Surry circuit contained more black Methodists, 705, than did any other circuit in Virginia. While the circuit was not precisely coterminous with the county, black Methodists clearly constituted a tremendous proportion of the area's black population. In the 1790 census, Surry County itself reported 3,097 slaves and 368 free blacks, more than half of whom probably attended a Methodist church.[36] It is meaningful, then, that manumitters wrote in the language of the Golden Rule, explaining that "it is my duty to do unto others as I would be done by in the like situation." They did not appeal to any of the scriptural arguments against "manstealing" to explain their actions or critique the clumsy argument from the Curse of Ham; instead they explained that through manumission they were trying to fulfill their duty to love their neighbors. While it is possible that this could have been an abstract expression of the unity of the family of man, given the documented conversion of Surry County blacks and the particular word choice that whites used to explain the manumissions, it seems far more likely that whites were trying to do justice to their new spiritual brethren.

African American Virginians may have helped advance the cause of liberty by simply joining Surry County Methodist churches, but they were often more assertive in their pleas for white evangelicals to look at slavery in a new light. Enslaved evangelicals constantly brought concerns intrinsic to the practice of chattel slavery—the fragility of slave families or the use of corporal punishment, for instance—before their congregations for discussion. Another way that slaves and free blacks influenced white evangelicals was by maintaining their autonomy as religious actors. African Americans continued to choose which church they attended, and they usually followed those evangelical leaders who took the most aggressive stances against slavery. When black Virginians shifted their allegiance to white ministers who took antislavery positions, this placed their white allies in a difficult position. On one hand, whites who argued against slavery felt empowered by the large constituency within the church that supported their position. On the other, the spiritual independence of black Virginians frightened slaveholders with the specters of insubordination and insurrection. African American evangelicals thus continued to create ideological challenges for their white brethren even though their churches refused to throw their influence against slavery. Blacks demanded from white evangelicals tangible evidence of goodwill, resulting in a series of ameliorative decisions by white churchmen.

In the three denominations best characterized as evangelical in the 1790s —Baptist, Methodist, and Presbyterian—leaders ultimately resolved internal conflicts over slavery and muted the divisive effect of their new antislavery constituencies in the same way, by forcing the discussion outside the church and into the statehouse. There, conversation about slavery's justice could cause only civil, not spiritual, discord. According to the similar settlements reached in all three denominations, neither supporters nor opponents of the institution of slavery were to use the churches as a venue through which to argue their positions. Whites chose not to demand that members emancipate their slaves, reserving the prerogative to act on such a divisive subject for civil authorities. By the same token, neither Baptists, Methodists, nor Presbyterians passed any resolution suggesting that slavery was a positive good. Converted blacks and their allies within religious communities militated against such a decision. The difference between formally embracing slavery and refusing to act against it was more than a semantic one. In the first instance, white churchmen would have needed to legislate their antagonism toward black evangelicals; in the second, they merely needed to allow civil processes to run their course.[37] Ecclesiastical inaction was nonetheless functionally proslavery, for white evangelicals' decision not to confront slavery corporately protected the status quo.

Virginia's white church members found easy and compelling support for their conviction that contrasting views of slavery should not divide their religious communities. Most of all, they found slavery in the Bible and determined that they could not intervene in an institution that both Old and New Testaments appeared to sustain. The patriarchs owned slaves; Jesus refused to condemn the institution; and Paul directly urged slaves to remain submissive. Indeed, the apostle seemed to have addressed the subject directly: "Servants, obey in all things your masters according to the flesh; not with eyeservice, as menpleasers, but in singleness of heart, fearing God."[38] Whites cited chapter and verse from both Old and New Testament descriptions of slavery in public petitions defending the institution. Even though the Old Testament only provided a precedent for the perpetual enslavement of those outside God's covenant relationship with Israel, Virginia whites uncritically cited Exodus and Leviticus to show biblical precedent for slavery in the abstract. The statute of 1667—which denied any connection between conversion and liberation—allowed this rhetorical sleight of hand.[39] Further compounding this conflation of Hebraic slavery with slavery as practiced in the late-eighteenth-century South, both foes and supporters of slavery approached scripture with a strict literalism that discouraged the contextualization of passages on slavery. Without a more critical or imaginative hermeneutic, white southern evangelicals simply could not have moved against slavery.[40]

Devereux Jarratt, the evangelical Anglican minister who played a critical role in sustaining the early Methodist movement in the commonwealth, typified the white evangelical response to conflict within the church over slavery. Too attached to the Anglican tradition to follow Methodists into ecclesiastical independence at the 1784 Christmas Conference, Jarratt joined the Protestant Episcopal Church instead. He remained in Virginia for a few years following the Great Revival, and before he left the state, he chronicled the religious changes that took place following the Revolution. In his letters, the Episcopal minister dealt carefully with debates over slavery taking place within Methodist churches specifically, and the Old Dominion's churches in general. He prefigured the Baptist, Methodist, and Presbyterian settlements over slavery in a March 1788 letter to Methodist Edward Dromgoole. Jarratt argued that because the Bible contained references to slavery and because the issue proved so divisive, white evangelicals should simply refrain from discussing it within the church.[41]

Jarratt opened by censuring those who attacked slaveholders. "Even allowing that those who retain Bondmen are wrong in so doing," he expounded, "yet I should think they ought not to be put upon a levil, (as they are now) with horsethieves & Hogstealers, Knaves, & c., nor to be insulted at every turn with the odious Name of Oppressors, Rogues, & Men destitute of even heathen honesty & c." He then appealed to scripture, strenuously arguing that slaveholders should not have to receive this sort of condemnation, "especially as they suppose they are warranted in their Practice by the Example of Abraham, Isaac, & all the antient People of God; & not only those, but by the writings of the Apostles, whose directions & Exhortations to Bond & free incline them to believe that such stations & relations were to exist under the Gospel, otherwise, 30 or 40 verses might as well be blotted out of the new testament, as being of no practical use. Nay they had much better be blotted, because, if the Practice is wrong, they very naturally tend to Lead Men into the Deception." Since the argument for slavery from scripture was so strong, and since supporters of slavery enjoyed the support of "the best & wisest of Commentators also," Jarratt concluded that "at least they ought to be judged honest men, & not put upon a footing with Thieves of every kind & c."

Jarratt was not seeking to render debate over slavery more civil; he hoped to squelch discussion of the issue entirely. As the deliberative bodies of Virginia Baptists, Methodists, and Presbyterians would each do within a few years of his letter, he declared that the best way to guarantee harmony among whites was to banish the discussion of slavery from the churches, without affirming or criticizing the practice. "I hope you wont understand that I am writing to you to prove the innocency or lawfulness of Slavery," he explained to Dromgoole. "No. I know not your opinion on it, nor do I wish to know. Be it your Opinion what It will, I do not even wish to alter it. If our sentiments should not be alike in it, I agree to disagree, & never say a word about it. I stand neuter, I neither persuade nor dissuade any one to this or that in the case." Virginia's evangelical leaders would permit their members to discuss slavery in their private capacity as citizens, but they ultimately followed Jarratt in eliminating discussion within their churches.

Virginia's white Baptists had welcomed the largest number of black converts in the Great Revival. Perhaps because they faced so many enslaved worshippers each Sunday, they were the first to make explicit the boundaries of their empathy and to echo Jarratt in defining emancipation as strictly a civil question. Antislavery Baptists tried to make their voices heard on both the congregational and the associational levels, but they were the most effective lobbying at the most rarefied level of Baptist polity, the General Committee. In 1785, Virginia Baptists were still divided into competing Regular and Separate factions and were busy campaigning against a general assessment and for religious freedom. A resolution from an umbrella committee of Regular Baptists declaring slavery "contrary to the word of God" does not appear to have gained much traction or generated many responses from congregations. A response from the Greenbrier Church in the Ketocton Association nonetheless forecast the Baptists' resolution of the antislavery challenge. The church admitted that many members felt slavery was wrong, even going so far as to state that "we believe it to be an evil in keeping them in bondage for life," but they also protested their association's request that they go on the record with their opinion and risk a painful argument. "Our church having but few [slaves]," they demurred, "we hope our Brethren will not think it hard if we lie neuter in this matter."[42]

The Regulars and the Separates combined in 1787, and each group sent representatives to an enlarged General Committee of Baptist Associations, a relatively weak body that became the chief organ for the denomination in Virginia. Antislavery Baptists, a significant minority, chose this flimsy organization rather than any particular local congregation as the best forum in which to advance their views. As early as 1788, a member of the committee posed the question of "whether a petition should be offered to the Gen. Assembly, praying that the yoke of slavery may be made more tolerable."[43] No one took up the debate that year or the next. In 1790, however, the committee finally agreed to "take into consideration the reference concerning the equity, of Hereditary slavery." Discussion among the twenty-odd clerics present, including nineteen official delegates from eight associations, proved inconclusive. The moderator, a native slaveholder named Samuel Harriss, cut off the contentious debate and appointed a committee of four to draft a resolution: William Fristoe of Ketocton, Reuben Pickett of Roanoke, David Barrow of Kehuckey, and John Waller of Orange. When this small group failed to craft a statement upon which all could agree, John Leland of Massachusetts offered one of his own. Perhaps out of desperation after almost three days of deadlocked discussion, the General Committee accepted Leland's resolution, which called slavery a "violent deprivation of the rights of nature, and inconsistent with the republican government," and urged Baptists to use "every legal measure, to extirpate the horrid evil from the land."[44]

Many Baptists rebelled against Leland's resolution, even though it already conceded the supremacy of civil authorities in matters concerning slavery by urging Baptists to pursue only "every legal measure" for its extirpation. Slaveowning Baptists rejected the strong insinuation in the resolution that slavery, in and of itself, was a sin. Less than a month after receiving word of the General Committee's statement, the Roanoke Association announced, "Tho' we are not unanimously clear in our minds whether the God of nature ever intended that one part of the human species should be held in an abject state of slavery to another part of the same species . . . we suppose neither the General Committee nor any other religious society whatever has the least right to concern therein as a society, but leave every individual to act at discretion in order to keep a good conscience before God."[45] The Roanoke Association must not have been the only reluctant group, for members of the General Committee quickly retreated from their resolution and sought to establish a position that would preserve the integrity of their faith while minimizing conflict among the churches, which was their primary goal. The committee remanded the issue to its constituent associations in 1791 and requested more input from them.[46] Meanwhile, firebrand John Leland left the state.

When white Baptists convened as the General Committee in 1793 to forge a new position on behalf of the denomination, there was more than one empty chair at the table. David Barrow, who had attended the meeting for the previous three years, had freed his own slaves in 1784, and had voted for Leland's resolution in 1790, was also absent. When the delegates revisited the question about "hereditary slavery," they doubtless thought of Barrow's Black Creek Baptist Church in Southampton County, where the pastor was engaged in his seventh year of acrimonious fighting over the place of slavery within the Baptist polity.

The minutes of Black Creek Baptist Church are ambiguous, but it was probably Barrow who posed the question at a congregational meeting in February 1786 that set off several years of intermittent debate over slavery. He, or one of his colleagues, asked, "Is it a ritious thing for a Christian to hold or cause any of the Humane Race to be held in Slavery?" After the church voted in November that it was indeed unrighteous, foes of slavery moved in February 1787 to distance the congregation further from slaveholding. Antislavery Baptists in the church asked if "a person who hires Slaves be Consider'd as one who hold or Causes any part of mankind to be held in Slavery." This question simmered for five months after its introduction until the church debated it and withdrew the question without an answer. Those who hired slaves remained members. Meanwhile, both slaves and slaveholders joined the church during the Great Revival and put the earlier resolutions about slavery to the test.[47]

Black Creek's African American members kept the moral challenges of slaveholding at the fore. While whites debated the resolutions about slaveholding and slave hiring, they also responded to claims of abuse and conducted a yearlong investigation of "Br. Tynes & Sistern Tynes" for "using Barbarity toward their slaves." The investigation of the Tynes family, probably but not definitively initiated by slaves themselves, began on 26 May 1786, just after Barrow had asked about the righteousness of slavery but before the congregation had reached a decision on the query. Whites thus debated how some of their own treated their slaves—a particular question—precisely at the same time and in the same meetings in which they debated a more general question about the righteousness of slavery. Even if black members did not initiate the case against the Tynes family, they were the key witnesses in it and had a hand in the couple's exclusion on 24 May 1787. The testimony of black members doubtless influenced how whites voted on the more abstract question as well.[48]

A new battle over slavery among whites began at Black Creek in February 1791, in the form of a certain Brother Jones's mysterious accusations against some of his brethren. Jones "openly charged Brn Stephen Lankford, John Suter, David Barrow, Benjamin Beal, and Sam Blackman with injuring him in his character, Property and Peace." Brother Jones's exact grievance remains unclear. It appears likely, however, that he was angry at certain church members for attacking his Christian character on the basis of his status as a slaveholder. Whites in Black Creek began debating the issue of slavery at the next business meeting on 24 June. Then, the clerk recorded that "Brn Norvel Vick's, Benjamin Beal's, John Johnson's Elizabeth Beal's and Sally Barrow's Difficulty was with a Part of the Church for holding Slaves and hiring them which caused a Debate which took up the greater Part of the Day. The Church agree to bear with them until a further hearing." The five antislavery advocates evidently earned probation for their attempts to hold the congregation to their 1786 ruling that slaveholding was not righteous, because at the 26 August meeting, the others returned them "to their privileges" as members. The tension over whether or not slaveholders should be accepted as members bubbled just beneath the surface for several more years and erupted again in November 1793 when Norvel Vick "absented himself from the Lords Table on account of Slaves being held by some of the Brethren."[49]

White members of Black Creek Baptist Church displayed in their treatment of Vick a new policy on slavery. Though they did not vote on a new resolution or even refute explicitly the 1786 decision that slavery was not righteous, they very clearly communicated that they valued white harmony more than their antislavery legacy. Whites pressed Vick to suppress his personal feelings about slavery, to rejoin the church, and to tolerate his slaveholding brethren. In other words, they argued that since slaveholding whites did not use the church to justify their ownership of human beings, so too should Vick refrain from using the church to advance his case against slavery. The solution was temporary, for Vick ultimately left the church for good in 1802. In 1793, however, he "agreed to content himself as much as possible under the care and in the Fellowship of the Church." Even a genuine opponent of slavery in the 1790s was not willing to risk the unity of his local congregation.[50]

At their 1793 meeting, the General Committee of Baptist Associations reached precisely the same position as had Baptists in Southampton County's Black Creek Baptist Church. They may have been thinking of David Barrow as they voted, and they might have been trying to insulate the commonwealth's churches against the kind of firestorm he had started in Black Creek. In what would become the uniform evangelical response to emancipationists within their midst, the ministers at the 1793 meeting of the General Committee eschewed any sort of proslavery proclamation but ordered congregants who were uncomfortable with the institution to take their concerns to the state. The delegates decided "that the subject be dismissed from committee, as believing it belongs in the legislative body." This assessment echoed the Roanoke Baptist Association's agnostic position on the justice of slavery and channeled the potentially divisive debate out of the churches and into the General Assembly.[51] Other associations swiftly adopted this noncommittal position; in 1797, the Dover Association decreed, "We sincerely sympathize, both as Christians and Citizens, with those unhappy people. . . . We would therefore recommend to our Brethren, to unite with the Abolition Society, in proposing a petition to the General Assembly, for their gradual emancipation."[52]

One of the many remarkable things about this decision to separate sacred jurisdictions from secular ones was that, only a decade before, it had been impossible to distinguish clearly between ecclesiastical and civil issues. Before its disestablishment in 1779 and the establishment of religious freedom in 1786, the Anglican Church had been an adjunct of the state. Its vestries had been the first step on the colonial *cursus honorum*, and its oversight was the business of the Virginia General Assembly. Baptists had played a critical role in changing this situation and had argued more forcefully than Jefferson himself that church should be sundered completely from state.[53] When they relegated discussion of slavery's future to the statehouse, Baptists were thus taking advantage of an altogether new ecclesiastical possibility: that some moral issues had such profound civil implications that they were off limits for churches to discuss. This was the ugly side of disestablishment; while it freed white consciences, it placed profound ideological obstacles in the way of evangelical action against slavery.

Jefferson did not cause white evangelicals to abdicate moral responsibility for slavery, but late in his life he did insist that ministers did not have the right to bring up controversial political issues before their congregations, precisely the position that evangelicals adopted vis-à-vis slavery. The chronology of the statement—Jefferson elaborated most fully on ministerial responsibilities in an 1815 letter—makes it impossible to establish any causal relationship between Jefferson's ideas and the evangelical settlement on slavery. But Jefferson had written on the need to separate church and state from the late 1770s, and his 1815 letter at least suggests that white evangelicals were drawing on current ideas about the proper role of churches in a republic in order to make their accommodation with slavery. Jefferson explained that it was wrong for ministers or parishioners to speak about contentious scientific or political issues, for ministers and congregations covenanted together for exclusively religious purposes. "Whenever, therefore, preachers, instead of a lesson in religion, put them off with a discourse on the Copernican system, on chemical affinities, on the construction of government, or the characters or conduct of those administering it," he maintained, "it is a breach of contract, depriving their audience of the kind of service for which they are salaried." "I do not deny that a congregation may, if they please, agree with their preacher that he shall instruct them in Medicine also, or Law, or Politics," he conceded, "but this must be with the consent of every individual; because the association being voluntary, the mere majority has no right to apply the contributions of the minority to purposes unspecified in the agreement of the congregation."[54] Since white Baptists did not find unanimity on emancipation, they steered clear of it in good Jeffersonian fashion.

Virginia Methodists boasted a stronger church hierarchy than did the Baptists and enjoyed more connections to churchmen outside Virginia, with the result that they endured a more protracted confrontation with antislavery forces within their denomination. Several scholars have traced that conflict in its full arc, from the publication of the initial *Discipline* in 1784, in which Methodists promised to expel members who bought and sold slaves and forbade traveling ministers to own slaves, through the General Conference's decision in 1804 to publish separate *Disciplines* for Methodists in slaveholding and nonslaveholding states. There were two significant Methodist pushes for emancipation in Virginia, each of which met with abject, humiliating failure. Those two initiatives were the attempt to win acceptance for the 1784 *Discipline* and the circulation by some Methodist ministers in 1785 of an antislavery petition for the General Assembly.

Ministers at the General Conference revealed their anxiety over Virginians' reception of the 1784 *Discipline* in the moment of its passage. They granted a two-year grace period for Virginians before they had to emancipate their slaves or face excommunication. This conciliatory move did little to make the plan acceptable to whites in the Old Dominion. While some manumitted their slaves, most laughed off the requirement. In 1785, participants in the General Conference recommended "to all our brethren to suspend the execution of the minute on slavery, till the deliberations of a future conference."[55] According to Virginia-born minister Jesse Lee, not even the revised rules stood a chance in his native state. The regulations "were so much opposed by many of our private members, local preachers, and some of the travelling preachers" that they were never implemented.[56]

Bishop Thomas Coke grieved the repeal of the minute on slavery and spearheaded an alternative assault on human bondage. He helped to write a petition to the Virginia General Assembly in 1785 and circulated it throughout the commonwealth. In it, the Methodist leadership urged legislators "to pass a law for the immediate or gradual emancipation of all the slaves." Coke miscalculated the reception that his document would receive. The House of Delegates treated the petition contemptuously and almost placed the proposal *beneath* the table. It would not be an exaggeration to say that the effort backfired completely, for angry slaveholders who saw copies of the petition circulating in their neighborhoods launched a much larger counterpetition drive.[57] Even Methodism's most sympathetic chroniclers conclude from the failure of the minute and of the petition that most white Virginia Methodists did not support the antislavery initiatives of their coreligionists at the state and national levels.

The case of the Virginia Methodists is illuminating despite the failures of 1784 and 1785 because of the way that black Virginians worked with a stubborn antislavery white minority to keep the issue alive within their connection. Within the Wesleyan fold, black believers displayed a very sophisticated awareness of where different parties stood on slavery. They voted with their feet for denominational leaders who promised to use the power of the church to work against hereditary servitude. They especially aligned behind minister James O'Kelly, one of several Methodist clergymen violently opposed to their bondage and the one most willing to take his fellow ministers to task for their complicity with a denomination that tolerated ownership of slaves.

O'Kelly earned a reputation in the 1780s as one especially concerned with the enslaved. He sealed this status in 1789 by publishing the widely circulated *Essay on Negro Slavery*, in which he laid out a vigorous, biblical plea for emancipation. In the terms in which he attacked chattel slavery, O'Kelly drew from both the colonial legacy of appealing to black Virginians in order to prove the authenticity of evangelical faith and the Revolutionary legacy of natural rights. Like colonial evangelicals, he argued that those who ministered to slaves were engaged in the most authentic possible expression of Christian faith. "This is feeding the hungry, clothing the naked, in the highest sense," he proclaimed of working for emancipation. "Our business is not only to free them," he added, "but to do all we can, respecting their souls and bodies." But onto this old, dissenter perspective he grafted the natural rights language that Jefferson and Tucker were promulgating. O'Kelly sounded less like a minister than a statesman when he added, "The gentlemen who formed our bill of rights call slavery *an inhuman negative*. Our revolution can be justified on no other principles. Our government stands on the basis of natural liberty, as the birthright of all human beings."[58]

Based on the written testimony against slavery that he left in his *Essay*, O'Kelly also drew from his interactions with black Methodists when formulating his antislavery position. He began his preaching career in Surry County, and his description of the emotional impact of beholding an enslaved brother or sister in Christ may have animated some of that county's many manumitters. "If it be a divine precept to *feel* for those of our brethren who are in bondage," he besought his readers, "certainly we ought to *deliver* them, if it be in our power; otherwise it would be dissimulation to pretend to feel part of their burdens." He drove home this theme of failed Christian brotherhood by referring often to enslaved Methodists, perhaps most poignantly in the gut-wrenching conclusion of the *Essay*: "O Almighty Goodness, hear the groans of my poor brethren; behold their blood spilling like water! How long will the bowels of a tender parent bear it? . . . Moses' disciples chastized thy enemies with rods, but Christians chastize thy friends with scorpions! Thy truth suffers, Lord Jesus, and so do thy creatures."[59]

When, in 1792, O'Kelly led a group out of the Methodist Church to protest their episcopal form of government and failure to act against slavery, black Methodists sustained him.[60] Black Virginians who had met the preacher in the course of his ministry proved themselves fully cognizant of the difference between his heartfelt antislavery convictions and the equivocal position other Methodists were adopting in saying that slavery was wrong but not acting on that judgment. In the eight Southside Virginia circuits that O'Kelly served as presiding elder in 1790 or later and for which there are returns each year, African American Virginians made the most of their freedom to join whichever church they wanted. In those circuits, blacks joined churches associated with O'Kelly after he published his *Essay*; whites in these circuits, not coincidentally, began to leave these churches. In 1793, the last year for which statistics were largely unaffected by the schism, there were 4,844 whites and 2,392 blacks in these circuits, which centered around Surry County. By 1796, there were only 3,663 whites and 1,117 black members in those same circuits; the white membership had fallen by almost one-quarter (24.4 percent), and the black membership had fallen by more than one-half (53.3 percent). The Surry County circuit, which contained in 1790 more black Methodists than any other Virginia circuit, literally vanished. The effect on black Methodists elsewhere in the church was much more muted: there were actually more black Virginians in non-O'Kelly circuits in 1796 than there had been in 1793. So many Southside black Methodists left the church that it took more than a decade for Methodists to recover, and even longer in Surry County. By 1804, the year in which the white membership of the Methodist Church in Virginia surpassed 1793 levels, black membership across the state still languished at 2,771. When the O'Kelly schism occurred, the Methodists and Baptists were competing on fairly even terms for black membership. Afterward, the number of black Methodists would never again approach the number of black Baptists.[61]

O'Kelly and African American Methodists thus placed the Old Dominion's remaining white Methodists on the horns of a dilemma: whether to alienate slaveholding whites or black Virginians. Slaves and free blacks had emphatically demonstrated that they would not join an actively proslavery church when an antislavery option was available, and slaveholders would not accept limits on their prerogatives as masters. Methodists did as the Baptists had done when confronted with this situation: they dodged the issue and relegated all discussion over slavery to the legislature. They determined that white men and women could disagree with one another about slavery and still be faithful Christians. In other words, they, too, accepted by the mid-1790s precisely the position that Devereux Jarratt had advocated in 1788. Virginia's white Methodists no longer tried to act for or against slavery, but they did retain a rhetorical posture against the institution more critical than Jarratt would have liked, probably as a salve to the angry passions of some of their black members. Virginia whites did not balk when national leaders included in an 1800 *Address of the General Conference of the Methodist Episcopal Church, to all their Brethren and Friends in the United States* a vigorous condemnation of slavery. They did, however, ignore its exhortation for Methodists everywhere to petition state legislatures for more lenient manumission laws. Recalling the disastrous 1785 petition drive, white Methodists refused to use the church or its agents as a vehicle for or against slavery. Any antislavery activity had to take place outside the auspices of the church if another experience as humiliating as the petition campaign or as crippling as O'Kelly's schism was to be avoided.

Virginia Presbyterians did not have many black members in their churches in the early national period, despite the legacy of Samuel Davies. They nonetheless silenced the few antislavery members within their denomination in the 1790s, preferring as did their Baptist and Methodist neighbors to agree to disagree on the controversial topic of slavery. The Presbyterian General Assembly made Virginia Presbyterians' acceptance of this position

Old Cypress Church (Surry County, Virginia). Black Virginians joined evangelical churches at three times the rate of white Virginians during the Great Revival from 1785 to 1792, guaranteeing that evangelicalism in the nineteenth century would be a biracial phenomenon. Nowhere did this process advance more quickly than in Surry County, where more than one-half of the black population attended a Methodist church like this one by 1790. This Surry County church was one of the first in which Methodist James O'Kelly, an outspoken opponent of slavery, ever preached. Black residents demonstrated their spiritual autonomy by following O'Kelly when he seceded from the Methodist Church in 1792. (Photograph courtesy of Elon University Archives and Special Collections, Elon, N.C.)

an easy one, for they proposed less controversial measures than did their Methodist counterparts. In reply to a question from antislavery Presbyterians in Kentucky over how to handle their proslavery brethren, for example, the General Assembly ruled in 1795 "that as the same difference of opinion with respect to slavery takes place in sundry other parts of the Presbyterian Church, notwithstanding which they live in charity and peace according to the doctrine and practice of the Apostles, it is hereby recommended to all conscientious persons, and especially to those whom it immediately respects, to do the same." Virginians echoed this perspective in their

Table 2. White and Black Membership in Methodist Circuits Served by James O'Kelly, 1790–1796

Circuit	Years O'Kelly served as presiding elder	1790 White	1790 Black	1791 White	1791 Black	1792 White	1792 Black	1793 White	1793 Black	1794 White	1794 Black	1795 White	1795 Black	1796 White	1796 Black
Brunswick	1783, 1787–92	676	266	627	200	677	233	653	161	586	216	520	181	500	187
Sussex	1784, 1787–92	690	145	606	208	565	168	448	206	1,285	1,069	820	240	664	180
Amelia	1787–92	740	158	651	132	645	139	645	139	545	103	433	63	396	41
Bedford	1788–89, 1791	370	150	383	89	499	43	474	102	345	41	441	72	366	59
Portsmouth	1788–90, 1792	949	693	819	574	787	557	729	439	651	367	665	537	610	380
Cumberland	1791–92	351	34	385	37	384	37	416	43	312	7	382	35	445	40
Greensville	1790, 1792	776	300	720	383	735	219	665	347	878	360	841	336	682	230
Surry	1790–92	677	244	770	705	831	800	814	955	Sussex and Surry merged.					
Total eight O'Kelly circuits		5,229	1,990	4,961	2,328	5,123	2,196	4,844	2,392	4,602	2,163	4,102	1,464	3,663	1,117
Total Virginia Methodists		12,668	3,387	12,248	3,757	12,857	3,494	12,825	3,683	12,896	3,420	10,706	2,505	11,321	2,458

Source: Minutes of the Annual Conferences of the Methodist Episcopal Church, 1773–1828.

Note: O'Kelly served other circuits as well during his tenure as presiding elder, but these are the eight for which there are statistics available for each year from 1790 through 1796.

own counsels. Delegates to the 1800 meeting of the Synod of Virginia lamented "that so many thousands of our fellow creatures should in this land of liberty, and asylum for the oppressed, be held in chains," but they believed that "to refuse to hold Christian communion with any who may differ from us in sentiment & practice in this instance would . . . be a very unwarrantable procedure."[62]

White Virginia Presbyterians had the occasion to affirm their policy of tolerance in 1815 when one of their ministers, George Bourne, tried to open a one-man crusade against slavery within the church. When away from his home state at the General Assembly, Bourne accused all slaveholders of being guilty of theft and tried to require that all Presbyterians manumit their slaves immediately. Bourne survived the assembly with his career intact but could not coax its members to vote against slavery. He ran into more serious problems when he returned to the commonwealth. White Virginians were especially angry that their delegate claimed to have seen a minister driving slaves through a town in his home presbytery, a statement that made "injurious impressions in the Assembly against the Presbyterian Clergy in Virginia." The language that Bourne used to defend himself did not help his case. In one letter, Bourne claimed that "the Devil can make better pretensions to be a christian than a Slaveholder," which grated against the ears of those who heard the missive read at trial. Proceedings against Bourne continued until the General Assembly of 1818, when he finally left the state in disgrace.[63]

White Virginians like Bourne, who could not abide the decision to remove discussion of slavery from the churches, left the state. Most, though, capitulated gently to the truce between pro- and antislavery factions, because they agreed with their proslavery brethren that saving souls took precedence over saving bodies. Evangelicals, Donald Mathews explained, "saw the Spirit of God in their own expansion and were therefore unwilling to place opposition to slavery above the need to bring all manner of folk—masters as well as slaves—within the community of faithful people."[64] Those who could not abide this position moved to Kentucky, Ohio, or somewhere else where they did not need to respect the convictions and property rights of slaveowners in their churches. These "migrants against slavery" left behind a few determinedly antislavery friends, but they considerably deradicalized the criticism of slavery in Virginia (and strengthened it elsewhere) by taking their advocacy out of the state and allowing ecclesiastical "gag rules" to stand.[65]

Some migrants could not resist a parting shot against slavery. Baptist minister David Barrow, who had been at the center of so much controversy surrounding slavery, published a forceful antislavery circular upon his departure for Kentucky in 1798. Barrow complained that his opposition to slavery made life in the commonwealth untenable. "I cannot comfortably support my family, educate my children, and attend so much to public calls, as I have done, with my means, in this poor country," he wrote, "without falling into the line of speculation, or that of holding slaves, or sticking closely and personally to my farm." Barrow would not go back to slaveholding after emancipating his slaves in 1784, because "holding, tyrannizing over, and driving slaves" he viewed "as contrary to the laws of God and nature."[66] Barrow, whose parallel political and religious creeds showed again the mutual reinforcement of evangelicalism and republicanism, joined in the Bluegrass State a significant cohort of expatriate Virginians who were trying to make certain that Baptists combated slavery more effectively in their new home than they had in their former state. Though they ultimately met failure both within their communion and on the civic front, antislavery members of the Elkhorn Association in 1791 manfully declared their opposition to slavery and tried to throw their association's weight behind an effort to pressure the nascent state government to forbid the institution. The three clerics who lobbied the constitutional convention on the association's behalf, Augustine Eastin, James Garrard, and Ambrose Dudley, were all Virginia Baptists who had migrated in opposition to slavery.[67]

More often the protest was private, either in letters to evangelical friends or in parting sermons. Methodist Edward Dromgoole, who was debating migration himself, received many letters in the first decade of the nineteenth century from fellow clerics who had decided to migrate to Ohio. After helping to lead revivals in Powhatan and Buckingham counties, Philip Gatch left Virginia in 1802 and wrote Dromgoole that he was "unwilling to lay my Bones there, and leave my children whom I tenderly loved in a land of slavery, not knowing what there evils thereof would amount to in there time." John Sale wrote that in Ohio, "we have a fertile soil & salubrious air that is not contaminated with *Slavery*." Bennett Maney asked "whether it be right in the sight of god for you to die there [in Virginia] and leave your children and grand children in that land of oppression."[68]

Just before leaving his native Virginia in 1794, Presbyterian minister Cary Allen, whose father had trained under Samuel Davies, delivered what his first biographer treated as his valedictory sermon to a houseful of slaves and their white owners. He presented an otherwise unremarkable message to the white auditors before abruptly changing gears at the end of the sermon and addressing the slaves directly. While Allen may have led in coarsely, asking, "Do you think that such poor black, dirty-looking creatures as you can ever get to heaven?" he turned his message to one of radical spiritual equality. "But I can tell you," he assured them, "that the blessed Saviour shed his blood as much for you as for your masters, or any of the white people. . . . Your masters may make some sort of excuse for serving the devil, because they have many of the good things of this life, with the pleasures of sin for a season. But what have you to make a heaven of in this world?" he asked. "You may become religious, and find peace with God as easy as white persons, and I think easier too, for you have not got half so many temptations in your path."[69]

The vast majority of black evangelicals were enslaved and could not leave the commonwealth in search of antislavery churches. For a few hundred persons, O'Kelly provided an alternative in his Republican Methodist Church, soon to become the "Christian" Church, but most black Virginians did not have an O'Kellyite congregation nearby. Instead of abandoning evangelicalism altogether after it became clear that their white coreligionists would not act against slavery, black evangelicals remained in evangelical churches and shaped whites' understanding of their obligations toward the enslaved from within evangelicalism.[70] A huge majority of black evangelicals gathered in Baptist churches, which became the most important sites of racial interaction in this period. By their presence and the explicit requests within these churches, African American believers forced white evangelicals to define how they would behave in a world with slavery, even if they would not take a stand on the justice of slaveholding itself. Moreover, black evangelicals made certain that whites rendered complacent by the settlement over slavery did not close evangelical churches to people of African descent. This must have seemed like a real possibility to black Virginians who had witnessed white evangelicals' steady retreat from the language of racial inclusion and who lived in a nation whose citizenship benefits were sharply limited to whites only. It was black Virginians who kept the churches biracial and prevented an ecclesiastical version of a turn to herrenvolk republicanism.[71]

Williamsburg's Gowan Pamphlet, while weathering accusations that he was conspiring with Haitian émigrés against slaveholders, channeled considerable energies into fighting for ecclesiastical inclusion. He confounded whites who might have moved to exclude or marginalize black believers following the Great Revival when he sought representation for his African Baptist Church in the Dover Baptist Association in 1791 and gained acceptance to that association in 1793. It is impossible to construe the admission of Pamphlet's church into the nation's largest Baptist association as a strategy for social control on the part of whites, because black members of the Williamsburg church initiated the process themselves. The secretary for the Dover Association recorded that "the Baptist church of black people at Williamsburg, agreeable to their request, was received into this Association, as they could not have done better in the circumstances than they have." Pamphlet and the emerging cohort of black leaders whom he gathered around him in Williamsburg made the most of this victory. They extended their activism from the local to the regional level and brought a vocal black presence to the Dover Association's annual meeting each year. Pamphlet himself served as a delegate to the association at least twelve times between 1793 (the year he received his freedom) and 1807. His protégés accompanied him and succeeded him after his 1807 retirement; Charles Bryan, Simon Gullet, Israel Camp, Lewis Armstead, T. Maise, Benjamin White, Thomas Mars, and James Roberts all served as delegates for the church.[72]

Other black men were also pushing for new roles within the Baptist Church during this period. Benjamin White and James Roberts were serving as delegates for the Williamsburg church at the Dover Association in 1813 when they had the pleasure of helping to welcome Elam Baptist Church from Charles City, another independent black Baptist community. Free black pastor Abraham Brown had founded Elam in 1810 and reported forty-two members in 1814 when he joined the Dover Association's small black caucus. In King and Queen County, Toney, a black Baptist preacher, established a new church in 1782 and nurtured its growth to 110 members by 1793. Black Baptists also formed two new churches in the city of Petersburg, Gillfield and Harrison Street Baptist. Members of the Gillfield Baptist Church joined the Portsmouth Association. In 1815, they even hosted the annual meeting of that predominantly white body.[73]

While independent black churches may have been relatively rare, the remarkable success of a few congregations accurately symbolized the strength of black evangelicalism, or at least African American Baptist life, at the turn of the century. Baptist churches in Portsmouth, Petersburg, and Williamsburg alone initiated more than 1,000 new black Virginians into the faith between 1792 and 1812, continuing the trend of surging black Baptist membership and outstripping white growth. Black men and women even gave Methodism a second chance in the first decade of the nineteenth century. Within the Virginia Conference, the largest of several jurisdictions containing Virginia Methodists, the number of black members increased from 3,794 in 1803 to 6,334 in 1813, a growth of 67 percent. By comparison, the number of white Methodists in the same conference increased from 13,099 to 19,817 during the same period, a growth of only 51 percent.[74] In an important survey of black church development, Luther P. Jackson also concluded that black men and women swarmed to, instead of fled from, evangelicalism after the settlements on slavery in the post-Revolutionary period. He estimated that, while the black population of Virginia increased by 69 percent between 1790 and 1830, the number of black church members increased by 131 percent.[75]

Virginia's black evangelicals, particularly Baptists, proved themselves active members of the congregations that they joined by submitting to communal discipline and by using the procedures set up for church discipline to initiate cases of their own. In examples like that of the Tynes family over their "barbaric" treatment of slaves, discussed above, members of evangelical churches in the South (more so than did evangelicals in the North) evaluated one another's behavior and sanctioned one another for perceived violations of God's law. Voting members of the church, almost always white men, made the final decisions in these cases, but female or black members would sometimes investigate the alleged sinful behavior and make preliminary reports to the church body. Though some scholars have suggested that white evangelicals used ecclesiastical courts primarily to achieve social control over black church members, most recognize that black evangelicals could expect before such tribunals far more respect for their persons than they enjoyed in any civil setting.[76] On rare occasions slaves tested the limits of their equality by initiating cases against whites, usually their masters. These were exceptions, perhaps one in a hundred cases. They represent what must have been dire situations in the lives of the enslaved initiators, who surely knew to expect brutal recriminations at home if their accusations were not sustained—perhaps even if they were. Only those already expecting punishment or who suffered from especially painful abuse would be willing to bring suit against their owners.

But slaves did not need to win cases against their owners to win moral victories or to challenge the dehumanization of their enslavement. Each time a slave appeared before a court as a defendant or as a complainant against another slave, he or she held up the institution of slavery itself to white inspection and forced slaveholding and nonslaveholding whites to consider their duties toward slaves. The access slaves had to a formal process that adjudicated complaints about their behavior showed them that the church both respected their testimony and theoretically provided some limits to the physical authority of white owners. Furthermore, blacks could expect the same treatment as whites accused of moral offenses; the Tussekiah Baptist Church in Lunenburg County tellingly resolved in 1786, "Black Member to be dealt with as a White one."[77] As Vernon Burton put it, "Social control worked both ways. . . . Once the slaves were converted, the masters themselves were obliged to obey biblical injunctions."[78] Some black evangelicals found disciplinary proceedings empowering even if they could not hope to sit in judgment over their white coreligionists. The situation ecclesiastically was generally better than it was in civil courts, where slaves could not even give testimony against a white person.[79] Presbyterian churches may have been more restrictive than Baptist or Methodist congregations in the use of black testimony, though, for the Hanover Presbytery ruled in October 1791 "that any person who is admissible in Courts of Justice to give Testimony ought to be admitted as witnesses in Church Judications," limiting the power of black members.[80]

Whites brought so many cases against African American members of Buck Marsh Baptist Church in the 1790s that the thesis of racial control seems to fit more snugly for that congregation than most. Even there, though, enslaved blacks brought cases against one another as well. These instances of intraracial discipline reveal both disturbing divisions among African Americans within the church and the ennobling aspects of church discipline. In March 1793, the church recorded a "complaint by Bro. Ned against Sister Sarah (svts. to Mr. Larue) that Sarah had taken some meat from her master which he conceiv'd was not honestly come by." On one hand, Ned was cruelly indicting Sarah for an act that most slaves regarded as completely justifiable, but, on the other, they were both eschewing the capricious discipline of the slaveowner for the measured judgment of the church. Indeed, the church's findings were remarkably balanced. After hearing all of the evidence, including testimony from both parties, the church agreed that "the charge is wrong & that it proceded from other matters which happened between them some time before & those the complainers (viz.) Ned, Ellick & Kilt be sensur'd [censured] until they shall give the church full satisfaction for such a conduct." A few months later, "Harry a black brother," who may have been free, since no owner appears in the records, "made confession at different times that he had been guilty of very disorderly behavior with a Black Sister Molley belonging to Capt. Ball." Again, the church distinguished itself well by trying Harry and Molley separately and by bestowing more dignity on Molley (whom it is not clear they ever excluded) than she could have received elsewhere.[81]

In Buck Marsh and other churches, whites in the 1790s also debated the impossibly complex questions about marriage that black men and women brought before them. Slaves chafed at being persecuted in ecclesiastical courts for violations of the marriage covenant when white statesmen prohibited them from marrying and when white owners—sometimes members of evangelical churches—routinely broke up slave unions through sale.[82]

When enslaved evangelicals (who were predominately but not exclusively Baptist) submitted their cases before their churches or defended themselves against charges of sexual impropriety, they forced white evangelicals to think of the most charitable and just manner in which they could treat black evangelicals, given the brutal realities of slavery. The discussion in Buck Marsh began in October 1791, when the church took "into consideration the proceeding of the Black Members parting with wives & taking of others." It tentatively resolved the issue, concluding that "in future that such members shall be call'd to acct for such conduct & also all such as shall (& has been encouragers of such a conduct) shall be equally chargeable for so doing." This equivocal response did not satisfy some church members, for the church minutes show that the issue resurfaced at each meeting until 31 March 1792, when they had a fresh discussion of the topic and concluded again that "Black Members parting from their wives and taking others" was "sinful."[83] Other evangelical churches would find this conclusion inadequate.

So many Baptist churches found the issue perplexing that they raised the question at association meetings. The trouble was defining what it meant to "leave" one's spouse, in a world where so much black movement was not voluntary. The Portsmouth Association framed it this way in 1792: "Is it lawful and agreeable to the Word of God, for a black Man servant, (or Slave) who has been Married, and his Wife removed from him a great distance, without his or her consent to marry another Woman during her Life or not?" Without making any headway against this question, they came at the problem from the angle of white responsibility at the 1793 meeting, wondering, "What ought Churches to do with Members in their Communion, who shall either directly, or indirectly separate married Slaves, who are come together according to the custom as Man and Wife?" Alas, even this question "was thought by a Majority to be so difficult, that no answer could be given it."[84] At their 1793 meeting the Dover Association also considered this issue, phrased in a more pragmatic way: "What is advisable in the case of a separation among slaves, between man and wife, which is forcibly made by their owners?" The Dover Association gave permission for churches to soften strictures against adultery by giving individual congregations authority to judge on a case-by-case basis. "Where men and their wives, being slaves, are so far removed from each other, as not to have it in their power to discharge the mutual duties of man and wife," they ruled, "that in all such cases, churches act discretionarily."[85] Presbyterians in the Hanover Presbytery came to an even more tolerant conclusion. "And in case where either of the parties may have had a former companion, and sold or removed by his or her Master at such a distance as to prevent all intercourse between them," the presbytery ruled, "the connexion being thereby as much dissolved to either of them, as if the other was dead, they ought not to be deprived of Church privileges, even in case he or she should take another companion."[86]

Whites tried in other ways to make the behavior of slaves and slaveowners within the church conform to standards of evangelical morality. Enough churches debated how vigorously whites could discipline enslaved and free African Americans that the issue made it to the association level. The Tynes case was not the only one in Black Creek. In February 1792 that church tried two different whites for separate instances of "beating a free Negroe." Brother Henry Jones "acknowledged his fault," and the church allowed him to remain a member. Brother James Johnson, on the other hand, showed no remorse. The church held over his case for another four months but excluded him from membership over the incident in June.[87] At the same meeting in which it argued that emancipation was a civil issue, in 1790, the Roanoke Baptist Association agreed that "it is the indespendsable [sic] duty of masters to forbear and suppress cruelty, and do that which is just and equal to their servants."[88] Members of the Dover Baptist Association, who made room for creative interpretation on the issue of slave marriage in 1793, hedged again on the difficult question of slave discipline. They phrased the question as directly as possible—"Is there no restriction on believing masters, in the chastisement of their servants?"—but were unable to come up with a good answer. Delegates to the association voted in 1796 that, though it was "impossible to fix a certain rule in these cases," there were conceivably occasions on which Baptists should censure one of their own for wielding "an unreasonable authority" and that "churches should take notice of such as they may think improper and deal with the transgressor, as they would with offenders in other crimes."[89]

In sum, white evangelicals found that black evangelicals made it impossible for them to ignore the issue of slavery, even if whites had decided not to discuss the institution in the abstract in an ecclesiastical context. Instead, African American churchmen offered through word and deed an endless series of queries about how best to govern the relationships between slave and free, black and white. Always in response to queries from or about the enslaved, whites worked to define the mutual responsibilities of masters and slaves to one another. They accepted the ideas that God put restraints on the power of owners and that slavery ultimately had to be a Christian institution. They also acknowledged that slaves were moral agents and committed themselves to a sustained dialogue with them over their position within evangelical churches. In the process, whites and blacks forged in the

1790s an ethic of slaveholding that historians have identified as paternalism. White evangelicals at first employed paternalism to explain responsibilities to black members of their churches at a time of uncertainty over slavery. Because paternalism was imbued with the same language of moral responsibility with which abolitionists would later attack slavery, southern whites later employed the concept as part of a self-conscious defense of their exploitative labor regime.

Eugene Genovese gave the word "paternalism" its meaning relative to American slavery in *Roll, Jordan, Roll,* and his definition enriches the analysis here. One of his great insights was that the negotiated ethic of paternalism meant very different things for slaves and slaveowners. By asserting that they owed to their slaves compassionate treatment and Christian discipline, slaveholders were effectively redefining their seizure of black labor as a legitimate exchange. At the same time, the slaveholders' "need to see their slaves as acquiescent human beings constituted a victory for the slaves themselves. Paternalism's insistence upon mutual obligations—duties, responsibilities, and ultimately even rights—implicitly recognized the slaves' humanity." Moreover, Genovese also saw that paternalism only developed in the context of intimate and sustained white and black interaction, for "the existence of the community required that all find some measure of self-interest and self-respect."[90] The most important community for these interactions was not the plantation but the church, defined both as a physical place and as a body of men and women sharing the same conversion story and committed to following the same savior. Furthermore, paternalism was only one of the frameworks for understanding slavery that whites forged in response to their black coreligionists, and its history therefore requires more chronological and geographic sensitivity.[91]

White evangelicals doubtless were also responding to a variety of nonecclesiastical trends in constructing an ideology of paternalism. Demographic changes were among the most important. Since slaves had stopped coming into the commonwealth from abroad in 1778, Virginia slaveholders by the early national period presided over a largely native-born slave population.[92] This was true even in the Piedmont, where African slaves were still arriving by the hundreds each year as late as the 1760s. In two Piedmont counties, Amelia and Chesterfield, the proportion of African-born adult slaves had already declined to 27 percent by 1782, indicative of substantial creolization.[93] Furthermore, Virginia slaveowners consolidated their holdings in slaves onto larger plantations in the closing decades of the eighteenth century. This concentration of African American labor had important social repercussions for enslaved Virginians, for on larger units of production they could create semi-independent communities with more stable families.[94] These demographic changes were useful preconditions for owners' development of paternalist strategies, but they were not sufficient to explain them. Owners without an ideological incentive to treat their slaves with some measure of humanity might have answered the same demographic changes through strategies other than paternalism. They might have dehumanized slaves still further, for example, and demanded continued access to African imports to compensate for a higher mortality rate. Alternatively, they could have capitalized on the cessation of the African trade in the Upper South and become more intentional about slave breeding. In biracial evangelical churches, whites and blacks negotiated the set of reciprocal obligations that characterized paternalism and made such unsavory turns unlikely.[95]

On a more or less conscious level, evangelical whites who acknowledged the boundaries of their power over slaves were compensating for their refusal to work for the liberation of those same persons. The Dover Association made the connection between ecclesiastical inaction on slavery and amelioration explicit in a 1797 resolution. The white ministers present declined to sponsor a plan for gradual emancipation but felt the need to soften the blow on the association's thousands of black members and their white allies. They therefore stressed that they "sincerely sympathised, both as Christians and Citizens, with those unhappy People," and that they "would not wish to be backward, in promoting their happiness and liberty, upon cautious grounds."[96]

In a provocative study of the Tucker family, historian Philip Hamilton has shown how this mental shift could happen on a very personal level. In the decade after patriarch St. George Tucker published his *Dissertation on Slavery*, members of his family embraced evangelical Protestantism and contented themselves with forging warm personal relations with slaves rather than working for emancipation. By 1814, Tucker had convinced at least himself that benevolent paternalism—with all of its assumptions of racial hierarchy—was an adequate substitution for antislavery. As if desperate for some accomplishment to measure once legislated emancipation had become unlikely in the commonwealth, Tucker asserted that "the treatment of Slaves in such Cases is infinitely more humane [now] than before the Revolution."[97] Often, antislavery whites who agreed not to press for ecclesiastical action against slavery became the most vocal paternalists, because they wanted to be certain that slaveholders at least treated their chattel humanely if they would not remove their chains.[98] In this way, paternalism facilitated the agreement to disagree.

There was continuity between paternalism as articulated in the late eighteenth century and the message that ministers concerned with the salvation of slaves had articulated in the colonial period. When Godwyn, Fleetwood, Whitefield, Davies, and other divines had tried to convince owners to allow them to convert their slaves, they had explicitly used the argument of mutual responsibility. Whitefield, for example, chastised owners for failing to provide for their slaves. "My Blood has frequently almost run cold within me," he wrote with characteristic vigor, "to consider how many of your Slaves had neither convenient Food to eat or proper Raiment to put on, notwithstanding most of the Comforts you enjoy were solely owing to their indefatigable Labours.—The Scripture says, *Thou shall not muzzle the Ox that treadeth out the Corn.*" By the same token, he reminded owners that scripture enjoined upon slaves certain responsibilities: "Do you not read that Servants, and as many as are under the Yoke of Bondage, are required to be subject, in all lawful Things, to their Masters; and that not only to the good and gentle, but also to the froward?"[99] This language of mutual responsibility across unequal relationships, in other words, already existed, both in scripture and in evangelical parlance. What was new in the 1790s was that this language moved from the fringes of southern religious practice to the center, and that white evangelicals employed it not in dialogue with Anglican slaveholders, but in negotiation with enslaved evangelicals.[100] What's more, because of large-scale black conversions, white evangelicals in the late eighteenth century could no longer explain slavery through appeals to distinctions between heathen and Christian and relied more heavily on paternalism to explain slavery's righteousness.

Divines within the Baptist, Methodist, and Presbyterian churches in the 1790s elaborated on the central themes of paternalism in sermons and in published work, explaining that white men at the top of Virginia society owed spiritual and physical nurture to the slaves, children, and women beneath them. While Baptist churches were the most important sites of interracial interactions, all white evangelicals took up the theme. At the same meeting where Dover Association Baptists voted that churches could sanction slaveowners for disciplining their slaves too vigorously, they sent out a circular letter explaining in great detail the duties that white adults owed to children and to slaves. In order to bring still more black Virginians into evangelical fellowship, the association urged whites to reform how they interacted with the enslaved. To give their proselytism "the greater impression, they ought to take every opportunity to shew them acts of humanity and tenderness, and to adapt as mild a discipline as possible, to shew a spirit of forgiveness for faults, and by no means to exercise wrath nor cruelty in chastisement." The Baptists quoted Colossians 4:1 to sum up their argument, reminding readers that "masters ought to 'give unto their servants that which is just and equal, knowing that they also have a master in Heaven.'"[101]

Presbyterian William Graham also appealed to scriptures to drive home the point of mutual responsibility. Paraphrasing the same passage in Colossians, he taught that the apostle Paul "always expects [masters] to treat their servants with gentleness and good usage, which becomes masters as Christians and which servants have a right to expect."[102] Methodists, who had endured the most costly internal debates over slavery, accepted the notion of reciprocal relations within a fixed hierarchy more slowly than the others. Jeremiah Norman revealed the precise pathway that antislavery Methodists finally followed to paternalism in his journal entries for October 1793. In that month, he experienced a "melting time round ye Lord's table" when he spoke of the mutual obligations of "Wives & Husbands. Children & Parents. Servants & c." In contrast, when Methodists spoke more aggressively against slavery, he noted that "people had made a vow against hearing ye Methodists any more." Preaching paternalism, he learned, both kept the door open to more white converts and ensured relatively harmonious relations among blacks and whites already in the church.[103]

White evangelicals even dug through the annals of their short history in the United States to find support for the idea that white and black evangelicals owed one another mutual obligations despite their unequal stations. They found and republished in the early 1800s several documents that contained the seeds of paternalism. In 1809, William Gray, for instance, republished Samuel Davies's *The Duty of Masters to Their Servants*. Episcopalian William Meade, soon to lead his denomination's effort to join the ranks of Virginia evangelicals, compiled a more exhaustive volume in 1813. His *Sermons Addressed to Masters and Servants* contained six addresses on the topic, Cotton Mather's resolutions concerning slaves, the Decalogue, and sundry passages of scripture. Meade assembled the material to reinforce the emerging evangelical consensus that "the indispensable obligation of every Master and Mistress" was "bringing up their slaves in the knowledge and fear of Almighty God."[104]

Precisely how significantly white, evangelical paternalists managed to change slaveholders' behavior by preaching about their duties to slaves remains an open question. Some white evangelicals did become deeply invested in improving the spiritual and physical lives of the enslaved. Both John Poindexter and John Self developed an aversion to slavery after experiencing evangelical conversion. As Poindexter said in 1797, "I have been an advocate for Slavery, but thanks be to God, My Eyes have been Opened to see the impropriety of it." Neither freed their slaves as a result of their realization of slavery's evils, despite the ease of doing so according to the terms of the 1782 statute, but they demonstrated their changed hearts by improving their treatment of enslaved men and women. Landon Carter, who employed Self as an overseer, described Self's changed attitude toward slaves in his diary: "News just came John Self at Rings Neck turned a Baptist, and only waits to convert my people. He had two brethren Preachers and two other with him; and says he cannot serve God and Mammon, has just been made a Christian by dipping, and would not continue in my business but to convert my people."[105]

For every slaveowner like Poindexter or Self, there were others who did not accept the premise of paternalism, that whites owed spiritual and physical nurture to enslaved men and women. The cruel evangelical slaveholder is almost a stock character in slave narratives published from the 1820s through the Civil War, indicating that paternalism never completely carried the day. Charles Peyton Lucas, for one, was not impressed by the paternalist tendencies of his owner in Loudoun County. "My master never sent me to school," he reported from Canada, "nor gave me any instruction from the Bible, excepting one passage of Scripture which he used to quote to me,— 'He that knoweth his master's will, and doeth it not, shall be beaten with many stripes.' He was a Baptist Minister—and after he had quoted the text, he would take me to the barn-yard and give me a practical explanation with raw hides. My mistress used to beat me over the head with a dairy key about as big as a child's fist."[106] Peter Randolph cataloged the deprivations of several slaveholding Virginia clergy in his own narrative, taking special delight in narrating the untimely end of one of them. "One of the Baptist ministers was named B. Harrison," Randolph explained. "He owned slaves, and was very cruel to them. He came to an untimely end. While he was riding out one afternoon, the report of a gun was heard, and he was found dead,—his brains being blown out."[107]

Those slaveholders who professed no evangelical commitment, a significant minority late into the antebellum period, did not need to conform to paternalist standards at all, nor did their slaves expect them to do so. Thomas Anderson, born near Davies's former haunts in Hanover County in 1785, was not surprised at his unbelieving owner's cruelty. "My master who owned me at that time having no knowledge of God or godliness," he explained, "supposed my religion was all a fancy, and said he could and would whip it out of me. He took me up and tie me, and scourged me until feeling of flesh was almost gone."[108] The power of paternalism to ameliorate the condition of enslaved people must not be exaggerated.

All whites may not have accepted or acted upon paternalism, but black evangelicals nonetheless found the concept useful because it gave them a solid foundation from which to critique even nonbelieving slaveholders. The efforts of white evangelicals to maintain biracial community and their clear articulation of their own responsibilities gave African Americans a convenient measure with which to judge them. This ability confidently to condemn whites for failing to live up to their own standards kept evangelicalism attractive to black Virginians, even when they revolted at the idea that slavery was a divine institution. Henry Atkinson, like many black evangelicals, felt simultaneously disgusted and empowered by going to biracial churches. At Norfolk's First Baptist Church, he noted that whites studiously avoided portions of scripture that suggested emancipation. He was able to hear better things between the lines though, for when he "heard the white minister preach," it made him realize the justice of his frustrations with human bondage. "I think slavery is the worst and meanest thing to be thought of," he determined. "It appears to me that God cannot receive into the kingdom of heaven, those who deal in slaves." David West even more perfectly articulated the way that slaves held whites accountable to their paternalist promises. "I have often tried to love my minister and brethren in Pokaroan church," he wrote, "but when I heard them say, 'Do unto others as ye would that others should do unto you,' and saw what they were doing to their own brethren in Christ, I thought with the disciples, 'Who, then, can be saved?' I never knew in all my living in the South, a colored man to separate a family of whites by sale or in any way, but have often known this to be done by the whites."[109]

The meaning of church discipline subtly changed as whites closed their churches to conversation about emancipation and articulated the sort of paternalist ideals that West complained they rarely lived up to. Whites had initially found some cases of black church discipline troubling, for they had highlighted inconsistencies between slavery and Christianity. The more they embraced paternalism, the more they began to see the opportunity to discipline black members as a validation of African Americans' need for Christian direction and nurture. When black men and women ran afoul of church law, whites reasoned, they showed that they needed whites' control. This control was, by the turn of the century, officially white and male. The Dover Association's treatise on the topic of authority in cases of church discipline in 1802 effectively demolished any lingering voting privileges retained by women or black members. For a variety of reasons, among the most revealing the contention that "no person is entitled to exercise authority in the Church whose situation in social life renders it his duty to be under obedience to the authority of another—such as minor sons and servants," the Dover ministers urged "that none but free male members can properly exercise authority in the Church."[110] Whites' developing sense of spiritual oversight did not destroy entirely the elements of discipline that enslaved people found affirming of their humanity—particularly their rights to due process or the assertion that whites, too, were under God's law—but it did neutralize the subversive element of communal accountability.

Church discipline became an instrument of racial control, but only on an ideological level and not as a direct strategy to control the behavior of individuals. As a direct method of controlling slaves or free blacks, church discipline was dreadfully inefficient. Not only did church discipline give the accused the chance publicly to state his or her side of the story, but it also required too much time. Even simple cases of discipline often dragged on for months, and most churches only heard cases several times a year. In other words, it was impossible through the churches to get the sort of immediate punishment necessary to maintain order in a slaveholding household. Moreover, the most common sanction in church courts was expulsion, removing precisely those individuals whom whites would be interested in controlling from the influence or "watchcare" of the church. In terms of direct racial control, then, church discipline had many disadvantages to the lash.

Ideologically, though, church discipline helped to affirm the moral basis of owners' authority over slaves. The church defined as sinful many behaviors characteristic of everyday slave resistance: stealing food, running away, or being insubordinate, for example. Despite the concession that sale to the Deep South released slaves from their marital promises, white evangelicals also held slaves to expectations of marital fidelity that were unrealistic in a world in which slave marriage was illegal and slave residences were too often impermanent. By defining much slave resistance and sexual activity as sinful, whites probably did not reduce the incidence of these behaviors one iota, but they did guarantee that slaves would constantly violate church rules and would appear for discipline in a steady stream. The more black faces whites sanctioned, the more confident whites were that blacks needed the discipline of slavery. In this indirect way, church discipline was a potent instrument of racial control. When Chappawamsic whites excommunicated Ben and James for "taking of wheat . . . and carrying it to Chapman's mill to grind in meal," or when Mill Swamp Baptist Church "declared from under the watch and care of this church" a man named Phil for "breaking into a house & stealing corn," they lost control of these individuals but gained the conviction that blacks in general were not suited for freedom.[111]

White evangelicals in the early national period, while refusing to act against slavery, thus responded to the concerns of African American evangelicals who sought to be full participants in the growing evangelical movement. In the context of so much black spiritual initiative, it is curious that white evangelicals did not seriously consider the possibility that their black brethren might take up arms against slavery. Black believers dared to seek redress through church discipline for the worst abuses of slavery, and they voted with their feet for the preachers most friendly to their interests. White evangelicals, along with unchurched whites, ignored signs that churched blacks might also be more likely to flee or to rebel. Instead, white Virginians focused most of their anxiety about their security within a slave society on the presence of free blacks. In his ill-fated revolt of 1800, Gabriel Prosser, a Richmond-area slave, delivered what should have been a warning to whites about the potentially insurrectionary dimension of evangelicalism. Whites did react to Prosser, but not to the religious elements of his conspiracy.

Prosser hired himself out as a blacksmith and therefore enjoyed considerable liberty for an eighteenth-century slave. In the last months of the century, he made weapons in his shop and recruited volunteers for an insurrection using a web of contacts along Virginia's rivers. On several occasions, his brother Martin quoted scripture at presumably racially exclusive black Baptist worship services in order to convince the men and women present to join their plot. This—combined with Gabriel's published warning that "Quakers, Methodists, and French people," groups with a history of antislavery or concern for black welfare, were not to be harmed—revealed the synergy between black religious commitment and rebellion. Some black revolutionaries clearly considered evangelical Protestantism and slavery to be incompatible. Only the combination of a torrential rainstorm, which washed out bridges and prevented mobilization on the night of the intended insurrection, and of slave informants who exposed the plot to white authorities before the insurrection could be rescheduled made Gabriel's rebellion a failure. A subsequent plot in 1802—tellingly named the Easter Conspiracy— revealed the persistence of complicated connections among religion, race, and rebellion in early national Virginia.[112]

In their response to these two failed rebellions, white Virginians indicated that they did not yet comprehend the relationship between religion and rebellion. In a pattern that would hold for decades, Virginia's political and religious leaders blamed free, and not evangelical, blacks for instability among the enslaved population. Slaves who had been carried by their owners from Haiti in the 1790s also received some blame, but for their direct experience of revolution and not for their religious convictions. When political leaders communicated news of the insurrection to governors in other slaveholding states, they revealingly failed to mention religion, speculating instead "that this alarming business *probably* had its origin in *foreign* influence."[113] On 21 January 1801, lawmakers enshrined into law their suspicion that free blacks were to blame by compelling all free blacks to register with local authorities. They also tried to eliminate the quasi-free category to which Prosser had belonged, the self-hiring slave. In the following session, the General Assembly also passed stiffer laws designed to prevent ship captains from carrying slaves or free blacks without first seeking the permission of civil officers.[114]

Representatives seemed deeply unwilling to acknowledge the possibility that black evangelicals had a hand in the insurrection. George Tucker did suggest that because "fanaticism is spreading fast among the Negroes of this country, and may form in time the connecting link between the black religionists and the white . . . it certainly would not be a novelty, in the history of the world, if Religion were made to sanctify plots and conspiracies."[115] And yet, the closest that delegates to the General Assembly came to recognizing the link between religion and rebellion at all was in January 1804, when they passed a law "that all meetings or assemblages of slaves, at any meeting house or houses, or any other place or places, in the night, under whatsoever pretext, shall be deemed and considered as an unlawful assembly." As the text of the law clearly indicates, the timing of the meetings and the lack of supervision over them were more important than their purposes.[116]

White evangelicals showed that they, like their legislators, missed the connection between religion and rebellion by seeking to repeal even the relatively modest police regulations put in place after Prosser's failed rebellion. At their 1804 meeting, members of the Dover Association made concrete plans to fight the new law against evening meetings. One constituent church forwarded the question to the body, "Would it not be expedient to present a memorial to the next assembly, praying a repeal of a certain law, declaring what shall be deemed an unlawful assembly of slaves?" Members of the association, who had a decade earlier refused to participate in any petition for emancipation, readily agreed to participate in this paternalist campaign. They recommended "that Elder Robert B. Semple, prepare a memorial and present it to the Goshen association, for their concurrence, and then to be delivered to Elder John Courtney, and thro' him presented to the next general assembly." Though Baptists were unsuccessful in their efforts to get the measures repealed, their sense of urgency evaporated when time revealed that secular authorities would not interfere with religious meetings. In 1808, the Baptists noted, "The laws of Virginia are probably the most unexceptionable of any in the world; that which respects the unlawful assembling of slaves, is not so well as we could wish; but being no where put in force, as to the improper parts, we feel no inconvenience."[117]

Free black Virginians, a population growing steadily as a result of the manumission law of 1782, bore most of the long-term repercussions of Gabriel's rebellion. In January 1806, legislators added restrictions on manumission that limited the growth of the free black population. According to the new law, freedmen and -women had to leave the state within twelve months of gaining their freedom or risk reenslavement.[118] Some white Virginians believed free blacks to be so dangerous that they contemplated removing not only the newly free but also those already free from the state in a program of colonization. In a secret letter to then-president Thomas Jefferson, Governor James Monroe inquired in 1801 about the possibility of creating a colony "to which free negroes or mulattoes, and such negroes or mulattoes as may be emancipated, may be sent or choose to remove as a place of asylum."[119]

In sum, neither white churchmen nor white statesmen proved willing to act against slavery in the early national period. But neither could white evangelicals altogether ignore the issue of slavery or, more importantly, the slaves themselves. Black men and women had made evangelical congregations, especially Baptist and Methodist ones, biracial during the Great Revival from 1785 to 1792 and refused to leave them, even after whites shunted the divisive debate over emancipation to the civil sphere. When Methodism in Virginia whitened considerably in the aftermath of James O'Kelly's 1792 departure, Baptist churches became the most important sites for interracial dialogue in the commonwealth. In direct response to the actions and petitions of their black brethren, white churchgoers in these congregations fleshed out existing ideas about hierarchy into a paternalist understanding of the relationship between master and slave. Whites became so invested in fulfilling their responsibilities in this paternalist relationship that they were not willing to consider that they might make their slaves and those of their neighbors more likely to rebel by introducing them to evangelical Protestantism. Whites thus stood by as enslaved converts within their churches began to take ownership of their professions of faith and to build upon a tradition of black spiritual leadership in the tradition of Gowan Pamphlet and Gabriel Prosser, one thoroughly at odds with their status as chattel.

Chapter Three

THE FLOURISHING OF BIRACIAL
CHRISTIANITY, 1815–1831

Behold, how good and pleasant it is for brethren to dwell together in unity!
—Psalm 133:1

Politicians and evangelical clergymen pulled the country in different directions in the years between the War of 1812 and the Southampton Insurrection in 1831. Representatives of slave and free labor regimes competed in Congress for access to western lands and, in 1819, rehearsed the fatal debate over slavery's expansion when Missouri applied for statehood. There was no corresponding cataclysm in the nation's evangelical churches, however, no "fire bell in the night."[1] Northern and southern evangelicals actually cooperated more closely in this period, building rather than tearing down bridges between the sections. Southern white evangelicals, particularly in places like Virginia, where they had agreed to disagree over slavery, did not suspect that conflict over slavery would disrupt their communion with their northern brethren.

Virginia's white evangelicals celebrated in the 1810s and 1820s their most exciting triumphs since the Great Revival of 1785 to 1792. They cheered growing membership rolls, resolution of internal disagreements over slavery, and the inauguration of a number of benevolent enterprises. Moreover, whites from different denominations began to forge common bonds with one another. Presbyterians who had initially resisted identification as evangelicals, particularly those from the Valley, and Episcopalians who had languished after disestablishment, now worked to identify themselves as evangelicals and to share in the fruits of the evangelical ascendancy. Thanks to the efforts of black men and women in the previous decades to keep evangelicalism biracial, one of the most important issues that new evangelicals needed to consider was how they might better advance the conversion of African American Virginians.

As a result of white evangelicals' widespread emphasis on promoting black conversion, black believers enjoyed considerable freedom to preach, to organize, and to worship during this period. Blacks joined whites in several benevolent enterprises, none more significant for evolving white ideas about slavery than the ambitious attempt of the American Colonization Society (ACS) to settle American blacks on the west coast of Africa. The participation of black evangelicals like Lott Cary in the ill-fated colonization movement had devastating consequences for black Virginians. It enabled those white evangelicals most sympathetic to the plight of slaves to imagine colonization—notwithstanding its racist assumptions and devastating mortality rate—as a compassionate, biracial approach to the problem of slavery.

The attempt to plant a colony of freedmen and -women on the west coast of Africa was only one way that the logic of paternalism unfolded during the so-called Era of Good Feelings. So long as black evangelicals did not press for either civic privileges or equality within the biracial church, their white coreligionists were willing to open to them a relatively wide field of activity. Concern for the spiritual welfare of blacks was a central part of the self-professed obligations of whites as paternalists, and evangelical whites generally regarded the increasing activity of black preachers as a healthy indicator of growing African American religiosity. Though they feared slave rebellion and regarded events such as the flight of black Virginians during the War of 1812, George Boxley's planned rebellion of 1816, and the 1822 Denmark Vesey plot in Charleston with grave concern, the commonwealth's white evangelicals continued to see free blacks, and not the African American ministers maturing in the 1810s and 1820s, as threats to their security. But all was not as it seemed; some enslaved and free black Virginians were using the privileges white evangelicals afforded them in the name of Christ to create potentially insurrectionary spheres of activity. Not until the bloody events of 1831 would white evangelicals come to terms with the growing gap between their perceptions of black evangelicals and reality. Even then, the favorable impression that black evangelicals made on their white brethren in the 1820s ironically determined the tactics with which whites responded to Nat Turner.

Following the War of 1812, white Virginians experienced the same economic and cultural upheavals as did their peers in other states. The headlong rush to connect individuals to the market through an expanded transportation network, for example, reached every corner of the Old Dominion. In 1816, the General Assembly created the Fund for Internal Improvement and the Board of Public Works to help bring canals, steam travel, and even railroads to the commonwealth. In the most ambitious of the projects that received state funding, the James River and Kanawha Canal Company improved a 250-mile stretch of Virginia's most important waterway. The company did not succeed in connecting the James and Kanawha rivers, but it greatly reduced the cost of bringing the agricultural produce of the Piedmont to market via the James. Virginia's urban centers, primarily Richmond, Petersburg, and Norfolk, grew dramatically in order to service the expanded export economy. By 1820, Richmond had already grown to 12,067 residents; Petersburg, to 6,690; and Norfolk, to 8,478.[2] Adding to the prosperity of the Old Dominion's whites—but with tragic effects for Virginia blacks—Virginia slaveowners also discovered a market for their slaves in the new states of the Southwest. White migrants to Louisiana (1812), Mississippi (1817), and Alabama (1819) purchased slaves by the thousands from the Upper South and gave Virginia slaveholders a valuable source of income.[3]

Virginians participated in the deceptively named "Second Great Awakening" as well as the postwar flurry of economic development. Like the First Great Awakening, which occurred in fits and starts over a span of a half century in Virginia and hardly deserves to be called a discrete movement, the Second Great Awakening was also in some ways a nonevent in the commonwealth. There was no single, galvanizing personality, no cluster of revivals fixing the phenomenon to any particular chronology. But there was an important change in theology that matched very closely the shift inaugurated in the Northeast by ministers such as Charles Grandison Finney. Following the War of 1812, Virginia evangelicals were much more willing to employ "means" to achieve conversions and to fight corporate sin. By acceding to the use of means, which they understood to be devices or practices designed to compel belief, evangelicals were acknowledging human agency and, therefore, human responsibility. In the words of Finney, "The preacher is a moral agent in the work he acts; he is not a mere passive instrument; he is voluntary in promoting the conversion of sinners."[4] The Baptist General Meeting of Correspondence, which succeeded in 1800 the General Committee of Baptist Associations, anticipated Finney's later formulation at their 1815 meeting when they affirmed the use of specific strategies to win converts. "It is with great cordiality we unite with the Dover Association, and sundry other Associations, in recommending and encouraging Missionary Societies," delegates resolved. "Under God, we are persuaded that these efforts will greatly advance the spread of the Gospel of our Lord."[5]

Evangelicals in Virginia and across the nation followed their acceptance of means to its logical conclusion by establishing benevolence societies to facilitate the conversion of nonbelievers and to improve society. Virginia

Baptists were on the leading edge of this national movement. They formed in Richmond in October 1813 the Virginia Baptist Society, also known as the Foreign Missionary Society of Virginia.[6] Methodists already possessed in their system of itinerancy the most effective missionary organization in the United States, yet Virginians in that denomination also cooperated with their General Conference and undertook new initiatives. In 1816 they authorized the publication of *Methodist Magazine* and, in 1817, established the Methodist Tract Society. In 1819 they proved that Methodists, too, believed in international missions by establishing the Missionary Society of the Methodist Episcopal Church.[7] At the same time, white evangelical Virginians rushed to create state or local affiliates of new national societies: the American Education Society in 1815, the American Bible Society in 1816, the American Sunday School Union in 1824, the American Tract Society in 1825, and the American Home Missionary Society in 1826.[8] Increasingly, support for these agencies designed to promote conversion was a characteristic of evangelical identity.

Some believers felt alienated from this development in evangelicalism. The critics fell into two broad categories: the Campbellites, who, under their founder, Alexander Campbell, insisted that there was no scriptural foundation for the new benevolent organizations, and the antimission Baptists, who argued that the doctrine of predestination made benevolent organizations presumptuous and wasteful. Alexander Campbell began his critique of Baptists in 1823 with the publication of *The Christian Baptist*, in which he called Missionary, Bible, Sunday School, and Tract societies "engines" of "priestly ambition." Campbell continued to upbraid Baptists through the 1830s, by which time his antidenominational movement had achieved a quasi-denominational status of its own. The Disciples of Christ, as they were known, soon boasted their own seminary, newspaper, and missionary organization. Antimission Baptists, or "Primitive Baptists," were appalled at Campbell's inconsistency. They criticized benevolent organizations because they rejected all human agency in the spread of the Gospel. Their integrity in resisting the use of "means" to achieve conversion cost them their numerical significance, however, and supporters of missions overwhelmingly won the contest for Baptist hearts within the commonwealth.[9]

Presbyterians and Episcopalians got in on the act, too, as part of a sea change in these denominations as they worked to integrate lessons from the more successful Baptists and Methodists. William Meade, a strong evangelical presence in the Episcopal Church from the time of his ordination as a deacon in 1811, dated his denomination's transformation to the convention of 1814, the convention at which they called evangelical Richard Channing

Moore to the episcopacy. From that moment, Meade declared, "as to the great benevolent and religious institutions of the age, our Ministers felt that they were doing well to encourage their people to a lively participation in them. The Missionary and Bible Societies, the Colonization and Temperance Societies especially, received their most cordial support, and they considered it a subject of devout thankfulness to God, if their congregations took a deep interest in the same."[10]

Presbyterian John Holt Rice was the most important advocate in his denomination of benevolent work and evangelicalism. He not only helped organize the national board of the American Bible Society (and contributed personally to the Norfolk and Richmond branches), served on the board of the American Home Missionary Society, and exhorted his congregants to join such organizations, but he also tried to tie Virginia's emerging evangelical community together by beginning publication in 1817 of the *Virginia Evangelical and Literary Magazine*. Though not the first use of the word "evangelical," the journal signaled the arrival in common American parlance of a term to describe the emerging united front of converted, benevolence-minded Protestants. In a definition of the term that appeared in the inaugural issue, Rice showed the increasing emphasis on the application or living out of one's faith, in addition to the necessity of conversion. He explained that "the principal articles are: 1. The total depravity of man. 2. The necessity of regeneration by the Holy Spirit. 3. Justification by faith alone, and 4. The necessity of holiness as a qualification for happiness."[11] Both Rice and Meade saw in benevolent work the prospect of revitalizing their own traditions and creating harmony among competing denominations.

For good measure, the Presbyterians and Episcopalians also hastened to "get right with the Revolution," as had the upstart denominations before the Great Revival of 1785 to 1792. Rice penned the most important statement of Presbyterianism's Republican nature himself, in 1816. Inscribing the work "To the . . . Members of the House of Delegates of Virginia, the Constitutional Guardians of the Rights and Privileges of the Citizens," he argued strenuously "that the principles of the whole [Presbyterian] society in the United States are decidedly republican."[12] Rice wrote in defense of Presbyterian efforts to incorporate a seminary in Richmond, but he seized the specific occasion of the charter debate to catalog Virginia Presbyterians' fidelity to the Revolution, quoting documents from as far back as 1776. Meade, for his part, helped the Episcopalians to move closer to the legacy of the Revolution by recasting his denomination as a victim, not a beneficiary of the colonial establishment. Instead of lamenting lost privileges, he apologized to his fellow Virginians that his church ever had them. Meade claimed that the Church of England would have been better off without legal protection, lamenting, "Many were the disadvantages under which she had to labor, during the whole period of her existence in connexion with the Government of England."[13]

No evangelical initiative during this period was more important for the development of proslavery Christianity or more evenly shared across denominational lines than African colonization. Whites in Virginia and the Upper South still agreed to disagree over the future of slavery, but they found common ground with one another and with antislavery northerners in the ideologically capacious ACS. White Virginia evangelicals helped to cobble together an unlikely coalition of economic modernizers, proslavery activists who feared the presence of free blacks, and antislavery moderates who wanted to establish an "entering wedge" against the institution in the winter of 1816–17. The founders of the society deliberately refused to discuss emancipation, especially after Henry Clay forcefully warned them at their organizational meeting that they would not receive any support from white southerners if they did so. They suggested instead a program to help free blacks remove from the United States to a colony to be established on the west coast of Africa.[14] While evangelical white Virginians were not the only members of the ACS, they assigned it a special role as the institutional embodiment of their paternalist posture toward enslaved persons.

Black Virginians also participated in the ACS and other benevolent enterprises. In declining to throw their churches' influence behind emancipation, white evangelicals had conceded that their black neighbors had the right to hear the Good News and to worship their maker. Moreover, when blacks expressed a desire to spread the Gospel by preaching, attending meetings of some benevolent society, or—in the case of free blacks—emigrating to Africa, evangelical whites gave them a wide berth to allow them to participate in these spiritual initiatives. Black men thus had no more open theater in which to distinguish themselves than the pulpit or the mission field, and African American evangelicals provided powerful models of black achievement as they set about doing what they understood as God's work.[15] Many whites interpreted black spiritual successes as evidence that paternalism was working, and a significant minority even concluded that people of African descent were learning the skills and habits requisite for freedom.

White Presbyterians and Episcopalians pursued black members and supported colonization as part of their efforts to become more evangelical. There was a theological core to evangelicalism, one that Rice had summarized. But beyond this there was an aesthetic component to the movement, a "look and feel" that successful evangelical churches exhibited in the early national period and that Presbyterian and Episcopal churches tried to imitate after the War of 1812. Black Virginians, by refusing to leave their churches when abolitionism was stillborn in them, had shaped decisively this aesthetic. Whites understood that evangelicalism was biracial, both in the sense that evangelicals typically worshipped in racially mixed groups and in the sense that black Virginians had influenced the character of worship itself. Presbyterians and Episcopalians sought to adopt this biracial aesthetic as they emulated Baptists and Methodists in their bid for a share of nineteenth-century converts.

The very presence of African Americans, especially slaves, in evangelical Baptist and Methodist congregations sent a powerful message about what evangelicals valued. Virginia whites systematically denigrated African American men and women in civic life, but, relative to their civil status as chattel or half-citizens, blacks enjoyed good standing in evangelical communities. When those who attended evangelical churches saw black faces around them—and they would have seen many, for African Americans constituted more than one-quarter of evangelicals after the Great Revival—they received strong reinforcement of the idea that salvation came from a personal relationship with Christ and not from any worldly achievements. Enslaved evangelicals were walking morality tales for unregenerate observers who saw in their skin tones evidence of degradation but in their attendance at church evidence of salvation. White evangelicals recognized the symbolic function of their black brethren, and most accepted it warmly.

In modes more than symbolic, black Virginians shaped the actual practice of evangelical worship. Scholars have debated vigorously the precise contributions of African Americans to evangelical rituals, finding both European and African antecedents for most ecclesiastical practices. Even if few things that happened in an evangelical church were of exclusively African origin, Africans and African Americans transformed certain existing practices, including baptism and singing. Baptism in the Christian tradition was always a sacred event. It is one of the two sacraments clearly required by scripture and marks the engrafting of the baptized person into God's covenant people (the church) and their receipt of the Holy Spirit. Calvinists and Arminians, supporters of full immersion and those who merely sprinkled, Catholics and Protestants—all give the ritual a central place in the life of the church. Black evangelicals, then, by no means invented baptism. But they did celebrate the transformative power of the act itself to an unusual degree and made the administration of the sacrament a more raucous affair than it was in most white churches. Not because they were by nature more emotional than white worshippers but because they believed the "marking of anyone's passage from one stage to another was a cause for communal celebration," black evangelicals cheered wildly at baptisms and even shouted encouragement to the candidate if he or she appeared hesitant to follow through with the sacrament.[16] White Presbyterians and Episcopalians, who did not usually baptize by immersion, sometimes did so for slaves, so pronounced were African Americans' preferences on this front.[17]

Enslaved men and women also changed how white evangelicals sang. Black men and women sang on their own, either at work or in praise meetings, and they sang together with whites in church. Again, black men and women neither invented the singing of hymns nor the practice of singing without a hymnal. Whites lined out songs and as early as the eighteenth century wrote hymnals that allowed for a broad range of musical expression. But, again, black believers breathed new life into a familiar form. As one scholar has noted, "The most important evidence of the African contribution to the spirituals is in the ritual that accompanied the singing: the moans, shuffles, and ring shouts central to African American religious expression."[18] Few whites allowed ring shouts in their worship services (and the shouts may have been concentrated on and around the South Carolina Sea Islands), but they could not keep the motion and extratextual lyrics that black men and women offered out of their praise music. This was true from the first stirrings of evangelicalism in the commonwealth; recall John Todd's efforts to obtain a more "evangelical" hymnal for his black congregants and Samuel Davies's insistence that "*Negroes* above all of the human species that ever I knew, have an ear for Music, and a kind of extatic delight in Psalmody."[19] Nonevangelical churches, even those armed with inspiring Watts hymnals, simply sounded different on Sunday mornings.

Paternalism became in the late eighteenth century as important to this biracial aesthetic as were spirituals or dramatic baptisms. Whites who wanted to affiliate with an evangelical church after the complex negotiations at the turn of the century knew that to do so meant accepting the premise that whites and blacks lived under mutual obligations to one another. Moreover, it meant tolerating black Virginians' initiatives as ministers of the Gospel. White Presbyterian William S. White explained in his biography of "Uncle Jack," an enslaved Baptist preacher who was an intimate of White's family, why whites across denominational lines allowed considerable independence of operation to black divines. "As a preacher of the gospel," White wrote, "he gained the good will and secured the confidence of all who were capable of appreciating true excellence of character, gained admittance into the best families, and was there permitted to enjoy a freedom of intercourse that

I never witnessed in any other similar case."[20] The social privileges that "Uncle Jack" gained through his spiritual prowess betrayed white evangelicals' struggles to come to terms with paternalism's logic in this transitional period of proslavery. Implicit in their self-identified charge to teach African Americans Christianity, whites acknowledged the fact that blacks could learn the faith and take ownership of it. They therefore puzzled over both the degree of black agency that was acceptable in a slave society and the level of evangelical attainment that black men and women could reach without making repugnant their status as slaves.

Evangelical whites proved surprisingly willing to tolerate black preachers, so long as the ministers professed a common faith. Indeed, Virginia whites licensed more slaves and free blacks to preach during the 1810s and 1820s than at any other time before the Civil War. Notwithstanding the limits that white males placed on black participation in church governance around 1800, whites were nonetheless willing to show "good will" and "confidence" in black evangelicals by ordaining some black men to preach the Gospel, usually among other black Virginians. Varying degrees of ordination, particularly in the Baptist denomination to which to most slaves belonged, make it difficult to identify exactly when an ordination took place in a rigorous theological sense—when the requisite number of elders, presbyters, or bishops laid hands on the candidate. Often the process seems to have been rather informal, and black Virginians held positions ranging from that of minister in the full possession of sacerdotal powers as identified by one's denomination to "slave preacher." Slave preachers were those whom clergymen, devout slaveowners, and sometimes other slaves commissioned to attend to the spiritual welfare of plantation communities. Depending on the source of their commission or ordination, these men might or might not have been connected to a biracial evangelical church. Nor were they necessarily tied to any specific denomination, though they were typically Baptist by default. Sometimes slave preachers appear in the records as "exhorters." Technically speaking, the rank of exhorter was a formal position within the Baptist and Methodist churches in which an individual had a right to preach sermons of encouragement but not to propound doctrine.[21]

Taking the wide range of ministerial opportunities open to black Virginians—from overseas missionary to settled preacher to exhorter in a slave community—it is impressive how many blacks received full ordination from whites. Presbyterians ordained at least one black man during this period, and Baptists and Methodists called scores of black Virginians to the Gospel ministry. Presbyterians did not have a strict prohibition against the ordination of black members, but they had such high educational bars to ordination that few southern blacks could meet the requirements under a slave regime. The exception was John Chavis, who worked as a minister for the Synod of Virginia from 1801 after training at Liberty Academy in Lexington, Virginia. Many more black Methodists received ordination. Richmond free black David Payne was not the first Virginia Methodist of color to labor under the auspices of the Methodist church in his state—Harry Hosier, John Stewart, John Charleson, and scores of lesser-known black Methodists had preached before him—but he was the first to receive orders as a deacon, in 1824. Many African American Virginians followed Payne as exhorters or deacons. Two Maryland men, Joseph Cartwright and James Harper, gained the higher office of elder in the Baltimore Conference, a conference whose jurisdiction stretched south in Virginia all the way to the Rappahannock.[22] None of these men were enslaved at the time of their ordination, but several did not gain their freedom until adulthood.

Baptists, who boasted the oldest tradition of ordained black leadership, continued to consecrate African American ministers in the 1810s and 1820s, including several enslaved persons. Richmond's First Baptist Church alone produced five black preachers and seven black exhorters during this period, all formally ordained and set aside for the ministry. Black Baptists also ran the state's dozen or so exclusively black Baptist churches, including new churches in Petersburg, Richmond, and Norfolk, in addition to the older communities in Williamsburg, Charles City, and Sandy Beach. All of these congregations flourished because they were situated in the midst of large concentrations of slaves and free blacks, usually in urban areas. This created a difference in the religious outlets open to black Virginians; an increasing proportion of urban slaves had the opportunity to worship in semiautonomous bodies numbering several hundred or thousand, while most rural slaves settled for plantation chapels, brush arbors, or white-dominated biracial churches. This explains one historian's finding that 60 percent of urban slaves converted, while only 40 percent of rural slaves did so.[23]

African American preachers in urban churches did a great deal to narrow the gap between the religious experiences of urban and rural slaves. They systematically took their message out into the countryside, where they placed "slave preachers" over satellite groups of the faithful clustered on rural plantations.[24] Urban black Baptists also approximated something like the Methodists' circuit system, in which religious leaders regularly traveled on preaching tours through the countryside. Charles City slave Pleasant Randall illustrated the pattern. He went "into Prince George County, one Saturday, to preach for a couple of days" and traveled a circuit in which he encountered hundreds of slaves.[25] Lott Cary, too, was engaged in such activity before earning fame through his participation in an expedition to Liberia. As one contemporary biographer wrote, Cary "became a preacher several years before he left this country, and generally engaged in this service every Sabbath, among the colored people on plantations a few miles from Richmond."[26] When he began preaching several years later, John Jasper probably followed a similar circuit as did Cary, for he was well known within a "radius of eight or ten miles" from the city.[27]

The itinerant black preachers helped to build connections between the slave Christianity of the quarters and black evangelicalism when they were acting as agents of churches in communion with evangelical whites. An unknown number of black men acted instead on behalf of the invisible church, operating outside the supervision of white evangelicals and largely outside the historical record. After 1831, when more slave preachers had to practice their calling in secret, there are more references to these men and women because whites regarded them more suspiciously and took more careful note of them. Between 1815 and 1831, when there were more white-sanctioned outlets for ambitious black ministers and when whites at least passively supported black ministerial efforts, information on these individuals is sparse indeed. Henry Box Brown recalled one such underground minister from his youth, "John the Baptist." This appropriately named gentlemen did not have a fixed relation to any local church but preached regularly and routinely baptized his converts.[28] Ben Harding, in describing the religious practices of slaves in neighboring Kentucky, gave further testimony to the presence of such spiritual leaders outside visible evangelical churches. "Almost every neighborhood had its Negro preacher," he wrote, "whose credentials, if his own assertion was to be taken, came directly from the Lord."[29]

The frequent movement of slaves from one plantation to another within Virginia created additional connections between the religious experiences of urban and rural slaves and reduced the gap in belief and practice between visible and invisible churches. When slaves who had lived in an area with a particularly strong evangelical church were moved to new locations, they tried to re-create spiritual communities. The example of slaves from Hanover County who grew up in the Presbyterian community first gathered by Samuel Davies in the 1740s shows both the geographic mobility and spiritual resilience of slave preachers. Many of Davies's initial converts had hailed from one plantation, that of Col. Byrd, an estate that finally broke up around the turn of the century. Two men who ended up in Charlotte County "were very particular in teaching their descendants the Catechism, and the principal truths of the gospel, had the privilege of attending preaching, and the liberty of teaching as many to learn to read as desired." The death of their new owner shattered this reconstituted community of enslaved Presbyterians soon after the War of 1812, when executors of the will sold them. The displaced evangelicals became spiritual leaders in their new homes in more than a dozen locations.[30] None apparently went as far from home as "Aunt Jane," who spread the Gospel she had learned in Virginia to a Virginia-born friend in Louisiana. The convert, Charlotte Brooks, credited Jane with saving her soul, remembering "it was Aunt Jane's praying and singing them old Virginia hymns that helped me so much."[31]

Internal migration did not entirely erase the conflict between black evangelicals and champions of the more independent slave Christianity. In rural areas where most slaves lived, some of the self-proclaimed preachers ran into conflict with black evangelicals who worked within a more orthodox tradition. Whatever the subtext was for these conflicts, usually competition for influence in a particular geographic area, they sometimes took the form of theological disputes. The paternalist biographer of "Uncle Jack," the Baptist patronized by so many well-known Presbyterians, recounted with evident pride one such contest, between the "African Preacher" and "a coloured preacher whose name was Campbell." Campbell won large numbers of slave converts in southeastern Virginia but refused to read the Bible, "as so many of his people were deprived of this privilege" of literacy. Campbell himself could read but nonetheless burned his Bible as an expression of solidarity with the majority of his enslaved auditors. He squared off against the evangelical "Uncle Jack," who challenged him to a debate in front of a Sabbath assembly of slaves, most of whom were quite taken with Campbell's implicitly antiwhite message. Jack defeated Campbell in the debate, not by stressing his greater fidelity to white Virginians, but by publicly shaming his opponent with his superior knowledge of scripture and forcing Campbell to resort to ad hominem attacks when he could not compete theologically.[32]

Black preachers associated with both biracial evangelical churches and secret hush arbors drew inspiration from individuals in the North who were pioneering independent black denominations. While some courageous black Virginians were forging independent congregations in their home state, Richard Allen and other African American Methodists in the North were doing something far more radical: they were building an entire autonomous denomination. Having seceded from Philadelphia's St. George's Methodist Church in 1787 because whites there forced blacks to sit in subordinate positions, Allen in 1816 gave his rebellion against white racial prejudice geographic breadth when he joined his large Pennsylvania following with Methodists in the care of Baltimore's Daniel Coker. Though the election was close, the delegates at the denomination's organizing convention chose Allen as their first bishop. The African Methodist Episcopal (AME) Church, as Allen, Coker, and their fellow priests called their connection, did not establish any churches in Virginia, but it still became a beacon for black Christians everywhere. Black Methodists in Charleston, South Carolina, even sent two of their own, Morris Brown and Henry Drayton, to be ordained by the famous Bishop Allen. The church that the Charlestonians established back in their home city quickly gained 3,000 members, at least half of whom were enslaved.[33]

The commonwealth's evangelical whites tolerated native black religious virtuosos in part because they were so effective at bringing people to the faith. Even though agents of the invisible church diverted a huge proportion of converts made by black evangelicals—as many as one-half—away from Baptist, Methodist, Presbyterian, or Episcopal congregations, Virginia's black apostles nonetheless substantially increased the number of black men and women officially enrolled in their state's evangelical churches.[34] Of the 469,757 slaves and 47,348 free blacks who appeared in the 1830 census, Luthur P. Jackson determined that 30,000 individuals, or one in seventeen, were members of a church recognized by whites. Making adjustments for adherents, Jackson's numbers suggest that almost one-quarter of black Virginians attended an evangelical church regularly by 1830. This represented a doubling of the proportion of black churchmen since 1790, when about 11.5 percent of black Virginians belonged to an evangelical church.[35] Leaders of black evangelicals were simultaneously earning the respect of their white brethren and building a broader and deeper base of support within their own communities each year.

Whites allowed African American evangelicals considerable latitude to preach and worship in part because they were confident that they could moderate any unruly or seditious activity through church discipline. Black members in Stafford County's Chappawamsic Baptist Church were so active in recruiting new members that their white coreligionists contemplated in 1816 setting them off as a quasi-independent unit. Instead, the white Baptists decided that they could best regulate the thriving black portion of their congregation if they kept them as members of the same body. White members began focusing an extraordinary amount of attention on black discipline after voting down the proposal to separate out black members; of the fifty-eight total cases that the church heard before the proposal, from 1772 through May 1816, only 20 percent had involved a black member. Of the thirty-two cases heard after the proposal, from 1816 through 1831, 85 percent involved a black member.[36] Even in this instance where church discipline does seem to have been a fairly overt strategy for white racial control, the amount and efficacy of white oversight must not be exaggerated. While discipline of African American evangelicals was a routine occurrence for those who meted it out, whites at Chappawamsic sanctioned only a tiny fraction of the black membership. Of the 132 men and women of color who joined the church between 1800 and 1815, only 13 ever came under church discipline during their entire tenure at the church, at a rate of less than one case per year.[37] Church discipline thus served as much as a salve for white concerns that black religious expression might become unregulated as it did an actual check on black behavior.

Whites during this period did not inaugurate new missionary efforts to the slaves to recruit black members, perhaps because black evangelicals themselves were already bringing in converts at a furious rate. Church records and slave narratives do not give enough detail to reconstruct the personalities or strategies of black evangelists with any precision, but they do give enough to show that black men and women (women were certainly involved) sought new church members from among their peers. Black evangelicals, not whites, were the primary vectors of evangelical knowledge among slaves in this period, and many black Virginians converted as a result of the persuasive efforts of other blacks. In Chappawamsic, this was never clearer than at the church meeting on 8 May 1819. A significant group of at least ten black men and women announced to the church that they wanted to be admitted as members. Whites in the church clearly did not know these men and women at all, and none of them had an owner or a white sponsor to speak for them. As a result, the white church members stumbled a bit as they tried to sort out the prospective converts' professions of faith. They "held a conference" at which they "heard a number of experiences related by the black people and after a lecture delivered by Brother P. Spiller at the request of the church, 9 of the Blacks were Baptized by the hands of Brother Spiller." Whites had decided at the last moment to deny church membership to one of the candidates. "A Black woman Re[b]ecca by name who related an experience by which the church was deceived was detected by Sister Grimes and [forbidden] to be Baptized. She belonged to Mr. Moncure. A man by the name of Isaac belonging to Mr. Moncure came forward with a note but the Church [had] information through Sister Grimes that his moral character was inconsistent with a profession of Religion as adopted by us." Chappawamsic's whites had not catechized these men and women, worshipped with them, or introduced them to the Gospel, or else they would have known Rebecca's character before the eleventh-hour intervention by the vigilant Sister Grimes.[38] African Americans had brought the group to the church.

An enslaved preacher the likes of London Ferrill probably caused the disorder at Chappawamsic that day. In about 1810, Ferrill converted to evangelical Protestantism and received baptism at the hands of a white, Baptist minister. He soon thereafter received permission to preach from a biracial congregation in Hanover County, which commissioned him "to go and preach the gospel wherever the Lord may cast your lot and the doors open for you." After that, Ferrill did most of his preaching away from whites, at slave funerals, in the quarters, and in places outside the regular, biracial meeting. In his words, he "commenced preaching, and the people appeared to receive the word gladly." Ferrill was enormously successful, and "when he had gained about fifty converts who were ready to be baptised which ceremony he was not authorised to perform by the Virginia law, he procured the services of [white] Preacher Bowles, and he baptised them." Though things appear to have gone well when Preacher Bowles conducted the baptisms, Ferrill had put him in precisely the same situation in which some unknown agent had put the Chappawamsic Baptist Church. He had requested him to baptize converts whose spiritual biographies neither Bowles nor any white knew personally.[39] The narratives are full of such examples, from the perspective of both black ministers and their auditors. William J. Anderson may have been one of Ferrill's converts, for he was born in Hanover County in 1811, shortly after Ferrill's conversion. Though he did not join a church until later, he attributed his conversion to the secret "prayer meetings and preachings" of his Hanover County youth.[40]

Black spiritual initiative was also evident in the passes that white owners increasingly sent to churches of which they were not members but which they granted their slaves permission to join. The very existence of these documents suggests vigorous black proselytism, for the whites who authored the passes by definition did not share the same religious convictions as the African Americans for whom they wrote. Indeed, the writers to Upper Goose Creek Baptist Church routinely deferred to the judgment of the church as to the spiritual status of black men and women, indicating that they had not conversed with their slaves deeply about the topic. In 1827, John Bowie wrote, "My black Woman Amy is desirous of Joining the baptist Society, if they have no objection. I say with pleasure Ive none. She has for some length of time been very obedient to me and so far as I can Jud[ge] she [is] truly seeking religion." Hannah Keeble wrote later that year, "My Ben tells me that he has A noshan of Joinin your church and if you thinks proper to Receive him I have No objection to his Bein Baptised." Turner Ashby, father of the Confederate cavalryman, gave Maria permission to talk to the church. "I have no objections to them hearing what she has to say," he explained, "and deal with her as they may deem she merits."[41]

The letter Thomas Anderson's resolutely irreligious owner wrote for Anderson to join a Baptist church sounded similar to Ashby's letter. "That the church should judge for herself, for he was not a judge," the author reasoned, "but if they thought best to receive him he had no objections; and for his part, he thought if there was a Christian in the world, Tom was one." Because the text of Anderson's letter comes from his own narrative and not from a church minute book, it provides a direct window into the sort of black religious initiative that is only suggested in the Upper Goose Creek letters. Anderson confirms that a groundswell of black religious activity lay behind black requests to join evangelical churches. Before he sought his owner's permission to join a church, Anderson had already converted to Christianity and decided to work as a preacher. In other words, the most exciting chapters of Anderson's spiritual biography had already concluded before he announced his intent to join a biracial church. Long before requesting a letter, Anderson had already gained "confidence to talk to the white or the black folks, and tell what the Lord had done for my poor soul." Furthermore, he reported that "a great many come to me about religion, some good and some bad folks: for it was generally known that a great change had come over Tom."[42] Thomas Anderson was a successful black recruiter for the church even before he joined it.

African American preachers enjoyed a variety of privileges that facilitated their capacity to make converts, even if whites did not distribute all of those privileges for purely religious motives. In the mid-eighteenth century, just as evangelicals were first beginning to make inroads in the Old Dominion, slaves had won the unofficial right to refrain from work on Sundays. Fugitives from slavery such as Henry Banks testified that some owners resisted the practice long into the nineteenth century, so the right was not an absolute. In 1855, Banks recalled that "Sundays differed little from other days" and that sometimes his owner "would give us Sunday or part of a Sunday; but if he were in the least angry, we had to work all day."[43] Even non-evangelical whites generally granted the time off, however, because they conceived of the day of rest as an effective way to maintain the health and morale of their labor force. Owners originally intended slaves to cultivate their own plots of land and thereby supplement their diet, to mend their clothing, and to visit any "abroad" family on the Sabbath. Slaves did all of these things before the day became a sacred one for them, even turning

Sundays into important market days on which they sold the fruits of their weekend and after-hours labor for a small bit of discretionary money.[44] The Dover Association recognized the prevalence of these secular pursuits in 1816 when it addressed the question, "Is it according to Gospel Order for Professors of Religion to trade with Slaves on the Sabbath day?" The association decided "that such conduct is contrary to the spirit of the Gospel and the profession thereof."[45]

Sundays off assumed a new meaning as more and more slaves used the time to worship in the evangelical tradition. Whites interested in slaves' spiritual welfare and African American evangelicals interested in converting other slaves and free blacks began to consider the Sabbath a day of special opportunity for blacks as well as whites. Temple Mason received a letter from his mother in 1816 in which she admonished him to "give your poor slaves who work in the field, Saturday to sell what they make, that they may have it in their power to go to worship on Sunday."[46] What was significant here was the freedom to "go to" worship, not simply to worship; whites allowed evangelical blacks to travel. In an extreme example, James L. Smith recounted that while still enslaved he once traveled twenty-four miles on the Sabbath in order to minister to slaves in Heathesville, Virginia:

> I remember in one instance that having quit work about sundown on a Saturday evening, I prepared to go ten miles to hold a prayer meeting at Sister Gould's. Quite a number assembled in the little cabin, and we continued to sing and pray till daybreak, when it broke. All went to their homes, and I got about an hour's rest while Sister Gould was preparing breakfast. Having partaken of the meal, she, her daughter and myself set out to hold another meeting two miles further; this lasted till about five o'clock, when we returned. Then I had to walk back ten miles to my home. How I ever did it, lame as I was, I cannot tell, but I was so zealous in the work that I did not mind going any distance to attend a prayer meeting.[47]

While Smith's Sabbath did not involve a great deal of physical rest, it did involve a relaxation of the normal restrictions on black mobility.

Smith's narrative shows that women, too, traveled on the Sabbath and actively helped to organize worship services, even though men usually served as nominal leaders of both the visible and invisible black churches. In Smith's account, Sister Gould provided more than just a place to worship; she was important enough to the organization of a successful meeting that she accompanied Smith to his second appointment. Narratives contain numerous accounts of such female spiritual leadership. Francis Fedric's grandmother, for example, took delight in counseling slaves on the Sabbath. He described how "she would speak of her home, far away beyond the clouds, where there would be no whipping, and she would be at rest. This seemed to be her greatest, indeed her sole comfort, in the hour of trial. This would be a source of joy, when seated, on a Sabbath evening, under the shade of the peach trees, she talked to her fellow-slaves, or to those who came from the neighbouring plantations to see her."[48]

Some blacks also learned to read on the Sabbath as a part of their pursuit of evangelical piety. Noah Davis, born into slavery in Madison County in 1804, remembered how his father "on those Sabbaths when we remained at home, was to spend his time in instructing his children, or the neighboring servants, out of a New Testament, sent him from Fredericksburg by one of his older sons. I fancy I can see him now, sitting under his bush arbor, reading that precious book to many attentive hearers around him."[49] Peter Randolph learned indirectly at the hands of white, not black, instructors. "I used to go to the church to hear the white preacher," he recounted. "When I heard him read his text, I would read mine when I got home. This is the way, my readers, I learned to read the Word of God when I was a slave."[50] There were few avenues to literacy available for slaves, and evangelicalism provided most of them.[51]

As a result of all of this religious activity, many Virginia slaves and free blacks found in evangelicalism a new way to organize their communities. Eugene Genovese, struck both by the institutional possibilities created by widespread slave participation in worship services and, even more so, by the messages of hope and resistance inherent in Christianity, early defined evangelical Protestantism as the foundation of "a protonational black consciousness."[52] More recently, James Sidbury, Sylvia Frey, Betty Wood, Peter Hinks, and others have traced the development of slaves' religious identities with more chronological and geographic precision and have argued for the coalescence of an African American evangelical community in Virginia by the first decade of the nineteenth century.[53] Walter Rucker and Michael Gomez also argue that evangelical Protestantism formed a new basis for organization within slave communities, but they stress the retention of African belief systems and date the transformation later, to the late 1820s.[54] Notwithstanding these subtle differences of chronology, there is substantial agreement among most scholars that Virginia slaves used evangelicalism as a way of bridging cultural differences among them grounded in different ethnic African heritages. In other words, the widespread acceptance of evangelical Protestantism facilitated the creation of a pan-ethnic racial consciousness among people of African descent.[55]

Yet, even in the second and third decades of the eighteenth century, when slaves and free blacks joined evangelical churches at a rate surpassing that of white Virginians and exercised considerable freedom of worship, the equation of slave religion and slave community must not be overstated. In important ways, slaves brought diversity and, sometimes, conflict to their communities by joining evangelical churches. Though the fiction of solidarity in the face of white oppression is inspiring, admission to an evangelical church sometimes undermined racial cohesion. The most fundamental division that black evangelicals created was between those "saved" and "unsaved."[56] Some black men and women resisted conversion to the point of alienating family members or friends. These individuals did not join the secret or open worship meetings that might have served as important building blocks for communal consciousness. Francis Fedric's father articulated very clearly why some slaves chose not to attend religious meetings or associate too closely with religious slaves. "How," he challenged his converted son, "can Jesus be just, if He will allow such oppression and wrong? Don't the slaveholders justify their conduct by the Bible itself, and say, that it tells them to do so?"[57] Even converted slaves disagreed about whether or not they should join churches governed by white males. The rapid growth of autonomous black churches after the Civil War suggests that many blacks who were otherwise sympathetic to Christianity had not been willing to join the visible evangelical church as long as most of its branches were controlled by whites.

The intention here, then, is not to idealize black evangelical resistance to slavery, but simply to underscore the spiritual initiative of black evangelicals and their many points of contact with white evangelicals, those most responsible for the formation of a religious proslavery argument. In the 1810s and 1820s, bonded evangelicals impressed their white counterparts by their success in winning converts. Whites saw black evangelical progress as a strong endorsement of the delicate position on slavery that they had adopted in the early national period and as a natural outgrowth of their paternal care for the enslaved. To a great extent, black evangelicals by their hard work on behalf of the Gospel therefore strengthened the paternalist justification for slavery. At the same time, black initiative created an ideological problem for the most thoughtful white evangelicals. In a paternalist framework, did there come a time when enslaved men and women learned the lessons of the master class well enough to deserve freedom?

Whites did not worry about the answer to this question enough to reopen the discussion about slavery within their churches. The ban on debate over emancipation was still absolute, as white members of Black Creek Baptist

Church revealed when they turned on one of their own who tried to break it. At a church meeting in December 1825, Jonathan Lankford, who had been preaching for the church but had not been called as its pastor, "this day openly declared to this conference that he cannot in justice to his conscience, administer the ordinances of the Gospel to this Church any longer, owing to his opposition on the subject of Negro Slavery, a Part of the Church being slave holders." In rather bold fashion, Lankford had tried to make emancipation a topic of church discussion once more. Members of the church worked patiently for the better part of two years in a "brotherly and affectionate" manner to reason with Lankford and to encourage him to define emancipation as a civil issue. They finally excluded him from their congregation in September 1826 but still hoped that eventually they would be able to restore him to fellowship. When they could not convince him to retract his demand that the church debate slavery, though, their condemnation was absolute.

In a scathing December 1827 report, the church strongly echoed the Jeffersonian idea that churchmen, especially ministers, had no business dividing the church by raising nonreligious issues. "The Church contained slave holders when he became a member thereof," the committee appointed to look into Lankford's case explained, "has continued to do so ever since, and notwithstanding, there has been a small majority of non slave holders, the Church has moved on harmoniously, each member regulating this subject to his own conscience, as he might think Proper, without interfering with that of his brothers, untill the present case." Lankford's disruption of the church's peace was downright sinful, the committee found. Indeed, the committee felt "compelled to believe that Jonathan Lankford, has through the vain influence of improper impressions, yielded too much to the delusion of Satan, and thereby lost sight of the Duties of the Gospel." As if following Satanic promptings was not reason enough to dismiss Lankford, whites in the church also explained that their disgraced preacher had breached his contract. "He was at perfect liberty to enjoy his own opinion; but they cou'd not suffer him to controul them, upon an important question, over which they considered he had no cognizance, further than as regarded his own conscience."[58]

In response to the spiritual achievements of black evangelicals, then, white evangelicals did not reopen a discussion of slavery or entertain the possibility of wholesale emancipation. Some white evangelicals, though, did begin to search for a middle way, a course of action through which they could simultaneously honor their decision not to discuss slavery and acknowledge the extent to which black evangelicals had exceeded their paternalist expectations. For these men and women, African colonization seemed to offer the perfect opportunity to act on their consciences without disrupting their local congregations.

White Virginia evangelicals do not bear sole credit or blame for giving the idea of colonization institutional form with the establishment of the ACS in 1816–17. Many different constituencies, each with its own motivations and hopes, wanted to remove black Americans from the United States to a foreign country. Scholars have added to the confusion about the origins of the ACS by describing the society's goals in very different terms. Some have attributed to colonizationists an economic motive and depicted the scheme as a component of the National Republicans' plan to revitalize the country's economy by establishing a national bank, funding internal improvements, and setting a protective tariff.[59] Others have made sense of the movement by stressing its continuity with enlightened, Jeffersonian Republicanism.[60] Still others have made white racism and the attempt to free the country of people of African descent the primary story, while some—following abolitionist William Lloyd Garrison—have interpreted colonization primarily as a proslavery scheme to remove free blacks subversive of the slave regime.[61] Finally, there are those who have depicted colonization as an earnest antislavery effort by conscience-stricken slaveholders.[62] Colonization defies easy interpretation because it was all of these things.[63]

In addition to being ideologically capacious, colonization was also painfully flawed and internally inconsistent from the start. Historians and even some contemporary observers have excoriated the program for its assumption that America could never be a multiracial nation, for the catastrophic death rates in Liberia, or for the logistical impossibility of removing from America even the natural increase of a rapidly growing black population.[64] These flaws, however, did not stop many white evangelicals from setting enormous store in the program. Evangelical statesmen from across the Upper South seized upon the idea of subsidized emigration as the best way to balance the scriptural and constitutional rights of slaveholders, the pleas of the enslaved, and the scruples of antislavery whites. Scholars have finally restored colonization to the center of national debates about the future of slavery between 1816 and the late 1840s and recognized its tremendous national appeal. Northern moderates joined white, southern evangelicals in their support of colonization and seized upon the program as the single best hope for sectional compromise on the issue of slavery.[65] National newsmen trumpeted the work of the ACS, and the editors of the *Christian Spectator* even proclaimed in 1824 that "it appears to us to be the *only institution which promises any thing great or effectual for the benefit of the black population of our country.*"[66]

White Virginians freed more slaves and facilitated the passage of more free blacks to Liberia than did citizens of any other state. Black Virginians comprised roughly one-third of the total number of emigrants. Virginians' reasons for supporting colonization are therefore particularly important; if there was any state in which whites actually tried to implement a colonizationist agenda, it was the Old Dominion.[67] Though information on the religious affiliation of each of the 186 known Virginia emancipators is not available for an accurate assessment of the proportion of evangelicals among them, evangelicals held a disproportionate share of the leadership positions in colonization societies and doubtless also constituted a majority of emancipators. Presbyterian Benjamin Brand was treasurer of the state colonization society, and Richmond's First Baptist Church sponsored the first emigrants to Liberia in 1821. Philip Slaughter, an Episcopal priest, wrote the first history of colonization in Virginia in 1855. In *The Virginian History of African Colonization*, Slaughter recorded the names of the officers for thirty-two of the state auxiliaries of the ACS in existence between 1817 and 1828, when colonizationists in the state reorganized as the Colonization Society of Virginia. Over one-fifth of the 111 presidents and vice presidents were ordained clergy in an evangelical church.[68] Another evangelical Episcopalian, future bishop William Meade, served as the first agent for the ACS in Virginia.

In his capacity as an agent, Meade explained with sublime clarity the relationship between paternalism and African colonization. In a letter he wrote to a friend back in Virginia while on the road for the ACS in Charleston, S.C., Meade depicted colonization as the natural end of a steadily ameliorating paternalist regime of slavery. "So far as true Christianity predominates," he reported, "as many new hearts created by divine grace as we find, so do we discover a desire to do something which sooner or later may benefit Africa, raise the condition of the Negro race and relieve our children." Some things were already happening: "The religious instruction of Negroes, the teaching them to read, the feeding & clothing of them, and the whole condition of the slave, (tho at far below what justice & religion requires) is but I am told on good authority, [annually] improving." But current efforts were not enough, Meade implored:

> While this should rejoice our hearts let it stimulate us to do more & more for those whom Providence has entrusted as talents to our care. Let us

look upon them my good friend as immortal beings, brethren & sisters, dependent upon us for the means of improvement and for whom we are in a great measure responsible before God, and while a proper degree of labor and a due discipline is necessary for them as well as profitable for us let us not consider them mainly as property but rather as unfortunate beings thrown upon our clemency, whom we [are] to cherish and cultivate and in return for which their obedience, and their labor is permitted by Providence to be ours.

Meade went on to argue that paternalist whites were training blacks for a new destiny. "How much better & happier would it be for us & them would we regard them as so many objects of charity, so many candidates for eternity, so many pensioners on our bounty, so many children of a free school to be trained up for Heaven than as sources of revenue beasts of burthen whose only province it is to minister to our pleasures or our avarice," he pleaded. The new destiny that Meade proposed was a return to Africa as missionaries.[69]

The support that white Virginians showed for colonization, so ably explicated by Meade, can only be understood in the context of their relationships with black evangelicals. Out of deference for their black coreligionists, white evangelicals at the turn of the century had worked for an amelioration of slaves' conditions and helped to form a paternalist ethic. In the 1810s and 1820s, moderately antislavery white evangelicals had few strategies available through which to assist enslaved believers short of disastrously circumventing the ban on conversation about emancipation or breaking the laws of the state. At best, they could only hope to attack slavery very indirectly, in a way that preserved intact the rights of slaveholders. Colonization was the best available option. It was made even more attractive by the fact that some of Virginia's black evangelicals assured antislavery whites that the scheme was a benevolent one. African American church members encouraged Virginia whites to free their slaves for emigration or to give money to a local affiliate of the society.

Black and white evangelicals worked together closely in the colonization enterprise from the beginning. Colonization was unique among benevolent societies, for whites could accomplish nothing without the active participation of their black brethren. White colonizationists refused to send anyone to Africa without their consent, so would-be émigrés had to buy into the vision and become a critical part of the planning process. Both slaves and free blacks emigrated, and therefore both took part in the preparation. Free blacks first expressed their interest in emigrating and then worked with whites and other prospective emigrants to gather supplies, raise funds, and recruit additional companions.[70] Since this process could take more than a year, white colonizationists screened free black candidates for emigration and tried to make certain that those who wanted to leave were of sound religious character and were willing to see the task through to completion. Thus, at a meeting in Richmond at the First Baptist Church in which twenty-six free blacks volunteered for Liberia, whites refused to recommend one of the candidates, David Login.[71] Slaves, too, were active participants in the process of preparation, though they volunteered themselves less often. More frequently, slaves' connection to a colonization society came when their owners made plans to free them. As Eric Burin has made clear, whites typically manumitted slaves to go to Liberia as part of long-term plans, which usually "entailed subjecting carefully selected bondpersons to unspecified amounts of religious indoctrination, educational instruction, and occupational training." Thus, interracial interaction only increased after enslaved men and women agreed to go to Liberia, for they had to receive extensive training from whites before their manumissions would become a reality.[72]

In this way, both free blacks and manumitted slaves—who made up one-third and two-thirds, respectively, of Virginia's 3,444 total emigrants between 1820 and 1860—had regular contact with whites. This intense communication often continued once the settlers arrived in Africa, for many migrants established a regular correspondence with whites and blacks involved in the ACS. At every stage, blacks and whites were in intimate contact, and—in this enterprise in particular—whites could view the growing spiritual assertiveness of African Americans in a positive, nonthreatening light.[73] Both in the heady early stages of the enterprise, when many blacks participated, and in the 1830s and 1840s, when white recruiters had to work hard to overcome negative messages coming from earlier emigrants, whites saw slave and free black co-laborers in colonization as brothers and sisters in Christ—and as the first fruits of paternalism.

The earliest and most influential instance of this sort of interracial cooperation occurred in Richmond, Virginia, in the African Baptist Missionary Society. Black and white members of the city's First Baptist Church formed the group on 26 April 1815 with the goal of converting the congregation's growing interest in overseas missions to Africa into concrete action.[74] This group, which predated the ACS, was initially interested in sending black missionaries from the First Baptist Church overseas, not in establishing a permanent colony. The African American Baptists who participated in the group, most prominent among them Lott Cary, Collin Teague, and John Lewis, formed close relationships with the white evangelicals who also ex-

Lott Cary. This engraving of Lott Cary, from Carter G. Woodson's *History of the Negro Church* (1921), shows the multitalented Baptist at the height of his influence. Cary was born into slavery outside Richmond in 1780 and purchased his freedom in 1813. Once free, he mobilized black and white Baptists in the First Baptist Church of Richmond to found the African Baptist Missionary Society. Cary and his family were among the first missionaries whom the group sent to what would become Liberia, in 1821. (From the copy in the Rare Book Collection, The University of North Carolina at Chapel Hill)

pressed an interest in Africa. Whites such as David Roper and the brothers William and James Crane found in the society the opportunity to get to know their black coreligionists in a more intimate way than was possible at the weekly services, which were packed with more than 1,000 African Americans. Roper and the Cranes further developed this intimacy by introducing black members of the society to other white evangelicals in the community who were interested in Africa and African Americans. For the small, predominately urban cadre of evangelical whites who considered in the 1810s through the 1830s strategies to ameliorate or to end slavery, the black missionaries turned colonizationists became representatives of an entire race—interracial confidants whose friendship confirmed the benevolence and wisdom of colonization.

Lott Cary, born a slave in about 1780, was the most influential of the black colonizationists and a critical figure in the early history of African colonization. After moving from the countryside to Richmond in 1804, Cary managed to purchase his freedom and that of his two children in 1813. He worked in a tobacco warehouse where he learned to read, write, and maintain complex business ledgers, skills that he put to use as the most prominent African American member of the city's biracial First Baptist Church. He was the prime mover behind the African Baptist Missionary Society and took minutes at the society's first meeting. Without Cary's strong leadership and interest in establishing a benevolence society that focused exclusively on Africa, it is doubtful whether men such as Roper or the Crane brothers would have willingly diverted their energies from the Richmond Missionary Society, founded less than two years earlier and the darling of white Baptists. Black evangelicals in Petersburg also formed an African Baptist Missionary Society for the purpose of preparing the city's blacks for service on Africa's shores as missionaries.[75]

Since they already possessed the goal of going to Africa, members of Virginia's black evangelical elite were willing partners of the ACS after its formation. Cary, Teague, and their wives were among the first to go to Liberia in 1821, as soon as the African Baptist Missionary Society raised enough money for their passage. Whites celebrated the black families' departure and exalted Cary in particular as an example of the possibilities of racial uplift inherent in evangelicalism. Cary was fully "trained up for heaven," a disciple of Christ who was capable of manly assertions for the sake of the Gospel. Impressed by his faith, whites had allowed him to learn to read, to have considerable authority at work, and to preach to slaves on the Sabbath. Sympathetic evangelical whites therefore understood his departure as the logical end of paternalism; by making good on all of the opportunities afforded him, Cary had unsuited himself for life in a slave society.

Cary's white admirers tolerated his revulsion against slavery and his love of temporal freedom because he displayed such impeccable spiritual credentials. A white Baptist minister who supposedly interviewed Cary upon his departure reported with respect on the missionary's ambition. "I am an African," he quoted Cary as proclaiming, "and in this country, however meritorious my conduct, and respectable my character, I cannot receive the credit due to either." "I wish to go to a country where I shall be estimated by my merits, not by my complexion," Cary continued, "and I feel bound to labor for my suffering race." In his going-away sermon in 1821, before a racially mixed audience, Cary further identified himself with the martyrs of old and professed the spiritual goals that made so many whites trust him. "I long to preach to the poor Africans the way of life and salvation," he intoned; "I don't know what may befall me, whether I may find a grave in the ocean, or among the savage men, or more savage wild beasts on the Coast of Africa; nor am I anxious what may become of me."[76]

Four years later, when the *Hunter* carried more black Virginians to Liberia, white and black evangelicals still viewed colonization in complementary, providential ways. From whites' perspective, colonization marked the moment when they had fulfilled their paternalist duties to certain favored slaves and readied them for a return "home." From blacks' perspective, colonization marked a divinely provided opportunity to strike out on one's own. Before the *Hunter*'s departure, a biracial congregation met in Norfolk's First Methodist Church to sing a hymn that accommodated both blacks' and whites' providential understandings of colonization. The singers praised colonization as a wholly divine program, situated by God in history at a particular time:

Come on my fellow comrades, come—
Let's hasten to our new given home,
The time's arrived, the signal's given
For us to seek our destined haven.

In Africa, the black man's land,
Given by him whom none withstand,
We'll build an altar to HIS *grace*,
And strive to save a heathen race,

There all our troubles will be o'er;
Upon that long neglected shore
Our vines will spread, *our* corn will grow,
Our fields will smile and plenty flow,

Our children *free* will round us play,
As happy as the live long day;
No force, no violence they'll fear,
For God will claim them as his care.[77]

The vision described in the hymn was considerably better than the reality for the first settlers. When Cary, Teague, and the twenty-six others who accompanied them completed their transatlantic voyage, they found to their dismay that Liberia did not yet exist. Agents of the ACS who had promised to procure land had either died prematurely or failed in their negotiations with native Africans. Though unfortunate, this situation ultimately created more opportunities for Cary to impress his transatlantic observers. But first he had to wait; the expatriate Virginians encamped at the British colony of Sierra Leone while Lt. Robert Field Stockton of the U.S. Navy traveled inland to "negotiate" with native rulers for access to land. Holding one of them, King Peter, at gunpoint, Stockton forced him and five other chieftains to deed part of their dominion, Cape Mesurado, to the ACS. Less than two months later, on 7 February 1822, the small African American community in Sierra Leone moved south along the African coast to take possession of the plot.[78]

Black Virginians who remained at home did not immediately hear of this inauspicious beginning—or of the devastating mortality rate and economic deprivation that characterized the first years of settlement.[79] Many of them thus remained open to the possibility of emigrating until they established more consistent correspondence with emigrants. Since the ACS only raised enough funds to send 324 men and women to Liberia before 1825, that feedback loop was slow in coming.[80] Free African Americans' almost universal condemnation of the program from the early 1830s through the Civil War must not obscure a brief window during the late 1810s and early 1820s when blacks, especially southern slaves, displayed a willingness to travel to Africa.[81] Some bondmen and bondwomen very understandably hoped that colonizationists, some of whom had promised to free their own slaves in order to send them out of the country, were setting in motion a process that would end slavery. Even though they were not enthusiastic about the specific destination of Africa, the free people of color from Richmond believed in 1817 that it would "tend to the benefit and advantage of a great portion of our suffering fellow creatures, to be colonized."[82] Thomas Smallwood, a Maryland slave granted his freedom at the age of thirty, remembered the optimism that surrounded the first acts of the ACS: "If my memory be not at fault, I was from the year 1822 or 23, up to about 1830, an advocate of African Colonisation, because I thought the object of that Society was the entire abolition of slavery in the United States; and which I thought would lead to its final extinction every where else."[83] That optimism faded when bitter letters and broken persons began to return to the South. Isaac Williams of King George County, Virginia, remembered that his own hopeful feelings vanished when "some colored men who had been once and returned told very different stories about fevers, hostile tribes that fought to drive the colony away, and other discouragements."[84] Gilbert Hunt, a member of Cary's former church, became part of this negative feedback loop; he traveled to Liberia in 1829 but returned to Virginia with some relief in 1830.[85]

Enslaved Virginians may have looked favorably on colonization in part because the alternatives they faced were increasingly abysmal. They considered voluntary migration to Africa in the context of the forced migration of tens of thousands of their friends, partners, and family members to the American Southwest. Slaveowners had begun to carry their chattel out of

Virginia even before the Revolutionary War, but the movement did not become epidemic until Andrew Jackson had cleared the Gulf States of American Indians during the War of 1812 and thereby opened the land to cotton production. Then began what Ira Berlin has called the "Second Middle Passage," the greatest forced migration in American history. Slaveholders who migrated in search of a fortune based on white gold carried their slaves with them against their will, and whites who stayed in Virginia sold their slaves south to work in the cotton fields of strangers. Virginia became a slave exporter, sending more than 35,000 individuals out of the state in the 1810s and 30,000 in the 1820s.[86] Paternalist whites justified this horrific trade by arguing that they were only selling disobedient individuals who corrupted their households or—when purchasing—that they were rescuing slaves from a cruel market.[87] Enslaved men and women did not accept this flimsy rationalization and may have hoped for the chance to go to Liberia rather than Mississippi.

Those who did go to Liberia and survived became, for white evangelicals, larger-than-life symbols of the benevolent functions of slavery. Whites rejoiced with black colonists at their every achievement, primarily because the success of Liberia confirmed a place in God's plan for whites' paternalist system of slavery. Over the years, a pantheon of primarily Virginia-born heroes emerged in Liberia, black men who worked steadfastly to spread the Gospel and to administer the colony. This group included future Liberian president Joseph Jenkins Roberts, who converted at Petersburg's Union Street Methodist Church in 1826 before emigrating, and Hilary Teague, a Richmond resident, Liberian newspaper editor, and author of the Liberian Declaration of Independence.[88] For several years before Lott Cary died in 1828, the Virginia-born minister was at the center of this remarkable pantheon, the unmistakable symbol of the possibilities of colonization. Sometime before 1824, Cary's companion, Collin Teague, despaired of making the colony work and returned to Sierra Leone, which left Cary as the most visible representative of the founding generation. King Peter, the African potentate from whom Stockton had extorted the original land grant for the colony, provided an early opportunity for Cary to impress transatlantic observers when he tried to retake Cape Mesurado in late 1822. The white ACS agent, Jehudi Ashmun, had landed in May of that year and, like most new arrivals, had promptly developed a severe case of "African Fever," likely malaria. Though partially recovered when 1,500 African soldiers attacked the thirty-seven colonists, Ashmun basically abdicated the defense of Liberia entirely to Cary, who took command and demonstrated outstanding personal courage. In his understated official report, even the self-centered Ashmun had to acknowledge Cary's role, conceding that "the movement of the main body [of African warriors] was disordered, and impeded; and an opportunity afforded the Agent, assisted principally by the Rev. Lot Cary to rally the broken force of the settlers."[89]

A military hero, Cary made himself further indispensable to the inchoate colony by becoming the only person in it with any medical knowledge. He learned from a few books and from trial and error enough medical skills to keep a slightly larger proportion of immigrants safe from the fever; so indispensable did he become that both he and Ashmun were too "apprehensive" about his absence for him to leave Africa for a visit to Virginia in 1826. The general and doctor was also a priest, farmer, trader, and—when necessary— revolutionary. Though Cary's relations with Ashmun were generally cordial, Cary seized weapons from the colonial storerooms and led a coup of sorts in December 1823. Without shedding a drop of blood, he overruled the ACS's stingy distribution policies and allocated foodstuffs and construction supplies to his fellow settlers. Recognizing the ultimate efficacy of Cary's actions, the ACS forgave and forgot the incident; they even made Cary vice regent of Liberia in 1826.

White readers of the *African Repository and Colonial Journal*, a paper established by the ACS in 1825 to spread news of the Liberian mission, positively exulted in Cary's triumphs.[90] They followed his success carefully and found in it confirmation that colonization was of God. They read, for example, in July 1825 a letter from Cary in which he described the conversion of an African native to Christianity. Cary closed the letter with a moving appeal to members of Richmond's African Baptist Missionary Society: "Tell the Board to be strong in the Lord and in the power of his might, for the work is going on here, and prospers in his hands; that the Sunday School promises to be a great and everlasting blessing to Africa." In other words, he wanted to tell them that the plan was working—and that divine blessings were showering upon the experiment of colonization.[91] Cary was the darling of the paper by October, when the *African Repository* ran a hagiographical biography of him that they borrowed from the *Family Visitor*. The editor described Cary's success as integral to the progress of evangelical Protestantism. "Other facts than those enumerated," he gushed, "might be mentioned to the honour of this servant of Jesus Christ, especially his liberality to newly-arrived emigrants, and his numerous disinterested sacrifices and unwearied labours for the general good of the Colony. May Heaven long preserve his life for his brethren's sake, and for the Christian cause."[92]

The *African Repository* also ran articles exhorting white readers to fulfill their spiritual obligations to their slaves, with no reference to colonization. These articles show the continuity of paternalist and colonizationist thought in the minds of nineteenth-century evangelicals. Thus, readers encountered an article from the *Religious Intelligencer* in December 1825 in which the author complained that "while on a visit some time since to a professedly religious friend, I had an occasion to notice, with much grief, a want of Christian-like conduct toward his domestics. Instead of a becoming kindness of manner and language, there was a tone of harshness and tyranny in every thing he said to them." The contributor reminded readers that "without good, kind, and judicious masters and mistresses, there can never be affectionate, faithful, and useful servants."[93] The point was made again the following month, in a sermon titled "Benefits of Religious Instruction to the People of Colour."[94]

African Americans in Liberia provided another conduit of information regarding colonization when they wrote to their emancipators or, if free when emigrating, to contacts in the United States. In their private correspondence with white evangelicals, these black men and women affirmed whites' decision to manumit them and reinforced their commitment to colonization. Sometimes this encouragement was incidental in letters primarily about other things. In Mars Lucas's March 1830 letter from Liberia to Loudoun County, for example, he told his former owner, "I feel myself very much indebted to you, for my Freedom, more than under an oblagation, to you for Immancipating me. I am very much pleased with this Country."[95] At other times, black men wrote for the express purpose of shoring up white faith in the enterprise. Cary wrote to the Virginia society's treasurer, Benjamin Brand, in 1827, both to soothe Brand's doubts about the wisdom of colonization and to steel him against the rising black protest against it. As Cary explained, the program required considerable faith, and white colonizationists had to believe in its long-term prospects in order to be able to bear up under whatever voices might rise against them. "I am confident that all the colored people in your city," Liberia's most famous son assured Brand, "will regret the loss of time when they are convinced of the great mistake that they labor under for I am of the full belief that you might go out in your streets and take a list of names of the first hundred men that you saw and send them out and in twenty four hours after they arrived in Monrovia there would not be one found among them that would be willing to return to America."[96] This dynamic was present in the late 1820s but became more important in the 1830s, as criticism of colonization increased domestically and more scrupulous white evangelicals began to second-guess the program.

For many white evangelicals, unfortunately for enslaved black Virginians, the corollary to the conviction that colonization was of God was that slavery, too, must be divinely ordained. There was no colonization without bondage, no mission to Africa without the dialogue between blacks and whites that accompanied chattel slavery. Even those white evangelicals who had been squeamish about slavery before colonization saw in the survival of Liberia evidence that slavery was part of God's plan. Those who did not own slaves (or who had never had reservations about the practice of slaveholding) were even quicker to draw the conclusion that slavery and colonization were mutually reinforcing. John Gray of Fredericksburg perceived that "a superintending God . . . sent these people here to get a knowledge of a saviour—and he is sending them back again to spread that knowledge in their own country." Unless he did so anonymously, Gray did not emancipate any slaves for colonization or have any direct dealing with the ACS.[97] Like many other white evangelicals, he was participating vicariously in colonization through reports published in the *African Repository* and spread by word of mouth. Thus, whites miraculously derived from the potentially antislavery program of colonization a powerful proslavery idea, that blacks in America were learning the religious and secular lessons necessary for them to play their part in the salvation of African peoples. The ACS actually encouraged this thinking. In the 1825 broadside that it sent to local ministers to urge them to devote the collections from their 4 July offerings to colonization (an annual tradition), the Petersburg auxiliary of the ACS praised slaveowners for teaching people of African descent "Christianity and civilization." They introduced the society as one that "proposes to rescue the nominally free negro, from his state of degradation and semi-slavery in America, and to place him, reinvested with the dignity of manhood and of freedom, in the land of his ancestors; carrying with him, to Africa, as the wages of his servitude, the rich treasures of Christianity and civilization."[98]

Members of Virginia's white antislavery vanguard were among those for whom good news from Liberia delayed or, in some cases, entirely prevented a move toward immediatism. Some of the most active and influential evangelical colonizationists, including Brand, William Crane, Anne Page, Mary Minor Blackford, William Meade, and John Hartwell Cocke, were on record against slavery itself and clearly regarded colonization as a tactic to advance black liberty. Brand, as befit his role as an officer of an organization that some whites found seditious, was circumspect in the way that he argued for emancipation. "My prayer is that the Lord may take the colony under his particular care and protection," he confided to Lott Cary, "and make it a blessing to the tribes of Africa, and to *all* the colored people in the United States." The emphasis on "*all*" was Brand's.[99] William Crane began work while in Richmond on *Anti-slavery in Virginia: Extracts from Thos. Jefferson, Gen. Washington and Others Relative to the "Blighting Curse of Slavery". Debates on the "Nat Turner Insurrection,"* though he did not publish it until he was safely ensconced in Baltimore in 1865.[100] Page prayed fervently against slavery, crying out to God in 1823, "Thou seest how thy grace has taught me to desire above all earthly things, the abolition of slavery." Her prayer bore some fruit when she emancipated and sent to Liberia thirty-three slaves and convinced her daughter of the impropriety of slavery. When Sarah W. Page married Charles Andrews, another colonizationist committed to ending slavery, she signed over her inheritance in slaves to her mother, "so that she may have it in her power to liberate & send them to Africa or elsewhere whenever she desires to do so," and so that her new marriage would not bear the stain of slavery.[101] The existence of an outlet for their hostility toward slavery, one apparently approved by evangelical black Virginians, was enough to keep these men and women from becoming immediatists.

Contemporaries of Cary, particular black Americans in northern cities, recognized colonization as an obstacle to black liberty. They argued that African American colonizationists hurt the cause of emancipation by endorsing the idea that blacks could never be equal citizens and by frittering away their energies on foreign soil. Cary did not see it this way. In 1827, he drafted a remarkable letter home in response to criticism of colonization that he heard emanating from free blacks in Philadelphia and Baltimore. Ostensibly because he was concerned about errors in composition, but more likely because he realized that he had struck too combative a tone, Cary did not send it to a newspaper editor. Instead, he sent it to his fellow colonizationist Benjamin Brand and requested that Brand "use it in any way that you think will be likely to promote the Interess of the Cause If you should have it published please to have all the erors rectified and what ever expences are incured charge them to my account."

In the letter, Cary blasted in disconcertingly harsh tones the inactivity of free blacks in Philadelphia and Baltimore and praised the opportunity for self-advancement in Liberia. "You will never know, w[h]ether you are men or monkies so long as you remain in America," he challenged. He also attacked one by one the objections raised to emigration, including the complaint that "there is no guarantee given them of the Liberation of those who are at present in bondage." Neither the ACS nor the government, Cary reasoned, had promised emancipation. It was therefore useless for northern free blacks to sit on their hands and hope that one of these agencies would change its mind. In his view, it was far better to alter the calculus of the situation and to increase the likelihood of a general emancipation by creating a safe haven for freedmen. "If the General Government was to say to you, that if you free people will emigrate to Africa, we will liberate all the slaves in the Union Would that induce you to come?" he asked, "and if it did[,] would they be more able, on that account[,] to send you or do you think that you, would be more able to Govern, two Millions of uncultivated persons; than you would a few hundred in the commencement?" Cary went on to enumerate the cracks that colonization was already causing in the slave system, citing in particular its work against the Atlantic trade and the increasing number of manumissions. Finding Cary's open hostility to slavery and his harsh tone too alarming, Brand did not publish the letter.[102]

Keeping this one letter secret, though, was not enough to prevent some white Virginians from expressing concern about the expanded activities of evangelical African Americans following the War of 1812. Especially for those who were not evangelicals themselves, it was easy to see subversive possibilities in the ideas that black evangelicals were articulating and in the privileges they were accruing. Some slaveholding Virginians, virtually all of them outside the church, attacked even the relatively innocuous program of colonization. These men and women recognized the antislavery intent of many of the ACS's northern (and some of their evangelical Virginian) supporters. They therefore blasted the organization for endangering their property in persons. No humanitarian or spiritual mission, in their minds, was worth destabilization of the slave regime. Some Southside reactionaries labeled colonizationists "mischievous intermeddlers, whose principles and designs were calculated to disturb . . . relations of master and servant." Anticolonizationists feared that even the modest act of sponsoring emigration from the United States would serve as an "entering wedge" against slavery and lead inexorably to emancipation.[103]

Some white slaveowners lashed out not just against colonization but against black evangelical agency in general. These men and women recognized what evangelical whites did not: that black men and women could exploit the privileges that they earned on the basis of their religious commitment for revolutionary purposes. Since southern whites enjoyed relatively unrestricted authority over their chattel, unchurched whites were free to employ any number of techniques to circumscribe black evangelical agency. Francis Fedric's irreligious owner, for example, physically punished his slaves for any demonstration of Christian commitment. Fedric remembered when "my grandmother having committed the crime of attending a prayer-meeting, was ordered to be flogged by her own son. This was done by tying her hands before her with a rope, and then fastening the rope to a peach tree, and laying bare the back. Her own son was then made to give her forty lashes with a thong of a raw cow's-hide, her master standing over her the whole time blaspheming and threatening what he would do if her son did not *lay it on*."[104] Even when whites were willing to resort to such measures, it was difficult to arrest black religious expression entirely. As Peter Randolph recalled, although other slaves on his plantation knew they were not "allowed to hold meetings on the plantation, the slaves assemble in the swamps, out of reach of the patrols. They have an understanding among themselves as to the time and place of getting together. This is often done by the first one arriving breaking boughs from the trees, and bending them in the direction of the selected spot."[105]

Whites outside the church had only limited success when they tried to use the force of law to curtail black evangelical prerogatives. Blocking black agency where it fell into their power to do so, on their own plantations or in certain legal situations, for example, these skeptics could not touch those activities that took place inside churches. In Richmond, proslavery secularists in the General Assembly voted down an 1822 petition from the city's blacks requesting "that your honorable body will pass a law authorizing them to cause to be erected within this city, a House of public worship which may be called the Baptist African Church." This legislative veto actually underscored the impotence of those hostile to slave participation in the evangelical movement, for black Virginians continued to worship and to build semiautonomous organizations within the existing, racially mixed church, First Baptist.[106]

White evangelicals circumvented legal restraints on black evangelical activity because they were generally confident in their ability to prevent African American religious expression from becoming violent. Some among them, though, did begin to fear in the 1820s that seditious men or women outside the visible church might use a heterodox message to mobilize violence against whites. In other words, white evangelicals began to fear the invisible church that functioned as a shadowy auxiliary to biracial evangelicalism. In 1825, Virginia Presbyterian John Holt Rice noticed the proliferation of unordained black preachers and warned evangelical whites and blacks of the potentially dangerous consequences of allowing men to preach who did not have the sanction of the church. "The preachers among them, although extremely ignorant, (often unable to read a verse in the Bible or a line in their Hymn book), are frequently shrewd cunning men," he cautioned. "They see what influence misdirected religious feeling gives them over their brethren and they take advantage of it. Many of them feel their importance, and assume the post of men of great consequence." In an admonition that proved clairvoyant, he went on: "I venture to predict, that if ever that horrid event should take place, which is anticipated and greatly dreaded by many among us, some crisp-haired prophet, some pretender to inspiration, will be the ringleader as well as the instigator of the plot." In addition to his concern over heterodoxy, there appears in Rice's editorial a definite awareness that black men throughout Virginia—as they had elsewhere in the Atlantic world—were linking resistance to slavery and evangelical piety.[107]

Rice failed to attract much notice with his warning, but free black tailor and revolutionary David Walker drew a great deal of attention in 1829. Walker never actually lived in Virginia—he moved from Wilmington to Charleston and, finally, to Boston—but he did recognize the emerging black evangelical leadership as the best hope to bind black Americans together. Peter Hinks, in his superlative treatment of Walker, *To Awaken My Afflicted Brethren*, showed how Walker used scripture to justify violence against whites and used the idiom of evangelical Protestantism to encourage black unity. He strove to rein in the centrifugal forces tugging at black evangelicals and counseled corporate action at every turn. "Your full glory and happiness, as well as [that of] all other coloured people under Heaven," Walker assured blacks, "shall never be fully consummated, but with the *entire emancipation of your enslaved brethren all over the world*." Born in 1796, Walker was of the same generation as Lott Cary and had committed to evangelical Protestantism as a young man. Also like Cary, "a colored preacher named Campbell," Collin Teague, and so many hundred unnamed contemporaries, he believed that the Bible and slavery were fundamentally incompatible. Walker published these beliefs in his 1829 *Appeal to the Colored Citizens of the World* and smuggled them to Virginia and other slaveholding states. White officials in the commonwealth discovered that a free black man had been circulating them and called an emergency closed-door session of the General Assembly on 7 January 1830 to address the problem.[108]

Across the Old Dominion in the late 1820s, white evangelicals worried that black Christians who decided to remain outside the biracial evangelical church might not be their allies in the pursuit of black souls, after all. There were, in fact, ominous signs that some black men were interpreting evangelicalism in a manner that flouted white authority. A Southampton County slave, for example, bypassed the biracial Black Creek and Raccoon Swamp Baptist churches near his home and started an independent ministry of his own. When the enslaved man converted a white neighbor in 1828 by sharing with him prophetic visions, evangelical whites showed their disdain for his ministry by refusing to baptize the convert. The bondman was not discouraged by this affront to his spiritual independence and simply baptized the man himself. The black preacher's name was Nat Turner.[109]

Chapter Four

THE SPIRITUAL CHALLENGE OF NAT TURNER, 1831–1835

The spirit of the Lord God is upon me; because the Lord hath anointed me to preach good tidings unto the meek; he hath sent me to bind up the brokenhearted, to proclaim liberty to the captives, and the opening of the prison to them that are bound; To proclaim the acceptable year of the Lord, and the day of vengeance of our God.—Isaiah 61:1–2

Hark, Henry, Nelson, Sam, Jack, and Will arrived at Southampton County's Cabin Pond early on Sunday, 21 August 1831. Like most other slaves in the commonwealth, they had the Sabbath off from work. Many African Americans marked the day by attending one of several churches in the county with a high proportion of African American members—including the Raccoon Swamp or Black Creek Baptist churches—or by listening to itinerant preachers. But this particular group of friends was celebrating their weekly respite with a roast pig and some apple brandy. Perhaps because their friend Nat Turner had spent the morning preaching or worshipping, as was his habit, or because he wished for some time alone before carrying out plans long contemplated, he did not join them until three o'clock in the afternoon.[1] Together, the friends enjoyed barbecue and conversation for several hours before heading back to their respective farms before sundown, which signaled the end of their liberty.

Sunday afternoon's apparently lighthearted festivities must have concealed some sober planning, for the entire group reconvened a few hours later, at two o'clock on Monday morning, for much more deadly activity. This time, they carried with them hatchets, axes, and a resolve to use force of arms to end white hegemony. Many Southampton County whites were away at a camp meeting in neighboring Gates County, and Turner and his friends may have determined over pork and brandy that their absence created a window of opportunity to strike a blow against slavery.[2] Whether by intent or by coincidence, the group of black revolutionaries began their campaign at a time when the county's white population was particularly vulnerable. They first entered the home of Turner's owner, Joseph Travis, and killed all seven whites whom they found inside. The rebels then collected a few new recruits and some supplies before marching to a nearby farmhouse and performing a similar slaughter. They suffered their first casualties on the afternoon of the twenty-second in a "battle" near the home of James W. Parker but pressed on toward the county seat of Jerusalem, where they planned to gather additional weapons and ammunition. By the morning of the twenty-third, notwithstanding the setback in "Parker's Field," Turner and his companions had killed almost sixty Southampton County whites and sent a wave of terror rolling across Virginia and the slaveholding states.[3]

Whites met Turner's violence with violence of their own and crushed the rebellion later that afternoon. Local whites, half-organized into militia units, brought the rebellion to an abrupt end by killing or capturing most of the insurgents and chasing Turner himself into hiding. Long after the insurgents had dispersed, armed whites continued to arrive on the scene, and some 3,000 "troops" eventually assembled to fight in a possible race war. U.S. Marines were among the first to respond and rushed to Southampton County from Norfolk, while militia units from as far away as Richmond also offered their services. Too late to participate in any set battles against Turner or his men, scores of the white soldiers engaged in bloody reprisals against the county's slaves and free blacks. They beat or murdered both those whom they suspected of having participated in the revolt and a good number of those who simply happened to be in the wrong place at the wrong time— or who demonstrated a too-independent spirit. In these vigilante actions, completely independent from the legal proceedings that would begin on 31 August, whites took the lives of more than 100 African Americans.[4]

Nat Turner shocked white evangelicals into looking at their black brethren in a new light. Whereas in the 1820s they had been willing to accord black men in particular a certain latitude in their pursuit of new converts, after the Southampton Insurrection white evangelicals looked upon independent black spiritual activity with horror. Whites had already begun to regard with suspicion black spiritual activity that remained outside the visible church. After Turner, white evangelicals broadened that mistrust to include all black Christians, even those within the embrace of evangelical congregations. For many months, white evangelicals struggled to reestablish a sense of spiritual fellowship with blacks. They never did rebuild the same level of trust, cooperation in ministry, or interracial fellowship that had existed in the 1820s. This did not mean that whites forgot about the presence of black believers; to the contrary, they became even more preoccupied with them. After Nat Turner's rebellion, white evangelicals threw themselves wholeheartedly into missionary work among the enslaved. They tried simultaneously to attract new black members and to undercut the authority of African American leaders already within an evangelical church. The challenges inherent in this balancing act explain why white southern evangelicals became so angry at comments by northern evangelicals that jeopardized white southerners' fragile rapport with black Virginians.

After the Southampton Insurrection, whites quickly realized that the constant application of military power was neither an adequate guarantee that there would not be future rebellions nor a course well calculated to calm frayed nerves. Indeed, the overwhelming response by white vigilantes and militiamen may have only intensified fears in the commonwealth and in neighboring states. Nightmares of further carnage haunted whites as they anticipated additional revolts, and enslaved persons dreaded further reprisals. A wagoner camped just outside Petersburg in early September discovered that white Virginians' anxieties were still at a feverish pitch when he innocently tapped out a rhythm on his drum as a gentle lullaby. Eliza Meyers explained that the sound alone was enough to trigger rumors of another slave revolt. "It happened to be in the dead of the night," she wrote to Rachel Lazarus. "The warlike sound was heard, & the alarm was in an instant spread through the town, that a body of negroes 500 strong were rapidly marching down the Halifax road. The bells rung out violently, & the streets were filled with women & children."[5]

Sometimes correspondents made it clear that the sight of military power itself was discomfiting, for it made the threat of race war seem more imminent. This was true for many close to Southampton, who witnessed the mobilization of so many troops. "Only think for a moment my dear Louisa," worried Helen Read of Norfolk, "that from two to three hundred men on guard at the Court house and prison and a hundred light Horsemen riding through the town all night. O my Louisa through all my long life and two wars I never witness[ed]·such seens before."[6] Mary McPhail, also in Norfolk, had the double fright of witnessing the soldiers and watching her own father's preparations to meet what he thought would be his end. She confided to Mary Carrington that "I did not expect to see the next day, and there were such crowds of soldiers and horsemen going about the town that I thought there must be more cause for alarm than I had heard of." Her father, who was "very seldom alarmed at such reports," spent the evening "loading pistols and sharpening swords." Mary put on a brave face, suggesting on 30 September, "the alarm has now entirely passed"; but she gave additional space in her letter to the new fortifications that she hoped would make the town "as safe as man can make it."[7] Rocked by the events of 22 August, Virginia whites perceived a desperate need to render their peculiar institution safe and to restore order to their lives.

Heightened military alert and increased slave patrols in the weeks and months following "the tragical events at Southampton" were only a small part of the white response. Turner had challenged the ways in which Virginia whites understood their spirituality as surely as he had threatened their physical security. White evangelicals wondered what it meant that the rebel had claimed to be a preacher and second-guessed their long tolerance of black religious assertion. They questioned, too, how Virginia slaves could have interpreted the Gospel in a manner that sanctioned such revolutionary activity, and how they might need to alter their religious practices to prevent their black brethren from making these connections. By the time of the Southampton Insurrection, evangelical churches were the most powerful cultural institutions in the state. Whites therefore worked through both their churches and their legislature to reorder the world that Turner had turned upside down.

Contemporary newspaper accounts suggest that most white and black Virginians immediately recognized the religious dimension of the Southampton Insurrection. After his capture on 30 October, "General Nat" gave the events an even more undeniably spiritual cast. Warned by an executive order from Governor John Floyd not to harm the fugitive without due process of law so that authorities could interrogate him about the extent of the insurrection, captor Benjamin Phipps and Southampton officials managed to keep the revolutionary safe from angry mobs long enough for Thomas Gray, a planter's son, attorney, and one of several men tasked with constructing a thorough investigation of the case, to record his "Confessions."[8] In the words that Gray transcribed, Turner depicted the uprising that he had led as an explicitly Christian act. He argued that his knowledge of Christianity had both prompted and enabled him to succeed so spectacularly. As events after Turner's 11 November execution would reveal, religious commitments just as surely conditioned how whites responded to the insurrection.

In the "Confessions," Turner claimed that God had prepared him for great things from childhood, when a "very religious grandmother" and doting parents concluded that he "surely would be a prophet." As he moved into adulthood, he self-consciously cultivated this spirit of prophecy, and "the Spirit that spoke to the prophets in former days" spoke to him and convinced him that he should lead an uprising against the South's ruling race. He observed that his apparent intimacy with God gave him additional authority in the thriving spiritual community of the slave quarters, and he used this power to attract coconspirators. "Knowing the influence I had obtained over the minds of my fellow servants, (not by the means of conjuring and such like tricks)," he explained, "I now began to prepare them for my purpose, by telling them something was about to happen that would terminate in fulfilling the great promise that had been made to me." The revolutionary was not simply exploiting religion to gather manpower for a political project; rather, Turner conceived of the entire insurrection as an act of faith, not unlike his 1828 baptism of a white man. "When the white people would not let us be baptised by the church," the prophet explained in reference to Etheldred Brantley, "we went down into the water together, in the sight of many who reviled us, and were baptised by the Spirit." The same Spirit, he insisted, commanded him to lead the 1831 revolt.[9]

Even if, as some have speculated, Thomas Gray authored some of Nat Turner's "Confessions" himself, the repeated references to Turner's devout faith do not lose any of their haunting power, and neither would they have lost any for nineteenth-century whites. While Gray may have violated his own promise to "commit his [Turner's] statements to writing, and publish them, with little or no variation, from his own words," he nonetheless crafted a vivid and plausible account of how adherence to Christianity could empower Virginia's slaves to rebel.[10] In the widely circulated words of the "Confessions," Virginia whites saw how Christian theology and Christian practice could enable the bondmen among them (469,757 persons, or 39 percent of the total population in 1830) to act with more boldness and autonomy than they had ever imagined.[11] It made little difference to white Virginians that Turner himself did not belong to an evangelical church. They saw that Turner had taken advantage of the freedoms that they allowed evangelical blacks and that the cross-pollination of the visible and invisible churches upon which they had relied for new converts was not always benign. Indeed, none of the steps that Turner claimed to have followed to become a revolutionary were foreign to mainstream evangelicalism. Turner's belief in the Bible led him to pursue a dangerous literacy; his perception of divine favor bred in him a lethal confidence; and unsupervised Sabbath assemblies enabled him to spread deadly information. In Turner's boast that he had baptized a white man, whites saw with fresh eyes how empowering it could be for blacks who adhered to the Christian faith to wield spiritual authority over whites. Evangelical whites reached the conclusion that they had allowed black believers to take Gospel freedom too far.

Whites were especially frightened because they could easily draw comparisons between the personalities of enslaved preachers in their own communities and the personality Gray described in the "Confessions." They worried that blacks whom they knew might also be appropriating evangelicalism to their own ends. Whites blamed black evangelicals for encouraging their peers to blur notions of spiritual equality into notions of civil equality—and for abusing the liberty allowed them as agents of evangelical ministries. Legislators, indulgent owners, and church leaders everywhere cursed the permission they had given Virginia slaves to participate in religious services and to exercise such a high degree of ecclesiastical autonomy. The huge weekly assemblies, the networks of slave preachers, and the mobility allowed to Sunday worshippers suddenly seemed malevolent prerequisites to Turner's deviltries. White evangelicals felt betrayed; they had sown the Gospel and reaped the whirlwind. Editors in nearby North Carolina were among those who gave voice to this perception of betrayal. The *Fayetteville Journal* called whites' leniency toward black evangelicals an "indulgence," and the *Miners and Farmers Journal* interpreted the rebellion as proof of the destabilizing influence of evangelicalism. "We believe it has generally been the case," the editors explained, "that in all attempts at insurrection in the southern states, the plans of organization for murder and rapine have been concocted and matured at professed religious meetings."[12] The two obvious antidotes to this toxic combination of slavery and evangelicalism were to remove either the burden of slavery or the boon of the Gospel from the enslaved population. In the first startling months after the rebellion, stunned white Virginians soberly considered each of these extreme alternatives.

By March 1832, though, Virginia whites had successfully avoided the extreme options of either emancipating their slaves or outlawing mission work among them. Lawmakers and pastors instead snatched formal spiritual authority from the hands of African American clergymen and prescribed for all Virginians a refined brand of proslavery Christianity. Much more important than the message that God had blessed the institution of slavery—historians have been too preoccupied with some white southerners' definition of slavery as a "positive good"—were the limits that white evangelicals at this time placed on black initiative and black interpretive authority.[13] Turner's claim to spiritual leadership made whites loath to entrust ecclesiastical power to any slave, however loyal, especially to enslaved men. They therefore resolved to increase their supervision of blacks within their churches and to bring the invisible institution out of hush arbors and move it indoors. After pastors recovered from their initial fright at the specter of a more general insurrection, they began increasingly systematic attempts at oral instruction of the slaves within their reach. Meanwhile, legislators (many of whom were evangelicals themselves) did their part by changing the law to forbid all unsupervised religious activity by slaves or free blacks and to encourage owners to assume more active spiritual oversight of their slaves.[14] Legislators had ironically just completed a significant revision of Virginia's slave code in April 1831, so the post-Turner adjustments to the law that they made in early 1832 reveal very precisely Nat Turner's influence on the law. Virginia slaveholders refused to choose between the equally untenable choices of abolishing slavery and restricting the spread of the Gospel, though Turner's insurrection forced them to consider both possibilities. The elevation of a proslavery Gospel characterized by outreach and supervision enabled slaveowners to meet both of their goals, though it did introduce new challenges into the relationships between white and black evangelicals and between northern and southern whites.

There was little new theological content to proslavery Christianity as espoused by Virginia evangelicals in late 1831 and 1832, only new practices with different ecclesiastical and political ramifications. White evangelicals still insisted that blacks possessed eternal souls and deserved access to the Gospel, and most in Virginia still refrained from describing slavery as a positive good. But white evangelicals no longer regarded the invisible church as a harmless auxiliary to the blacks formally enrolled in biracial evangelical churches. Instead, they saw it as insurrectionary and made co-opting unchurched black Christians a prominent goal. White evangelicals also continued to support the work of the ACS. But the meaning of their support changed; they did so despite massive black resistance to the colonization program and not as part of a paternalist program to help distinguished black evangelicals emigrate. After Nat Turner, white colonizationists had to work very hard to convince themselves and black Virginians that their work was anything other than a crusade to rid Virginia of potentially dangerous free blacks. Finally, whites in the post-Turner dispensation denied black men the sort of leadership and educational opportunities that they had found within the biracial church of the early national period.

Whites may not have forged a new theological understanding of slavery following the rebellion, but they did develop new habits that inured them to criticism of the institution. Most importantly, white Virginia evangelicals after Turner's rebellion directed so much of their ecclesiastical energy to the evangelization of slaves that they bound together in their own minds the perpetuation of slavery and slave missions.[15] They included under the broad heading of "missions" any intentional, church-sponsored effort to bring enslaved Virginians into their churches and to teach them a form of Christianity that did not legitimate resistance to slavery. Just as white evangelicals in an earlier generation had assumed that slavery was a necessary precondition for colonization, the post-Turner generation began to see slavery as a necessary precondition for effective mission work. The post-Turner arrangement was therefore functionally proslavery.

This connection between slave missions and the defense of slavery was only weakly developed at the outset, however. In its first incarnation, proslavery evangelicalism was a significant liability in nascent battles with northern abolitionists. It opened Virginia whites to new charges of inconsistency—for blocking slave ministers from the pulpit, for demanding colonization as an answer to slavery when so many blacks decried the plan, and for making it more difficult for slaves to attain literacy and to read the Bible, for example. White evangelicals saw little choice after Nat Turner, though, and they invited northern criticism rather than risk black rebellion.

It took white evangelicals some months to realize the relational cost of the new restrictions that they put on black religious expression, but whites soon learned that they would have to work harder to lure black Virginians into their churches after changing the terms of spiritual fellowship so significantly. Their predecessors had been keen not to offend their black brethren or one another and had therefore banished discussion of emancipation from the churches to the civic sphere. But there could be little finessing the defrocking of black ministers or the invasion of formerly private prayer meetings. Black churchgoers noticed that whites regarded them with fear and suspicion, which eliminated the cooperative feel of much evangelical worship. Whites managed to avoid the poles of gradual emancipation or the suppression of the black church, but in the process they ironically made more difficult the tasks they were then most eager to accomplish: reaching unchurched blacks and controlling black religious leadership.

Already by 1830 the task of supervising the vast numbers of African American evangelicals was a heavy one. As documented in Chapter 3, roughly one-quarter of black Virginians, or 115,000 persons, had accepted the message of salvation through Christ and worshipped at evangelical churches by the time of the insurrection. Tens of thousands more practiced an identifiable Christian faith outside the visible church. Enslaved men and women had grown accustomed to helping their fellow bondpersons mark life's most important passages—birth, marriage, and death, for example— with Christian ceremonies. White evangelicals interested in watching over every act of black evangelical devotion had a numerical advantage, but one narrow enough that it made the task of supervision demanding. Without interdenominational cooperation, the task would have been impossible, for blacks outnumbered whites in many Baptist and some Methodist churches. Building on partnerships formed in the benevolent work of the 1820s, white Presbyterians and Episcopalians were just as eager as Baptists and Methodists in the commonwealth to take on the invisible church and to rein in the insurrectionary potential of black evangelicalism. White Presbyterians and Episcopalians did not have many black members in their churches, but in their capacity as slaveowners they cooperated with Baptists and Methodists in supervising black believers.

Until Turner cataclysmically altered their perspective in 1831, Virginia whites had worried more about the potentially subversive actions of free blacks than about the revolutionary potential of slave Christianity. Independent black worship services had concerned white Virginians insomuch as they gave blacks a place to meet away from white eyes and to the extent that they had allowed free blacks to intermingle with slaves. The General Assembly's heavy hand against free blacks after Gabriel's rebellion, legislators' attempt in 1806 to banish free blacks from the state, and the Virginia Colonization Society's persistent efforts to send free blacks to Africa indicated the widely shared conviction that free blacks were the single most dangerous source of insurrectionary activity among the state's African American population. Even when the evidence pointed manifestly to the contrary, before 1831 whites elsewhere in the South also feared free blacks more than they did evangelical bondmen.

The case of Denmark Vesey's attempted revolt in Charleston in 1822, when whites could not ignore that enslaved and free black evangelicals had acted together as revolutionaries, only highlights the myopia of most white southerners. Although scholars disagree exactly what Vesey, a free black, had planned, all concur that he and intimates from the city's AME Church publicly discussed a desire for liberty.[16] In 1816, Charleston's Morris Brown and Henry Drayton had traveled north to Philadelphia, where they had received ordination as ministers in the AME Church, a denomination composed entirely of black men and women. The two ordained African Americans returned to their hometown in 1817 and promptly organized two AME congregations by siphoning black evangelicals—who composed over 90 percent of the city's Methodists—from racially mixed churches. Vesey led a "class," or devotional group, of these AME Methodists and shared with them a vision of racial liberation. Upon Vesey's arrest in 1822 for conspiracy to rebel, vengeful whites showed that they understood the liberating power of black Christianity and utterly destroyed the black church buildings, took many AME leaders into custody, and forbade the congregations to meet again. Morris Brown fled north in fear of his life.[17]

For all of the drama exhibited by white South Carolinians in their crackdown on the AME churchmen suspected of conspiring with Denmark Vesey, the response of whites was more localized than systemic. Only on a comparatively small scale did South Carolinians initiate the types of religious reforms that Nat Turner would compel Virginians and other white southerners to enact. White Methodists focused the brunt of their vengeance on the autonomous black churches of Charleston, though a few scattered slaveowners from that denomination did take the additional precaution of restricting the access of itinerant white ministers to their chattel. Divines from other evangelical denominations with large followings in the city, especially Baptist Richard Furman and Episcopalian Frederick Dalcho, worked to ease any fears of black evangelicalism by reassuring the white population of South Carolina that slavery actually reinforced the social order. By 1829, Methodist William Capers was experimenting with a nonthreatening form of missionary work among the slaves in which he stressed the need for "servants to obey their masters," relied on oral instruction, and carefully supervised the exercise of religious authority.[18] In this, Charleston-area evangelicals prefigured many of the developments that would happen in Virginia only a few years later. But because a slave informed on Vesey before he could begin his crusade, while Nat Turner's men successfully killed almost sixty whites, the evangelical response to Turner was much more comprehensive. White southern evangelicals launched a systematic attempt to make evangelical Protestantism compatible with slavery in 1831, whereas they only offered localized, piecemeal measures in 1822. In locales outside Charleston in the 1820s, whites had continued to see free blacks rather than religious blacks as the primary threat to their safety.

Before Nat Turner, Virginia legislators and churchmen made only indirect attempts to govern slaves' religious activities. Following the 1829 discovery of a copy of David Walker's *Appeal*, legislators moved to curtail black literacy but did not act against black evangelicalism, per se, notwithstanding Walker's overt calls for black Christian resistance to slavery. Walker could not have been more explicit, calling "the man who would not fight under our Lord and Master Jesus Christ, in the glorious and heavenly cause of freedom and of God," worthy of being "kept with all of his children or family, in slavery."[19] On 7 April 1831, the General Assembly passed a thorough "Act to amend the act concerning slaves, free negroes and mulattoes." In this act, politicians reiterated their intent, first expressed in 1806, to exclude all newly freed slaves from the state and made illegal "all meetings of free negroes or mulattoes, at any school-house, church, meeting-house or other place for teaching them reading or writing."[20] The legislators stopped short of making an explicit connection between religion and disorder; they only expressed the awareness that churches and other prominent community buildings could be the sites of dangerous slave meetings. White evangelical leaders themselves wavered at this time on the amount of control that they needed to exercise over black congregants. Even though they did not interfere with the daily administration of the all-black Williamsburg or Charles City churches, for example, members of the Baptist Portsmouth Association nonetheless required for the first time in 1828 that the black churches send a white representative to the yearly association meetings.[21]

Virginia whites concluded in late 1831 that they had misjudged the role played by black evangelicals in the threat to whites' safety. An enslaved preacher—and not a free black—led the bloodiest revolt in the nation's history. After the gruesome deaths of three-score white citizens, Governor John Floyd, newspaper editors, lawmakers, and churchmen unanimously blamed black distortions of Christianity for the uprising. Gripped by fear and mistrust for several months, white Virginians struggled to adjust to the sobering fact that converted slaves could unleash such savagery. Some, particularly nonslaveholders from the western portion of the commonwealth, suggested that only a general emancipation could save the state from racial Armageddon and pushed for a constitutional convention to consider such a measure. Others, including some white evangelicals still shocked by August's carnage, favored simply denying slaves the privilege of religious expression. Stark choices: emancipation or an end to evangelization. Within two years, however, white evangelicals had found a way to move forward without either destroying black religion or freeing their slaves. No single ideologue emerged to articulate the new policy of constant white supervision right away; politicians and churchgoers independently stumbled toward the formula of aggressive oversight and proselytization.

The first newsmen to react to the rebellion demanded a change in how whites treated black Christianity and in some ways set the agenda for the social changes that followed. They wrote copy and reprinted letters from observers close to the scene that clearly stated Turner's connections to evangelical Protestantism and suggested the need to reform slave religion. Some writers doubted the sincerity or the orthodoxy of Turner's beliefs, but none denied that he spoke in an evangelical idiom and had used freedoms available to him because of his professed faith to organize the insurrection. John Hampden Pleasants, the editor of the *Constitutional Whig* and a member of the Richmond militia unit dispatched to help crush the rebellion, reported in a letter dated Saturday, 27 August, "My own impression is, that they acted under the influence of their leader, Nat, a preacher and a prophet among them; that even he had no ulterior purpose, but was stimulated exclusively by fanatical revenge, and perhaps misled by some hallucination of his imagined spirit of prophecy."[22] The editors of the *Richmond Compiler* similarly warned their readers that "a fanatic preacher by the name of Nat Turner (Gen. Nat Turner) who had been taught to read and write, and permitted to go about preaching in the country, was at the bottom of this infernal brigandage." The *Richmond Enquirer* was more explicit still in its calls for religious reform: "The case of Nat Turner warns us. No black man ought to be permitted to turn a Preacher through the country."[23] On 3 September, Pleasants had returned to Richmond and expressed in print his settled conviction that Turner had manipulated evangelical Protestantism to his advantage. "It is more than probable," he wrote, "that this mischief was concerted and concocted under the cloak of religion."[24]

In private correspondence as well, white Virginians made it clear that they perceived a dangerous connection between religion and the Southampton Insurrection. Those in the Southampton area who knew or knew of Turner were especially quick to identify the potentially incendiary combination. E. P. Guion wrote to Thomas Ruffin, a North Carolina supreme court justice, on 28 August: "It is strange to me that men can be so blind and Infatuate as to be advocates of Negroes Preaching to negroes no dout that these veery Slaves would have Remained quiet but for this fanatic Black that has excited them in this diabolical deed."[25] On 21 September, another Southampton man added even more shocking details to the public perception of the event with a letter to the *Richmond Enquirer.* "Pretending to be divinely inspired, more than four years ago," he revealed, Turner "announced to the Blacks, that he should baptize himself on a particular day, and that whilst in the water, a dove would be seen to descend from Heaven and perch on his head."[26] The image of a rebellious slave mirroring the actions of Jesus Christ whipped Southampton whites into a frenzy.

Beck, a young slave girl from Southampton County, confirmed white evangelicals' worst fears in trials for some of the captured men. In the first two weeks of September, before Nat Turner surrendered his body to Benjamin Phipps and his confession to Thomas R. Gray, Beck testified at the Southampton and Sussex Courts of Oyer and Terminer in the trials of others accused of participation in the rebellion. She claimed that blacks in Southampton and Sussex counties had planned their uprising for a year and a half, and that black church members were among its ringleaders. Most incendiary was her testimony that at "the last May meeting" of Sussex County's Raccoon Swamp Church, she heard black members—all of whom were apparently enslaved—plotting together. Two of the men said "that they would join the negroes to murder the white people," and a third stated that "he would join too, for God damn the white people they had been reigning long enough." Even though white authorities years later doubted the veracity of Beck's testimony, she had made it difficult to ignore the possible connections between religion and revolution and—most importantly—had connected the Southampton Insurrection to black members of biracial evangelical congregations.[27]

Those outside Southampton took for granted the implication of black evangelicals in the rebellion against slavery. Less than a week after the insurrection had commenced, Cornelia Jefferson Randolph relayed to Mrs. Joseph Coolidge Jr. her understanding of events. "The papers say," she reported, "that after a camp meeting instead of returning home they went out to rob, & murdered, the last accounts say 30 persons." Randolph did not believe that the revolt had been premeditated but that something had happened while Tidewater slaves assembled together for Christian worship that pushed a few of them to desperate acts.[28] What happened once, many feared, could happen again. As Cornelia's kinswoman Martha Jefferson Randolph explained, whites did not have to believe in the authenticity of the rebel leader's claim to intimacy with God in order to believe that black preachers posed a threat to whites' safety. According to Randolph, Nat Turner had only "pretended habitual intercourse & conversation" with the Lord in order to bring "success to his enterprise." Though she hoped that "the tragical end of the whole business and of the prophet also [would] convince his race that God had no hand in it," she confessed that "those agents of the *black gentleman* the editors of the '*Liberator*' and 'Walker's Pamphlet & c.'" may have been important instigators of Turner's decision to rebel.[29] Just over the state line in North Carolina, Solon Borland communicated to his governor his impressions, based on extensive correspondence with those in Southampton. "Their leaders, who you know are preachers," he reported, "have convinced many of them that to die in the cause in which they are engaged affords them a passport to heaven—many have said so when about to be put to death."[30]

Whites showed their awareness of the potential danger from black "religious fanatics"—preachers of any or no denominational affiliation—by executing them or taking them into custody. Lott Cary, were he still in Virginia, would have found a much less appreciative audience for his spiritual talents in 1831 than he did a decade earlier; indeed, to some slaves it seemed that whites were systematically attacking all of the "brightest and best men" during the reprisals.[31] On 4 September, William Campbell of Norfolk communicated to his friend Col. Baldwin that whites in his hometown had been interrogating local black male religious leaders. "A Black Preacher of the name of Grimes was examined yesterday," he informed Baldwin. "The testimony against him bears more evidence of plan of revolt than any thing I have known—But in the present state of excitement a little [illegible] on one side goes a great way."[32] Also in September, Randolph Harrison Sr. informed John Hartwell Cocke of the internment of at least two preachers. "With regard to the insurrection below," he related, "we learn by a letter from Polly, that 5 of George Harrison's men, one a preacher, have been apprehended, and it was supposed would be all executed." He added, "One of Willm. Harrison's a preacher of the name of Jerry, has been also apprehended. They were to have set out on their journey up here on Monday last, but she says W. Harrison cannot come away till he is better satisfied that all is quiet."[33] Though they also expressed their wrath against whole congregations of black evangelicals, whites deduced from Nat Turner that black religious leaders were the most dangerous of all slaves.

Governor Floyd, then, was only voicing the consensus of white Virginians in his address to the General Assembly on 6 December 1831, wherein he decried the deadly admixture of slavery and religion that white residents of the commonwealth had allowed black Virginians to concoct in the previous years. "The most active among ourselves, in stirring up the spirit of revolt," he explained, "have been the negro preachers." In his estimation, preachers "have been the channels through which the inflammatory papers and pamphlets, brought here by the agents and emissaries from other States, have been circulated amongst our slaves." Though white support of black preachers may have been well intentioned, the chief executive conceded, whites would pay a high cost for their charitableness. "Through the indulgence of the magistracy and the laws," he warned, "large collections of slaves have been permitted to take place, at any time through the week for the ostensible purpose of indulging in religious worship, but in many instances the real purpose with the preacher was of a different character."[34] Convinced, then, that the leader of the Southampton Insurrection had both manipulated and been inspired by evangelical Protestantism, Floyd urged Virginians to take concrete measures to guarantee that such violence would never happen again.[35]

Privately, at least, Floyd prayed for emancipation as a potential way to end the threat of violence. He confided on 21 November 1831 to his diary, "Before I leave this Government, I will have contrived to have a law passed gradually abolishing slavery in this State, or at all events to begin the work by prohibiting slavery on the West side of the Blue Ridge Mountains."[36] Statesmen like Floyd from the western portion of the state, across the Blue

Nat Turner's Bible

Nat Turner's Bible. Nat Turner demonstrated a mastery of scripture in the "Confessions" and claimed to have baptized a white man, Etheldred Brantley. Southampton County's white evangelicals insisted that Turner did not belong to one of their congregations, but whites across the state nonetheless identified him as a "slave preacher" and associated him with black evangelicalism. When William S. Drewry traveled to Southampton County in the late 1890s to collect photographs and interviews for a history of the insurrection, local residents produced this Bible as proof of Turner's religious commitment. (Speech and photographs relating to Nat Turner's Insurrection, MSS 10673, Special Collections, University of Virginia Library)

Ridge Mountains in the Shenandoah Valley and in the trans-Allegheny region, feared insurrection more than emancipation and were especially willing to consider antislavery proposals. Their constituents owned far fewer slaves than did whites in the Tidewater and Piedmont; in 1830, 11 percent of the state's slaves and 46 percent of the state's whites lived west of the Blue Ridge.[37] Not only did white residents of the interior stand to suffer less financially by emancipation, but they were also increasingly aware that easterners were taking advantage of their property in persons to gain political advantage. As recently as the Virginia constitutional convention of 1829–

30, residents of the Tidewater and eastern Piedmont had insisted on using the high number of slaves in their region to increase their share of seats in the General Assembly.

Eastern slaveholders at the 1829–30 convention fought bitterly against the apportionment of seats on the basis of the white population. Westerners finally convinced the slavery-conscious easterners to use white population figures from the 1820 census to apportion members, but not before men like Abel P. Upshur had laid bare some planters' preferences for the protection of slavery over democracy. Upshur insulted the mountain representatives by insisting that slaveowners required artificially high representation in order to protect their interest in slavery. "*Our* property demands *that kind of protection* which flows," he explained, from "possession of power." So recently bruised by proslavery politicians such as Upshur and the even more disdainful John Randolph, western representatives who favored curbing slaveholder power at the 1829–30 convention saw in the wake of Turner's rebellion a fresh opportunity to strike against slavery.[38]

White evangelical Virginians with antislavery sentiments also took advantage of the moment of political uncertainty to press for emancipation through the political process. Though this sort of individual civil activism was seldom pursued, evangelical churches had always permitted it according to the denominational settlements of the 1790s. Meriwether Lewis believed by October "that the people of that county [Buckingham], to a considerable extent, are awakened to a sense of their danger from the black population around them." Moreover, he believed that they "would readily cooperate in bringing the subject before the Legislature, & recommending the adoption of some plan of emancipation."[39] From Buckingham and other quarters came calls for Virginia politicians to consider drastic measures to prevent another Southampton. John Hartwell Cocke, already a cautious enemy of slavery through colonization, was willing at this critical juncture to cooperate in bizarre schemes to bring antislavery measures to the assembly's attention. Cocke's friend Charles A. Stuart convinced the Fluvanna County reformer to solicit and/or plant petitions from women in order to appeal to statesmen's sense of masculine responsibility for female safety. Cocke received a memorial from at least one of his female correspondents, Virginia Cary of Norfolk, who worried that she had perhaps "been too plain in declaring the apprehensions under which many females of our state are now suffering *seriously*."[40] Stuart had no luck recruiting female writers, but he eventually took up his own pen and assumed the persona of a woman in urging the General Assembly to end slavery. In Stuart's highly stereotyped piece, he begged from a position of domestic helplessness for the leaders of the commonwealth to remove the specter of race war: "The bloody monster which threatens us is warmed and cherished on our own hearths," he opined. "O hear our prayer & remove it, ye protectors of our persons, ye guardians of our place!"[41] Actual women wrote as well, and a passionate plea came from 215 Augusta County women "for the adoption of some measure for the speedy extirpation of slavery from the Commonwealth."[42]

When they arrived in Richmond on 5 December 1831 for the regular legislative session, Virginia's political elite responded swiftly to the concerns of Floyd, Cocke, and the Augusta County women. Without first pausing to consider other matters, legislators inaugurated the most thorough, exhaustive debate on the future of slavery in the commonwealth's history. A special committee chaired by William Henry Broadnax—a devout Episcopalian from Dinwiddie County—collected hundreds of memorials and petitions from across the state, including petitions from women recruited by Cocke and Stuart. Evangelicals and nonevangelicals agreed that the permissive attitude that white evangelicals had maintained in the 1820s was no longer appropriate. Ideas were pouring in about how to make white Virginians safe again, ranging from ending slavery to strengthening the black codes. There was no little irony in Broadnax's role as chair of this important committee; just a few months earlier, he had commanded the militia forces in Southampton. Wielding procedural rather than military power by late 1831, Broadnax and his committee considered ideas that would have seemed extreme only a few months before, including a petition from Hanover County Quakers demanding immediate abolition.[43]

On 11 January 1832, a freshman delegate from Albemarle County, Thomas Jefferson Randolph, brought the discussion of abolition out of Broadnax's committee and before the entire house. Doing what his more famous grandfather and namesake had failed to do, Randolph submitted for consideration a concrete plan for gradual emancipation. Under his proposal, all slaves born on or after the symbolic date of 4 July 1840 would receive their freedom—but only after they served for eighteen to twenty-one years in order to remunerate their owners. So startled by Nat Turner's attack were Virginia politicians that a majority of delegates were willing to entertain the proposal—in stark contrast to the way that they had laughed down a similar scheme by Virginia Methodists in 1785 and abruptly tabled St. George Tucker's detailed plan in 1796, as outlined in his *Dissertation on Slavery*.[44] In political councils white Virginians were at last doing what they could not do in their churches: discussing the possibility of legislated emancipation.

Despite the enthusiastic support of delegates from the trans-Alleghenies, Randolph's proposal and others like it met decisive legislative defeat. Representative Samuel McDowell Moore, of Rockbridge County and a member of Broadnax's committee, predicted in a private letter of 5 January 1832 that the house as a whole would refuse to pass any meaningful legislation toward emancipation: "A proposition to emancipate all the slaves in the Commonwealth and send them away will be discussed in the House of Delegates, but cannot be carried." He further speculated that "after the proposition to remove them from the whole state" failed, "another will be made to prevent the importation of colored persons (free or slaves) into that part of the state west of the Blue-ridge. And to remove all of them from it. For this most if not all of the western members will vote, but I fear it cannot carry."[45] Moore's calculations proved correct, and Mary Jefferson Randolph's prayer that the people of Virginia would "continue to keep their eyes open after the excitement of the present moment is over & until they have taken measures to remove the evil" went unfulfilled.[46]

As part of their debate over the future of slavery in the commonwealth, legislators also discussed the colonization movement. Colonization had stalled in Virginia prior to Nat Turner's rebellion, partly because Richmond and Petersburg colonizationists had made the mistake of asking the General Assembly to tax slaveowners to fund their activities but mostly because African American Virginians became more reluctant to participate the more they heard from Liberia.[47] In the early 1820s, most white colonizationists had considered manumission and emigration the logical end of paternalism. The whites who reenergized colonization immediately after Turner's rebellion did not, though, act in a paternalist manner. They were simply eager to remove blacks, especially free blacks, from their communities and thus to lessen the chance of another insurrection. The Southampton and Norfolk branches of the Colonization Society of Virginia were the prime movers in this effort; they hastily gathered up approximately 350 Southampton County blacks, mostly free persons who survived the post-Turner reprisals, and sent them to Liberia in December 1831.[48] Even though the Southampton emigrations were more deportations than deeds of cooperative benevolence, some longtime supporters of colonization took heart at the colonists' departure and hoped it was a harbinger of renewed public support for their cause. M. F. Robertson of Norfolk was among the most optimistic. "Judging from the number of applications which the Colonization Society here has received, particularly from Southampton County, I should suppose that it would result in a great increase of immigration to Liberia," she speculated, prayerful that "a merciful Providence [would] overrule the whole of this affair for good."[49]

Virginia legislators understood better the tenor of post-Turner colonization activities than did Robertson, for one of their own was the head of the Virginia Colonization Society. The same William Broadnax who vetted the petitions before their discussion by the larger assembly chaired the 11 January 1832 meeting in which Virginia colonizationists clarified their mission in a post-Turner world. Virginia colonizationists had founded the Virginia Colonization Society in 1828 to supersede local auxiliaries of the ACS, which some Virginians worried was becoming an invasive branch of the federal government. The Virginia society had not been very active between its founding and the Turner rebellion. When it roared to life in 1831, it took care to distance itself from the cooperative vision evangelical colonizationists had espoused in the 1820s: "On motion it was resolved that the Society deems it expedient at this time to renew its pledges to the public strictly to adhere to that *original feature in its constitution which confines its operations to the removal of the free people of color only*, with their own consent."[50] When the General Assembly considered colonization after 1831, then, it was as a possible public safety measure and not as a way to realize the ends of paternalism. In the session of 1832–33, the legislature finally appropriated funds to help the society, $18,000 per year, but stipulated "that no payment shall be made by the said board under the provisions of this act, for the transportation of any other than persons of color who are now free, and born and residing in this commonwealth, or their descendants."[51] In other words, the General Assembly had endorsed only antiblack colonization, not colonization as antislavery reform. White evangelicals would subsequently fight a rearguard action to preserve the illusion that colonization was a benign, paternalist enterprise, but the momentum had clearly shifted.

While legislators contemplated emancipation after the rebellion, the most extreme option available to them, white clergymen experimented with the most extreme option available to them, denying black churchgoers the right to participate in any sort of worship. This move would have represented a dramatic reversal: white evangelicals would have forfeit generations of outreach to and fellowship with enslaved Virginians. In the immediate aftermath of the bloodshed, though, it seemed the most likely course. White members of the Raccoon Swamp and Black Creek Baptist churches, those located closest to the killings, did not feel comfortable allowing slaves or free blacks to worship with them for weeks after the incident. At the Raccoon Swamp Church, whites faced a "perplexed situation" in regard to their black members on 30 October and "thought it best to forbear the Administration of the Lords Supper."[52] They still had not resolved their fears and frustrations by 12 November and launched a full investigation of the African American members of their church, "to make inquiry relative to the general course pursued, in time of the Horrid Insurrection and the character they supported as professors of godliness."[53] The Black Creek Church, too, "agreed that the sacrament be Postponed in consequence of the unpleasant feeling the white Brethren have toward the black Brethren."[54] Other churches in Raccoon Swamp and Black Creek's Portsmouth Association also felt immediate hostility toward blacks in their midst, as did churches further abroad. At the Goshen and Middle District Association meetings, the delegates resolved to recommend "to the churches ... to discountenance all unlawful assemblies of colored persons, and that they deal with any coloured person, who persists in exercising any gift in public."[55]

So universal was the hostility toward African American evangelicals that whites wondered openly whether this alienation was desirable and/or permanent. The Portsmouth Association, home to many of the Baptist churches in the area of the insurrection, sent out the following report in its 1832 letter of correspondence:

> The high character for godliness claimed by many of the insurgents, and the extensive religious influence they actually possessed, (though we believe none of them were Baptists,) have destroyed, with many of our Brethren, all confidence in that class of persons. Some of our Churches have therefore made no report from that department, and others have reported separately, with remarks expressive of their suspicions and alienation. We regret to be obliged to add, that some Churches have complained to the Association, that since the insurrection, the great body of their coloured members have constantly exhibited a most rebellious and ungovernable disposition, and which, wherever it has existed, has resulted in the worst consequences. Whether in those Churches a union can ever be restored between our white and coloured members, or whether they must be separated entirely, and continue to exercise toward each other no feelings of fraternity or communion, are questions which can be decided only by the great Head of the Church.[56]

For almost a year after the violence in Southampton, white evangelicals in the neighborhood expressed little interest in the spiritual welfare of their slaves or of local freedmen.

Evangelical whites and blacks experienced strained relations in other locales and denominations after the Southampton Insurrection. Whites in Williamsburg, for example, shut down the Williamsburg Baptist Church, the state's most famous autonomous black congregation, after almost forty years of continuous operation.[57] As an obvious sign of black power and an ongoing testament to the courage of men such as Moses and Gowan Pamphlet, it could not stay open in the nervous climate of 1831. The Methodists, for their part, found congregations broken along racial lines throughout the Southside. Benjamin Deany, whose circuit took him near Southampton, reported, "My predecessors on this circuit the past year had a very fine revival in successful operation until the late Southampton disturbance. This put an entire stop to the religious excitement; and many of our houses of worship were almost deserted."[58] Methodists John Holstead and James Boatright similarly reported that the "far-famed Southampton tragedy" had "produced such a general commotion that it was difficult to meet and worship peaceably and profitably. And as it regards the colored part of our societies and congregations in this circuit, we have not been enabled to convene them together, and take the proper oversight of them, as it was possessed before that event took place."[59] This relational break between whites and blacks, which whites would aggravate by their new ecclesiastical policies, was a key development in the history of proslavery Christianity.

White evangelicals did not stop responding to the spiritual decisions of black evangelicals after the Southampton Insurrection, but they set more modest goals for their interracial relationships. Before Southampton, whites accepted blacks' partnership in ministry, so long as African American evangelicals did not demand that whites discuss slavery in church. In several important ways, whites before Southampton even tried to compensate for their failure to free their brethren by insisting on paternalism and supporting colonization. After Southampton, whites paid closer attention to black Virginians than ever and remained interested in making evangelicalism attractive to African Americans. But the new objective was not fellowship; it was security. While there doubtless remained some white men and women who sought real fellowship with their black brethren, most whites after 1831 wanted to pay only enough attention to the spiritual lives of black Virginians to convince them to join their churches. Their primary goal was to wrench the veil from the dangerous invisible church and to bring tens of thousands of unchurched blacks to Sunday services.[60]

Full of doubt about the intentions of their black brethren and faced with fractured congregations, white evangelicals were just as divided on how to respond to Turner as were white statesmen. Some initially believed that emancipation was the best way to resolve the conflict between slavery and faith, while others thought that stamping out slave Christianity would be just as effective a solution. A correspondent to the *Religious Herald* best reflected the mood of this more draconian segment of white evangelicals when he asked the editors in October 1831, "Would it be proper to cut off the coloured members from our churches?" The inquirer, who self-identified as a "Lover of Religion" without any sense of irony, added that "since the insurrection the minds of the people have been so exasperated with the blacks that many of them cannot reconcile it to their feelings to admit them any more to church membership, and say it would be best to cut them off."[61] Henry Berry, a Jefferson County slaveowner, echoed this harsh perspective in the General Assembly on 2 January 1832: "We have as far as possible closed every avenue by which light might enter the slaves' minds. If we could extinguish the capacity to see the light, our work would be completed; they would then be on a level with the beasts of the field and we should be safe! I am not certain that we should not do it, if we find out the process, and that on the plea of necessity."[62]

By early 1832, both churchmen and statesmen had regained their composure and pursued a compromise course. Almost sheepishly forgoing the radical possibilities of general emancipation or spiritual tyranny, legislators set to work on new laws to regulate slave behavior, while religious officials began the process of restructuring church life. In legal and spiritual forums alike, whites emphasized supervision as the key ingredient to a viable post-Turner biracial evangelicalism; at all times, whites had to be a part of the black religious experience. Though there was no formal coordination between lawmakers and evangelical clerics, the program that each suggested was remarkably similar: whites would fight independent expressions of African American spirituality wherever they found them and curtail attempts to teach literacy en masse. In addition, whites would expend increasing amounts of time and energy to gather black evangelicals into supervised congregations. Missions to the slaves would become the hallmark of white evangelicalism.

This program found immediate and widespread support. Whites who had considered ending slavery following the Southampton Insurrection found in the program of aggressive white intervention in black religious life a publicly sanctioned avenue through which they could minister to slaves and advocate on their behalf. Those most concerned with security, who had led the crackdown on slave religion in the months following the insurrection, found the intense supervision of proslavery evangelicalism an adequate guard against rebellion. After all, as one historian has observed, "so long as the slaves were listening to a trusted white preacher, they could not (at least for the moment) be listening to a subversive black one."[63] Only as a secondary consideration, and one discussed in the following chapter, did whites realize that every hour and every penny that they spent spreading a sanitized, supervised Gospel helped to defend themselves against mounting northern criticism of slavery.

The General Assembly completely rewrote its April 1831 "Bill concerning slaves, free negroes, and mulattoes" following the insurrection and enshrined in its place a legal version of proslavery Christianity. On 15 March 1832—following the *almost* revolutionary debate over the fate of slavery in the commonwealth—lawmakers passed "An act to amend an act entitled, 'an act reducing into one the several acts concerning slaves, free negroes and mulattoes, and for other purposes.'" In this revised legislation, they replaced a clause from the 1831 statute against slave meetings and training in literacy with specific prohibitions against exactly those types of religious activity that Turner had used to organize his revolt. Remembering the Sabbath beginning of Turner's rebellion and the rumors that he had spread word of his plans by preaching as far away as Richmond, Wilmington, and Norfolk, they stipulated "that no slave, free negro or mulatto, whether he shall have been ordained or licensed, or otherwise, shall hereafter undertake to preach, exhort or conduct, or hold any assembly or meeting, for religious or other purposes." As if to drive home the point, they assigned specific sanctions for those who attended such a meeting. The new version of the law warned that "any slave, free negro or mulatto, who shall hereafter attend any preaching, meeting or other assembly, held or pretended to be held for religious purposes, or other instruction, conducted by any slave, free negro or mulatto preacher" would be whipped by the magistrate.[64]

As important as its restrictions on slaves' religious practices, and what made the Virginia statute so ideologically compatible with evangelical interests, were the positive recommendations that legislators included in the bill for slaveowners. They prescribed for masters an active involvement in the religious lives of their slaves, the cornerstone of proslavery evangelicalism. Using the bully pulpit of the law, delegates and senators beseeched white Virginians that "nothing herein contained shall be so construed, as to prevent the masters or owners of slaves, or any white person to whom any free negro or mulatto is bound . . . from carrying or permitting any such slave, free negro or mulatto, to go with him . . . to any place of religious worship." Moreover, they made it clear that they did not seek "to deprive any masters or owners of slaves of the right to engage, or employ any free white person whom they may think proper, to give religious instruction to their slaves."[65] Thus, Virginia legislators explicitly encouraged white men to take personal responsibility for the religious education of their slaves. Virginia Baptists clearly heard the message; they noticed that "it will be at once perceived that the law fully extends to all denominations the privilege of giving religious instruction to our colored population," and that it was "an admission of the principle that religious instruction can, at least, do no injury with respect to the relations that exist between masters and slaves."[66] The framers of the bill intended to pull more and more blacks out of the invisible church and into a web of white-supervised evangelical fellowship, where slaves and free blacks could harmlessly express religious devotion. By expanding from one-quarter the proportion of black Virginians who participated in biracial evangelicalism, legislators intended to prevent future Southamptons.

Evangelical leaders rebuked those within their denominations who were reluctant to worship alongside black Virginians after Southampton and urged reengagement with black Christians. When letters, including that of the "Lover of Religion," flowed in questioning the right of African Americans to participate in church life, Eli Ball, editor in chief of the *Religious Herald*, struck back. On 14 October he urged readers to keep trying to bring more slaves under the influence of Christianity for both spiritual and practical reasons. "We know of no instance, in the New Testament, of any person being excluded from a church for such a reason as is suggested by our correspondent," he reasoned. Less idealistically, he added, "the exclusion of the coloured members from our churches at this time, would put it out of the power of the churches to watch over them and correct their errors. . . . If any situation in life be more likely to engender diabolical thoughts and plans for insurrection than another it is that of excluded members from our churches."[67] At the same time, Ball rose to the public defense of the state's most prominent minister involved in mission work among black Virginians, John Kerr of Richmond's First Baptist Church. "Folks apparently spread the rumor that Kerr accepted bribes from blacks to admit them to First Baptist, and that he had been thrown in jail on the eve of Nat Turner's insurrection for a meeting with blacks," he wrote. Ball then not only refuted the fictitious charges but also defended Kerr's decision to allow slaves to meet, even though "the meeting may have been contrary to the letter of the law."[68] Ball was interpreting the spirit of the law to mandate getting black men and women under white supervision.

In their pastoral letter of 1832, Methodists in the Virginia Conference confronted the reluctance of whites to converse with black evangelicals or African American potential converts. The traveling preachers noted that their conference's membership had been severely affected by the "unpleasant occurrences of the past year," which had resulted in a loss of 934 black members in contrast to a gain of 2,225 white members. They counseled their white followers that revolution had not undone their paternalist responsibilities to black Virginians. "In regard to your servants, we are aware of the delicacy of your situation," the denominational leaders conceded.

But we are equally certain that nothing can absolve you from the obligation to teach them the fear of God. And however circumscribed your means of doing this may be in other respects, it is still your right, with which no human authority should or can interfere, and it is made your solemn duty upon the authority of God himself, to extend to them all the benefits of family religion. And we may add, that it is also your privilege and duty to take them to the house of God with you, and we particularly advise, where this cannot be done on the Sabbath day, that they be taken to our circuit preaching in the week.[69]

While denominational leaders needed to remind some whites about their obligations to black Virginians, other white evangelicals found in the 1832 laws themselves sufficient inspiration to become involved in the religious lives of black Virginians. Reflecting on his long career with Richmond's First African Baptist Church in 1880, Robert Ryland wrote plainly about the connection that he perceived between the state's post-Turner laws and his own decision to begin missionary work among enslaved African Americans. "Since the passage of a law by the Virginia Legislature, forbidding all colored preachers to minister to their people in divine things," he recalled, he "felt that all the ministers of Christ, and especially those of [my] own denomination, were called on to put forth new efforts to evangelize the people of color."[70] Other Baptists also cited the passage of the laws as a powerful inducement to increase their attention to African American Virginians. Addison Hall offered a resolution explaining as much to the Dover Association in May 1834, which that body unanimously approved: "Whereas the General Assembly of Virginia did, in March 1832, pass an act, 'Entitled an act, to amend an act, Entitled an act, reducing to one the several acts concerning slaves, free negroes and mulattoes, and for other purposes,'" Hall proposed, "Therefore, *Resolved*, That it be recommended to the pastors and members of our churches, to take into consideration, the propriety of adopting, in conformity with the provisions of the law aforesaid, a more systematic course of oral religious instruction for the benefit of coloured persons."[71] Even the angry gentlemen in the Portsmouth Association eventually came to support a supervision-heavy approach to slave Christianity. At their May 1833 meeting, representatives from the Black Creek and Raccoon Swamp churches joined in passing a unanimous resolution that "this Association earnestly recommend to the Churches composing this body to make it the duty of their Pastors to assemble at stated seasons, and at their respective places of worship, the coloured portion of their members and congregations, for the purpose of preaching to them, and giving them other suitable religious instruction."[72]

Once the state and the churches had agreed to increase their supervision of black evangelicalism, whites across denominations faced the socially awkward task of simultaneously defrocking black ministers and bringing slaves more closely into the lives of their churches. Since most people of African descent in Virginia were Baptists, Baptist communities faced the most upheaval. Richmond's First Baptist Church was not the only congregation that had to change course very rapidly; the church had licensed five black preachers and seven exhorters in 1828 but reversed its policies and defrocked the ministers in 1832.[73] One Norfolk bondman, Cyrus Branch, was still furious about the white response to Turner more than three decades after the insurrection. To a postbellum interviewer, he described " 'Nat Turner's insurrection' as fresh in his mind, because the slaves after that were more strictly watched than ever, their usual privileges denied them, and their hardships greatly increased." But Branch also remembered why many stayed involved in a biracial church, and his rationale suggests either that whites tried to soften the blow by increasing their personal attention to black coreligionists or that black evangelicals had formed a strong enough cohort within evangelicalism that they were able to make the best of a flawed ecclesiastical situation. "The State Government soon after enacted a law prohibiting colored men entirely from preaching and exhorting, or even gathering for prayer meetings, except at the leaves of their respective owners," he explained. "These were hard laws to submit to, their situation as slaves being made bearable to some only by the soothing counsels and influence of their christian brethren."[74]

Even though Presbyterians had only one black licentiate, their treatment of him revealed the same pattern of tightened racial control and "soothing counsels." White Virginians had paid to educate John Chavis, a free black, at Liberty Hall and helped him to launch a ministry in Virginia and North Carolina. He was under the charge of North Carolina's Orange Presbytery at the time of the Southampton Insurrection and was dismayed when his sympathetic white superiors "recommend[ed] to their licentiate to acquiesce in the decision of the Legislature referred to, until God in his Providence shall open to him the path of duty, in regard to the exercise of his ministry." The same hand that took away then attempted to give, if not to Chavis personally, then to black men and women in general. The Orange Presbytery that had stripped Chavis of his right to preach immediately thereafter resolved "that every minister and licentiate of this Presbytery, be earnestly requested to preach at least one sermon on each Sabbath, to the black people, and that they call to their aid in giving religious instruction, in conducting their meetings, and in watching over the spiritual interests of the black congregation, such intelligent, prudent and active laymen, as they may need."[75] Soon enough, whites followed their paternal logic to its conclusion and aided Chavis personally. At their annual meetings, Presbyteries throughout North Carolina and southern Virginia took up collections for Chavis, transforming him through their giving from a symbol of white intolerance and spiritual blindness to a symbol of paternal kindness. In 1835, for example, at the Orange Presbytery, "the case of Mr. Chavis was brought before Presbytery, and subscriptions for his support taken up."[76]

John Chavis survived the public humiliation and frustration that came with his removal from the clergy, but his resilience belies how devastating the implementation of post-Turner rules was to black believers who valued both their spiritual autonomy and the privileges that accompanied it. Some were even so angry that they lashed out against Turner himself. One slave, Fields Cook, was especially bitter about the new restrictions that whites put in place; he was "a boy about the time of nat Turners insurrection who had better never been born than to have left such a curse upon his nation I say that he had better never been born."[77] Harriet Jacobs, forty miles away from Southampton in Edenton, North Carolina, captured some of the pathos in her community. "The slaves begged the privilege of again meeting at their little church in the woods, with their burying ground around it. It was built by the colored people, and they had no higher happiness than to meet there and sing hymns together, and pour out their hearts in spontaneous prayer. Their request was denied, and the church was demolished." The compensation whites offered clearly did not measure up, in Jacobs's analysis: "They were permitted to attend the white churches, a certain portion of the galleries being appropriated to their use. There, when every body else had partaken of the communion, and the benediction had been pronounced, the minister said, 'Come down, now, my colored friends.' They obeyed the summons, and partook of the bread and wine, in commemoration of the meek and lowly Jesus, who said, 'God is your Father, and all ye are brethren.' "[78]

Other narrators stressed how reluctant the black preachers whom they remembered were to surrender their privileges. Henry Box Brown of Richmond wrote how "one of that class in our city, refused to obey the imperial mandate, and was severely whipped; but his religion was too deeply rooted to be thus driven from him, and no promise could be extorted from his resolute soul, that he would not proclaim what he considered the glad tidings of the gospel."[79] Though the story is extraordinary and perhaps apocryphal, Cyrus Branch remembered that the slave preacher Pleasant Randall challenged white authority even more directly. Because he "deemed his commission to make the Gospel known to sinners" was "from the Lord, and not from man," Randall continued to preach openly. Arrested and tried under the post-Turner laws, he went before the governor and proclaimed that he meant "to preach as long as the Lord God gives me breath." The governor supposedly freed Randall, believing that to do otherwise would be "a scandal to Virginia."[80]

Many black Virginians simply decided to hold their meetings in secret, swelling the ranks of the invisible church, rather than risk direct confrontation with white authorities. Thomas Johnson, born after the law went into effect, learned early to conceal his religious devotion. "I often met with the slaves in some secret place for prayer," he said, "though we knew, if we were found out, we would be locked up for the night, and the next morning receive from five to thirty-nine lashes, for unlawfully assembling together." Johnson, like other slaves, also showed a minute knowledge of the regulations, remembering that "over five constituted an unlawful assembly. At night, no slave was allowed to be out without a pass from his master."[81] James L. Smith, who admired Turner as a "captain to free his race," took some precautions to hide his preaching from white eyes but was willing to confront whites when discovered. He described a meeting in "some of the quarters" that a slaveowner interrupted. Smith was among the "few, who were more self-composed" and stood their ground. The slaveowner "wanted to know what we were doing there, and asked me if I knew that it was against the law for niggers to hold meetings. I expected every moment that he would fly at me with his cane; he did not, but only threatened to report me to my master. He soon left us to ourselves, and this was the last time he disturbed us in our meetings. His object in interrupting us was to find out whether we were plotting some scheme to raise an insurrection among the people."[82]

Black men who lost access to formal leadership positions within the church resented the new laws the most. Evangelical whites had welcomed the manly assertiveness of black evangelicals in the early part of the century, but in sermons and devotional literature produced after Nat Turner, white divines praised feminine piety as the most exalted quality. The very men and women who had praised the masculine valor of Richmond free black Gilbert Hunt for rescuing white women and children from a burning theater in 1811 and who had helped send Lott Cary and Collin Teague to Africa as missionaries in 1821 now balked at any situations in which enslaved men could demonstrate evangelical assertiveness. Instead they praised the example of older women, whom they deemed less inclined to lead a revolt. "Mammy," as depicted in a collection of biographical sketches assembled in the 1840s, became the model evangelical slave. "Mammy Chris" and others like her, who "preferred to be in Virginia, with the name of slave, to the freedom of the north," were the role models whom white evangelicals presented to their black counterparts.[83] On the leading paternalist John Hartwell Cocke's own plantation, Bremo, black men registered their resentment at the conflict that whites created between masculine honor and evangelical piety. In the mid-1830s, many men in the Cocke labor force refused to join evangelical churches because they believed that to do so would undermine their manhood, a testimony to the effectiveness with which white evangelicals feminized slave conceptions of the Christian life. Most of the female slaves on the plantation were evangelicals, but no age cohort of male slaves possessed a majority of believers.[84] Some whites had a hard time enforcing the laws, since doing so risked creating the sort of resentment that poisoned the waters against conversion at Bremo. Selective leniency, as explained in Chapter 5, therefore became a strategy for recruiting and retaining black members.

Episcopalians did not have a large black membership to alienate in 1831, nor any black ministers to shame by defrocking. They nonetheless became extremely active participants in the campaign to convert unchurched black Virginians and to make slave Christianity safe. In some ways, the Episcopalians may have been more energetic than other white Virginia evangelicals precisely because they did not first have to heal relations with black members within their communion. Whatever the reason, priests and laymen joined in the wholesale effort to bring the invisible church under white supervision by offering African Americans religious instruction, and they accepted it cheerfully when their black pupils ultimately chose to affiliate with other denominations. Moreover, their episcopal form of government gave Virginia Episcopalians the most bully pulpit in the commonwealth from which to advocate slave missions.

William Meade, assistant bishop of the diocese of Virginia from 1829, signaled the beginning of Episcopalians' crusade for the spiritual welfare of Virginia's enslaved blacks at the convention of 1833 in Richmond. After cataloging his own private efforts to instruct "servants" each Sunday afternoon, Meade prayed that God would bless the new mission to the slaves upon which white evangelical Virginians from all denominations appeared ready to embark: "May he who made of one blood all nations upon earth, grant his blessing to every effort in behalf of the poor and ignorant that they may become rich in faith and wise unto salvation, for Jesus Christ's sake." Ministers from St. Thomas (Orange Courthouse), Lexington, and Nelson parishes also boasted of their private ministrations to the "coloured people" in their midst, echoing their leader. The convention gave much rhetorical support to slave missions in that year but committed no resources to the task other than continuing to set aside offerings from the Sunday before Independence Day for the colonization society.[85]

The following year, however, Virginia Episcopalians devoted substantial time, treasure, and energy to the campaign to incorporate blacks into the visible church. By the May 1834 convention in Staunton, the Episcopal Church had decided to swing its growing cultural authority behind proslavery evangelicalism as formulated after Turner's insurrection. In his opening address, Meade exhorted his hearers to initiate more intentional outreach to the commonwealth's enslaved residents. "I know the difficulties of the task," he challenged them, "but I know that both ministers and people are far too ready to magnify these difficulties, and satisfy themselves with very insufficient excuses for its neglect." He then reminded listeners of the reason why Virginia's white evangelicals could not simply deny blacks the potentially revolutionary power of the Gospel: "If the love of immortal souls, which is the true spirit of Christ, did but reign in our hearts as it ought to do, we should be more apt to teach these, our poor ignorant fellow creatures, and less apt at finding out excuses for our neglect of them. I commit the feeble effort in their behalf to God and your consciences, hoping that it may not be altogether in vain."[86]

The divine should not have worried. His churchmen were already working harder than ever to bring more slaves into their congregations; almost two-thirds of the parishes represented at the 1834 convention reported new initiatives to the slaves during the preceding year. Antrim Parish of Halifax County, for example, was eager to call attention to a second service that the rector had initiated, "held on Sunday, chiefly for the benefit of the coloured population. A growing interest in the religious improvement of this part of the community is manifest." In support of this last claim, the rector added that "one gentleman designs building a chapel exclusively for the benefit of his servants." From Fredericksburg, Edward M'Guire noted that, in his church, too, "something has been done of late for the spiritual improvement of our coloured population. The time seems to have arrived with us for successful efforts in their behalf. Recent endeavors to instruct them by preaching, have been attended by the most encouraging indications of usefulness." Similar accounts sprang from other Episcopal parishes. C. C. Taliaferro of Cumberland Parish in Lunenburg County shared that "for the last 6 months I have paid renewed attention to the colored people of my neighborhood, preaching on the afternoon of every other Wednesday and Sunday, with the most pleasing prospect of success. The masters of the servants feel the duty of providing for their spiritual welfare so great, that they contemplate building a Church expressly for them."

In solemn assembly, Virginia's Episcopal leaders energetically affirmed these local missionary initiatives among the state's slaves. Participants in the Staunton convention erased any doubt of the Episcopal Church's soundness on the new orthodoxy of proslavery evangelicalism, with the co-option of the invisible black church at the center of their agenda. President Adam Empie of William and Mary College, also the rector of Bruton Church and spokesman for the influential Committee on the State of the Church, denounced abolitionism—"the merest machinery and excesses of fanaticism"—and exhorted his codenominationalists to respond to the "affliction" of slavery by paying more attention to the salvation of their bondmen. In no uncertain terms, he reminded whites of their profound responsibility as the master class: "For their moral and spiritual wants, we are as imperatively bound to provide, as for their temporal." Willing and eager to act on this imperative but uncertain how to instruct slaves and free blacks without increasing the risk of rebellion, the delegates requested help from the indomitable Meade. Sensing that the venerable shepherd understood the delicate balance of Christian empowerment and Christlike submission called for by a proslavery faith, they requested "that the Assistant Bishop of this Diocese, with the aid of any of the Clergy or Laity whom he may call to his assistance, be and are hereby requested to prepare, from time to time, such tracts or sermons as they may deem suitable for the religious instruction of servants." Finally, in order to create accountability for its now very public commitment to the mission to the slaves, the convention of the Protestant Episcopal Church in Virginia closed its meeting by resolving to distinguish between black and white communicants in all future documentation. Like the Baptists and Methodists, white Virginia Episcopalians wanted measurable results.[87]

Meade fulfilled his charge and made certain that his codenominationalists did not forget their pledge by immediately penning and publishing a pastoral letter "on the Duty of Affording Religious Instruction to Those in Bondage." In what would become an important theme of the mission to the slaves in all evangelical denominations, he instructed his flock that it did not matter with what church black converts affiliated, so long as they converted. "It will not be a sufficient excuse for any of us to say that they belong not to our communion," he chided, "and that all their partialities are to some other." In another important development, Meade, who had been such an important early advocate for colonization, also retreated from his enthusiasm for the project. While many white evangelicals clung stubbornly to the belief that colonization was a scheme ordained by God, notwithstanding the devastating reports of many emigrants, Meade was attentive enough to black sentiment regarding colonization to know that whites overestimated its promise. Moreover, he may have reacted against the decidedly unpaternalist turn that colonization had taken in Southampton after Nat Turner. Instead, he tried to direct attention domestically, gently remonstrating, "We cordially sympathise with those who are endeavoring to convert one of the heaviest calamities into a means of great good, by cherishing the American Colonization Society; but we fear there are those, who, in their zeal for this philanthropic and magnificent scheme, forget that there are other and most important duties required by Almighty God." By these other duties, Meade meant domestic missions to the enslaved.[88]

While fewer white evangelicals actually emancipated their slaves for colonization after 1831, some clung to their paternalist vision of the plan after Meade had begun to grow skeptical of it. In practice, though, colonization became little more than an idea. African Americans gave white Virginians the opportunity to believe anything that they wanted about the plan by overwhelmingly refusing to leave their native state—and therefore reducing the contemplation of removal's benefits to abstract theorizing. Outmigration from Virginia to Liberia slowed substantially after the brief flood of Southampton and Norfolk émigrés left in 1832.[89] Colonization became an article of faith held tightly by white evangelicals who may otherwise have adopted a more forthright antislavery position.

White evangelicals who continued to believe in colonization attributed to it an increasingly mystical quality. Just as they anticipated Christ's triumphant return, they prayed that—in his own mysterious timing—God would signal an end to the servitude of Africans and would restore them to their native continent as a free and Christian people. But God was not to be rushed. As Meade explained, "What [this world's] millennial state may be, or how soon it may arrive, I undertake not to say, for I am not skilled to interpret prophecy which is not fulfilled. But I expect not in our day to see all men free and equal, or every barren wilderness turned into a blooming Eden."[90] The proslavery function of this version of colonization as millennialism was that it relieved men of the obligation to do anything about slavery, for God was using the practice for his own purposes and would not require whites to free any slave until all had accepted his Gospel.

Men like Cocke, who still hoped in 1832 that colonization might provide the "double blessing of the removal of slavery from our Land & christianizing & civilizing benighted Africa by the self-same operation," were increasingly rare.[91] Eric Burin, in a careful tally of manumissions for colonization, found that most of the late (post-Turner) manumitters were aged members of the Revolutionary generation.[92] Cocke fit this description and in 1833 granted freedom to Peyton Skipwith, his wife, and six children. Skipwith had come to share Cocke's evangelical faith and enthusiasm for Christian benevolence enterprises, particularly temperance reform. Perhaps receiving his training before the passage of the March 1832 legislation designed to prevent slaves from learning to read, Skipwith was also literate. Convinced that this literate, skilled, and—most importantly—devoutly evangelical slave and his family were ready for independence, Cocke helped them sail for Liberia. Cocke's willingness to send his slaves and his slaves' willingness to go were both rare by the 1830s. Most owners seemed to require a clarion call from the Lord himself before determining that their laborers were "Christian enough" for colonization, and most blacks, both slave and free, preferred Virginia to an unknown land. The many fond letters between Skipwith and Cocke after Skipwith's emigration placed the two in a fading tradition of interracial cooperation. Like Lott Cary's letter to Benjamin Brand, they also gave Cocke assurance that he was doing the right thing by his slaves.[93]

The role of colonization changed, but there were other important continuities between pre- and post-Turner evangelicalism. First, white evangelicals affirmed that they owed spiritual responsibilities to their enslaved brethren. White evangelicals tried to salvage their tradition of paternalism, scarred though it may have been by the threats of some whites to bar blacks from fellowship in the weeks and months following the attacks. Second, white evangelicals tried to maintain the ban on the discussion of slavery within their denominations. The *Religious Herald* wrestled with this early in January 1832, amid the revitalization of the colonization society and the General Assembly's debates over slavery. "Though we feel in common with every other citizen of our country, an anxiety that some measure should be adopted for relieving our land from one of its heaviest burdens [slavery]," they wrote, "we have always considered it, and we do still consider it, our duty to leave the subject where it ought to be left, in the hands of politicians." Methodists agreed in the *Christian Sentinel*, calling Virginians back to the terms of the post-Revolutionary settlement: "It then appears to be the duty of all christians to regulate their own private conduct in accordance with these heaven-inspired precepts," they taught, "and not to engage in the political controversies which may arise out of the subject of slavery as existing in our country."[94]

There were some indications, though, that the post-Turner mission to the slaves might be eroding this ban on "political" conversation about slavery.

In the same essay in which Baptist leaders insisted that statesmen, not clerics, had the authority to discuss slavery, they staked out one issue related to the peculiar institution that they believed evangelicals had a right to address. "But there is one subject upon which we think it our duty to speak out," they warned; "it is the importance of communicating religious instruction to the people of colour. On this subject we should think there would be but one opinion."[95] In the years to come, this conviction would give white evangelicals grounds to critique abolitionists, who they believed made it more difficult for them to win black converts.

Another thing that changed by 1835 was the relative weight that white evangelicals gave to missions to the slaves in their self-identification. The flurry of public debate about slavery within and, ultimately, outside of Virginia made whites very conscious about their stance toward black Virginians. The mission became the most important ecclesiastical priority. Virginia Baptists framed the evangelization of African Americans as a direct command from God. "We have also heard a voice from heaven saying to us, 'Go ye into all the world and preach the gospel to every creature,'" a contributor to the *Religious Herald* wrote. "We have heard and we must, and we will obey."[96] The same urgency was present at the first annual meeting of the East Hanover Presbytery's brand new Domestic Missionary Society in April 1834. Amasa Converse, also the editor of the *Southern Religious Telegraph*, "asked the attention of the meeting to a statement in the report— '*That more had been done last year, than in any year previous, by our missionaries for the religious instruction of our colored population.*'" But Converse did not have self-congratulations in mind. Indeed, "he regarded this subject as most intimately connected with the progress of religion. Our church had been sleeping over these heathen which surround her on every side, without scarcely an effort for their salvation. With the guilt of this neglect and inexcusable indifference resting on her, it was not surprising her progress had been slow." Converse then went on to connect the evangelization of Virginia slaves with the temporal and eternal fortunes of the Presbyterian Church. "Should her ministers and members awake from this criminal sleep," he prophesied,

> and look on the colored people as immortal beings, on their souls as precious above all price, as sinners for whom Christ died—we might *expect* the blessing of God. It was a distinguishing characteristic of the gospel, when preached by its blessed Author, that *it was preached to* THE POOR. And who are so poor as the colored race whose souls we have neglected? Let the church, in view of their worth, and in the spirit of our

Lord, imitate his example—and new life and power from Heaven will descend upon her, will accompany her ministry, and spread the triumphs of the gospel through the spiritual desolations of our southern country.[97]

Converse's jeremiad was an extraordinary illustration of how tightly white evangelicals tied their own spiritual fortunes to the success of the mission. They cultivated a vision for their region in which Christ was king—but in which there was little place for colonization and none at all for emancipation. Thus, the mission to the slaves, by its very nature, was proslavery.

By May 1834—months before the famous abolitionist mailings of 1835—the leadership of each major denomination in Virginia had committed to a mission to the slaves. White Virginians were responding first to the internal threat of slave rebellion and only second to the external threat of abolitionist invective. Most white Virginians had probably heard that an unbalanced northern reformer had begun publication of the *Liberator* in January 1831. And many honor-sensitive southerners and thoughtful proslavery exegetes of scripture did engage their northern brethren on the righteousness of their "domestic institutions." But Virginia's white evangelicals offered in those debates ideas that they forged at home, particularly the idea that slavery facilitated Christian benevolence.

White evangelicals across the South applauded Virginians' response to Nat Turner: increased mission work among the slaves, with new safeguards for white safety. Several state legislatures peremptorily passed laws in imitation of Virginia's 1832 statute. North Carolina, Georgia, Alabama, and South Carolina, for example, issued complete bans on slave literacy and freedom of assembly within the year.[98] Scores of white ministers, including Virginia's Robert Ryland, published very simple catechisms to aid laymen in their oral outreach to slaves. White churchgoers of all denominations across the South raised thousands of dollars to fund Sabbath schools and missionaries for the new project. In 1834, Presbyterians in Alabama and Mississippi proclaimed, "During the past year the condition and wants of the colored population, have occupied more of our attention than at any previous period, and in future we hope to be more untiring in all our efforts."[99] Charles Colcock Jones spoke for the Presbyterian synods of South Carolina and Georgia in December 1833 when he stated "that we deem religious instruction to master and servant every way conducive to our interests for this world and for that which is to come" and "that we cannot longer continue to neglect this duty without incurring the charge of inconsistency in our Christian character."[100]

In short, Nat Turner, his companions, and less dramatically the tens of thousands of enslaved men and women who led, hosted, or participated in worship meetings inside the visible or invisible church presented white evangelicals with a dilemma in August 1831. They forced whites to choose between slavery and faith. Initially divided—some for emancipation, others for a moratorium on slave Christianity—evangelicals and other white Virginians ultimately came together on a variation of evangelicalism that supported more fully the institution of slavery. They encouraged rather than limited expressions of black spirituality but supervised far more closely communal acts of African American worship. Out of fear that a Nat Turner would appear in their own jurisdictions, legislators across the South sharply curtailed slave worship privileges. Once committed to oral instruction and supervision of enslaved evangelicals, whites in Virginia discovered in other states pioneers in the endeavor, especially South Carolina Methodist William Capers and Georgia Presbyterian Charles Colcock Jones. The mission to the slaves became a shared regional crusade, as more and more white evangelicals contributed to the cause of converting bondmen and -women to a safe brand of biracial evangelicalism.

Chapter Five

THE SECTIONAL CHURCH, 1835–1856

Then he said to them, "Suppose one of you has a friend, and he goes to him at midnight and says, 'Friend, lend me three loaves of bread,' . . . I tell you, though he will not get up and give him the bread because he is his friend, yet because of the man's boldness he will get up and give him as much as he needs."—Luke 11:5, 8

Nat Turner not only forced Virginia's white evangelicals to rethink their relationship with their black brethren, but he also set in motion a chain of events that caused them to rethink their relationship with their codenominationalists in the North. In response to the insurrection, evangelical whites in the South devoted an increasing amount of time and money to missionary efforts among the region's slaves, an activity about which northern evangelicals were increasingly skeptical. Many northerners doubted whether white southerners could convey an authentic faith under the legal constraints put in place after the Southampton Insurrection. They were suspicious about any program of religious indoctrination that reinforced rather than challenged the practice of slaveholding. In the 1830s and 1840s, Virginia's white evangelicals thus found that they had much in common with their white coreligionists across the South and little in common with northern churchmen. Southern white evangelicals were united after Turner on the need to maintain the safety of white persons while "saving" the souls of resident blacks. In the pursuit of these goals, they exchanged hundreds of letters, catechisms, and instruction manuals across state lines in which they discussed the best methods to attract slaves to church.

Black, evangelical Virginians lost some of their influence within biracial congregations, but they continued to shape the development of proslavery Christianity. Whites wanted more than anything to increase the number of African Americans enrolled in evangelical churches so that they could better police African American worship. This task was impossible without cooperation from black evangelicals, who had been so effective at bringing their peers into evangelical churches from the Revolution through Nat Turner's rebellion. African American Virginians sought major concessions from whites before they consented to stay in or join post-Turner churches. They both fought for exemption from some of the most obnoxious post-Turner restrictions and pushed hard for the right of segregated worship. Whites granted black Virginians the ecclesiastical space they needed to carry on their work of evangelization once they became convinced that doing so was the best—perhaps the only—way to continue to increase black church membership. They enforced the 1832 laws governing slave worship selectively and funded separate services for black evangelicals. Some black Virginians still spurned on principle any worship service that enjoyed white sanction, but many more African Americans flocked to the new, quasi-independent congregations. Through it all, black Virginians kept white evangelicals focused on the one issue, recruiting new black members, that distinguished their ecclesiastical agenda from that of northerners.

These two, interconnected processes—the growing alienation of southern, white evangelicals from northern, white evangelicals, and ongoing negotiations among Virginia's white and black evangelicals regarding ecclesiastical privileges—came to a head in the mid-1840s. At that time, the two largest denominations in the nation, the Baptists and the Methodists, split over the issue of slavery. As if to drive home the connection between the mission to the slaves and ecclesiastical conflict over slavery, the single most important interregional conference on the evangelization of black southerners met immediately following the schisms. Presbyterian Charles Colcock Jones, who had become the foremost advocate of slave missions, presided over the meeting in Charleston in 1845 for the purpose of sharing "best practices" across state and denominational lines.

White Virginians found the mission to the slaves ideologically useful in the escalating conflict with northern antislavery evangelicals. In their minds, the mission's success in making new Christians proved that God intended to use slavery for good. White southerners' continuous search for evangelistic strategies that attracted black southerners further strengthened whites' conviction that slavery was just. Whites came to believe that they alone knew how to meet the unique spiritual needs of African Americans. White southern evangelicalism had become thoroughly proslavery, though some ministers still professed an abstract dislike of the peculiar institution. Evangelical blacks inadvertently abetted the development of proslavery evangelicalism. When they joined an evangelical church—even a separate black congregation—they validated white evangelicals' conviction that chattel slavery and Christianity could go hand in hand. Seen this way, the concessions that blacks won for more ecclesiastical autonomy were only a short-term victory, for their enlistment in the evangelical ranks was increasingly valuable to apologists for slavery.

Virginia's white evangelicals thought a great deal about the mission because they were always having to defend it. Northern evangelicals, fugitives from slavery, and a few expatriate white Virginians assaulted slavery on explicitly religious grounds in the 1830s and 1840s. This outside criticism created additional pressure for evangelical whites in the Old Dominion to prove the integrity of their faith by caring for the spiritual needs of their slaves.[1] Virginia whites did not feel opportunistic in using the mission to answer northern criticism of slavery for two important reasons. First, in their minds, the mission predated intense sectional religious conflict over slavery. Second, the commonwealth's white evangelicals had to fight secular proslavery advocates within their own state for the right to proselytize Virginia slaves. Defending the mission from slavery's most rabid supporters at home gave Virginia's white evangelicals a feeling of integrity when defending their treatment of slaves from critics abroad.

The volume of criticism from the North increased as the abolitionist movement grew. Tutored by free blacks such as David Walker on the inadequacy of colonization as a benevolent response to slavery, whites who had formerly cooperated with southern colonizationists were instead calling for immediate emancipation. African American foes of emigration convinced William Lloyd Garrison in 1830, James G. Birney in 1834, and Gerrit Smith in 1835 to reject colonization as a bigoted and impractical answer to the problem of slavery.[2] ACS secretary Ralph R. Gurley tried in vain to rehabilitate his institution's image among antislavery northerners by finding proof that colonization was accelerating gradual emancipation. White Virginians disappointed Gurley, and even colonization stalwart John Hartwell Cocke could not vouch for the ACS's capacity to produce manumissions. "The difficulties with those who are sincerely anxious to promote the ends of your society are greater than one who is not the inhabitant of a slave state can well conceive," reported Cocke sadly.[3] Northern abolitionists, unlike prior generations of northern antislavery activists, could not find common ground with colonizationist or gradualist white southerners. Of great concern to white, southern evangelicals, some abolitionists even introduced resolutions against slaveholders into the national councils of their respective denominations.

Some white Virginians did not become aware of how much more confrontational black and white abolitionists had become until 1835. In August of that year Virginians got a thorough education on the new militancy when

they received the American Anti-Slavery Society's massive mailing of abolitionist pamphlets. Garrison, Arthur Tappan, and other immediatists had
founded the society as an umbrella group for northern abolitionists in 1833,
and the hundreds of thousands of tracts they put in the mail represented
their attempt to take their message to a southern audience. White authorities in the southern states staged an aggressive interdiction effort and guaranteed that few of these pamphlets reached their destinations. In Charleston, Richmond, and towns and cities across the South, local officials led
posses, often armed, in burning piles of the subversive documents.[4] White
Virginians responded as vigorously as did members of the South's ruling
race anywhere, and the capital city's evangelical ministers played a key role
in the counterattack.

On 28 August 1835, leaders from the Baptist, Methodist, Presbyterian,
and Episcopal traditions met in the offices of the Virginia Episcopalians'
newspaper, the *Southern Churchman*, and took the extraordinary step of
forming a Committee of Correspondence, just like those their forebearers
had formed for the defense of republican liberties before the American Revolution. They met for two days and crafted a public proclamation in which
they roundly condemned northern evangelicals for their presumptuous act
and for their mistaken criticism of slavery. They also assured their Virginia
audience that white, southern evangelicals were already fulfilling their
Christian responsibilities toward slaves. Most importantly, the committee
"resolved, *unanimously*, That we earnestly deprecate the unwarrantable
and highly improper interference of the people of any other State, with the
domestic relations of master and slave." Taking care to honor, at least formally, their now well-established agnosticism "on the abstract question of
slavery," the clerics did not call chattel slavery a positive good. Instead, they
counseled white evangelicals to accept slavery as a legal institution and to
devote their energy to evangelizing slaves. They cited the "example of our
Lord Jesus Christ and his Apostles, in not interfering with the question of
slavery, but uniformly recognizing the relations of master and servant," and
they urged readers to give "full and affectionate instruction to both" slave
and free.[5] The Presbytery of Winchester, in its own statement on the mailing, put whites' concerns that abolitionists were poisoning the incipient
mission to the slaves even more clearly. "In view of the effects of abolition
efforts upon the moral condition of the slave, in depriving him of religious
opportunities which he before enjoyed with little, if any, molestation," they
explained, "we are constrained to pronounce the abolitionist the worst enemy of the Black man, whatever his intentions may be."[6]

White evangelical leaders not only criticized the abolitionists but also tried to differentiate themselves sharply from them. Virginia clerics, they realized, were so vocal about the need to minister to people of African descent that unsophisticated or unchurched auditors might easily mischaracterize them as abolitionists. The evangelicals' fears were not unwarranted; another community watch organization set up after the mailings, Richmond's Committee of Vigilance, had already accused certain ministers of abetting the abolitionist cause. Baptist William Broaddus was deeply concerned that he and other white evangelicals would lose access to potential slave converts if they did not rebut the Committee of Vigilance's charges convincingly enough. He therefore urged "that Christian Ministers and Christian communities throughout the South, for the sake of the cause of religion, and for the good of the slaves themselves, should most expressly discountenance the doctrines above referred to."[7] The evangelical Committee of Correspondence published in the *Religious Herald* a similar resolution one week later, assuring readers "that the suspicions which have prevailed to a considerable extent against Ministers of the Gospel and professors of religion in the State of Virginia, as identified with Abolitionists, are wholly unmerited, believing as we do from extensive acquaintance with our churches and brethren, that they are unanimous in opposing the pernicious schemes of Abolitionists."[8]

In one of the many proslavery consequences of the mission to the slaves, the small minority of white evangelicals who doubted slavery's justice and poured their empathy into the mission effectively became proslavery ideologues by simply trying to distinguish themselves from abolitionists. Baptist Robert Ryland, for instance, had genuine reservations about slavery and later proved himself to be a surprising ally of black Baptists. But in August 1835, Ryland felt that he needed publicly to counter the abolitionist argument that slavery was unscriptural. Ryland's scriptural argument was straightforward; he asserted that God implicitly sanctioned slavery by regulating it in the command that masters give to servants their due. Though it is uncertain whether his feelings were real or affected, Ryland claimed discomfort with his public stance that the Bible affirmed slavery. "The other parts of the article on slavery are manly and just," he conceded. "The views are sound and liberal, and the conclusions logical. I do not wish to be considered an advocate for slavery, though I *appear* to be, in the above remarks. I feel the perplexity of the subject."[9]

Andrew Broaddus, the most prominent Baptist advocate of slave missions in Virginia, also reluctantly became a proslavery ideologue in defense of his instruction of black Virginians. Remarkably, he was still willing to acknowledge antislavery sentiments even after the content of the mailings had been revealed. "I am a friend to the rights of the human family," he defiantly proclaimed; "I am, in principle, opposed to slavery, and, consequently, I am in favor of emancipation." But Broaddus chafed at the manner in which the American Anti-Slavery Society had demanded immediate emancipation without considering the ramifications of such a plan, and he argued that the South should be left alone. "In conclusion, permit me to say to you," he declared, "that the South knows its own situation better than you know it;— that the people are more capable of estimating the consequences of your scheme of Abolition, than you can be;—that you are running a fearful career —and that you ought to stop, or change your course."[10]

After the abolitionist mailings, Ryland and Broaddus played new roles in the sectional contest over slavery, but they did not change their basic understanding of the ban on the discussion of slavery or of the mission to the slaves. In the four years between Turner's insurrection and the mailings, Ryland and Broaddus had helped their fellow evangelicals to develop a post-Turner regime of white supervision and proselytization. In 1832, spokesmen for their denomination had even affirmed Baptists' continued determination not to discuss the sensitive issue of slavery in their capacity as churchmen. The only exception to this rule, and the line they drew in the sand, was that they would defend in every venue the "importance of communicating religious instruction to the people of colour."[11] In 1835, Ryland and Broaddus thought that they were defending their right to spread the Gospel, not inventing new, spurious arguments to protect their material self-interest in the court of public opinion. By the 1830s, regardless of what they intended or how they got there, though, Ryland, Broaddus, and other white evangelicals invested in the mission nonetheless found themselves rebutting the arguments of slavery's critics in denominational and secular papers. Their program had a new political salience, even if its roots were in the relationship between white and black Virginians and not in the rhetorical contest between northern abolitionists and southern defenders of slavery. Moreover, slaveholders without strong religious convictions quickly appropriated the arguments that Ryland and Broaddus made on behalf of their work. In their clumsier hands, what originated as a defense of mission work became a defense of slavery per se.[12]

To appreciate the distinction between a defense of mission work and a defense of slavery in the abstract, it is important to rehabilitate a picture of the mission to the slaves as an earnest evangelistic endeavor. In the accounts of many former slaves and in several histories of the period, the mission comes across as only a shallow strategy for racial control. Beverly Jones, for example, remembered that he heard endless sermons on Ephesians 6:5,

"Servants, be obedient to them that are your masters according to the flesh, with fear and trembling, in singleness of your heart, as unto Christ." "Can' tell you how many times I done heard that text preached on," he recalled in a scathing indictment of white evangelicalism. "They always tell the slaves dat ef he be good, an' worked hard fo' his master, dat he would go to heaven, an' dere he gonna live a life of ease."[13] There is a core truth to this perspective: white evangelicals did believe that the mission proved their righteousness in holding slaves. Such a reductive view of the mission is also misleading, however, for it does not explain why the number of black evangelicals in Virginia doubled between 1830 and 1850, nor does it accurately portray the amount of time and energy that white evangelicals spent trying to introduce black Virginians to their faith. Any accurate reconstruction of the mission to the slaves, then, must somehow capture both its attractiveness to enslaved persons and its hypocrisy that they later critiqued so forcefully.[14] White evangelicals left three decades worth of letters, newspaper articles, sermons, catechisms, and resolutions that make such a reconstruction possible.

In an article titled "Highly Important," Baptist Andrew Broaddus laid out in the pages of the *Religious Herald* in February 1835 an early plan for the religious instruction of black Virginians, one that heavily influenced those to follow. While acknowledging that individuals might have to adjust the method as their experience dictated, he hoped that his article would "furnish hints that may open the way for practical operation" of slave missions. Abolitionists looking for grounds to criticize Broaddus for perverting the faith would have been disappointed at how closely he stuck to orthodox Christianity. Broaddus built his lesson around a basic introduction to the Bible, and the main alteration that he made to normal Baptist worship was the inclusion of more definitions. He urged ministers to explain, for example, that "there are four writers, who have each given an account of our Lord Jesus Christ. These are Matthew, Mark, Luke, and John—called Evangelists." If anyone was scandalized, it would have been proslavery Virginians who demanded scrupulous adherence to the laws forbidding slaves to preach, for Broaddus hinted at a gradual erosion of that prohibition in closing. He suggested that whites may "let one of the gifted colored members be called on to pray, having previously selected one for that purpose. This may serve to give an additional interest among the colored people to the exercises of the meeting." Broaddus encouraged the readers of the *Religious Herald* to take the paper to church with them and to present his suggestions before their congregations.[15] Eager readers could find a helpful or encouraging morsel regarding slave missions in almost every issue of the *Herald*, and in many other papers as well. Presbyterians published in the

Southern Religious Telegraph one of the first catechisms specially designed for black Virginians in June 1834.[16]

The Episcopal *Southern Churchman* went so far as to publish sample sermons that white ministers or slaveowners could use when preaching to enslaved men and women. This may have been Bishop Meade's way of fulfilling the charge given to him at the 1834 convention that he provide guidance to churchmen who wanted to preach to their slaves. To the credit of Meade or the *Southern Churchman*, the editor selected sermons on the basis of how accessible the material would be for unchurched ears, rather than for how well it reinforced the slave regime. In 1835, the first year of the *Churchman*'s impressive publication run, these sermons appeared under the heading "Domestic Assistant." Some, such as the sermon printed on 20 February 1835, were clearly intended primarily for slaves. The lesson was based on Ephesians 6:8, "Knowing that whatsoever good thing any man doeth, the same shall he receive of the Lord, whether he be bond or free." Most lessons were much more general and contained material intended for either slaves or children. For example, a story on temptation that echoed Augustine's classic encounter with the orchard appeared in the "Domestic Assistant" for the following week, reprinted from the Portland Sabbath School Instructor. This relatively color-blind series ended sometime in late 1837. By 1838, the editors had replaced the "Domestic Assistant" with "Stories for Servants: The Pious Negro Family" and always targeted black audiences. In these stories, the authors generally developed one of two complementary arguments why African Americans, particularly slaves, should join the church. On one hand, they appealed to blacks' sense of justice by forthrightly stating that it would be more difficult for rich men (that is, their owners) to get to heaven; on the other hand, they directly targeted blacks in the invisible church who had some knowledge of scripture by arguing that the Bible obligated church membership.[17]

The drift in the *Southern Churchman* from the "Domestic Assistant" to "Stories for Servants" showed how the process of trying to lure black men and women to evangelical churches could reinforce for whites notions of racial hierarchy. The more convinced that whites became that they needed to form a separate and distinctive mode of religious instruction for black Virginians, the more they accepted that black men and women were fundamentally different from white men and women. The editor of the *Religious Herald* put it like this: "Children in intellect, they require to be treated and instructed like children." But African Americans, he argued, were not altogether like children; "they have peculiar vices which require to be exposed and pointed out, as repugnant to the Christian religion."[18] Even writers like Andrew Broaddus who demonstrated surprising empathy displayed this same, heightened sense of racial essentialism. "That this class of people stand in need of *special* religious instruction, in order to a due degree of religious knowledge, is a position which appears to me so obvious as hardly to require an effort to make it plainer," he wrote.[19] Whites inferred this lesson from experience, for it is nowhere to be found in scripture. As Mark Noll has demonstrated, white southerners brought assumptions of racial difference to their reading of the Bible, literally "coloring" everything that they did, including missions to the slaves.[20]

The *Southern Churchman* and the *Religious Herald* were the main print organs of the Episcopal and Baptist churches in Virginia, but white evangelicals of all denominational backgrounds from Virginia and—courtesy of the nineteenth-century practice of reprinting articles from elsewhere—from other southern states read the papers. This was emblematic of the strong spirit of ecumenism that characterized the missions. What began after Nat Turner's rebellion as discrete conversations within each denomination about the mechanics of slave missions quickly became a broader discussion, and white evangelicals took advantage of an expanding evangelical print culture to share news across sectarian and state lines.[21] Dozens of evangelical ministers from every denominational background published catechisms or manuals specifically designed to facilitate the oral instruction of slaves. Virginia Episcopalian William Meade issued dozens of sermons on the topic; South Carolina Methodist William Capers published a catechism and several sermons; Virginia Baptist Ryland issued his own catechism; and many others contributed in their own way.[22]

Methodist Holland M'Tyeire was a son of the South, more than of any single state, and his peripatetic proslavery career exemplified the extent to which white churchmen cooperated across state lines in the proslavery mission to convert African Americans. Born in South Carolina, M'Tyeire graduated from Smith's Randolph Macon and had had appointments in Virginia, Alabama, and New Orleans before taking charge of the printing press of the Methodist Episcopal (ME) Church, South, in Nashville. M'Tyeire made the mission the framework for his most important proslavery treatise, *Duties of Christian Masters*, which he first drafted in 1849, in order to enter an essay contest on the duties of Christian slaveowners sponsored by the Baptist State Convention of Alabama. Very ecumenically, the Baptists of that state had "assigned the duty of making the award to a committee selected from the leading religious denominations of the Southern and Southwestern states," and they did not blush to award a share of the prize to an expatriate. The Southern Baptist Committee published the essay in 1851, along with two others. By the time that M'Tyeire decided to republish it on his own initiative in 1859, he had considerable additional material to add, including several letters from Methodist bishop James Andrew on the topic. Lest his readers suspect that he had relied too heavily on the Methodist perspective, however, M'Tyeire advertised that, because "Christian masters are confined to no particular branch of the Church," he had written with a particular eye to "catholicity." He explicitly acknowledged debts not only to Virginia's Episcopal prelate William Meade but also to Presbyterian J. C. Young of Kentucky and to Baptist C. F. Sturgis of Alabama.[23] The religious instruction of slaves and free blacks was the issue of the day, and men like M'Tyeire were very aware that they were writing for a regional, evangelical community.

Georgia Presbyterian Charles Colcock Jones was unquestionably the brightest light in the regional mission to the slaves. Like many other prominent participants in the mission, Jones was initially opposed to slavery but resolved his sympathy for slaves by determining to do all that he could to ameliorate their condition and to spread the Gospel among them. While in school at Princeton in 1829, Jones wrote like an abolitionist. He railed against slavery in a letter to his cousin and fiancée, calling it "a violation of all the Laws of God and man at once" and "a complete annihilation of justice. An inhuman abuse of power, and an assumption of the responsibility of fixing the life and destiny of immortal beings, fearful in the extreme."[24] Once he returned home to Georgia, Jones decided not to attack slavery directly but to target instead its abuses and to share the Gospel with its victims. Jones was methodical in his approach to the task and, after his start in 1830, made Liberty County, Georgia, a laboratory for the most innovative techniques in mission work. In this, he soon solicited the assistance of like-minded evangelicals from across the region. In the second edition of his catechism for the instruction of slaves, for example, he credited a network of southern reformers with refining his original manuscript into a usable form. "There are Plantations, and Plantation Schools, and large Sabbath Schools, in different parts of the country, that have gone *entirely through* the Catechism, and have reviewed, and re-reviewed it accurately and intelligently," he wrote in 1837.[25]

In 1842, Jones published the most ambitious, thoroughly researched, and influential volume on slave missions, *The Religious Instruction of the Negroes in the United States*. Jones gave a historical sketch of white efforts to convert slaves and free blacks, described obstacles to the task, outlined the obligations of white evangelicals, and recommended specific procedures to increase the effectiveness of white missionaries. In the historical sketch, he cited examples from every denomination and every slaveholding state, implicitly emphasizing the opportunity for white evangelical union on the issue. Although he testified that tens of thousands of African Americans had converted during the course of their 222-year residence in the United States and cataloged the formation, especially after 1831, of more missionary groups, Jones also took his fellow evangelicals to task for the lukewarm quality of their efforts. "It is a remarkable fact in the history of the Negroes in our Country," he challenged, "that their regular, systematic religious instruction, has never received in the churches at any time, that general attention and effort which it demanded." In other words, the pastor wanted evangelicals to move beyond piecemeal measures to a more comprehensive, institutional approach to slave Christianity.[26]

Prominent evangelicals in Virginia corresponded with Jones, underscoring the cooperative nature of the mission. Cocke read all of Jones's published reports on missions in Liberty County and in June 1844 initiated a correspondence with him. "I have often been upon the point of writing & soliciting your correspondence" in relation to the instruction of slaves, he wrote, thanking Jones for his leadership in the field before offering his own ideas about how best to proceed. "I am satisfied that the most successful system of instruction, must commence in the form & manner of Infant Schools," suggested Cocke. "An intelligent female of the plantation can soon be made competent to the operations of this system, many of the most useful parts of which are mainly mechanical."[27] Presbyterian Samuel J. Cassells tried to implement Jones's ideas without modification. He chaired a committee on domestic missions for the Synod of Virginia and used his position in 1843 to recommend "that a committee be appointed either to obtain a supply of Jones' Catechism, or of some other suited to the purpose, so that persons duly authorized may be enabled to enter at once upon the work of instructing the colored people."[28]

Baptist Ryland never became as famous as Jones, but he also demonstrated the cooperative, interstate nature of the mission when he scripted his catechism. Ryland first tried to use existing catechisms, presumably including Jones's, during his ministry at Richmond's First African Baptist Church in the 1840s. "As none of these precisely suited his plan of instruction, he had determined to prepare one for his own use, when he learned that the Rev. A. W. Chambliss of Alabama was about to publish a work which would meet the wants of the case." Even the Chambliss volume was disappointing, however. "Having lately examined that production," Ryland explained, he "found it larger and less simple than he desired, (though it has many excellences)." Only after trying these alternatives from evangelicals in Georgia and Alabama did Ryland write his own, which was different from preceding editions in that he framed each question to require a yes or no answer and provided quotations from scripture to back up each response. Ryland's catechism, like all the others, was functionally proslavery in two ways. First, Ryland included a brief section on the mutual responsibilities of "Masters and Servants." Second, through the very act of creating and disseminating a catechism, Ryland was making the case that a well-regulated system of paternalist instruction—not abolition—was the best way that owners could care for their slaves.[29]

African American Virginians' continued preference for Baptist churches in some ways necessitated cooperation among denominations in the commonwealth. In 1860, an estimated 90 percent of Virginia's African American evangelicals were Baptists, while only 38 percent of enslaved Christians nationally affiliated with the Baptist Church.[30] Though white Presbyterians, Episcopalians, and Methodists became more and more interested in attracting black Virginians to their respective traditions, they generally conceded that their most important role came in attracting slaves to evangelicalism in general, not to their particular churches. As Presbyterian William Gaines explained of his own efforts to convert slaves on his plantation, "We have not endeavored to make Methodists or Baptists, or Episcopalians, or Presbyterians, or Reformers—but we do try to make Christians of them. 'Tis true that every one would have his heart delighted, that his servants when they become Christians should join his own Church; but our aim is to make them *Christians*; and then leave them to their own choice."[31] The crusade was thus both personal and institutional; whites outside the Baptist tradition urged slaveholders in their ranks to read the Bible to their slaves and to instruct them orally in the rudiments of evangelical faith—and then to permit them to attend a Baptist (or occasionally a Methodist) church. Virginia's white evangelicals thereby embraced a practical ecumenism in their missions to the slaves and grew closer to one another, even as they drifted apart from their northern coreligionists.

Presbyterian and Episcopal slaveowners got used to worshipping apart from the men and women whom they claimed to own. At the Ballenger Creek Baptist Church, in Albemarle County, this caused an awkward situation. The church's membership rolls were so full of black members in 1855, with 247 African Americans heavily outnumbering 54 whites, that one of the church officials felt compelled to offer some sort of explanation to denominational leaders for the imbalance. Either the clerk or the pastor (John Morris or Charles Wingfield) appended a handwritten note to the statistics that he submitted to the Albemarle Association. "It may be wondered at by some why there are so many more coloured member than white," he observed, "one reason is there are a great number all round the Church, some of whose master own from fifty to a hundred, and whilt the master belongs to the Episcopal Church or some other the servants all come to the baptist."[32] Presbyterians who responded to an 1843 survey that asked, "Is any thing done specifically for the religious instruction of the colored people?" explained that they were doing some work, but that others were reaping the benefit. The East Hanover Presbytery, for example, reported that, though there was "no special Missionary for the colored people," "a few catechetical classes have recently been formed among them, and most of our Pastors preach to them apart from the whites occasionally. They are very numerous among us, but are for the most part Methodists and Baptists."[33]

White evangelicals traded enough ideas back and forth—and responded to enough similar prompts from black Virginians—that the mission eventually took on a similar form regardless of denomination. There emerged a core of common ideas and practices, though the precise way in which whites went about seeking black members always varied depending on one's ecclesiastical tradition. All evangelicals believed that whites should simultaneously encourage and monitor their slaves' religious worship, that paternal care for slaves was a piece with proselytization, that oral instruction was the safest method of religious indoctrination, that whites should supply worship places and worship times especially for blacks, and that whites should recruit white southern men and women to conduct services to compensate for the lack of slave preachers. Presbyterians, Methodists, Episcopalians, and Baptists all also generally favored the establishment of Sunday schools for black residents of the community, and they encouraged ministers and laymen to preach the Gospel in "plain" terms to black members.

Within this broad consensus, Presbyterians and Methodists were the most willing to fund special missionaries to aid in the work of evangelizing the slaves. In this, they largely followed the examples of Jones and his South Carolina Methodist counterpart, William Capers. Jones called for whites to fund missionaries as a complement to the work of settled pastors. Though he was explicitly interdenominational in his call, even suggesting that "two or more churches, of one or more denominations contiguous to each other, might unite and support a missionary to the Negroes connected with them," Presbyterians took him the most seriously and repeatedly considered such a plan. In Virginia, at least, they always stopped short of implementing it.[34] From 1829, when he had colluded with Episcopal planter Charles Cotesworth Pickney to launch a formal Mission to the Slaves, Capers had also urged Methodists to appoint special missionaries to slaves. By 1840, Capers was head of the Southern Department of Missionary Work in the Methodist Church and presided over eighty missionaries committed to working exclusively among the region's bondmen. The number of Methodist missionaries in the slaveholding states peaked in 1861, at 327.[35]

Episcopalians, with the tradition of family worship using the rubric provided in the Book of Common Prayer, tended to emphasize household piety as their preferred angle of attack in the mission to the slaves. Episcopalians were by no means the only ones who pursued household devotionals—such attention to the spiritual concerns of one's human property was a part of the paternalist attitude of many slaveowners—but they played a more important part in the Episcopal incarnation of the mission. Episcopal clergy such as William Huntington and Frederick Goodwin regularly made the rounds of their neighboring plantations to conduct these services, but many owners conducted worship themselves. One of the practical advantages to this approach, from an Episcopal point of view, was that Episcopal owners could influence enslaved men and women in the home even if their bondmen and -women would never set foot in an Episcopal church. In his collection of anecdotes about faithful slaves, Meade recorded several such examples, of which the account of "Aunt Margaret" was typical. " 'But, "Aunt Margaret," you are not an Episcopalian, are you?' " asked a white acquaintance of the woman in question. " 'No, madam, I am a Baptist, but my dear old mistress in Virginia was, and she used to read the Bible to me, and I used to hear the Church service read. And, madam, I know I shall never hear better prayers, until I go where prayer is turned to praise.' "[36]

Baptists, as the anecdote above illustrates, already enjoyed considerable success in attracting black members before the post-Turner phase of white missionary outreach began. As a result, white Baptists were the slowest to experiment with new practices in search of African American converts. Instead, they took advantage of systems or institutions already in place to extend their ministry to African Americans. Their greatest assets were the large congregations that contained both free blacks and slaves. Though the General Assembly had theoretically stripped black Baptists of their leadership and autonomy, significant communities of African American Baptists remained in many of Virginia's cities. In some locations, such as Petersburg and Norfolk, the congregations had been fully autonomous before Turner and continued with only nominal white leadership. In other places, the churches were biracial but included large black majorities. The biggest of these churches were urban, but there were also rural congregations that fit the description. In the much more rural Albemarle Association, for example, blacks were a majority in at least seven of the thirteen churches that reported membership statistics in 1833.[37] Rather than setting up "mission churches" or designing innovative outreach programs, white Baptists prioritized the growth of these existing biracial or quasi-independent communities of African American faithful.

The challenge for white Baptists was to encourage the growth of existing faith communities while at the same time enforcing the laws of the state. This was most challenging in the immediate aftermath of the Southampton Insurrection, when enforcing the laws meant removing black men from power. Since all of the state's completely independent black churches— Elam, Gillfield, First Baptist of Norfolk, and the Harrison Street Church in Petersburg—identified themselves as Baptist, it fell to the Portsmouth and Dover associations to make sure that black men did not again resume control of these churches. The Dover Association promptly shut down the Williamsburg church, and whites at the Old Mount Zion Church (also in that association's jurisdiction) pulled their slaves from the Elam church, leaving only free blacks. The Gillfield church and First Baptist Church of Norfolk confounded whites in the Portsmouth Association for several years by obeying the letter of the law and electing white pastors, though those pastors were unaffiliated with a white Baptist church and therefore free from white ecclesiastical censure. To close this loophole, Portsmouth Association delegates passed tighter legislation in 1839 and again in 1844, forcing the head of these black churches to be a member of the nearest white Baptist church.[38]

Black Baptists' creative resistance to white ecclesiastical control in the Gillfield and Norfolk churches was only one instance of African American resistance to the post-Turner regulations. At every turn, black evangelicals sought to retain or regain ecclesiastical privileges that they had enjoyed in the 1820s. They had no legal leverage on whites at all, but they could refuse to join biracial churches and thwart the entire purpose of the mission to the slaves if whites did not grant them some relief from the 1832 regulations, particularly the restrictions on slave preaching, literacy, and assembly. Though evangelical whites did their part to prevent the most flagrant violations of the law, they acquiesced in a surprising degree to black Virginians' desire for a return of some measure of spiritual autonomy.

The ecclesiastical negotiations between black and white Virginians that took place in the 1830s through emancipation were different than they had been in the early national period. In the 1790s, white evangelicals had refused to consider emancipating the black men and women who had joined their churches, but they perceived that these persons had real claims to justice and had offered an olive branch in the ethic of paternalism. In the 1820s, white evangelicals believed it possible for black evangelicals to "graduate" from slavery and participated alongside black believers in the ACS. A few white evangelicals in the late 1830s and 1840s still perceived bonds of fellowship strong enough that they tried to overthrow the post-Turner legislation because black evangelicals appealed to their consciences. Most white churchmen, however, did not make concessions to their African American brethren in the late antebellum period because of any relational motive. Rather, they were simply willing to do anything that they could to bring black men and women into evangelical congregations where they could supervise them.

Whether the motive was empathy or self-interest, white evangelicals were nonetheless still responding to the spiritual initiatives of black evangelicals. In this way, lay black Virginians contributed as much to the shape of the mission as did ordained white Virginians. They compelled whites to add several elements to their outreach to slaves that they would not otherwise have offered. The commonwealth's African Americans pressed white evangelicals to give them permission to preach, even if the law prevented them from receiving formal ordination. They called for private instruction in literacy. They sought permission to assemble for irregular prayer services. And, above all, they sought the right to assemble separately from whites for Sunday worship, in environments in which they could hear from other African American evangelicals, could worship with their friends and family in the format most agreeable to them, and could escape the racial posturing of evangelical whites.

Black men continued to preach after 1832 and compelled white evangelicals to adjust their understanding of the law against black preachers. Though whites initially seem to have interpreted the law as a blanket prohibition of black spiritual leadership, they began to interpret more leniently the provision "that no slave, free negro or mulatto, whether he shall have been ordained or licensed, or otherwise, shall hereafter take to preach, exhort or conduct, or hold any assembly or meeting, for religious or other purposes."[39] White evangelicals allowed blacks to preach, exhort, and conduct meetings, as long as there was a white present. This was essential in the bid to recruit black converts. Some whites approved of black preaching even when there were no whites present. In surviving explanations of this flagrant violation of the law, whites granting the approval seem to have calculated the cost of intervention, the likeliness of rebellion, and the possibility that leniency would gain more converts.

When Englishmen Andrew Reed and James Matheson visited the United States in 1834, they recorded many examples of black Virginians preaching, nominally, if at all, under white supervision. In Lexington, Virginia, they witnessed their first black worship service, in "a poor log house, built by the hands of the negroes." Though there were two whites present, black men ran the service and delivered the sermon and exhortation. "The senior black, who was a preacher among them, then offered prayer, and preached," they noted with approbation, to the point that one remarked, "I know not that while I was in America, I listened to a peroration of an address that was superior to the one I have briefly noted." At a Northern Neck camp meeting that Reed and Matheson attended, black participants exercised even more autonomy. When the meeting became unruly late at night, the 300 or so black Virginians in attendance "separated themselves from the general service, and sought their own preacher and anxious seat. A stand was presently fixed between two trees; a preacher was seen appearing and disappearing between them."[40]

Reed and Matheson were simply observing what they saw, but some participants in the mission actually encouraged black men to exercise this sort of spiritual authority. In the same way that Andrew Broaddus had suggested that blacks would be more open to evangelicals' message if white ministers encouraged black men to conduct prayers, others gave their assent to the quasi-ordination of black men. Anthony Burns, for example, was a "quasi-pastor or preacher": "without being formally set apart to the sacred office by any rite of ordination, they yet receive a sort of recognition from the church with which they may happen to be connected." Whites and blacks in Burns's church openly affirmed his gifts, and Burns carried out a thriving ministry among Virginia slaves both in secret hush harbors and in the presence of sympathetic whites. As his biographer wrote, "Gathering a little congregation of slaves, sometimes in the kitchen of a friendly white person, sometimes in the rude cabin of a slave, he would lead them in their devotions and speak to them of the Gospel. These meetings, however, as well as all other assemblies consisting exclusively of slaves, were violations of Virginia law."[41] Noah Davis, who preached as a slave in Madison County until 1845, also described his ordination as if there were no legal restrictions to it whatsoever:

I related my convictions of duty to my brethren, and particularly to one who was always held in high esteem for his piety and excellent character— a colored brother, Armistead Walker. My case was first brought by him before the colored portion of the church; and after a full hearing of my statement, by the white brethren, with regard to my call to preach, &c., I was licensed to preach the gospel, and exhort sinners to repentance, opportunity might be afforded. I had ample opportunities at that time, for doing good, by preaching to my fellow men, both in town and country.[42]

"Colored preachers" like Burns and Davis appear throughout the written record in both white and black sources despite the post-Turner ban.[43]

The accounts of black ministers flouting the 1832 edict come from church minutes as well as slave narratives. The biracial congregation of Chappawamsic Baptist Church, for example, seemed willing to allow black men to preach so long as the church licensed them. In June 1843, "the Church being informed by Bro West that Charles a Servant of Thos. Cannon & Ralph A servant of Wm. H. Fitzhugh, were in the habbit of preaching in publick without License from the church; appointed Jesse Jasper & Thos. Cole to cite them to the Ch. at the next Meeting to answer for the same." Though there is no record of an actual licensing, Charles continued to preach until 1852, when the church expelled him for "False Doctrine (in preaching)."[44] The First Baptist Church of Norfolk called Lewis Tucker to preach in 1845 and licensed him in 1859.[45] Even when whites were not explicit about the ecclesiastical processes involved, they still affirmed black ministers. In September 1849, at Mill Creek Baptist Church, "Br. Charles Adams a coloured preacher applied for admittance and was received on Confession of his Faith in the Lord Jesus Christ."[46]

White evangelicals also ceded ground on literacy. In Virginia and in a few other slaveholding states, evangelical whites campaigned for a repeal of the antiliteracy laws and allowed considerable evasion of the rules.[47] Although revising the law to allow black evangelicals to read was a popular cause among white evangelicals, including prominent Baptist Jeremiah Bell Jeter, whites' nonevangelical partners in the proslavery Gospel—men and women who simply wanted to remove every potential spur to rebellion from the Christian message as delivered to the bondmen—refused. Remembering with distaste the inflexibility of the laws regarding slave literacy, Jeter recalled the justification that his fellow citizens offered following the Southampton Insurrection: "I then thought, and I still think, that the laws were more severe than was demanded by the exigency of the times, but they certainly found a plausible defense in the excited state of the public mind and in the defenseless condition of the women and children in the rural districts."[48] White evangelicals repeatedly revisited the issue throughout the late antebellum period. In 1852, some white Baptists even petitioned the legislature for "the education of colored people in Richmond." The response was still no.[49]

Teaching slaves to read never became an essential or universal part of proslavery evangelicalism, but many white evangelicals were willing to push the boundaries of the law for the sake of the mission and in response to the desires of their black coreligionists. There is ample evidence, for instance, that Robert Ryland designed his *Scripture Catechism* in part as a primer for his black congregants.[50] Some evangelical slaveowners, either as a part of their plans to colonize some of their slaves or because their consciences or their black neighbors convinced them it was important, also taught slaves to read.[51] The image of the plantation mistress teaching her slaves to read the Bible had some basis in fact in antebellum Virginia, at least according to the editors of the *National Era*, based in Washington, D.C. Gamaliel Bailey and his staff on the abolitionist newspaper surveyed access to literacy across the slaveholding South in 1847 and rated Virginia favorably. They reported that whites in Virginia were different from whites in the Cotton South when it came to allowing slaves to read the Bible as a part of their spiritual development. Bailey found it remarkable that "the Virginia Baptist and Foreign Bible Society" had resolved "that the Board be authorized to furnish copies of the Bible for gratuitous distribution among such of the colored members of our churches as are able to read, and are unable to purchase them." One of the paper's correspondents noted that during fourteen years in Virginia, he "knew of cases in which the slaves of Christian masters, and of gentlemen not members of the church, were taught to read the Bible. And he never knew or heard of any Protestant denying them this right." Though there were laws on the books, "the laws are not rigidly enforced, and the Bible might be circulated to a considerable extent among the slaves."[52]

The greatest single concession that black Virginians won from whites was the right to establish quasi-independent churches, functionally autonomous but nominally under the oversight of white ministers. In *The Religious Instruction of the Negroes*, Charles Colcock Jones advocated keeping white and black worshippers together: "It is best that both classes worship in the same building; that they be incorporated in the same church, under the same pastor, having access to the same ordinances, baptism and the Lord's supper, and at the same time; and that they be subject to the same care and discipline; the two classes forming one pastoral charge, one church, one congregation."[53] Virginia evangelicals had felt much the same way immediately following the Nat Turner rebellion, but they had already begun to experiment with all-black congregations by the time that Jones wrote in 1842. Black Virginians found in these churches enough opportunities to control their own spirituality that they joined despite their reservations about white oversight.

Whites in urban areas with large populations of slaves and free blacks were the first to abandon this principle, in the early 1840s. Some whites favored separation of black and white evangelicals because it relieved them of what had become for them the most distasteful part of the mission—the burden of spending much of Sunday morning outnumbered by what seemed to them noisy, ill-behaved black churchgoers. Whereas some Baptists and Methodists in the post-Revolutionary period had perceived interracial religious experiences as sacred expressions of the Gospel's universality and essential parts of the evangelical aesthetic, many white evangelicals by the late antebellum period saw African American believers as distractions from the service. Beth Barton Schweiger best explained why urban white evangelicals obsessed with notions of progress and respectability began to find their relations with black believers strained: "The very success of the Gospel among slaves and free blacks—for whom, most whites were convinced, religion could bring neither social, intellectual, nor material progress—raised troubling questions among those for whom racial inequality was just as firm a principle as progressive religion."[54]

Richmond white Baptists proved in 1841 that by establishing separate black churches they could kill two birds with one stone: they could simultaneously achieve more "respectability" and attain a more effective outreach to blacks. Black evangelicals in the capital city had long been active in the area's Baptist churches and had been interested in forming their own congregation at least as early as the 1820s, when they petitioned the legislature for the right to establish one. The city's whites did not grant African American Baptists this wish until it also served their own purposes of respectability, or until they outgrew their sanctuary at College and Broad streets. At that time, on 3 October 1841, whites left their old sanctuary to the exclusive use of Richmond's black Baptists, but only under the rules set following Turner's rebellion. In an elaborate schema constructed primarily by the leadership of the First Baptist Church, a committee of twenty-four whites exercised final authority over the decisions of the new First African Baptist Church, and a white pastor, none other than Robert Ryland, performed all of the services and preached all of the sermons.[55] Some nonevangelical whites were still concerned about the wisdom of setting up a church with such limited oversight, but those evangelicals most committed to the mission seem to have been united in support for the plan. Presbyterian William S. Plumer, for one, assured First Baptist's pastor Jeremiah Bell Jeter, "I wish you to understand that in any difficulties you may have concerning the African church I am to go halves with you."[56]

In Richmond's First African Baptist, blacks exercised considerable spiritual authority despite Ryland's nominal headship. In the church hierarchy, a board composed of thirty deacons selected by members of the First African Church from among their own ranks handled all cases of discipline and church governance.[57] Ryland allowed the deacons enough leeway that these men became the most important leaders in antebellum Richmond's black community. Slaves outnumbered free blacks in the church by about two to one, but members of First African Baptist elected to the deacon board those who embodied their ideas of success, mostly free blacks with some property. At least two slaves, James Holmes and Isaac Turner, worked alongside these free blacks to serve their congregation and the black community at large. With so many blacks in the city attending regularly—the church reported 2,076 members in 1844 out of a total slave and free black population of roughly 10,000—the deacon board functioned as a primitive representative government for city blacks.[58] Deacons served as the community's judges, patrons, and ambassadors. One vehicle that these churchmen used to serve other Richmond blacks was the Poor Saints Committee, a group formed in 1848 to provide financial relief for poor church members. Five deacons from each of Richmond's three wards served on the committee, an arrangement that fostered among the deacons a sense of responsibility to particular constituencies. With a total annual budget that reached $3,000 in the late 1850s, the deacons were able to feed hundreds of the hungry, patronize free black businessmen for church-related services, and even help purchase at least three fortunate souls from slavery.[59]

Black Richmonders endorsed the First African Baptist Church and the chance to reclaim some autonomy so overwhelmingly that whites elsewhere moved to allow similar congregations. The church grew by literally hundreds each year, from a starting membership of approximately 1,000 in 1841, to 2,076 in 1844, to 2,457 in 1846. The church continued to increase in size despite spinning off enormous daughter churches such as Second African Baptist, which itself numbered 770 in 1855 and hit 3,260 in 1860.[60] Friends of the mission who tried to reproduce the experiment found the most success in areas where there had been independent black churches before 1831, in Norfolk, Petersburg, Williamsburg, and Portsmouth. The willingness of whites to allow blacks a measure of responsibility and independence in worshipping on their own in these communities accomplished a chief goal of the mission, bringing members of the invisible church into the open and under supervision. This supervision, though, was marginal at best; even if they had a white preacher, the congregants could set the tone in terms of worship style and exercise subsidiary forms of leadership, such as offering public prayers and voting on cases of discipline. Moreover, as the editors of the *Religious Herald* conceded in a discussion about the challenge of supervising the numerous black members of the First Baptist Church, "a number so large cannot be attended to faithfully by any one individual, however faithful and competent."[61]

These concessions by whites to black evangelicals in one sense represented significant African American victories in the continuing negotiations of slavery, but in a more profound sense, they represented an enormous victory for proslavery Christianity. Blacks did get their way on the ground and recoup some of the post-Turner losses. But, in the success of the quasi-independent churches, whites received an enormous boost in the intensifying sectional conflict over slavery. Three years after the First African Baptist Church had opened its doors, white Virginians used it and other congregations like it to turn abolitionists' complaint that slavery was the antithesis of loving one's neighbor as oneself on its head. "We recently saw a complaint in a northern periodical," an article in the *Religious Herald* stated, "that the colored Baptist churches were dwindling away for want of efficient ministers. Surely those brethren are not so intent on pointing out our duty, as thus so sadly to neglect their own. . . . We have many flourishing churches, and we hope that these will continue to increase, and others be raised up."[62] The editors of the Methodist *Richmond Christian Advocate* put it this way: "Which party most strictly conforms to the doctrines and practice of Christ and the Apostles? Those who seek to save the souls of the slave population of the country"—and who, thanks to the success of quasi-independent churches had hard evidence that they were succeeding—"or those who strive merely for their freedom?"[63]

The rhetorical trump card that whites gained from the huge success of quasi-independent black churches, effective though it was, was not the most important factor whereby the mission strengthened proslavery Christianity. Whites constructed in the mission an ideology of slaveholding so flexible that it reinforced the justice of the institution regardless of black behavior. Black Virginians were damned if they did and damned if they didn't accept the invitation of white evangelicals to join quasi-independent or biracial churches. If they did submit to some sort of nominal white religious oversight and seek membership in an evangelical church, enslaved Virginians reinforced whites' belief that slavery was a benign vehicle for Christianization. If they instead rejected the mission as proslavery garbage, bonded Virginians only offered more proof that slavery was necessary—that blacks needed more time in the refining fire of slavery to come to a saving knowledge of Jesus. The powerful proslavery effect of the mission was that white evangelicals could view every interaction with a black man or woman in a way that reinforced their perception that slavery was just.

When black men and women affiliated with white churches, white evangelicals saw proof that God had ordained slavery. Presbyterian Samuel Cassells was one of many who saw the early (and relatively modest) success of the mission as a sufficient rebuttal to abolitionist arguments. "In almost every place, they either worship with the whites in the galleries, or in seats appropriated for them, or, they have churches of their own. Several of these churches are larger and far better attended than even with the whites," he boasted. On the basis of this good news and despite countervailing examples of white cruelty, Cassells concluded,

> God *intends* the enslaving of the Africans among us for *great good*. His wise and powerful hand has been directing and controlling in this matter a great moral machinery, in the midst of which, it is true, many a feebler and worse hand has mingled. Still, however, will the *final* and *good* result be accomplished, and masters and servants, those who hold slaves, and those who condemn slaveholders—*all* will be constrained to admire those results of *civilization*, of *liberty*, and of *christianity*, which shall thus be wrought out for Africa, by an exiled and enslaved portion of her long humbled population.[64]

Later, on the eve of the sectional conflict, an anonymous Virginian was still connecting black church membership with white southern virtue: "The pharisaic spirit of the Abolition-tainted-portion of the North believes the South is semi-barbarian, but in all the characteristics of true and genuine Christianity she is more than equal to the North. Her slave population will compare most favorably in their moral and religious culture, with the class in society in the North that occupy the same place. The number of church members among the slaves, shews the attention paid by all religious denominations to that class."[65]

Black Virginians, by joining evangelical churches, thus inadvertently undercut the attacks of abolitionists. For one thing, they proved wrong one of the abolitionists' most poorly calculated charges, that it was "impossible to convert slaves to Christianity." White Baptists in Stafford County who read this charge from James G. Birney reprinted in their regional papers must have thought it particularly ludicrous. Three weeks after the article appeared in 1835, they held a worship service at which blacks outnumbered whites, then met to conduct church business. After some associational business, they "heard the Experience of Peggy a coulord woman belonging to Mr. Moncure and received her for Baptism"; then they "heard the experiences of Mary & Henson a woman & man Belonging to Miss Mary Hare and received them for baptism."[66] Even the very bitter recriminations of fugitive slaves rolled off white evangelicals who were insulated by their apparent success in meeting the spiritual needs of Virginia blacks. And so it was across the state; whites troubled by abolitionist charges could take comfort that more than 50,000 black Virginians did not openly criticize white evangelicals but instead submitted to membership in white-supervised churches with them.[67]

The most devastating proslavery element of the mission was its malleability. Even white evangelicals who failed to attract black converts derived a proslavery lesson from their experience, for they interpreted African Americans' resistance to the Gospel as proof of slavery's necessity.[68] Frederick Goodwin, an Episcopal minister who shared his denomination's commitment to instructing black Virginians, had every reason to be optimistic about his role in converting the enslaved. He taught in church and in private homes in the Piedmont almost constantly, often noting that his audience was "a good number, & very attentive." He even started a Sunday school for black Virginians, which thirty-eight enslaved women and twenty-four enslaved men attended, and boasted that "the improvement of the pupils has exceeded the most sanguine expectations of the teachers." But it took only one clear setback to convince him that slavery was black Americans' natural state. On 26 April 1845, he confided to his diary, "had service for the collored people at Grace Ch. in the eve. Had but 7 & 2 of them my own. I am entirely in despair about doing any thing for them."[69]

Paulina LeGrand, an evangelical plantation mistress, also read black resistance to her version of Christianity as evidence of blacks' suitability for slavery.[70] She was in many ways an exemplary supporter of the mission to the slaves. In her correspondence with Episcopalian William Huntington in 1838 she urged him to greater exertions on behalf of black Virginians, arguing, "If much is ever done for the salvation of there precious & immortal souls, they must be more particularly attended to, than they have ever yet been."[71] But, perhaps because LeGrand characterized slavery as a school of virtue and not as a forced labor arrangement, she interpreted day-to-day resistance to the chattel principle as evidence of slaves' moral weakness— and not of their humanity. When Catherine, one of her slaves, played sick repeatedly to get out of work, LeGrand interpreted the act as a spiritual failure—and therefore evidence that the mission needed to continue indefinitely—and not as a tactic in labor negotiations. "I am distressed to find that Catherine is acting so deceitful a part," she wrote. The situation reminded her what "trials upon trials will those have that have much to do with servants that have not got the fear of God before them."[72] Whatever religious choices black Virginians made, then, they reinforced white Virginia evangelicals' commitment to slavery and slave missions.

Black Virginians who had immigrated to Liberia also played a part in shoring up proslavery evangelicalism as it coalesced in the late antebellum period. They enabled white evangelicals to remain positive about colonization in the face of what became by the late 1830s withering abolitionist and black criticism. Whites privileged the few positive reports that arrived from Liberia and shut their ears against all other news. Good news from the African coast was attractive because it fit smoothly into whites' understanding of the mission. Slowly but surely, they believed, God was using slavery to Christianize and civilize African Americans. In the event that an enslaved man or woman demonstrated that he or she had learned all that white Virginians could offer, there was already a mechanism in place, colonization, that would facilitate that person's journey to Africa as a missionary without jeopardizing whites' property in persons one iota. Whites were, in essence, two-faced in their orientation to colonization; they made free blacks the targets of colonization recruitment but made manumittees the center of their theological narrative about how God was using slavery.

In their correspondence a small number of manumittees gave whites the resolve to stay the course for colonization despite the overwhelming turn of public sentiment against it. One reason for John Hartwell Cocke's enduring commitment to colonization was his continued receipt of encouraging news directly from correspondents in Liberia. After meeting with Liberia's first black governor, Joseph Roberts, who originally hailed from Petersburg, Cocke confessed relief in his diary: "But I was particularly gratified to receive from Gov. R's own lips a confirmation of the encouraging acct. lately published in the African Colonization Journal touching the Colony."[73] He drew additional affirmation from his continuing correspondence with the Skipwith family. After the deaths of several loved ones, Peyton Skipwith still found it in himself to write in 1844, "Dear Masters as to myself, I am as well satisfied as I can be in this little Community, & I must thank, you sir, for the care you had over me while I was young, for when I was young & knew nothing you studied my interests, I am blessed with a trade, for you has sent me to this country where I can speak for myself like a man & show myself to be a man, so far as my ability allows me."[74] Charles Wesley Andrews, the Methodist who may have outdone Cocke in enthusiasm for colonization, also received his encouragement from correspondence. His wife, Sarah Page Andrews, relayed to him in 1839 good news from former slaves in Africa. "They are all doing well," she summarized after reading two letters from manumittees: "the children going to school & improving. Sally sends her special love to her Grandmother Uncle Joe Aunt Mindy Eleanor, & tell her Brother (Billy) that he must come to Africa for that is the only place where he can enjoy *perfect freedom* & bring plenty of clothing with him. Do tell them all this."[75]

Since so many emigrants died and since free blacks composed a significant proportion of the group, few white Virginians had access to such personal encouragement. There were simply not enough manumittees who survived in Liberia to provide letters for many Virginians. So whites manufactured positive news or multiplied what little authentic news did trickle through. The *Southern Churchman*, for example, reprinted a series of "Colonization Sketches" from the *Petersburg Intelligencer* in 1837 in which the editors ignored the colony's difficulties and instead recapitulated the first, more promising decade of African colonization. They also reported joyfully on a meeting in Liberia in which those Liberians most dependent on white succor had affirmed the wisdom of colonization. The information, the editors were confident, would steel white evangelicals against anticolonization news. "It has often been said, by many ill disposed toward the colonization enterprise, that the colonists are dissatisfied and discontented. Even some who have returned form Liberia have joined in the cry. We are gratified to have it in our power to give the real sentiments of the colonists themselves." According to the report, reprinted from the *Liberia Herald*, those present at a public meeting resolved "that this meeting entertain the warmest gratitude for what the Colonization Society have done for the people of color, and for us particularly, and that we regard the scheme as entitled to the highest confidence of every man of color."[76]

Richmond Baptist James B. Taylor had his own way of recalling the good old days of colonization and wrote in 1837 a biography of Lott Cary. This hagiographical account, commissioned by the Maryland Colonization Society, concluded with a defense of colonization by J. H. B. Latrobe. "It is admitted now on all hands to be practicable," Latrobe asserted somewhat optimistically. "It is one of the noblest charities of the age. It frees one country from a stain and a crying evil. It restores to another the descendants of its children, rich in the glorious treasures of Christianity and civilization —nor can the success that has, in the main attended it, be better accounted for, when compared with the early settlement of this country, than by using the words of the founder of the society, the Rev. Robert Finley—who replied to all the ridicule that was heaped upon him while he advocated it, by saying, 'I know this scheme is from God.' "[77] By publicizing accounts of Lott Cary, who by that time had been dead for almost a decade, evangelicals were giving a wider audience the image of a willing black colonizationist and, in the process, affirming slavery's role in Christianization. Future governor Henry A. Wise repeated this argument with less subtlety in 1838: "*Slavery on this continent is the gift of Heaven to Africa*," Wise bellowed; "Africa gave to Virginia *a savage* and *a slave*, Virginia gives back to Africa *a citizen* and *a Christian!*"[78]

On the ground, white colonizationists were not so idealistic. In an examination of the career of Rufus W. Bailey, who served as agent for the ACS in the Shenandoah Valley between 1847 and 1853, Ellen Elsinger has shown the absurdity of whites' professions to be acting in concert with or on behalf of black Virginians. Bailey repeatedly misrepresented the situation in Liberia in search of more free black emigrants. In an unambiguous demonstration of his motives, he also proposed to use the power of the state legislature and the county courts to coerce free blacks into leaving the state after his best efforts at persuasion failed.[79] Bailey's free-black-centered, deceit-filled crusade was the harsh reality that somehow coexisted with the evangelical idealization of colonization as part of God's plan.

Southern white evangelicals became so invested in the idea that slavery facilitated Christian benevolence toward slaves that they began to distance themselves from institutions, even national ones, which did not share this perspective. While Virginia's and the South's most committed white evangelicals were celebrating the opportunity that slavery offered to carry the Gospel to a needy people, a vocal minority of northern evangelicals was criticizing that same institution. Cooperation in mission work and other benevolent causes had been the hallmark of evangelical cooperation from 1815 through 1831, and that cooperation necessarily deteriorated when southerners devoted more energy to slave missions and northerners questioned the propriety of slavery. Reformers in each region were pulling away from the center—missionaries to the slaves assumed slavery's longevity, while reformers in the North believed that the institution had to be destroyed immediately. So strained did relations between northern and southern evangelicals become over the issue of slavery that between 1837 and 1845 Virginia clergymen would participate in the dismantling of national Presbyterian, Methodist, and Baptist jurisdictions.[80]

The Presbyterian schism came first, in 1837. Unlike the subsequent Baptist and Methodist schisms, the Presbyterian break had a theological component. "Old School" and "New School" factions within the church had a long-standing dispute about revivalism and the governance of mission boards, but these doctrinal disagreements probably only resulted in schism because they coincided with differences of opinion on the abolition movement. In a treatise intended to prove "that the issue between the two parties in the late controversy in the Presbyterian Church was strictly a doctrinal one," James Wood explained the theological reasons why Old Schoolers mistrusted the benevolent organizations and revivalist practices of New Schoolers—primarily a belief in the sovereignty of God rather than in human agency.[81] The newest and most disconcerting crusade, of course, was antislavery, institutionalized in the American Anti-Slavery Society in 1833. Very conscious of the fact that abolitionist boosters of the New School were trying to force the Presbyterian General Assembly to make a stand against slaveowning, Virginia Presbyterians George A. Baxter and William S. Plumer, along with South Carolina divine James Thornwell, forged an alliance with northern conservatives and expelled four New England synods. In Virginia, as in other slaveholding states, about 85 percent of the Presbyterians remained with the Old School. In 1840, roughly 9,350 Virginia Presbyterians aligned with the Old School Synod of Virginia; 2,000, with the mirroring New School Synod.[82]

Virginia's Old School Presbyterians recognized that the removal of the New Schoolers had been a victory for those who believed in slavery, even if slavery per se was not the only issue involved. In advance of the schism, Plumer had launched a newspaper, the *Watchman of the South*, dedicated to protecting "Southern interests," by which he meant slavery, in the General Assembly. On 7 September 1837, the members of a Presbyterian church in Sussex, Virginia, likewise expressed their understanding that they opposed the New School primarily because they opposed abolition. In a session meeting, these Virginians urged their sister churches to support the Presbyterian General Assembly's decision to expel four New School synods. "The great body of Abolitionists who have heretofore disturbed and convulsed the whole Presbyterian church, and who have avowed it as their intention never to cease their efforts, until the General Assembly declare the holding of slaves to be sinful," they explained, "lies in the boundaries of the excluded Synods [Western Reserve, Utica, Geneva, and Genesee][;] we regard it as highly important to the Southern churches that the act excluding these Synods should be approved of by them; and . . . we also regard all the efforts of those who are laboring to repeal these acts, as tending directly to promote the interests of Abolitionists."[83]

Seven years later, southern Baptists and Methodists also split from their northern codenominationalists. In both cases, the precipitating issue had to do with missions to the slaves. After truces in the early national period in which slaveholding and nonslaveholding interests had agreed not to use churches as battlegrounds, a vocal minority of northern abolitionists was again demanding—in each denomination—that slavery be deemed a sin. This made some unchurched slaveholders fear the soundness of southern evangelicals on slavery. Moreover, northern Baptists and Methodists refused to fund slaveholding missionaries, the very kind of minister whom white southerners considered most useful in spreading the Gospel among the slaves. The champions of the South's efforts to Christianize slaves and free blacks had become obnoxious in the eyes of northern evangelicals, making communion virtually impossible.

The Virginia Baptists who had helped shape the mission to the slaves after the Southampton Insurrection led the call for disunion of the national Baptist Triennial Convention. Baptists, opposed in principle to centralized authority, had agreed to form their first national body in 1814 only with the understanding that funding missionary work would be the sole purpose of the Triennial Convention, named in full the General Missionary Convention of the Baptist Denomination in the United States of America for Foreign Missions. In 1832, Baptists had formed the American Baptist Home Mission Society to complement the Triennial Convention and to support domestic outreach. For southerners, of course, the chief domestic project was the mission to the slaves, and slaveowners preferred for slaveholding missionaries to do that work. Members of the American Baptist Anti-Slavery Convention, formed in 1840, worked to prevent the commissioning of slaveholders as missionaries, an issue that came to a head in 1844. In response to a query by Alabama Baptists, the board of the General Convention acknowledged that it was opposed in principle to funding slaveholding missionaries. Jeter, the architect of Richmond First African Baptist's innovative system of governance and an enthusiastic supporter of the mission to the slaves, immediately fired off a letter on behalf of the Virginia Baptist Foreign Mission Society, in which he called for an independent southern Baptist convention, to meet in Augusta, Georgia, the following year.[84] If their national institutions would not support the most important work going on in their region, white southern Baptists wanted no part of them.

White southern Methodists were also frustrated that slaveholders were not receiving the support of their General Conference, and Virginia Methodists led the charge to ecclesiastical disunion in that denomination as well. Like the Baptists, Methodists were frustrated in part because slaveholding ministers were forced to operate as second-class clerics within the Methodist hierarchy. Slaveowners, for example, had to restrict their operations to territories with slavery or give up their slaves. Abolitionists could accept calls to any state, but slaveholders could not minister in the free states unless they first gave up their chattel. John S. Martin of Lexington, Virginia, received an appointment to work in Pennsylvania in 1840, and his fellow cleric John Ruff reminded him how high the cost would be for accepting it. He counseled Martin to tell his superintendent, " 'send me wehir you please except to Pennsylvania or other free state' until I am convinced that slavery is sinfull & whilst it is sanctioned by the civil government under which plan, no Ecclesiastical Tribunal shall deprive me of the use of them."[85]

White southern Methodists wanted to clarify their status in the church as full members by electing a slaveholding bishop who would validate the integrity of their actions toward black southerners. Sections of the Methodist *Discipline* passed in 1784 and 1800 forbade slaveowners to hold such a position of leadership, but that prohibition did not sit well with a people so intent upon expanding the mission to the slaves. White southerners lived in continual hope that William Capers, the Methodist pioneer of these missions, would be appointed bishop. They were sorely disappointed in the meetings of 1836 and 1840. In 1844, the elevation of Capers became a secondary issue, for a bishop since 1832, James O. Andrew, inherited slaves through his wife. Northern Methodists rammed through a resolution at the 1844 conference demanding that Bishop Andrew "desist" from the exercise of his duties until he divested himself of those slaves. Virginia Methodist William A. Smith had advocated disunion from the moment he accepted editorial responsibilities for the *Virginia Conference Sentinel* in 1836 and became apoplectic at the censure of Bishop Andrew. After Smith delivered an impassioned speech about the collapse of Methodist fraternity, Capers— soon to be named bishop in the ME Church, South—put forth a resolution to divide the General Conference along slaveholding lines.[86] Virginia Presbyterians were delighted that Baptists and Methodists had followed in their footsteps by protecting slavery and the mission to the slaves. In an article titled "Our Methodist Brethren," William Plumer of the *Watchman of the South* praised the schism. "We feel a lively interest in all that concerns this branch of the Church of Christ," he wrote. "Its recent difficulties have increased rather than diminished our regards for many of its members and ministers. Nor have we disguised our strong sympathy for the Southern portion of this church in their contest for their *rights*."[87]

After the denominational schisms, white evangelicals rededicated themselves individually and corporately to the task of converting the slaves. A South Carolina correspondent with the *Richmond Christian Advocate* explained the link between the mission and schism. "The great impediment of this heretofore," the writer suggested, "has been the large number of Northern preachers among us tinctured with Abolition doctrines, and the occasional perversion of their sacred trust to dangerous seditious purposes. The late separation of the Methodists and Baptists of the South, from those of the North, has had a most happy effect in dispelling the just suspicions of slaveholders, and opening the cabin doors every where throughout the South to the blessed influences of the Gospel—so much so, that he would seem blind indeed who could not doubt that the guiding Providence of God had directed it."[88] Methodist ministers also believed that the formation of a new, southern jurisdiction of their church would advance the mission to the slaves:

> The delegates of the conferences in the slaveholding States take leave to declare to the General Conference of the Methodist Episcopal Church that the continued agitation on the subject of slavery and abolition in a portion of the church, the frequent action on that subject in the General Conference, and especially the extrajudicial proceedings against Bishop Andrew, which resulted, on Saturday last, in the virtual suspension of him from his office as superintendent, must produce a state of things in the South which renders a continuance of the jurisdiction of that General Conference over these conferences inconsistent with the success of the ministry in the slaveholding States.[89]

Because it was the chief enterprise that distinguished them from their northern antagonists, evangelizing slaves and free blacks became even more important to white evangelicals in 1844 and 1845. Since the mission had become so interdenominational, this sentiment affected Presbyterians and Episcopalians as well.

On 13 May 1845, veterans of the mission met in Charleston to discuss ways to augment their existing work among the enslaved. Though Charlestonians had convened the meeting and most of those present were from South Carolina or Georgia, the conference made it a point to consider ideas from across the South. Attendees discussed nineteen letters from slaveowners in other states, and the progress made by evangelicals elsewhere was a key point of discussion. The participants in this famous meeting "on the Religious Instruction of the Negroes" recognized first and foremost that their crusade had become a regional one with the division of the nation's churches. They assumed correctly that the denominational schisms had created distance between northern and southern evangelicals but had narrowed the gap between different evangelical denominations within the South. The convention modeled an interdenominational approach to slave missions by quoting from authorities as diverse as Virginia Episcopalian William Meade, South Carolina Methodist William Capers, and Georgia Presbyterian Charles Colcock Jones. "What is particularly a subject of gratitude is, that *all denominations* of Christians are entering the field," they concluded. "It is wide enough for all. It lies at our own doors, and God in his Providence and holy word, has laid the duty upon us to cultivate it. We can anticipate nothing but his displeasure, if we neglect it. Indeed, we look upon the religious instruction of the negroes, as THE GREAT DUTY, and in the truest and best sense, THE FIXED, THE SETTLED POLICY OF THE SOUTH."[90]

Back in Virginia, white evangelicals had been engaged in the mission to the slaves for many years. They nonetheless tried to accelerate their efforts after the denominational schisms and the Charleston convention. It was as if white evangelicals knew that they could no longer blame any failures in the mission on abolitionist influence and were therefore anxious to produce a high yield of converts. Delegates to the Episcopal Church's 1845 annual convention ramped up existing programs geared toward African Americans. An influential committee of clerics and laymen, the Committee on the State of the Church, reminded the delegates in Richmond of "a matter of *more than common importance*, [such that] we cannot consent to pass it by altogether without notice—we mean *the religious instruction of our colored classes*, children and adults, bond and free."[91] Presbyterians undertook a battery of new activities at the presbytery level, particularly the establishment of more Sunday schools targeted at black Virginians. The Presbyterian Synod of Virginia also reiterated "the expression of its deep and abiding conviction that the religious instruction of our colored population is a subject of vast importance, claiming the persevering attention of christian masters."[92]

The real change came in the Methodist Church, which—along with the Baptist Church—began building more quasi-independent churches to replicate in as many other communities as possible the success of First African Baptist in Richmond. Even though the Charleston convention of experts on slave missions had actually suggested the wisdom of making "provision for their worshipping with the whites," white Virginia Methodists knew from the example of Richmond's First African Baptist that meeting the demands of blacks for independent worship was a more effective strategy for making African American converts.[93] White Virginia Methodists therefore began breaking large biracial churches into separate black and white congregations and founding new, all-back "mission" churches throughout the commonwealth. Methodists in Virginia never caught up with Baptists in terms of the number of black members, but black Virginians signaled their approbation of the new Methodist willingness to allow semiautonomous worship by joining at a faster rate than at any time since the 1780s.

White Methodists were creative in the strategies they used to create black mission churches. They planted new congregations in areas with a high black population, siphoned black members from multiple existing congregations to create a single black church, and split large biracial congregations in two. By the 1848 meeting of the Virginia Conference, Petersburg and Portsmouth each reported thriving African American congregations, and the Virginia Conference in that year sent Allen Carver to Durantsneck and Pasquotank just over the state line in northeastern North Carolina to set up mission churches. The next year, Carver could report only twenty accessions to his rural mission. Whites kept open Carver's missions despite the modest number of accessions and reaped extraordinary results. In 1851, Durantsneck and Pasquotank claimed 457 black members (and no whites). Meanwhile, black Methodists in nearby Norfolk separated into their own body with 815 members. Richmond Methodists, desirous of replicating the success of their coreligionists in other corners of the state and of their Baptist in-town neighbors, reported in 1855 the formation of an African American congregation in that city. For this purpose, whites pulled all 275 blacks out of Trinity, Centenary, Union, Wesley Chapel Mission, Oregon Mission, and Clay Street churches. Francis S. Mitchell, who died the following year, orchestrated this consolidation of the capital city's black Methodists by raising funds among the city's whites and constructing a church on Third Street.

Mission churches accounted for most, but not all, of the growth in Virginia's black Methodist population. W. P. Harrison, a denominational historian of the late nineteenth century, carefully documented the establishment of mission churches within the ME Church, South. According to his statistics, at the time of the denominational schism in 1844, Methodists tallied only two all-black missions in Virginia, compared with a high of sixteen in South Carolina. Commonwealth Methodists increased their funding for these quasi-independent churches over fortyfold between 1844 and 1861, far surpassing the tenfold increase in the ME Church, South, as a whole. By 1861, there were twenty designated African missions in Virginia, and these mission churches contained 4,492 African American members.[94] There were other accessions, though, in Methodist churches that did not have full-time missionaries or that remained technically biracial with a small proportion of whites. In 1859, the statistical high-water mark of the Methodist outreach to African American Virginians, the Virginia Conference alone listed 7,828 blacks in full membership, with 967 candidates for admission receiving instruction. This represented a remarkable increase of more than 1,000 souls from the previous year. More impressive than the raw numbers was the roll call of communities now committed to the idea of a separate black church. Communities in Richmond, Petersburg, Norfolk, and Portsmouth still flourished, but by then Randolph Macon College, Nottoway, Lunenburg, Brunswick, and Suffolk also claimed separate, successful black congregations.[95]

Virginia's African Americans flocked to newly segregated black Baptist churches in even greater numbers, ensuring that denomination's continued stranglehold on African American membership. In 1844, the Dover Association recorded 4,384 white and 8,142 African American members. Each year after that, members of quasi-independent black churches made up a greater percentage of the prominent association's total enrollment. In late 1843, whites reorganized the Williamsburg African Church that they had snuffed out of existence in 1831, and blacks from the old capital city filed their first regular annual report in 1849, showing 203 members. Richmond's Second African Church opened in 1846, followed in short order by the that city's Third and Fourth African churches. Elam continued to flourish during this period, and a new black mission at Chickahominy came online in 1859. In 1860, blacks in exclusively African American congregations comprised 5,511 of the Dover Association's 13,882 black members. Since the split from northern Baptists, black membership in the association had climbed by 5,740; white membership, by only 1,072. Put another way, African Americans made up 84 percent of converts in the South's most important Baptist association during the late antebellum period.[96]

Many black Virginians joined Dover Association churches because white Baptists were learning not to take for granted their dominance of slave missions. White Baptists became more intentional in their outreach following the breakup of their triennial convention and the Charleston convention. In 1846, members of the Richmond-based Dover Association formed the Committee on Religious Improvement of Colored People in order to coordinate the various programs of their member churches and to enhance their churches' capacity to attract African Americans.[97] In 1847, delegates at the association's meeting urged more attention to slaves. "To our denomination almost exclusively God has committed the spiritual interests of this class of people in our State," they recognized. But slaves, they confessed "are Baptists, without any effort on our part to proselyte them. It becomes us gravely to consider and promptly to meet the responsibility thus thrown on us by Divine Providence." White Dover Association Baptists elevated slave missions to the level of international missions as a cause for denominational financial support. "We support the gospel in foreign lands, at great expense of life and toil and treasure," they reasoned. "Why should we not care for the souls that are found in our own houses—that understand our own language —that are accessible to our instructions?"[98]

Even white Episcopalians ultimately proposed separate congregations for white and black worshippers once they became convinced that black Virginians were more likely to join quasi-independent churches. Episcopalians conceived of their denomination as more catholic in its nature, so the idea of a fragmented parish at first seemed anathema to them.[99] Despite their best efforts, however, Episcopalians consistently failed to bring blacks into full membership in their biracial congregations. Dozens of parish priests had long conducted special prayer services and Sunday schools for slaves and free blacks, but African Americans still numbered only 114 of the state's 7,762 communicants as late as 1861.[100] Episcopalians were willing to allow black proselytes to join other denominations, it is true, but black Virginians were shaming white Episcopalians by avoiding their churches so completely.

Assistant Bishop John Johns proposed solutions to the problem in the diocesan convention of 1860. Drawing inspiration from the previous year's convention in Richmond, he addressed the assembled clergy and laymen on the virtues of independent black congregations: "I was privileged, in common with several of the Bishops and other clergy, to address the large and interesting congregations of colored persons assembled in the Baptist and Methodist African Churches. We have no such congregations there or elsewhere in the Diocese," Johns reminded them, "and for our delinquency in this I should find it hard to furnish a satisfactory excuse. It is to be hoped that the movement on this subject in our own Convention, and the incipient measures adopted by the Clergy and some of the zealous laymen in Richmond, will, under God's blessing, tend to the formation of a colored congregation in that city, which may serve as a model to the rest of the Diocese." Johns then acknowledged the report of a committee appointed in 1858 "to inquire as to the best means of securing the permanent attachment of the colored population to our Church." The men on the Episcopalian committee presented the single clearest statement of the evangelicals' plan for slave missions in the interlude between the ecclesiastical and political secessions. Significant in the statement is the frank admission that African American Virginians were fundamentally shaping Episcopal policy:

Our move, then, if we would accomplish anything, becomes obvious. Keeping the law of the State distinctly in view, and carefully conforming to its provisions, we must give [African Americans] their own stated and separate service. In a number of places, and in a qualified manner, this has been tried, and with decided effect. The information furnished by the replies to the circulars, authorizes us to say that where one colored person attends worship in the parish Church, ten attend the separate service. This manifestation is not to be mistaken, and must not be disregarded in our arrangement for their religious instruction. If they are to be taught, their presence must be secured, and this, as the experiment has fully proved, cannot be effected to any extent without stated separate services.[101]

In those communities where whites acceded to black preferences and set up quasi-independent churches, slave and free black enrollment grew at an extraordinary pace. Between 65,000 and 70,000 of the state's 490,865 slaves and 58,042 free blacks had joined an evangelical church by 1860. This represented more than a 100 percent increase in black evangelical church membership from 1830—simply incredible given that a quickening internal slave trade kept the total number of slaves relatively constant (the slave population actually decreased 4 percent between 1830 and 1840 as a result of exportation). To be fair, Richmond blacks accounted for a large proportion of this increase, for 15,805 African American Richmonders had joined a church by 1859. These numbers, representing only adult full members, understate the proportion of Virginia blacks who actually fell under the direct influence of white churchmen in 1860.[102] On any given Sunday in the midst of the sectional crisis, one-half of the blacks in the commonwealth worshipped in evangelical churches maintained and nominally headed by (if not attended by) whites. The creation of separate black congregations and the increased resources devoted to slave missions brought Virginia whites a large measure of success in their campaign to bring the invisible church into the open. At the same time, this success increased white evangelicals' confidence that they had done the right thing by leaving national denominational organizations.

Not all Virginia whites were comfortable with all-black congregations, and Virginia's white evangelicals occasionally had to defend their mission work among the enslaved against criticism from within the commonwealth. This internal criticism ironically functioned to enhance the proslavery value of the mission, for white evangelicals sharpened their sense of self-righteousness by defending the mission against secular white critics. White evangelicals received just enough resistance to the mission to convince them that they were sacrificing themselves on behalf of black Virginians and in the name of Jesus. This conviction of self-sacrificial service to the enslaved blinded white evangelicals to the self-serving function that the mission actually played in the controversy about the injustice of slavery.

By 1850, more than half of white Virginians attended an evangelical church. A few of those unaffiliated with a Presbyterian, Methodist, Baptist (Southern Baptist Convention), or Episcopal church were members of other denominations in the Christian tradition, and many of the remainder would still have claimed allegiance to some form of Christianity. But there were still tens of thousands of whites in Virginia who did not attend church or who attended evangelical churches for social reasons but did not join or feel bound by the church's ethical teachings.[103] Members of this cohort offered real resistance to the mission to the slaves, both in their attempts to deny enslaved individuals access to evangelicalism and in their attempts to fight the institutional growth of black churches.

Some slaveowners in the 1850s refused to allow their slaves to go to church. Albert Jones, of Southampton County, remembered that his owner was reasonable in some ways, but that "you better never let mastah catch yer wif a book or paper, and yer couldn't praise God so he could year yer. If yer doen dem things, he sho' would beat yer."[104] Henry Box Brown and his brother talked to some slaves who claimed that their owner said "negroes have nothing to do with God" and who prevented them from receiving any sort of religious training.[105] Bethany Veney eventually found her way around her owner's opposition, but he took advantage of his position of power to try to keep her from church after she had a conversion experience. "But there came a time when Master David said he was not going to have me running to meeting all the time any longer," she recounted. "He had decided to send me up to old Mr. Levers, two miles away, there to stay until I should get over my 'religious fever,' as he called it."[106]

Sometimes more secular whites were in a position to try to restrict black religious expression among persons whom they could not claim as their property. This was especially the case in their opposition to quasi-independent black churches, which some whites feared would become incubators of insurrection. In 1852, Basil Manly wrote from Richmond to Charles Colcock Jones, "in consequence of an atrocious & fearful murder recently committed by a woman, who at that time unfortunately happened to be a member of the African church in this city." He was concerned that white residents would "deny & denounce all efforts for their evangelization, & the immediate & special effect may be to close the doors of the African churches," and he wanted to recruit help from the region's premier advocate of slave missions. Manly argued that "to close the African church because it was not gifted with omniscience to discern the suicidal character of this woman when she offered for membership or to detect her as unworthy of the confidence they as well as her master & mistress reposed in her . . . seems to me a hard lot."[107] White evangelicals often tried to convince their fellow citizens that evangelization did not carry with it a danger to public safety. William Plumer pleaded of the mission in an 1848 publication, "It is entirely safe to do this. No facts can be established to the contrary, and many can be established in support of this assertion."[108]

In Lynchburg, Baptist David Shaver also found himself defending the right of blacks to worship. In this case though, Shaver was taking on his fellow white evangelicals who thought that quasi-independent churches had become too autonomous—those within his denomination uncertain about the lengths to which white Baptists were going to recruit black members. Whites in Lynchburg's Baptist Church, which theoretically enjoyed oversight of the city's African Baptist Church, excommunicated every member of the African church when they disagreed about how the African Baptists had selected a new minister in 1853. Shaver went before the city council to redress the wrong he perceived that whites had done black residents of Lynchburg. "Sincerely believing it to be a Congregation of Christians which merits legal protection, he begs to be heard by you in a recital of facts and considerations which, as he conceives, establish this position beyond controversy," he pleaded. Shaver argued that Lynchburg's white Baptists were out of line with the practice of Baptists elsewhere in the state and tried to convince city officials that the majority of white Virginia Baptists would sustain the protest of their black coreligionists.[109]

Shaver spent a significant amount of time rebutting the idea that quasi-independent black churches inculcated insubordination. He argued that civil and ecclesiastical insubordination were different things, and that white evangelicals aggressively policed the first even while they accepted some ecclesiastical conflict. "That Church pronounced them insubordinate, simply as Baptists, not as slaves," he maintained. "Now, insubordination as slaves is a far more grave criminal and dangerous offence than insubordination as Baptists; and it is a fair and necessary conclusion that the Baptist Church confined her censures exclusively to the latter because she believed the members of the Afr. Ch. guiltless touching the former." In so many words, Shaver was defending the creation of all-black congregations as a legitimate tactic in the larger post-Turner effort to draw black Virginians out of the invisible church and under white supervision. He reminded the city council that whites still maintained supervision of all-black churches: "Now, the Strawberry Association has already decided that Afr. Chs. must at least be 'under the superintendence of a committee of male members of some regular Baptist church or churches.'" This policy was more than enough, he assured them, to protect against either physical or ideological insurrection. "Your memorialist knows Va. Baps. too extensively," he promised, "and the Strawberry Assoc. too well, to question for a moment whether the rights of owners and the interests of white churches are safe in such keeping."

White Virginia evangelicals fought not only those who tried to limit slave missions but also those who proposed what they regarded as unscriptural proslavery arguments. In the early 1850s, northern intellectuals advanced the theory that either nature or the deity had created blacks separate and inferior to whites. Though this "scientific" discovery, championed by Josiah Nott and Louis Agassiz, would plainly have strengthened the slaveholders' rhetorical position, white evangelicals could not accept it on biblical grounds, for scripture clearly stated that God made all men from common stock.[110] In retaliation against Nott and Agassiz, Bishop Meade encouraged one of his flock, James L. Cabell, to write a scientific manifesto supporting the biblical position of one creation. Cabell, professor of anatomy, physiology, and surgery at the University of Virginia, readily obliged. In his 1859 work, *The Unity of Mankind*, first published in an Episcopal magazine, he struck at the scientific roots of polygenesis theory.[111] Virginia's white evangelicals risked social censure by standing up to other whites who sought to deny the humanity of African Americans or prevent them from hearing the Gospel.

Black evangelicals were not fooled. They made the most of their ecclesiastical freedoms at the same time that they recognized and condemned the proslavery implications of the mission to the slaves. While there is much to say on the contours of black Christianity outside the scope of this book, suffice to say that African Americans distinguished between authentic Christianity and that offered by the missionaries. They did not believe that their enslavement was justified because it had facilitated their conversion.[112] Black resistance to the idea that God sanctioned slavery highlights an important paradox: On one hand, African American Virginians converted in such significant numbers to evangelical Protestantism that white evangelicals felt confident that slavery was just. On the other hand, blacks from the commonwealth energetically rejected the idea that slavery was part of God's plan. This paradox could only develop as a result of the relational distance between black and white believers that formed after 1831, a distance that was increasingly embodied in separate churches. In order to bring black bodies into their churches, white evangelicals relinquished some control over black souls. They stepped back and allowed black evangelicals to continue to recruit new members. This relative disengagement allowed the mission to succeed, while at the same time it allowed black converts in the late antebellum period to look on their white brethren with disdain.

Fugitives from slavery were the most effective critics of white evangelicals, and they articulated what those still in chains only whispered. Many who escaped slavery in Virginia had been deeply involved in an evangelical church, and they did not hesitate to criticize the proslavery elements of their churches once free of them. Anthony Burns, who created a national spectacle when he fled from slavery in the Old Dominion to Boston in 1854, offered the most humiliating critique. He gained national notoriety because of the lengths to which the U.S. government had to go to retrieve him from Boston under the strengthened Fugitive Slave Law of 1850. Boston free black minister Leonard Grimes sympathized with Burns's plight and led an effort to purchase Burns from slavery as soon as possible after he was returned to Virginia. Once free, Burns wrote to the Baptist church to which he had belonged in Fauquier County to transfer his membership to Boston. When whites at Fauquier instead excommunicated Burns, he issued a public letter that turned white teaching on slavery on its head: "You charge me that, in escaping, I disobeyed God's law. No, indeed!" he proclaimed. "That law which God wrote on the table of my heart, inspiring the love of freedom, and impelling me to seek it at every hazard, I obeyed; and, by the good hand of my God upon me, I walked out of the house of bondage."[113]

Other black evangelicals offered criticisms just as scathing. David West, for example, from the safety of Canada, was just as confident in his criticism of white evangelicals for their hypocrisy. "I look upon slavery as a disgrace, and as breaking the laws of God: that no man can keep the laws of God and hold to slavery," he declared. "I believe my own master was as good a man as there is in the whole South: I loved him in health, and I loved him in death,—but I can read the Bible, and I do not see any thing there by which he could be justified in holding slaves: and I know not where he has gone to."[114] The great puzzle is that Burns and West, each of whom wrote so confidently against proslavery evangelicals, broke bread with them while enslaved in Virginia and retained their faith in freedom. They were able to separate the silver from the dross of proslavery Christianity and to hear life-affirming promises of salvation while rejecting the idea that God approved of their bondage.

Black evangelicals still in bondage in Virginia could not communicate their disapprobation of proslavery evangelicalism as forcefully as Burns or West, but they did so in more subtle ways. Whites rarely commented directly on the day-to-day interactions in which black evangelicals criticized their integrity, but the testimony of one white Episcopalian is revealing. He confessed that black evangelicals maintained a set of values so different from whites' that black evangelicalism sometimes seemed a different religion. The most disturbing element of black evangelicalism, to this particular white evangelical, was the certainty with which black evangelicals rejected the morality of slavery. "Talk to him now about his evil doings, and quote the Bible to him," the writer explained, "and he will probably answer, 'Don't care about what you say is in the Bible, King Jesus is here,' (thumping his breast.) He will not listen to any advice as to his moral duties, for he is a saint and can't go wrong, being inspired. He looks upon his master and mistress as poor deluded creatures, out of the pale of salvation; nay, worse than that, as hypocrites, however pure their lives may be in comparison with his own."[115] Such encounters both showed the limits of black solidarity with white evangelicals and fueled the intensity with which white Virginians defended the mission.

In sum, African American Virginians responded to the ecclesiastical regulations that white evangelicals put in place after the Southampton Insurrection in a way that inadvertently deepened white evangelicals' belief that slavery was ordained of God. They forced whites to direct much more energy and attention to the process of recruiting black converts and facilitating black worship, a development that heightened tensions between white northern and southern evangelicals to the breaking point. They compelled whites to relax some of the restraints on black worship—and then joined evangelical churches in such numbers that whites determined that slavery was central to God's plan for their region. White evangelicals involved in mission work fallaciously concluded that the practice of slaveholding itself was a reason for the dramatic increase in black conversions. Whites erroneously linked slavery and conversion in part because, according to their paternalist ethic, the status of black Virginians as "servants" obligated white Virginians as "masters" to care for their spiritual and physical needs. In other words, the mission was an outgrowth of a particular ideology of slaveholding, not of the general scriptural mandate to "make disciples of all nations."[116] White evangelicals still hesitated to argue that slavery was a "positive good," but they approximated this position when they accepted that God was using slavery to accomplish great and noble ends.

Chapter Six

RELUCTANT, EVANGELICAL CONFEDERATES, 1856–1861

Let every soul be subject unto the higher powers. For there is no power but of God: the powers that be are ordained of God. Whosoever therefore resisteth the power, resisteth the ordinance of God: and they that resist shall receive to themselves damnation.

—Romans 13:1–2

Virginia's white evangelicals helped to start a regionwide campaign for slave missions when Nat Turner compelled them to rethink the relationship between slavery and evangelicalism. In the years following the Southampton Insurrection, southern whites traded strategies for Christianizing the remaining unchurched slaves in their respective states and built a regional identity around the role that they assumed as stewards of black evangelical development. But solidarity among southern white evangelicals on the mission to the slaves belied division on the probity of Confederate nationalism. Though they stood shoulder to shoulder with their coreligionists in the Lower South on the justice of slavery and on the need for ecclesiastical separation from northern abolitionists, white evangelicals in Virginia and the Upper South emphatically rejected secession until the eleventh hour. Unlike their counterparts in the Lower South, who believed by late 1860 that white southerners could best obey God by forming a sovereign, slave-holding republic, Virginia clergymen continued to preach the sinfulness of disunion until Lincoln called for troops to suppress what he classified as a rebellion. Articulating the Unionist position held by a wide majority of voting Virginians, evangelical leaders in the Old Dominion stressed the biblical obligation of citizens to honor the federal compact at the same time that they affirmed the justice of slavery.

Black evangelicals, who so strongly influenced how white evangelicals understood slavery and master-slave relations from the colonial period through the Civil War, play a less conspicuous role in this chapter. African

American Virginians do not fade into the background because they had no part to play in the secession crisis. As William Link has demonstrated, enslaved persons in the commonwealth actually had a great deal to do with secession. By fleeing bondage, committing acts of arson, and assaulting slaveowners, they made whites more anxious about the security of their property in persons and less tolerant of political threats to slavery.[1] Through individual and collective acts, in other words, African American actors continued to shape how white Virginians felt about slavery and about politics throughout the secession crisis and the subsequent war.

The emphasis in this chapter, though, is on Virginia's white evangelicals, because they acted on their proslavery convictions in such surprising ways during the secession crisis. After a century of close engagement with black coreligionists, the commonwealth's white evangelicals felt more confident than ever in the 1850s that God approved slavery. A generation of church-goers grew up with the mission to the slaves and internalized the lesson that God was using the peculiar institution for beneficial ends.[2] But most pro-slavery white evangelicals did not favor secession, for they considered slavery and secession completely separate moral issues. While they feared the concurrent rise of the Republican Party and increase in black violence as much as other white Virginians did, evangelicals felt bound by scripture to combat disunion rather than embrace it as the answer to their fears. Instead of being responsible for secession as many historians have suggested, pro-slavery evangelicals actually restrained it in Virginia and the critically important Upper South.[3]

An account of the proslavery, antisecession stance of white Virginia evangelicals reveals two truths about the sectional crisis. First, the particular ecclesiastical history of evangelical Virginians prepared them to accept civil debates over the future of slavery with more grace than could their coreligionists farther south. While white Virginians ultimately proved unwilling to tolerate federal interference with the peculiar institution, they recognized discussion about it as constitutionally legitimate. Second, white Protestants' long defense of the Union persuaded them that they held the moral high ground when they finally did secede in April 1861. By waiting to secede until after Lincoln requisitioned troops, Virginia politicians changed the way that their evangelical constituents understood the moral issues of the war. White Virginians ultimately fought for the right to expropriate the labor of black Virginians, but waiting to secede until Lincoln had already committed to the use of force against the Confederacy enabled them to understand their rebellion as just resistance to a tyrant.

White evangelicals were not Unionists because they were religious, but many of them did understand their Unionism in spiritual terms. Like other white Virginians, they considered the economic and material interests of their communities when deciding whether or not to advocate for secession. But evangelicals also believed that whatever political course of action they proposed had to be consonant with sound biblical teaching. Since scripture clearly enjoined followers of Christ to "be subject unto the higher powers," any evangelical who would advocate disunion had to be prepared to explain exactly how federal officials had abrogated the federal compact and thereby nullified the spiritual obligation to submit to their authority. Virginia Unionists, including those in the western portion of the state who had strong economic and political reasons to contest secession, recognized the salience of religious concerns regarding the obedience to authority and repeatedly emphasized the moral strength of their position.[4] They framed the decision whether or not to support disunion as a religious problem and shored up the Unionist sympathies of evangelicals in general.

Few scholars have acknowledged the profound reservations with which evangelicals in the Upper South approached secession, largely because they have failed to differentiate between the perspectives of evangelicals in the Upper and Lower South. In the standard narrative of how southern churchmen came to support the Confederacy—which they manifestly did—the same, few Deep South clerics tend to stand for the entire antebellum southern church, with Louisiana's Benjamin Palmer, Georgia's Stephen Elliot, and above all South Carolina's ubiquitous James H. Thornwell representing all of southern Christendom. Virginia's Robert Lewis Dabney is now a sometime member of this pantheon, but his presence only highlights another bias, the tendency for historians to allow sharp-penned Presbyterians, a distant third in terms of membership to the Baptists and Methodists, to stand in for all evangelicals.[5] This homogenization of white evangelicals' approach to secession is ironic in light of the sensitivity that scholars have shown toward Virginia's distinctive political and economic position. Historians have been willing to acknowledge that Virginia's mixed economy and the commonwealth's role as a net exporter of slaves made the economic interests of Virginians diverge from those of the Cotton South.[6] In accounts of southern churchmen during the antebellum years, however, Virginia evangelicals march in lockstep with their Deep South brethren, falling more in love with both slavery and southern nationalism annually. Though as committed to enslaved African labor as their Deep South compatriots, white evangelicals were not the commonwealth's most active disunionists. Instead they were among the most "reluctant" of Confederates.[7]

It is tempting to conflate white southerners' support for slavery and their commitment to southern nationalism. Since the 1960s, after all, scholars have recognized the Confederate States of America as the political apotheosis of white southerners' commitment to slavery. They have generally described an individual's commitment to slavery as the best indicator of his or her opinion on secession. Specifically, scholars have used the intensity of the pronouncements of clergy in defense of slavery to gauge the depth of their disunionist sentiment, even though developments in the political sphere show that proslavery could be compatible with a variety of orientations toward the Union. One leading scholar, for example, cited ministerial ambivalence over slavery as proof positive of clerical reservations about secession. "We are concerned here with the holdouts, as it were, the leaders of the more conservative denominations who saw clearly the perils of disunion," Bertram Wyatt-Brown stated. As evidence of Unionist sentiment, he then quoted not these clerics' ideas about secession, but their ideas about human bondage; "Far from endorsing slavery's positive goodness, Presbyterian and Episcopal ministers in particular sounded various themes on the subject. None was hostile, but few called it holy."[8] But, for white evangelical Virginians, there was no such relationship between proslavery and prosecession ideas.

The commonwealth's white evangelicals were solidly proslavery by the late antebellum period. There was no antislavery cohort among whites within Presbyterian, Baptist, Methodist, or Episcopal churches equivalent to that which had been present in the early national period. Those men and women had either died, moved, or found in the success of the mission sufficient evidence that slavery was ordained by God. In their place, a new generation of evangelical ministers who had come of age during the thriving years of the mission proudly proclaimed slavery's benefits. These men, most prominently Baptist Thornton Stringfellow and Methodist William A. Smith, but also lesser lights such as Presbyterian William Plumer and Episcopalian Philip Slaughter, composed for a regional audience some of the most important proslavery literature in American history.

Virginia's most important proslavery ideologue, Thornton Stringfellow, placed white evangelicals' mission to the slaves at the core of the pamphlets and books that he authored in the 1850s to defend slavery. "The South did not seek or desire the responsibility, and the onerous burden, of civilizing and christianizing these degraded savages," he explained in *Scriptural and Statistical Views in Favor of Slavery*, arguably the single most influential proslavery text of the antebellum period, "but God, in his mysterious providence, brought it about."[9] In his preliminary studies of the issue, first in the pages of the *Religious Herald* and then in the 1850 *Brief Examination of*

Scripture Testimony on the Institution of Slavery, Stringfellow had already laid out his four-part agenda. The first three goals would have made sense without the mission; the minister simply tried to establish a scriptural basis for slavery in both the Old and New Testaments. But the fourth goal, to prove "that it is full of mercy," was conceivable only in the context of whites' sustained efforts to minister to black men and women. As he explained, slavery "has brought within the range of gospel influence, millions of Ham's descendants among ourselves, who but for this institution, would have sunk down to eternal ruin; knowing not God, and strangers to the gospel. In their bondage here on earth, they have been much better provided for, and great multitudes of them have been made the freemen of the Lord Jesus Christ, and left this world rejoicing in hope of the glory of God."[10]

In making this argument, Stringfellow showed how the proslavery tendencies of the post-Turner mission to the slaves had matured into a full-blown proslavery argument. He was not content, as some in the early national period had been, to argue that evangelicals could make the most of a flawed institution by trying to proselytize slaves. Instead, he assumed that slavery in the Bible perfectly corresponded to American slavery. Moreover, he asserted that the status of black Americans as slaves was a *necessary* link in the chain that led to their conversion. Breaking that link, as abolitionists threatened to do, would disrupt the mission and probably result in the catastrophic loss of life. "An officious meddling with the institution, from feelings and sentiments unknown to the Bible, may lead to the extermination of the slave race among us, who, taken as a whole, are utterly unprepared for a higher civil state; but benefit them, it cannot," he warned. In other words, because so many men and women of African descent were slaves when they professed conversion and sought membership in an evangelical church, Stringfellow—like a generation of white evangelicals who grew up with the mission—accepted at least three theological falsehoods: that race-based slavery was biblical, that slavery was necessary for the conversion of people of African descent, and that black men and women could not on their own attain true conversion.

Other scholars have documented with greater theological sophistication how white southerners like Stringfellow misread scriptural teaching on slavery as a result of their racist assumptions. Mark Noll explained that "one of the strongest indications of the prevailing racism of the mid-nineteenth century was that Bible expositors could not get Americans to take as seriously what Scripture said about the color of biblical slaves as what it said about slavery itself."[11] The success of the mission enabled this faulty hermeneutic. White evangelicals' glib use of scripture to justify an oppressive system seems opportunistic today, but white evangelicals—particularly in states like Virginia where the mission was so successful—had experiential reasons to think that God was using slavery. On any given day, they encountered more black converts to proslavery evangelicalism than they did white critics of their proslavery faith. Virginia Presbyterian William Plumer was thus only articulating the prevailing view when he explained that "the first step in the providence of God toward an amelioration of the spiritual condition of the negro race, was their dispersion among other races of mankind."[12]

Stringfellow and Plumer were not the only Virginians to participate in the regional elaboration of a defense of slavery based on the mission. Methodist William A. Smith also made the mission the cornerstone of his proslavery stance, best articulated in his *Lectures on the Philosophy and Practice of Slavery*. He did not publish these lectures until 1856, though he had been forging them for years in the classroom at Randolph Macon, where he educated young men for the ministry. In thirteen lectures, Smith mobilized several different arguments in defense of slavery, but his trump cards were the same as Stringfellow's and confirmed the emerging consensus among white, southern evangelicals that slavery was ordained by God. Like Stringfellow, Smith reasoned that slavery was necessary to facilitate black conversions and that African Americans would not be able to attain either Christianity or civilization on their own. As an alternative to abolitionism, which he dismissed as unworkable and dangerous, Smith offered the mission:

If any in the whole country be moved with sympathy for the race—as many think themselves to be—let them diffuse the charities of a pure gospel through the whole extent of our country. No field was ever more "white to the harvest," and none perhaps in which laborers could be employed to greater advantage in the cause of humanity. They will promote a charity which shall save the country from discord and civil war. They will give efficiency to those precepts of the Scriptures which enjoin the duties of masters and slaves. By doing this they will lighten the task of masters, and, at the same time, interest them more deeply in all that concerns the welfare of the slave. They will greatly improve the physical comfort of the slaves, and, what is of far greater importance, they will develop their moral natures, and therein add to their present cheerful and contented state, the enjoyment of that religion which, as it fits them for the higher walks of life on earth, at the same time fits them for the rest of heaven. In a word, they will effect all that the most devoted friend of the slave can reasonably desire.

Lest any object that the mission might succeed among a free people as well as an enslaved people, Smith echoed Stringfellow's unscriptural gloss on why slavery was necessary to accomplish conversion. He took the example of free blacks to "prove" that freedom did not advance either the Gospel or African Americans' material interests. "They are not prepared for self-government and therefore can derive but little, if any, benefit from its political and social advantages," he argued. "The crushing weight of ages of barbarism still presses heavily upon the intellect of the African, and in his present circumstances, to say the least, he is too feeble to rise. It is the accident of his position that he is free, and not the law of his intellectual and moral nature that makes him so. He is a slave in fact; and without the restraints of the domestic system, the tendencies of his barbarous nature are left, in a good degree, to take their downward way."[13]

Episcopalian Philip Slaughter's *Virginian History of African Colonization*, published in 1855, made the same arguments about the spiritual efficacy of slavery in the context of a history of colonization. Bishop William Meade had an enormous influence on Slaughter and strongly encouraged him to enter the Virginia Theological Seminary in 1833. At this time, Meade himself was retreating from his earlier enthusiasm for colonization because the program was losing its benevolent character. In contrast, Slaughter, who began his training as an evangelical minister in the heady beginnings of the mission to the slaves, embraced colonization precisely because he did not think that it was an antislavery enterprise. He praised the wisdom of "all-wise Providence, in permitting the black man to be brought here and subjected to the disciplines of slavery tempered by christianity, and regulated by law." Slaughter "unequivocally and indignantly" denied that colonizationists had any intention to free slaves and concerned himself only with the removal of free blacks, to whom he referred as "miserable creatures." Colonization was worthy of evangelical patronage, Slaughter argued, because it paired a desperate American problem—the presence of free blacks—with a benevolent evangelical solution, the conversion of Africa. Slaughter was almost hysterical in his repetition of the central thesis of his history, that colonization did not threaten slavery: "I repeat: In America, the black man never can be free!—he never can have the high-born feelings of a freeman,—he must ever be a political and social slave."[14]

A generation of Virginia's white evangelicals had grown up with the mission and had incorporated it into their justification of slavery. It would be very inappropriate to identify these clerics with the "Young Virginians" whose antebellum careers Peter Carmichael traced in his illuminating study: Stringfellow was born in 1788; Plumer and Smith, in 1802; and

Slaughter, in 1808. These evangelicals were all seasoned adults by the late antebellum period. They shared in common the experience of the mission to the slaves and the fact that during their tenure as ministers of the Gospel the proportion of black church members had more than doubled. Like their brethren in the Deep South, they approved of the mission and of African slavery.

White evangelical Virginians also agreed with evangelicals in the Deep South in their apprehension of the moral issues at stake in secession. Evangelical and nonevangelical Christians in all regions of the country believed that disunion and disobedience to civil authorities were sinful, unless some other party abrogated the federal compact and thereby released them from the obligation of submission. As devout Virginia Episcopalian William C. Rives explained before Richmond's Young Men's Christian Association in 1855, this belief came straight from scripture. Referring to Paul's injunction in Romans 13, he reminded his auditors of the reasons for obedience to civil authority in Holy Writ: "To the citizen it says, 'let every soul be subject to the higher powers, for the powers that be are ordained of God. Ye must needs be subject, not only for wrath, but also for conscience sake.'"[15] White, southern evangelicals professed this belief with almost complete unanimity, and it made Unionists of even future Confederate champions like South Carolina's James H. Thornwell well into the sectional crisis.[16] Geographic origin, in short, did not distort white evangelicals' apprehension of the moral issues relevant to the act of secession.

White evangelicals in the Upper and Lower South may have believed the same scriptural principles were at stake in secession, but they inhabited different political economies and therefore applied those scriptural principles to different situations. Clerics and laypeople in each subregion believed that if one party to the Constitution willfully broke its provisions, then the other party was no longer morally obligated to continue to submit to the federal compact. But ecclesiastical authorities did not consider themselves political experts and therefore relied on their elected officials to inform them of any such constitutional breach. Political leaders in the Upper and Lower South, for reasons beyond the scope of this book, gave their constituents different information on whether or not northerners had violated the national charter. Because a majority of Virginia congressmen and senators staged a spirited defense of the Union in its hour of peril while representatives from the Lower South conceded its early demise, the evangelicals amid their constituents reached different conclusions about when secession became a viable moral option.

Evangelicals in the Cotton South followed the judgment of their political leaders in considering the election of Lincoln sufficient evidence of a violation of the Constitution to warrant secession.[17] Georgia congressman Howell Cobb, author in 1856 of a *Scriptural Examination of the Institution of Slavery in the United States*, used profoundly religious language to discuss Lincoln's election. He believed that the elevation of a man who threatened the right of white southerners to expand slavery had destroyed the federal compact: "The broken Constitution and violated compact formed the only Union we ever recognized; and if you would still have us to love and preserve it, restore to it that vital spirit of which it has been robbed by your sacrilegious hands, and make it again what our fathers made it—a Union of good faith in the maintenance of constitutional obligations."[18] The editor of the *Daily Constitutionalist* in Augusta, Georgia, agreed that the Union was defunct. "Having failed to secure them in a Union where a controlling majority is against us," he intoned, "we must, as prudent men, seek new guards for future security."[19] Newspaper editors throughout the Lower South insisted that southerners did not owe allegiance to a Republican administration and interpreted the votes cast for Lincoln as votes against the South's rights and against the Constitution. A contributor to the *New Orleans Crescent* proclaimed, "The Northern people, in electing Mr. Lincoln, have perpetuated a deliberate, cold-blooded insult and outrage upon the people of the slave-holding states."[20]

Presbyterian Benjamin Palmer, in a sermon titled *The South: Her Peril and Her Duty*, offered from his New Orleans pulpit on 29 November 1860 guidance for how people of faith should respond to Abraham Lincoln's election. Palmer based his polemic on the interpretation offered by Lower South politicians that Lincoln's election itself was an unconstitutional attack on slavery. As his starting point, Palmer took it for granted that the constitutional compact had been broken. In the absence of a continuing moral obligation to obey federal authorities, for Palmer at least, the choice was clear. In language familiar to evangelical readers from Stringfellow, Smith, and others, Palmer claimed that "no calamity can befall [black southerners] greater than the loss of that protection they enjoy under this patriarchal system." He then leaped from the widely shared belief that God was using slavery for good to the more extreme contention that white southerners therefore had a particular responsibility to sustain the institution against all challengers. Slavery's functionality in the mission, in other words, made its defense against Republican threats a sacred obligation.

In a way, Palmer and some other white evangelicals from the Lower South did connect support for slavery and support for secession. The more passionate they felt about slavery, the more zealous they were to guard their constitutional rights to its practice. Palmer even concluded it was "the nature and solemnity of our present trust, to *preserve and transmit our existing system of domestic servitude, with the right, unchallenged by man, to go and root itself wherever Providence and nature may carry it.*" He added words to steel his countrymen for battle: "This trust we will discharge in the face of the worst possible peril. Though war be the aggregation of all evils, yet, should the madness of the hour appeal to the arbitration of the sword, we will not shrink even from the baptism of fire. If modern crusaders stand in serried ranks upon some plain of Esdraelon, there shall we be in defense of our trust. Not till the last man has fallen behind the last rampart, shall it drop from our hands; and then only in surrender to the God who gave it."[21] One Virginian acknowledged that Palmer's address had created "a very great sensation in the South," and the idea that white southerners had an obligation to protect the social arrangements under which so many of African descent had converted resonated with many. Palmer had rightly gauged the judgment of politicians in his adopted state of Louisiana that the Union was broken; South Carolina, Louisiana, and the five other states of the Deep South seceded in short order. But white, evangelical Virginians heard a more optimistic political report from their leaders and, unlike Palmer, therefore still considered secession immoral in late 1860. They agreed with Palmer that God was using the mission but could not accept his contention that the southern states would be justified in seceding.[22]

In the Upper South, evangelical whites followed the lead of their own political leaders and warned against secession. They were alarmed at Lincoln's election but were not convinced that white northerners had violated the Constitution by choosing him as president. The Constitution would remain the law of the land in Virginia unless and until the Lincoln administration used the force of arms to exert its will over the slave states. In their willingness to remain in the Union, Virginia's white evangelicals were not somehow forfeiting their interest in slavery. Men like Stringfellow and Smith were not backing off from their unqualified endorsement of slavery's benefits, but they were hoping that the president would keep his promise to adhere to the letter of the Constitution and refrain from interfering with slave property as it then existed. In the Upper South, whites were prepared to fight to protect slavery, but they did not yet believe that it had come to that.

Enough of Virginia's elder statesmen were optimistic that Lincoln would not break the Constitution that the state's clerics remained decisively Unionist long after the initial excitement of the election had passed. Based on the information provided by men such as William C. Rives, the most prominent Virginia politician of his generation, a majority of the commonwealth's evangelicals still believed the Constitution to be a binding document even after the secession of the Lower South. As he had in a May 1859 speech in the city of Richmond, Rives constantly assured Virginians that Republicans would not transgress constitutional safeguards for slavery. He boasted, "The supreme judicial tribunal of the United States has, by its solemn and irreversible judgments, surrounded the rights and institutions of the South, in the only points in which they have ever been supposed to be open to invasion, with an impassable wall of defence."[23] John Minor Botts, like Rives, was a Virginia Whig who fought for the Union. The national Whig Party was defunct by the late 1850s, and men like Rives and Botts joined together in an "Opposition" party in Virginia that restrained the more secessionist impulses of Virginia Democrats. Enough moderate Democrats, including Governor John Letcher, also believed that secession was unwarranted to give these Unionists a decisive majority.[24] Botts agreed with Rives that Republicans possessed odious views but had not shown any bad faith in their adherence to federal laws. "If there is no violation of the Constitution," he reminded Virginians, "you have no right to withdraw as a member of the body."[25]

Though some prominent Virginians were pessimistic about the Union and, like Edmund Ruffin, thought the Constitution long abrogated, a majority of statesmen believed that the crisis would pass peacefully. In his inaugural address on 7 January 1861, Governor Letcher suggested a national convention to negotiate a solution to the sectional conflict, and former president John Tyler published a more detailed proposal for what became the Peace Conference on 17 January. At the Virginians' request, a total of 132 delegates from 21 states convened in Washington, D.C., to seek a diplomatic solution to the debate over slavery's place in the nation. Most delegates favored the constitutional solution advanced by Kentucky senator John J. Crittenden, in which new amendments would guarantee slavery's future.[26] William C. Rives served as one of Virginia's five delegates to the Peace Conference and expressed his confidence to Virginians that their Constitution, the Union, and their slaves could all be saved. On 8 March 1861, Rives traveled to Richmond to report on the proceedings of the conference in person and assured his constituents that "by the proposed plan, every possible approach by which the rights and interests of the South could be threatened or assailed—every conceivable avenue through which the agitation of the slavery question could be renewed—is forever cut off and hermetically closed." He ended this particular speech with a sound evangelical flourish, a reference to Matthew 19:6: "What God has joined together, let no man put asunder."[27]

Based on the confidence of so many Virginia statesmen in a negotiated, constitutional solution to partisan conflict, evangelical clerics could not conclude that the Union had expired and could not agree with Palmer that secession was necessary. They therefore continued to demand obedience to the federal government for months into 1861. While white evangelicals in the Lower South advocated secession as a necessary step to protect slavery and the mission against an unconstitutional tyrant, those in the Upper South threw their support behind efforts to achieve peace while simultaneously preserving slavery. In an attempt to soothe sectional tensions after South Carolina had already seceded, one of Richmond's Presbyterian pastors, Robert Lewis Dabney, circulated "A Pacific Appeal to Christians" through the *Central Presbyterian* in January 1861. Several dozen leading Presbyterian ministers, sundry representatives of other denominations, and faculty members of the University of Virginia, the Virginia Military Institute, and Washington College also signed Dabney's decidedly Unionist letter. "All Southern Christians would deplore an unnecessary rupture of the Federal Union bequeathed to us by our heroic sires, as marring their glorious work, and showing ourselves unworthy of their inheritance . . . as covering the claims of American Christianity and republicanism with failure and disgrace before the world," the evangelicals declared.[28] The *Religious Herald* also did yeoman's work for the cause of Unionism. It ran repeated editorials about the costliness of war and printed a call for a January fast day, in hopes that "God may avert the judgments which our national iniquities have provoked."[29]

While they worked for the Union, however, these pastors warned against what Presbyterian Moses Drury Hoge called the "insane doctrine of coercion," which they understood would void the Constitution. They informed their flocks that any application of force by the federal government against a seceded state would signal the formal end of the constitutional compact and the beginning of rule by arms.[30] Even the Methodist *Richmond Christian Advocate*, the most bellicose denominational paper in Virginia, warned against coercion as late as 4 April 1861 rather than calling for immediate secession. The editors thought that it was still theoretically possible to prevent white northerners from violating the Constitution, though they feared the worst. The Methodists "argued that wise and peaceful behaviour might result in the prosperity of the land, and warned their Northern opponents that belligerent talk, so incompatible with the character of a christian journal, would only result in evil." At the same time they called for restraint on all sides, the Methodist editors also "defended the institution of Slavery upon Scripture grounds" and warned against coercion. They would not tolerate "those who would in the name of Christ draw the sword against their brethren."[31]

The tone of the *Richmond Christian Advocate* was antagonistic by April 1861, but the position was essentially the same conditional Unionist position that white evangelicals advocated from the beginning of the secession crisis. Some evangelicals leaned to secession, and others to union, but most agreed that secession was unwarranted unless Lincoln tried to use force against any of the seceded states—or until all constitutional methods of resolving questions about slavery's future had failed.[32] Baptist minister Jeremiah Bell Jeter belonged in the more southern nationalist camp, but even he did not think that Lincoln's election was sufficient cause to secede. As he explained to a South Carolina correspondent on 11 December 1860, "The sentiment of Virginia at the close of the presidential election was decidedly in favor of maintaining, if possible, the rights of the South in the Union; or failing to secure them, to leave it in concert with the Southern States."[33] One of the state's most Unionist papers, the *Charlottesville Review*, appealed to evangelical Virginians' moral sensibilities when rallying support against secession in January 1861. "We consider that we are citizens of the United States, and owe an allegiance to the Federal Government," they proclaimed. "Any resistance to the Federal authority we regard as rebellion."[34]

There is some evidence that evangelicals' commitment to obeying duly constituted authority, instead of simply reinforcing existing Unionist sympathies, may have actually held back secessionist desires. Episcopalian Nathaniel Beverly Tucker, a Winchester, Virginia, native serving in England as the consul of the United States, was a southern patriot. "Do you suppose that in the broad limits of the Southern Country there is a more loyal man to the South and her institutions than Bev Tucker?" he asked his brother in January 1861. "I will talk for them, write for them, fight for them and die for them as quick as any other they can trot out." Tucker, the father and grandfather of Episcopal bishops, did not think that Virginia had any right to secede, however. "Lincoln's election is constitutionally valid," he argued, "though he is a *sectional* candidate of the worst stripe. We entered into the fight with him—we met him upon the field—we acknowledged him worthy of our lance—*he* was victorious—we must abide the issue until *new cause* of quarrel arises."

Like most other Virginians, Tucker also believed that coercion was wrong and that slavery was right. In fact, his bedrock conviction of slavery's benevolence informed his thinking about secession. Since slavery was safe in the Union as long as Lincoln kept his promise not to touch the institution where it then existed, Tucker thought that Virginia would be foolish to risk the destruction of slavery by seceding. "Let me add," he wrote at the end of his exposition of the moral and political concerns surrounding secession in Virginia, "that it is because I love slavery & approve it & justify it, in all its relations moral, social, religious & humane, as elevating the master & ameliorating the condition of the slave—that I wish to see the *Union preserved if* it can be with honor to the South. Mark me—if the Union is broken up—the death knell to slavery in the South is, in time, sounded. . . . Keep this letter and see if I am not right."[35]

Theologically astute secessionists within Virginia clearly understood the spiritual concerns of Virginia Unionists. They therefore focused their arguments for disunion on the idea that the Union was already broken, and that Virginians like Tucker sympathetic to the formation of a southern nation therefore had no moral obligation to wait for an "overt act" on Lincoln's part before joining the Lower South. In the first of four anonymous essays promoting secession, Richmond lawyer James Lyons directly confronted the question, "Have the Southern States a Right to Secede?" Lyons stated the problem clearly: "It is said by some that the election of Lincoln is not sufficient cause for resisting, and we must wait for an *overt act*. But this doctrine is, I submit, founded in a total misconception of the case and want of just perception of the concrete ill which the election of Lincoln presents, and of the meaning of the very thing which the objectors call for, to wit, an overt act." He then reminded his readers "that the violation of the constitution by one section, absolves every other from its obligation to that constitution, and the government created by it." Since this abstract approach failed, Lyons in his next essay gave more attention to specific violations of the Constitution in an effort to convince Unionists that secession was already a morally viable option. He reminded Virginians that, before the Revolution, their forebearers had complained that the British were " 'enticing our slaves, by every artifice, to leave us, and then turning them against us.'" Jefferson considered Dunmore's proclamation a violation of the unwritten British constitution, Lyons reminded readers; did not abolitionists' actions represent a violation of the U.S. Constitution? "Has not this been done again, and again, and again—nay, have not our citizens been beaten, imprisoned and slain, in the effort to recover their property which has thus been enticed away from their owners? And have they not done more than 'turn them against us,' by hiring men to invade our soil, slay our people, incite our slaves to insurrection, burn our houses, and (in Texas) poison our springs. Could the devil and his legions if let loose upon us, commit more overt acts of deadly hate and war than these?"[36]

Secessionists did not convince enough evangelicals that the Constitution was already abrogated to move the state into the Confederacy with the first wave of secessions. Evangelical pastors successfully reinforced the political sentiments of cautious Virginia politicians, and the state remained decisively Unionist throughout the spring of 1861. In a special election called by the General Assembly, voters in the Old Dominion were able to show exactly how they felt about secession on 4 February 1861. Citizens on that day voted on two issues: they selected delegates for a statewide constitutional convention and signified whether or not they would require the convention to submit any proposed constitutional changes to a popular vote. Since South Carolina and its sister states in the Deep South had already seceded, voters knew that the constitutional convention would have to decide Virginia's place in the Union in addition to addressing long-standing constitutional disputes between the state's eastern and western interests. In an overwhelming rebuff to secessionist forces within the state, Virginians elected only about 30 outright disunionists out of 152 representatives to what became known as the "secession convention."[37]

Virginia's white evangelicals retained hope for the Union in part because they believed that it was appropriate for civil bodies to discuss slavery. In the early national period, they had channeled debates over slavery out of their sanctuaries and into the civil sphere. As recounted in Chapter 2, white members of all of the major denominations expelled the discussion of slavery from their ranks in order to promote internal harmony. Virginia Baptists, Methodists, and Presbyterians had each decided before the War of 1812 that the civil government had the exclusive prerogative to legislate on slavery.[38] Denominational leaders at no time suggested that the civil government was under any particular obligation to maintain the institution of slavery or to work for its abolition, only that slavery was in the Bible and therefore its continued existence was a civil rather than a moral issue. Some evangelicals even signed petitions calling for legislative action on slavery in the 1780s and 1790s, and evangelicals had generally affirmed the state's right to consider the issue in the session following Nat Turner's insurrection in the winter of 1831–32. Evangelicals in the Upper South, in sum, approved of slavery but acknowledged the right of the civil government to discuss the issue. It is true that by "civil government," white evangelicals most often meant the state government. But since Republicans only campaigned for nonextension and promised not to interfere with states' domestic institutions, white evangelicals in the Upper South tolerated even them.

The slave states of the Deep South had no analog to the turbulent period of antislavery agitation in Virginia in the early national period, with the result that they did not cultivate a similar tolerance for the discussion of slavery in the civil sphere. By the time evangelical settlers poured into the new Gulf States in the 1820s and 1830s, both the church and the institution of slavery had changed. Even transplanted northern clerics in the Presbyterian, Methodist, Baptist, and Episcopal churches knew better than to recommend abolition to their congregations in the Lower South, largely because the rapid spread of cotton production had made slavery profitable beyond any expectation and made the institution's boosters in the cotton-producing states ever more convinced of its desirability. While they entered ecclesiastical communion with Upper South evangelicals, whites in new Deep South churches had little personal and almost no institutional memory of internal discussions over slavery. Never having debated slavery within their own walls, churchmen therefore never banished debate to the statehouse, where it would not interfere with communal worship. White evangelicals in the Deep South never fixed an appropriate "space" for conversation about slavery.

To say that evangelicals from the Lower South lacked an ecclesiastical history of discussion about slavery is, in part, another way of saying that whites constructed polities there almost exclusively for the purpose of extending slave-based plantation agriculture. With the exception of Louisiana, where whites had a long and complex relationship with slavery and slaves, and Georgia, where idealistic proprietors had at first tried to keep slavery at bay, whites in general moved into the Lower South already enthusiastic about slavery and its economic benefits.[39] Not only did residents of the Lower South never discuss the possibility of emancipation as openly as had Virginians in the late eighteenth century and again in 1831, but they also lacked significant numbers of free blacks. Free blacks were an enduring, experiential reminder of paths not taken; their presence was a testimony to antislavery activism in Virginia's past and to the absence of such a history in the Lower South. Whereas 12.8 percent of blacks in the Upper South were free in 1860 (10.6 percent in the state of Virginia), only 1.5 percent of blacks in the Lower South were free.[40] When white evangelicals from the Upper and Lower South forged new sectional jurisdictions in the schisms of the 1830s and 1840s, Lower South evangelicals urged the new denominational bodies to adopt their more aggressively proslavery position. The ME Church, South, for example, went further than Virginians ever had and boldly declared that the practice of slaveholding was beyond the reach of *any* authority, ecclesiastical or civil. "We wholly disclaim any right, wish, or intention to interfere with the civil and political relation between master and slave," they resolved; "we consider the subject as having been put beyond the legislation, by the General Government."[41]

Virginia's white evangelicals, even after they cast their lot ecclesiastically with those less forbearing of antislavery voices, continued to tolerate more discussion of slavery in Washington than did their brethren in the Lower South. The commonwealth's Unionists doggedly insisted that mere conversation about the institution could not hurt them, even though conversation alone terrified many farther South. Botts, for one, urged Virginians not to worry about northern hostility to the peculiar institution until the Republicans put concrete actions behind their threats of interference. When Republicans' republication of Hinton Helper's *Impending Crisis of the South* caused a stir among southern nationalists in 1860, Botts tempered their rage with a reminder that Helper was impotent actually to separate a single slave from his master. "When they come here to take control of my domestic concerns, or attempt a practical interference with them, it will be quite time enough for me to find a remedy—it is always at hand, and it is not necessary to arm the State against Mr. Helper, Mr. Helper's book, or any sixty-eight endorsers of that or any other book in print."[42] As a result of their particular ecclesiastical history, white Virginia evangelicals were more willing to believe that words alone could not dissolve the federal compact and awaited coercive action before pronouncing the Union dead.

The case of Virginia Methodists in the Baltimore Conference illustrates how the state's white evangelicals tolerated civil but not ecclesiastical action against slavery. When southern Methodists withdrew from the ME Church and formed the ME Church, South, in 1844, a significant number of Virginia residents remained in conferences affiliated with the ME Church (i.e., the northern branch of the church). In 1850, there were 42,822 white Virginians and 6,128 black Virginians affiliated with the ME Church, South. There were about half as many of each affiliated with the ME Church, 25,253 whites and 3,835 blacks. The Baltimore Conference presented an especially fascinating situation, because it included members from both slave and free states and contained more slaves and slaveowners than any other conference in the ME Church. There were 12,048 white and 2,969 black Virginians in this somewhat anomalous jurisdiction.[43] As a result of this uniquely charged situation, Methodists in this unusual body learned to balance antislavery and proslavery sentiments very early, decades before the 1844 schism. They did not allow slaveowners to be preachers, but neither did they expel them from fellowship or label slaveholding a sin. This settlement differed from that adopted by other Virginia evangelicals in its prohibition of slaveholding ministers; otherwise, members of the Baltimore Conference had also agreed to disagree on the justice of slavery and to scrupulously abstain from discussion of the topic. In 1857, an antislavery minister complained, "It is true that they helped to suspend Harding for holding slaves; but when you come to touch the Methodist laity for holding slaves, that is quite another matter. To this they are as inflexibly adverse as Wm. A. Smith. They are opposed to discussion, to free speech on the subject."[44] While they were "inflexibly adverse" to any ecclesiastical conversations about slavery, however, members of the Baltimore Conference proved devoted to the Union, even when slavery was bitterly contested in national councils.

The Baltimore Conference self-consciously occupied a middle ground between northern and southern branches of the church. Members believed that avoidance of any discussion about slavery was the key to fellowship (among whites) and wanted to model harmonious, intersectional relations for their coreligionists. In 1843, members of the Baltimore Conference concerned about the possibility of a coming schism promised "to serve as a beacon of light, elevated far above the stormy elements of contention, and strife which are unhappily around her, by most bitter controversies concerning abolition and proslavery."[45] The conference continued to grow under this policy under the auspices of the ME Church, and by 1860 there were roughly 19,000 Virginians in the conference, including 15,000 whites and 4,000 blacks.[46] Virginia members of the Baltimore Conference continued in their precarious position until May 1860, when delegates to the ME Church's General Conference passed a resolution that condemned slavery as a sin. As a practical consequence of this resolution, slaveholding members of the Baltimore Conference would have to give up their slaves or forfeit their church membership.

In local meetings throughout the conference's jurisdiction, Virginia Methodists met to protest the resolution against slaveholding, which clearly violated their commitment to avoid discussion of the practice. Many whites, including those from the Methodist church at Staunton, emphasized their willingness to continue in fellowship with antislavery members of the Baltimore Conference but not with the ME Church. The Staunton group expressed their "continued and unabated confidence in the Baltimore Conference," in fact. But they could not stand the larger church's interference with their domestic institutions and resolved "that the time has fully come for a separation of the Baltimore Conference from the jurisdiction of the General Conference."[47] Slaveholding Methodists and those in the conference sympathetic to their interests penned statements at the annual meetings of both clergymen and laymen that amplified the Staunton group's concerns. Preachers speculated that they might still respect northern bishops but that they would no longer have anything to do with the General Conference. "This act of the General Conference," they claimed, "has destroyed its jurisdiction over the Annual Conferences, no one of which is bound by any of its legislative enactments."[48]

Laymen expressed even more clearly the conviction that the General Conference had gone too far in discussing slavery and swore they would not participate in any ecclesiastical council where slaveholders were forced to defend themselves against charges of sinfulness. "The Baltimore Conference has, by unanimous vote, again and again assured our people," they reminded area Methodists, "that it disclaimed having the least sympathy with abolitionists; that, on the contrary, it was determined not to hold connexion with any ecclesiastical body that made nonslaveholding a condition of membership in the Church, and that it was opposed to any inquisition in to the motives underlying the relation of master and slave. The people now demand a fulfillment of these pledges."[49] As had their southern neighbors in 1844, white Virginians in the Baltimore Conference demanded ecclesiastical separation when their codenominationalists tried to deprive them of their right to hold slaves. The result was the creation of two Baltimore Conferences: one based in Maryland, tolerant of abolition, and loyal to the ME Church, and one based in Virginia, proslavery, and in sympathy with the ME Church, South (which it would finally join in 1866).

Whites in the Virginia branch of the Baltimore Conference became ardent Unionists after their ecclesiastical division, demonstrating the difference between proslavery Christianity and southern nationalism. Six months after they voted nearly unanimously for ecclesiastical secession, in February 1861, white Virginians from the Baltimore Conference went to the polls to select delegates for the constitutional convention. This time they voted overwhelmingly in favor of Union—political union. Alexandria, Fairfax, and Jefferson each boasted Methodist churches of more than 400 members, and Augusta County contained over 600 Methodists associated with the Baltimore Conference. Voters from these four areas where Baltimore Conference Methodists made up a significant portion of the electorate chose 7 of the 152 men who attended the 1861 convention in Richmond: George W. Brent (Alexandria); William H. Dulany (Fairfax); Alfred M. Barbour and Logan Osburn (Jefferson); and Alexander H. H. Stuart, John B. Baldwin, and George Baylor (Augusta). These men worked steadfastly against secession throughout the Virginia state convention, to the point that all of them were willing to negotiate with Lincoln even after he had asked Virginia for troops to put down the rebellion in South Carolina.[50] Furthermore, residents in these communities voted overwhelmingly—6,891 to 1,378—to require the convention to submit any of its decisions to the citizens before they became law.[51]

The shattering of the Baltimore Conference was a sign that slavery was becoming more polarizing as a political and cultural issue in the late antebellum period. The actions of white Virginians in the conference were also a sign that many white evangelicals from the commonwealth were theologically committed to slavery but averse to secession. For those who followed ecclesiastical events carefully, there were other signs to be read as well. The Western Virginia Conference of the ME Church had almost as many Virginian members as did the Baltimore Conference. Those members did not revolt en masse when the General Conference acted against slavery. Westerners resembled easterners in their theological aversion to secession, but their continued affiliation with the ME Church threw into doubt their position on slavery. The question of the trans-Allegheny Methodists' loyalty on slavery went unanswered, for all eyes were on the capital city, where the constitutional convention convened on 13 February 1861.

The convention itself was a peculiar event, for the Virginia General Assembly charged delegates to address a number of issues, including but not limited to the secession crisis. Once again, tensions between white Virginians in the slaveholding Tidewater and Piedmont and the largely free-labor trans-Alleghenies had flared. Western delegates, not satisfied by adjustments made at constitutional conventions in 1830 and 1850, were demanding further redress of the low tax rates that easterners had set for their slaves. Although the average value of slaves had soared in the late 1850s, up to $2,000 for a young adult male, the 1850 constitution fixed the value of each slave for taxation purposes at $300. Most westerners tolerated slavery but were generally unwilling to expose their vulnerable counties to easy invasion by northern armies only to protect an institution in which they had little material interest. They therefore acceded to a "secession convention," like those held at roughly the same time in North Carolina and Tennessee, only on the condition that their concerns about taxation would also be on the table. Thus, men came to Richmond with different agendas—some to seek relief from an oppressive tax structure, others to help the nation avert war at all costs, and a small minority to try to pull the Old Dominion out of the Union as quickly as possible.[52]

Despite their different agendas, the delegates agreed on two things: that God's hand was in the troubling events of the day, and that coercion was anathema. In one of the few unanimous votes, delegates accepted on the convention's opening day the suggestion by Jeremiah Morton that they open each subsequent day's deliberations with prayer. "We all believe that the hairs of our heads are numbered. We believe that a sparrow cannot fall to the ground without a special Providence," explained Morton, quoting directly from Matthew 10. "I therefore, think it eminently proper that we should follow in the footsteps of our ancestors," he continued, "and, on an occasion like this, when we are deliberating not only upon the happiness of our State but the peace of this country, that the proceedings of this Convention should be opened in prayer."[53] Among the dozens of clergymen who responded to Morton's call by opening the proceedings with prayer were numbered Richmond's evangelical elite, including Presbyterian Moses Drury Hoge, Episcopalian George Woodbridge, Baptist Jeremiah Bell Jeter, and Methodist George W. Nolley. Significantly, not only was this group of ministers solidly evangelical and interdenominational, but it also included those prominent in the mission to the slaves. Nolley, who prayed on 21 and 23 February, did not have any white parishioners; he was then serving as the pastor of Richmond's black Methodists.[54]

Delegates at the convention of 1861 were united against any form of coercion on the part of the federal government. Though the assembly directed all questions about secession to the Committee on Foreign Relations, which did not present its report to the whole group for discussion until 9 March, many individual delegates warned from the floor that they would not tolerate coercive policies from the Lincoln administration. Union men such as Fauquier County's John Q. Marr were among the loudest anticoercion voices; on 16 February he deemed it "proper to declare through the Convention now assembled" Virginia's "opposition to the coercion, under existing circumstances, of any slave State, and an unalterable determination not to submit to any administration of the government in which her rights are assailed or not fully protected." In the hours before the day's session closed, five additional delegates proposed anticoercive resolutions.[55] Despite the fact that the convention did not issue an official resolution against coercion until 6 April, when it voted that "Virginia would never consent to federal power being used to subjugate a seceded state," the will of the convention against the use of force against the seceded states was clear from the beginning.[56]

Firmly against coercion, the delegates disagreed only about when that point had been reached. Some, like secessionist Henry A. Wise, believed that the Republicans' strong language against slavery, the personal liberty laws designed to provide succor for fugitive slaves, and other northern violations against the spirit of the Constitution were already tantamount to coercion. Others, like Augusta County's Alexander H. H. Stuart, held on to the hope that Lincoln would somehow reverse his course even after he asked for troops to assist in restoring federal control of South Carolina. Much of the convention's practical work thus consisted of identifying with clarity exactly when the federal contract had been violated. But discerning the point of no return proved no easy task for the delegates; many stories were unfolding at once, each with potential bearing on the probity of secession. Virginians, evangelical and otherwise, waited with bated breath to see how successful their peace initiatives were, how stable the nascent Confederate States of America would prove, and how aggressively Lincoln would act. Some scholars have seen Virginians' inaction as evidence of a lack of political will, but evangelical residents of the commonwealth knew their principles and were waiting not because of indecisiveness, but because they needed more information to see if the Constitution remained binding.[57]

When the statesmen at the Washington, D.C., Peace Conference failed to agree upon constitutional safeguards for slavery, Unionist Virginians became less certain that they would be able to avert secession. Initially, pro-Union delegates to the constitutional convention had been optimistic about the prospects of the Peace Conference. In a private letter to his brother, William C. Rives, who was a delegate at the conference, Alexander Rives (who was himself a delegate to the constitutional convention) conveyed absolute confidence that the South's leading figures, including James Guthrie of Kentucky and Thomas Ruffin of North Carolina, would "bring about a harmonious result."[58] Ironically, Unionists may have actually damaged their case for Union by being too enthusiastic about the possibilities for compromise in the Peace Conference. Their billing of the conference as the best hope for a political solution made its almost certain failure by 1 March a crushing blow to some of the more tepid Unionists. Edward C. Burks, for instance, cautioned that "if they fail to accomplish anything satisfactory, the failure will operate almost *irresistibly* to drive us *at once* into disunion."[59] Though he persevered in his hope for a constitutional adjustment, retired Methodist minister Overton Bernard, from Portsmouth, confided to his diary on 12 March, "The failure of the Peace Conference in Washington has increased the feeling in favor of secession in Virginia."[60]

Proponents and opponents of secession in the convention spent as much time debating whether or not coercion had occurred as they did discussing the potential consequences of their decision. They knew that the state's evangelical majority was looking to them to determine whether or not the Union could be saved, whether or not the Constitution was dead letter. Immediate secessionists made the case that the Constitution had already been violated, while the majority of Unionists and conditional Unionists

pointed to the absence of coercion and stressed Virginia's continued obliga-
tion to obey secular authorities. When South Carolina's John S. Preston
addressed the group on 19 February, he tried to convince Virginians of the
Deep South's position that Lincoln had already violated the Constitution.
By arguing that Lincoln's nationalist and antislavery interpretation of the
Constitution betrayed the document's original meaning, Preston wanted
to talk Virginians into seceding without additional evidence of coercion.
"Reverently let us invoke the God of our fathers," he beseeched the Virginians, "to guide and protect us in our efforts to perpetuate the principles
which, by his blessing, they were able to vindicate, establish and transmit to
posterity."[61]

Despite Preston's oratory, a majority of delegates to the convention re-
solved to wait until coercion took physical form before conceding that the
Constitution had been broken. Immediately following the South Carolin-
ian's passionate pro-secession speech, delegate Leonard S. Hall of Wetzel
County set forth this more cautious view: "The mere election of Abraham
Lincoln to the Presidency of the United States under the provisions of the
Constitution," he stated, "affords no just grounds for Virginia to resume to
herself the powers granted to the general government."[62] After six weeks of
debate, after the failure of the Peace Conference, after the establishment of a
Confederate government in Montgomery, after so many intimations that
disagreements between the North and the South might be irreconcilable, a
majority of the convention's delegates continued to oppose secession. In a
4 April vote on whether or not to substitute a vote on secession for the
convention's scheduled business, ninety delegates voted against the daring
act and only forty-five for it.[63] The center had held, and it was clear to all
involved that Virginians would not consent to leave the Union without
tangible evidence of coercion.

Jefferson Davis and Abraham Lincoln meanwhile pursued a collision
course that cataclysmically altered the balance of moral considerations facing white Virginians. Lincoln had abandoned most of the federal forts in
seceded states but had held on to Fort Sumter in Charleston Harbor and to
Fort Pickens off the west coast of Florida. A Union presence in these forts
was a constant affront to Confederate sovereignty, and Davis ordered Fort
Sumter "reduced" on 12 April. Firebrand Edmund Ruffin, who had decided
to leave his state because his fellow citizens were too slow to embrace the
dream of an independent southern, slaveholding nation, reportedly fired the
first shot in the massive artillery bombardment of the fort. Maj. Robert
Anderson, a Kentucky native and the officer in charge, surrendered the fort
to the Confederacy on 14 April. Having gained what he believed to be the

moral high ground by forcing the Confederate States to initiate hostilities, on 15 April Lincoln called for loyal states to contribute a total of 75,000 troops to suppress the rebellion.

A convincing majority of delegates to the Virginia convention considered Lincoln's request for military aid hard evidence of coercion and shifted their sympathies and votes to the Confederacy. Baptist Addison Hall, the only evangelical minister to serve in the convention, had defended the Union in the pulpit and in the convention, but the call for troops convinced him that Virginians were no longer bound to submit to a leader who had malice in his heart. A contemporary biographer explained that in Hall's "representative capacity he did all in his power in the Convention to prevent the State from seceding, until the United States Government attempted to coerce the seceded states and made a demand on Virginia to furnish her quota of troops for that purpose, when he became in favor of and voted for the Ordinance of secession."[64]

Dozens of additional delegates expressed outrage at Lincoln's request for troops and announced that they would switch their votes to secession. William Sutherlin, a Danville moderate, could not believe the news. He exclaimed, "I have been a Union man, but, my God, I have never been a submissionist.... I have a Union constituency who elected me by a majority of one thousand, and I believe now that there are not ten Union men in that county today." Samuel Staples of Patrick County also switched his vote. "Ten days ago, I was known as a Union man," he announced at the convention, but coercion meant that the convention "has no alternative left but to adopt an ordinance of secession."[65] On 17 April, William Preston reverently submitted an Ordinance of Secession for a vote, for Lincoln's act had convinced him that he no longer needed to obey the Constitution. "I shall go through all these struggles with a consciousness that I have done my duty to my country, and I believe I have done it to God," he said, "and I feel that in this contest God himself will be with us. I now submit the ordinance."[66] Only thirteen days after the overwhelming Unionist victory of 4 April, eighty-seven delegates voted for separation, with only fifty-five opposed. At least thirty-five delegates had changed their vote after Lincoln's request for men.[67]

When white evangelicals outside the convention heard of the call for troops, they roundly supported their elected representatives' conclusion that the Union had disintegrated. Amelia County's Presbyterian minister, Richard McIlwaine, had stayed up until midnight on 15 April trying to convince a fellow churchman of the justice of the Unionist position. But when he saw printed news of the president's proclamation the next morning, he "and the people of Virginia generally flopped over to the other side, became rabid Secessionists and were ready for a fight." Within a few days, McIlwaine helped to raise a volunteer infantry regiment and was elected its 3rd lieutenant.[68] Unionist John B. Minor wrote on 16 April to his even more Unionist cousin, "I devoutly thank God for the noble, moderate and conservative course so steadily pursued by this dear old commonwealth in the midst of the wild storm of obloquy and detraction by which some of her unworthy sons have sought to drive her from her course, so that now when Civil War has been inaugurated, it has been by no act of hers." He went on, "Nothing remains now to the Christian patriot but to strike strongly for the right, humbly invoking the aid and blessing of our fathers' God."[69]

Evangelical Unionists in most of the state endorsed a new political order. J. M. Broadus, a Baptist minister, declared, "If Virginia cannot belong to the Union without servile degradation from Northern aggression and domination, then I am for Virginia and nothing else at present."[70] William Meade, soon the senior Episcopal bishop of the Confederacy, explained his own shift to secession in his annual address to the denomination's General Convention: "I have clung with tenacity to the hope of preserving the Union to the last moment," he insisted, but "the developments of public feeling and the course of our rulers have brought me slowly, reluctantly, sorrowfully, yet most decidedly, to the painful conviction, that notwithstanding attendant dangers and evils, we shall consult the welfare and happiness of the whole land by separation."[71] Tennessee's Episcopal bishop, a Virginia native, was not as gentle as his apostolic senior. Writing to a friend in Bedford County on 17 July 1861, he fumed, "Your views, like mine, I doubt not, have undergone a great change in regard to the moral aspect of the contest. Since Mr. Lincoln's proclamation, and the attitude assumed, and the purposes proclaimed by the North, I have had no sympathy with the U.S. Government— no respect for its rulers—very little regard for the Northern people."[72]

Those in the trans-Allegheny west who protested the decision to secede also believed that they had God on their side. For white evangelicals in eastern Virginia, their faith had served as a barrier to precipitate secession, but they had no moral difficulty seceding once Lincoln called for troops. For white evangelicals in western Virginia, whose political leaders came to believe that the call for troops was justified, their faith reinforced their decision to continue to honor federal authority. It is possible that the same considerations of political economy that made statesmen from the western portion of the state unconditional Unionists—most notably its relative lack of slaves— contributed to their perception of the moral issues at stake. The mission to the slaves was much less important over the mountains, and western white evangelicals had not identified themselves so closely with its success. The overlapping Parkersburg circuits of the ME Church and ME Church, South, together contained 4,678 whites and only 56 blacks in 1850—hardly the kind of numbers that would have led local resident John Jackson to believe that God was using slavery for the conversion of multitudes. Whether or not the mission entered Jackson's thinking, he made an emotional appeal for Union when serving Parkersburg at the constitutional convention on 16 April in which he explained his position in profoundly spiritual terms. "I stand here to-day having taken the oath to support the Constitution of the United States twenty-seven times," he testified. "Was that an unmeaning ceremony? Was it of no consequence that I called the eternal God to witness that I would be true to the Constitution of Virginia as well as the Constitution of the United States?"[73]

Jackson could not bring himself to break his sacred promises for the sake of the Deep South, and he did not understand how others could, either. "Is it compatible with my obligations, not only to my country, but with my obligations of duty to God," he asked,

> that I shall obliterate this magnificent fabric of self-government, this Constitution of which we are so often reminded when we go to the door and look upon yonder Capitol [referring to the Capitol at Washington] that cost the Treasury millions upon millions—a Capitol founded on the counsel and the wisdom, not only of the most enlightened and distinguished men that were ever permitted to adorn the earth, but on a Constitution that had for its guiding star and direction the ever-blessed Spirit himself. I am called upon to obliterate that; to efface it from the memory of man. Will we not have to pause? Will not ordinary spirits fail as they enter upon the unholy task?

This same sense of spiritual obligation to the Union motivated Morganton's Waitman T. Willey, a Methodist lay leader who spearheaded the trans-Allegheny counties' drive for statehood. "But while I am no proslavery man," he wrote in 1862, "yet as a senator of the U. States, sworn to support the constitution of the U. States, no pressure of policy or expediency can so far stifle my sense of responsibility to my country and to God as to cause me to forget that oath."[74]

Those white Virginians who did secede continued to regard the developing conflict in moral terms, and there were several very important legacies of their evangelical Unionism. First, a reluctance to initiate disunion, sanctified by the church's teaching on submission to authority, had the paradoxical effect of making white Virginians among the stoutest defenders of the Confederate nation. In months of extremely well publicized debate, white evangelicals and their fellow citizens had reached a consensus that coercion would dissolve their obligation to obey federal authority and would reveal the iniquity of the Lincoln administration. When coercion came, white evangelicals who seceded therefore believed that they were engaging in a defensive, just war against northern aggression. Second, white evangelicals and their peers focused so much attention on the moral debate over secession that took place from December 1860 through April 1861 that they moved slavery to the margins of their understanding of the conflict. White evangelicals in eastern Virginia were so positive that Lincoln's decision to enforce federal authority was sinful that they forgot what lay at the root of the conflict in the first place, which was their determination to preserve and extend African slavery. Lincoln's tyranny alone, they came to believe, was sufficient cause for revolution.

White Virginia evangelicals displayed a great deal of indignation at the call for troops, to the extent that they often relegated the conflict over slavery to an afterthought in their understanding of the war's causation. Nelson County Episcopalian William D. Cabell fumed in his diary of 17 April 1861, "Lincoln having ordered up 5000 troops to coerce the seceding states I this day change my position and am for opposing him to the bitter end. Having been cool & conservative up to this date I now feel thrice armed for the combat—May the god of battles be with us!"[75] Three days later Mildred Gibson Lynch wrote in her diary about "the direst, most wicked war ever waged." While she at least obliquely acknowledged slavery, citing that northerners wanted to "rouse our own household to deeds of insurrection and bloodshed against those who had nurtured and cherished them," she reserved her sharpest words and the bulk of her diatribe for the administration's policy of coercion. "Even while we entrusted and hoped, the North prepared armies and fleets to seize our forts and wage war on our Southern Brethren, even demanded of *Va.* troops to subjugate these noble sons to their authority," she vented. "Did pen ever record wickedness & audacity like this? Where is their boasted freedom & liberty?"[76] Many—perhaps most—commentators, including an anonymous writer to the *Central Presbyterian*, did not even mention slavery in their appraisal of Virginia's righteousness. "N.E." warned that "a dragon stands ready to swallow us up, and if He does not help us, there is no help for us." Fortunately for them, "N.E." assured his readers that "we have a righteous cause, and may therefore look to him; for whatever may be thought of the commencement of secession, the proclamation to raise a horde of soldiers to overrun our soil and plunder and murder our Southern brethren, places us so strongly in the right, and gives us a conviction of the justice of our cause so deep, so intense, so pervading, that few can be found to question the course which Virginia has pursued. It has been remarked, and with truth, that the strongest union men make the hottest secessionists."[77]

Evangelical church leaders reinforced the message that Lincoln had demolished any obligations that white southerners owed to the Union and caused the war. Indeed, as many scholars have noted, white evangelical churchmen became the most important supporters of the Confederacy.[78] In the tense days following Lincoln's call for troops, when the advent of a full-fledged civil war was still uncertain, Bishop Meade used the occasion of the Episcopal Church's annual convention to brace his evangelical following for battle and convince them of the rightness of their cause. "A deeper and more honest conviction that if war should actually come upon us, it will be on our part one of self-defence, and therefore, justifiable before God, seldom, if ever, animated the breasts of those who appealed to arms," he preached.[79] White evangelicals of every stripe echoed Meade's conviction that the South's cause was beyond reproach, even holy.

For once, the Baptists may have outdone the silver-tongued orator in their rhetorical achievements in support of the Confederacy. At their statewide convention in 1861, after cataloging every wrong that white northerners had committed against the South in general in their abrogation of the Constitution, they turned to the state of their nativity. "Especially do we mention the noble efforts of our own State to preserve and restore the Union, in its original strength and beauty, with feelings of profound pleasure," they explained both nostalgically and with barely contained rage. "With earnest solicitation our State held out the olive branch, and besought for peace, until all hope was gone. With sad hearts Virginia's sons turned from their sacred temple, now desecrated by the prostitution of its holy columns of liberty to the cause of violence and wrong." In a great service to Jefferson Davis, the Baptist ministers made sure their congregations knew the implications of this narrative. "In consideration of these facts and many others that might be referred to, but which are familiar to the minds of all, we regard ourselves as identified with the States of the Southern Confederacy, as having the war *forced* upon us. We feel, furthermore, the sweet assurance that our cause is a righteous one, and we can appeal to the God of battles for help in this hour of darkness and peril."[80]

In state denominational meetings, in newspapers, in conversations by fence posts as their children marched off to war, and in their local congregations, white Virginians basked in the righteousness of their cause—and often left slavery out of their conversations altogether. The *Richmond Christian Advocate* reported proudly on "The Sentiment of Virginia" on 2 May:

> It is not often that a people can prepare for war under circumstances so creditable to their Christianity. No self-reproach unnerves the arm of Virginia; no retrospect discovers in her conduct an act of malice, disobedience to LAWFUL authority, or a plan devised in passion against her enemies.—When her soil was invaded, she arose indignantly, but calmly, and executed the offenders according to law; and now, when every right and interest of the State is threatened, she is rising by the simultaneous movement of every citizen, and girding herself for the conflict, feeling that the voice of Divine Providence has declared her duty distinctly, that every moral impulse is aroused, as naturally as if the whole body politic heard a summons to arms from the Captain of the Lord's host.[81]

Outside the capital city, evangelicals were no less willing to fight. The Elon Baptist Church passed a formal resolution in 1861 affirming its members' allegiance to the Confederacy, declaring "that the War which the U.S. government has forced upon us, involving as it does, our social and religious freedom, must be met with unfaltering determination and an earnest cooperation of every Christian."[82] J. G. Shepperson of Bedford County published in the *Central Presbyterian* in August 1861 a two-part sermon titled "The Defence of Our Country a Christian Duty," designed to make certain that members of that denomination did not lag behind their brethren in "Christian" support of the war effort.[83]

Once fighting was under way, white evangelicals aided southern nationalist ambitions both materially and ideologically. They did their part to meet the material demands of war by melting down bells for bullets, sewing uniforms, and opening churches to serve as hospitals.[84] But evangelicals also attempted to improve the Confederacy's chances by making it more godly. One way that they did this was to continue the mission to the slaves. Another was to launch an equally ambitious crusade to convert Confederate soldiers.

White evangelical Virginians may have avoided slavery in their accounts of the war's causation, but the events of the war—including emancipation, the massive flight of enslaved persons from Virginia plantations, and the service of black soldiers in the U.S. Colored Troops—made it impossible to ignore the fundamental conflict between slavery and freedom. As it had become during the late antebellum period, the mission to the slaves remained a bulwark for Confederates against Union criticism of slavery and, in the context of the war, against the Union embrace of emancipation as a war aim. White evangelicals continued the mission in wartime even though, in most communities, they experienced diminishing success. A committee of the state's Methodists, just before Virginia seceded, expressed "their conviction that a stern necessity exists, and for very obvious reasons more particularly now than ever, for the religious training of the colored population in our midst."[85] Though Methodists wanted to redouble their efforts, they were forced to reduce them. From twenty mission churches with 4,492 members in 1860, the figure had fallen to fourteen churches with 3,226 members by 1864.[86]

When evangelicals discussed the mission in the midst of war, they sometimes identified it as a theological strategy to protect the Confederacy from God's chastisement. Episcopal bishops from across the Confederacy met in 1862 and depicted the amelioration of slavery as a way to shield the Confederacy from any divine displeasure with the institution. They reminded their parishioners that "it is likewise the duty of the church to press upon the masters of the country their obligation, as Christian men, so to arrange this institution as not to necessitate the violation of those sacred relations which God has created and which man cannot, consistently with Christian duty, annul." Laws against slave marriage and the frequent alienation of children from their parents were particularly problematic. "The systems of labor which prevail in Europe and which are, in many respects, more severe than ours, are so arranged as to prevent all necessity for the separation of parents and children and of husbands and wives, and a very little care upon our part, would rid the system upon which we are about to plant our national life, of these unchristian features." The prelates hoped that secession would give them the opportunity to reform slavery. "We rejoice to be enabled to say that the public sentiment is rapidly becoming sound upon this subject, and that the Legislatures of several of the Confederate States have already taken steps towards this consummation. Hitherto we have been hindered by the pressure of abolitionism; now that we have thrown off from us that hateful and infidel pestilence, we should prove to the world that we are faithful to our trust and the church should lead the hosts of the Lord in this work of justice and of mercy."[87]

While white Virginians remained supportive of the mission, they simply could not allocate to it the same resources that they had provided before the war. They diverted some money and manpower from the mission to their soldiers, whom they targeted with an impressive barrage of devotional literature. In 1857, Virginia Baptists had founded the Sunday School and Publication Board to furnish their children and neighbors with readings in basic

Christian doctrine. Commissioners John L. Burrows, David Shaver, and William Sands vastly accelerated the operations of the Board after the firing on Fort Sumter and oversaw the printing of more than 50 million pages of devotional literature for Confederate soldiers. Eager to give their sons and brothers every rhetorical inducement to convert to Christianity before a cannonball or dysentery claimed their lives, Virginia evangelicals not only widened the distribution of existing publications but also inaugurated new ones aimed directly at the troops. By 1863, five additional religious newspapers, three of which were headquartered in Virginia, served the Confederate army and navy: *The Soldier's Friend* (Baptist; Atlanta); *The Army and Navy Messenger* (Evangelical Tract Society; Petersburg, Va.); *The Soldiers' Visitor* (Committee of Publication, Presbyterian Church in the Confederate States; Richmond, Va.); *The Soldier's Paper* (Soldier's Tract Association, ME Church, South; Richmond, Va.); and *The Army and Navy Herald* (Soldier's Tract Association, ME Church, South; Macon, Ga.). The Army of Northern Virginia did not falter for lack of inspirational reading material.[88]

Swarms of Confederate chaplains—a few paid by the government in Richmond, but most supported by their home churches or denominations—engaged in mission work in the camp rather than in the slave quarters. The men who labored for the souls of Lee's men displayed an extraordinary willingness to cooperate, extending the trend toward interdenominational work begun decades earlier. William J. Hoge of Richmond marveled at the smooth collaboration of southern evangelicals after participating in one particularly ecumenical service. "We had a Presbyterian sermon, introduced by Baptist services, under the direction of a Methodist, in an Episcopal church," he reported. "Was not that a beautiful solution to the vexed problem of Christian union?"[89] Evangelicals in Confederate service, torn from their home churches, joined together in "army churches" or "Christian associations," wherein prior denominational affiliation did not matter at all. These "churches" adhered to five basic articles of faith, representing the core theological beliefs around which evangelicals had begun to rally following the War of 1812: the authority of scripture; the existence of the Trinity; the fall, redemption by Christ, and renewing of the Holy Spirit; justification by faith; and a system of eternal rewards and punishments.[90]

Evangelicals' efforts to convert their nation's defenders bore fruit in higher Confederate morale, both on the battlefield and on the home front. Historians, who once debated whether Christianity in general strengthened or eroded Confederates' will to fight, now recognize how essential that evangelical Protestantism was to Confederate morale. The primary disagreement now is on exactly how evangelicalism aided the southern army. In addition to the convincing older argument that white evangelicals fought better because they believed in the righteousness of their cause, scholars have pointed to several other ways in which evangelicalism may have bolstered white, southern spirits. It enabled soldiers to process the emotional traumas of warfare, to imagine Providence intervening to reverse a desperate military situation, and to equate the battlefield deaths of their comrades (or themselves) with the self-sacrificial death of Christ.[91] Whatever the mechanism, Confederates depended on evangelicalism to keep their morale high throughout the war. The central role of faith in the maintenance of morale manifested itself in a series of spectacular revivals that began in the fall of 1862, in which thousands of Confederates professed faith in Christ while serving in the army.

Confederate civilians rejoiced to know that their soldiers and their military leaders were, or were becoming, men of faith. Evangelical leaders bestowed encomiums on the captains of Confederate arms, which gave many civilians hope that God would vindicate their cause. White evangelicals recognized Confederate soldiers, from the most exalted commanders to the lowliest privates, as godly men and drew from their example of selfless service inspiration for life on the home front. In July 1861, Virginia's new Episcopal bishop, John Johns, preached to the troops encamped at Manassas on the night before the battle. In 1862, Johns baptized and confirmed Jefferson Davis, placing an evangelical seal of approval upon the Confederate leadership.[92] In 1863, following the death of Stonewall Jackson from wounds sustained at Chancellorsville, Presbyterian Robert L. Dabney penned a hagiographical sermon for publication in which he depicted Jackson as an emblem of southern piety. Dabney gave to posterity an embellished account of Jackson's death, part tribute, part exhortation to others not to fear bodily harm. "He had always desired to die on the Sabbath, and this wish was kindly gratified," Dabney reported. "As his thoughts were wandering on some scene, earthly or heavenly, he was heard to murmur 'let us pass over the river and rest under the trees,' as if the bright unfading scenes on the other side of Jordan were dawning to his gaze; and before the shadows had grown long on that bright Sabbath noon, his noble and holy spirit had passed over the river, and was walking in brightness beneath the trees that fringe the banks of the crystal stream, and had entered upon that rest that remaineth for the people of God."[93]

Women, those most often left behind after the extraordinary mobilization of white, Confederate manpower, drew strength from the depiction of Confederate soldiers as men of faith. Judith McGuire, an Alexandria socialite displaced by the Union army and forced to seek refuge in Richmond, described in her diary her participation in government-ordained days of prayer and fasting, sewed socks and shirts for the troops with the women from her adopted Richmond church, and derived real comfort from the belief that her kinsmen were fighting as Christians for a Christian cause. A trip to church in March 1864 transported her into a rapture of joy; she saw a crowd of Confederate officers, all apparently in earnest prayer. "It is delightful to see them," she crowed, "all bending before high Heaven." Her delight swelled when she noticed that the commander in chief, Jefferson Davis, was in the congregation and still more at the report that Robert E. Lee had been spotted "at prayer-meeting, down upon his knees."[94]

Mildred Lynch did not see any generals, but she was able to endure the departure of beloved enlisted men for battle because she knew that her friends professed saving faith and that their cause was righteous. On 21 April 1861, she recorded in her diary,

> Mr. Head preached today from: "There remaineth therefore rest for the people of God." There was deep sorrow furrowed on his noble brow, and heart moving pathos in his tone as he took the sorrowing parents and friends, the brave sons to the God of strength and consolation, and scores of hearts went up with the prayer: in heaven unite us all as one family. Strong and tender wept bitter tears, but he made us see and feel the *rest* through Jesus, that remains for the people of God, and we were *comforted*. Oh! May the brave soldiers return to us, not only victorious, but may each one enlist under the banner of the Cross, and at last be enabled to say I have fought the good fight.[95]

McGuire, Lynch, and others like them stretched themselves in the Confederate service and tolerated high casualty counts out of the conviction, advanced by white evangelical leaders, that doing so was coterminous with serving the Lord.

In a lecture he delivered to Richmond's Young Men's Christian Association in May 1863, Virginia's Attorney General John Randolph Tucker offered his own explanation of why white evangelicals should support the war. Tucker ambitiously tried to create a narrative of the coming of war that had room for slavery and secession as distinct moral issues, with particular attention to the moral obligations of white evangelicals. In so doing, he summarized many of the arguments of this book. He revealed, for instance, how profoundly the prewar mission to the slaves had shaped white evangelicals' sense of the justice of slavery, and he insisted that Lincoln had given the Upper South a clear *causus belli* by calling for troops. Moreover, he betrayed the foundational assumption of black inferiority upon which he and other white southern evangelicals rested their arguments. His lecture, published as *The Southern Church Justified in its Support of the South in the Present War*, is a critical source for understanding the nature of evangelical support for the Confederacy.

Tucker began by defending the active role that southern churchmen played in maintaining Confederate morale during the war itself. By their own admission, preachers had become intensely involved immediately following the call for troops. With some pride, still a month before First Manassas, the *Richmond Christian Advocate* recorded that clergymen had already "offered their services to the country as officers, chaplains, or privates. It is not because they are in favor of war, or disposed to shed the blood of their fellow-men, but because they feel that a necessity is laid on them, in the providence of God, to uphold a cause that is interwoven with the progress of Christianity and the salvation of men, and they enter the lists not so much from a purpose to injure the invader as to identify themselves with those who suffer for right and virtue, and, if need be, to be offered up as witnesses for the truth."[96] Tucker made precisely the same case that the fate of the kingdom of God and the Confederacy were bound together. He stressed that "it is the right and the duty of the Church, entrusted with the interests of His religion, to sustain the State Power, when it is a shield against wrong— and to oppose it when it is a sword wielded for outrage and oppression."

In the case of the Confederate States, though, Tucker asserted that such theorizing about the proper relationship between church and state was moot. Theirs was "a war of *defence—not of aggression*," so Confederates required no apology or formal justification. The "*cause* of *secession*, the CAUSE OF THE WAR," he explained, "was outrage perpetuated, and threatened, upon the constitutional rights of these States, and a violation of the charter, which bound all the States together in the late Federal Union." In other words, coercion had loosed white evangelicals from any requirement to obey the Lincoln administration and made the current struggle righteous. To his credit, Tucker did not stop with coercion but directly confronted the more fundamental cause of the war, white southerners' insistence on perpetuating African slavery.

On a more fundamental level than partisan politics, Tucker asserted, white Virginians needed to fight because they had a moral duty to protect the mission to the slaves. With more subtlety than Benjamin Palmer, who had ignored actual African Americans while defending slavery in the abstract, Tucker maintained that the mission alone justified the creation of the Confederate nation. The war itself, he argued, was "the defensive holding of a talent, lent to promote the Divine glory—which cannot be surrendered without breach of faith and loss of character." The "talent" to which Tucker referred was the mission, uniquely facilitated by the institution of race-based slavery. He summarized the outlines of the mission to the slaves and stressed the real interracial engagement that whites undertook in their efforts to bring people of African descent into their churches (without, of course, acknowledging the prudential reasons that they had for doing so following the 1831 insurrection). "The christian slaveholder found his duty to his slave enjoined in the Bible; taught him the way of eternal life; made him a christian man; loved him, tended him in sickness, and promoted his well being and his happiness," Tucker waxed. Northern Republicans wanted to interfere with this fruitful master-slave relation, he complained, and the only recourse available to the southerner, "as a Christian, was in separation—in *Secession*." For the remainder of his rambling address, Tucker mixed arguments that northerners had trampled on the Constitution with examples of the success of the mission to the slaves. He especially boasted of how many African Americans had converted. Of 4 million slaves, he lectured, "in less than two centuries, *half a million are professing members of evangelical churches*. This fact is worth a thousand theories as to the savage nature of slavery. The home of the slave is the spot, whence, as yet, Ethiopia has stretched out its hands unto God."

In the end, though, Tucker's elaborate defense of white, Virginia evangelicals and his praise of the mission itself depended entirely on the a priori assumption that African Americans were inferior by nature. He described black Americans as "incapable of political or civil equality with the white race, by original inferiority, and the debasement of centuries; incapable of freedom, except to be licentious and brutal and savage, and only fit to be enslaved." The achievements of African American evangelicals during the 1820s alone gave the lie to this assumption, but upon it depended the entire Confederate argument. Evangelical whites who grew up with the mission had come to believe not only in white supremacy but also that white supremacy enabled a special bond between blacks and whites. White evangelicals hung their core rationalization for going to war upon the need to maintain this bond and to protect the "integrity of the social tie between master and slave." As Tucker emphasized in closing to his evangelical audience, "We are a superior race, with an inferior race to deal with. We are its guardians, and it is our pupil, and all this under God's good providence. As a Christian people, we have a work of evangelization to do."[97]

As fragile as it now sounds, Tucker's self-righteous account of the road to war proved durable enough to motivate Confederates throughout the conflict. White evangelicals who believed in the righteousness of their cause could tolerate the declining fortunes of Confederate arms with tranquility.

Since they believed that they were in the right, they believed that their God might shower destruction upon Federal armies at any moment. Moreover, they were so confident of God's favor that they derived solace from defeat as well as victory. Charles Minnigerode, rector of the Episcopal church at which Robert E. Lee and Jefferson Davis worshipped, taught his flock precisely this lesson, that God was using military reverses to teach them spiritual lessons. "The might and power which our enemies bring against us," he preached, "are not the might and power of God's spirit, we may be sure—except so far as they are permitted to chasten us for our sins and train us for the hardships of a godly warfare."[98] The ability of Confederates to greet tidings of either victory or defeat from a providential perspective is one reason why Confederate morale in 1864 and 1865 remained so high, and so detached from developments on the battlefield.[99] In March 1865, as Lee's lines stretched and starved around Richmond and Petersburg, pastors from each of the major denominations were still publicly offering "their services to the Government to address the people, encourage hearty support of the Government, moral firmness, and that faith which Christians may illustrate in such a cause."[100]

If he helped to craft a narrative that perpetuated a fratricidal war, Tucker at least brought a twisted moral clarity to the situation. He repeated the contention of white evangelicals that Lincoln's decision to use force absolved them of their duty to obey the Constitution. But, more importantly, he also recognized that constitutional conflicts were subsidiary to the conflict over slavery. White evangelicals in Virginia were on a collision course with whites in the North because of their views on slavery, not because of their constitutional theories. They believed that God had made them stewards of a benighted people, and that those who would deny them the fulfillment of that trust were godless and cruel. That this theological proposition enjoyed so much support for so long is a testament to both the intensity of American racism and the consuming nature of the mission.

EXODUS, 1861–1870

And I am come down to deliver them out of the hand of the Egyptians, and to bring them up out of that land unto a good land and a large, unto a land flowing with milk and honey.—Exodus 3:8

Virginia's African American evangelicals did not perceive the Confederate cause as a holy one. With the exception of occasional deeds of personal loyalty on behalf of their owners—modest acts, such as the protection of valuables, which whites celebrated far out of proportion to their frequency or meaning—blacks sought to retard the southern cause both ecclesiastically and militarily. The chief tool that black evangelicals used to combat the proslavery, pro-Confederate orientation of their white brethren was separation, both from slavery itself and from the white church. Almost half a million slaves from across the South fled from their owners during the conflict and sought succor behind Union lines.

Men and women in Virginia found it easier to reach the safety of federal lines than did enslaved people in other areas of the Confederacy, for the Union army maintained a presence on three sides of the state and made frequent incursions toward the capital city. By 24 May 1861, the first documented fugitive slaves of the war had already sought out Union troops at Fortress Monroe, near historic Jamestown, and had begun to work as military laborers.[1] Enough black Baptists in the commonwealth took advantage of the relative ease of escape that the Rappahannock Baptist Association, in which black members outnumbered whites by a two-to-one margin, ruled that fugitives from slavery be expelled from church membership. As their justification for this punishment, whites cited only the "general sanction which the Scriptures unquestionably give to slavery," forgetting the irony that white evangelicals had been among those questioning the teaching of scripture on the institution only a few generations before.[2]

Black evangelicals too far from the front lines to celebrate a "day of jubilee" by running from slavery at least slipped white control of their spiritual lives. They began during the war the process of transforming quasi-independent churches into fully independent ones and forming new African American congregations where there had not been any. By 1866, at least two-thirds of the African American men and women who had attended church with whites or under white supervision before the war worshipped in fully autonomous, all-black congregations. The actual proportion may have been higher, for black evangelicals changed their membership status too quickly for the documentary record to keep up. Those flawed statistics that exist give only enough information to indicate that black evangelicals began to take control of their lives ecclesiastically early in the war, and that the process dramatically accelerated with Confederate defeat. The five districts of the Methodist Virginia Conference that reported statistics for every year of the war recorded declining numbers of black members in five of six years following 1860, with the biggest drop coming between 1864 and 1865. By 1866, only 1,159 of 3,103 original black members remained, and the number of probationary black members had dropped from 223 to zero.[3]

What was happening in Virginia represented a regionwide trend, but the move to black ecclesiastical independence was happening fastest in the Old Dominion. Already by 1866, 84 percent of black Methodists in the commonwealth had abandoned their prewar churches. In the ME Church, South, as a whole, however, only 62 percent of black Methodists had left their prewar churches. The ME Church, South, in the former Confederate states—at least on paper—still boasted 78,742 black members in 1866.[4] African American South Carolinians and Georgians together accounted for more than 30,000 of the men and women still in an ME Church, South, congregation in 1866, suggesting that black evangelicals who did not encounter the Union army until late in the war may have been the slowest to organize their own churches. A small number of Virginia's black evangelicals, though, stayed in biracial churches even when black-run churches were available. This was the case in Farmville, where Curtis White and Nannie Carter remained in the Baptist church that White had helped to found. Fourteen black members passed in and out of Chappawamsic Baptist Church after the war, the last dying in 1891. Notwithstanding these and other exceptions, almost all black evangelicals in Virginia and in the South had left white-dominated congregations by 1875.[5]

Black evangelicals' willful separation from biracial communities undercut white evangelicals' boasts about the moral efficacy of slavery. As long as whites had forced the integration of their religious communities, they could boast that God was using an exploitative labor regime for the spiritual good of men and women of color. When it became apparent that the vast majority of blacks, left to their own volition, held white religiosity in contempt and preferred to organize their own churches, whites found their self-identity as benevolent paternalists shaken. Many slaveowners felt betrayed that the men and women for whose souls they had expressed such concern would leave them. Thornton Stringfellow was an old man by 1863 and had retired from the ministry, but he was still as confident as ever that slavery was "full of mercy." When the seventy African Americans whom he claimed as his chattel escaped en masse in that year, he was devastated. Historian Drew Faust has best captured Stringfellow's disbelief: "Unable to confront the thought that his servants had fled from his benevolent care," the proslavery theorist "insisted that they had been all but kidnapped by the Yankees."[6]

The rapid unraveling of the forced fellowship that white and black evangelicals had shared revealed much about the nature of their relationship before the Civil War. The stunning growth rate of African American churches following emancipation, for one thing, showed that some blacks with strong faith commitments had resisted enrollment in the integrated, proslavery church. Enslaved Virginians had been fully aware that white churchgoers were among the most stalwart defenders of human bondage. While some accepted fellowship with whites even under these circumstances, provided that they receive a modicum of ecclesiastical freedom, others protested a proslavery interpretation of the Gospel by remaining at home. Those who protested, who kept alive the invisible church despite whites' best efforts to eradicate it, willingly gave up their secret lives of faith as soon as worshipping in fully autonomous black churches became an option. Those who had been willing to join racially mixed congregations before the war enthusiastically left those communities as white hegemony cracked during the Civil War. Access to white houses of worship and white funds to pay for preachers and mission work were not adequate inducements to keep Virginians of color in racially mixed congregations.[7]

Black Virginians signified by joining black churches at a rate far greater than they had joined biracial evangelical churches that they preferred to be "under their own vine and fig tree." In 1860, between 65,000 and 70,000 of the state's 548,907 African Americans were full members of Virginia's evangelical churches, and many more attended regularly.[8] White reformers and white and black evangelists had made tremendous strides in recruiting black Virginians into the visible church, bringing roughly one of eight blacks into full membership and more than one-half into adherence. Their work, however, paled in comparison with the extraordinary outreach of postemancipation African American churchmen and -women. The data on religious adherence collected for the census of 1890 indicates that of the 635,858 black men and women living in Virginia, 238,617 were members of identifiably black churches. Looser postbellum requirements for church membership are not sufficient to account for this staggering increase. Both in terms of absolute numbers and as a percentage of the total black population, African American church membership soared following the war.[9]

The steps black evangelicals took toward ecclesiastical autonomy in one Piedmont town, Charlottesville, illustrate the path most of Virginia's African Americans chose during and after the Civil War. In Charlottesville, as elsewhere, the process through which black church members formed independent congregations was uneven, characterized initially by incremental changes but ending in a headlong rush by African Americans for autonomy.[10] As evangelical whites had done after the Revolutionary War, African American evangelicals following the Civil War made ecclesiastical autonomy a signpost of their new freedom.[11] They rushed in celebration of emancipation to build spaces and institutions in which to worship without reminders of prewar oppression. These new black churches were overwhelmingly Baptist, reflecting both decades of African American preference for the Baptist tradition in the commonwealth and the ease with which blacks could set up new Baptist churches. Lewis Bayley, who was an enslaved member of the Ivy Creek Methodist Church located just west of Charlottesville before the war, left that congregation just after blacks in town created an independent Baptist church. The notation by his name in the Albemarle Circuit's register suggestively reads, "Gone Baptist." All told, including newcomers and longtime members, 83 percent of the 238,617 black church members in Virginia in 1890, and a similar proportion in Charlottesville, were Baptists.[12]

Charlottesville's African American Baptists had deep roots in the biracial proslavery churches of 1831–61. Between April and June 1861, the white pastor of the town's racially mixed Baptist church, A. B. Brown, had baptized 225 new black members, bringing the total black membership of his congregation to over 800. A membership of this size made First Baptist Church by far the most significant institution among Albemarle County blacks. Statistics from the 1870 census, in which enumerators for the first time compiled statistics on the town of Charlottesville, indicate that there were 1,473 "blacks" and "mulattos" in the town proper, with 2,773 additional African Americans in the associated township. Adding conservative numbers of adherents to the official membership total of 842 for 1861 suggests that more than half of the county's slaves and free blacks had a personal connection to the First Baptist Church on the eve of the Civil War.

Charlottesville's "African Baptists," as they termed themselves, took the first steps toward self-rule very cautiously. They expressed their initial desire to separate from the white church so mildly and with such courtesy that, for a time, whites did not understand precisely what was happening. Meeting on 20 April 1863, in response to a petition submitted by the black members on 16 March, a special committee of whites interpreted the demands of the "colored members" as a desire to reconfigure a still-dependent relationship. All the African Americans hoped for, white members A. P. Abell, John Hart, J. T. Randolph, C. L. Thompson, and B. W. Snead reported, was (1) to acquire "a place of worship for themselves," (2) "to select their own Pastor, Deacons, Clerk, Treasurer, and their delegates," (3) "to decide all matters of membership and discipline according to Baptist usage," and (4) "to select the trustees to hold the property for them," since state law made property ownership notoriously difficult for black Virginians.[13]

Encouraged by the willingness of blacks to retain the white pastor, John T. Randolph, and to continue meeting in the First Baptist Church building, whites initially acceded to the petition of their African American brethren. White members understood the separation as a pragmatic step to win more black souls, a continuation of the antebellum ministry to the slaves.[14] A thriving quasi-independent black congregation would bring Charlottesville into the ranks of other commonwealth towns and cities that had allowed the charter of such churches in the late antebellum period. Whites in Charlottesville were familiar with the semi-independent model and could not conceive that black evangelicals would want to establish a wholly distinct church. When white church members discovered that this was precisely what black Charlottesvillians had in mind, they rushed to clarify to the secessionist blacks in June "that the organization proposed would not place the colored brethren beyond the care and control of this church."[15] The link between care and control is telling; whites expected that their paternalist patronage of the new African American body would guarantee the black Baptists' ecclesiastical submission. In this, the white Baptists were sorely disappointed.

Free blacks and some outspoken slaves in the more independent black congregation complained almost immediately about Randolph's ministry and demanded their own, separate minister. Randolph, it seems, did not know how to relate to his congregation as a community of equals. He showed favoritism toward the least confrontational slaves, whom he doubtless perceived as more pliable to his wishes—and who reinforced his idealized conception of himself as a paternalist master engaged in a benevolent mission. Conversely, he treated free men and women of color with suspicion. A majority of church members protested against this display of partiality. At some point between 1864 and 1867, black Baptists left Randolph and his prejudices in the basement of the white church. They moved downtown into the Delevan building, a vacant structure that colonizationist and evangelical John Hartwell Cocke had owned from 1825 until his death and that had been used as a Confederate hospital during the war. Refusing to be derivative of their white brethren even in name, Charlottesville's African American Baptists christened themselves the "Delevan Church" and in 1868 hired a full-time black pastor.[16]

In defiance of a contributor to the *Religious Herald*, who wrote that Virginia blacks did not have the "intelligence [or] self-control demanded in conducting the business and discipline of the Church," Charlottesville's evangelical African Americans flourished apart from white supervision.[17] They planted a new church, Mount Zion, in 1867, and by the 1870s both Mount Zion and the Delevan Church had embarked on ambitious campaigns to construct new sanctuaries.[18] Upon the completion of their brick building in 1884, proud parishioners of the Delevan Church renamed themselves the First Baptist Church. W. E. B. Du Bois could have been referring directly to this bustling congregation when he described in *The Souls of Black Folk* the "typical church in a small Virginian town." "It is the 'First Baptist'—a roomy brick edifice seating five hundred or more persons, tastefully finished," he wrote. "This building is the central club-house of a community of a thousand or more Negroes. . . . At the same time this social, intellectual, and economic centre is a religious centre of great power."[19]

Very early on, Freedman's Bureau officials operating in Albemarle County recognized the officers of the black First Baptist Church as the undisputed leaders of the freedmen, validating Du Bois's description and underscoring the importance of the church in postwar life. In a letter dated 12 March 1867, Captain William Lewis Tidball, an assistant superintendent for the bureau, featured Baptist leaders prominently in his survey of influential freedmen in the area. Of the eight names that Tidball forwarded to his supervisor, six were officers or preachers in the Baptist Church, and at least one of the remaining two was a member. The list included both men who had purchased their own freedom long before the war began and men enslaved until Union victory. William Gibbons, who served the First Baptist Church after the short-lived pastorate of John T. Randolph and became its full-time pastor until his departure for Washington, D.C., in 1870, received central billing.

"Gibbons, a mulatto," wrote Tidball, "is a farmer, and was formerly a slave. He, too, is a Baptist preacher. . . . As a preacher he is very popular, and has a large influence."[20]

In the process of withdrawing from white churches and forming their own local and regional institutions, Virginia blacks such as William Gibbons played the dominant role. Across Virginia and elsewhere in the former Confederate States, northern interlopers who rushed in to meet the spiritual and physical needs of the freedmen and -women generally found that freedpeople needed more physical than spiritual assistance. In some communities, missionaries from white northern churches or from predominantly black traditions such as AME and AME Zion did manage to channel existing black congregations into their denominations. Even this feat was relatively rare in the commonwealth, where African Americans like Gibbons took the lead in organizing denominationally.[21] In 1863, black Tidewater Baptists acted on their own initiative to form the Norfolk Union Baptist Association, and the Richmond-area Baptists followed in their steps by establishing the Shiloh Association in 1865. As a result of the tens of thousands of dollars white evangelicals had spent on spreading the Gospel among the slaves and of the development of a strong, Christian culture within slave communities, most freedmen and freedwomen had already accepted the religious message carried by northern missionaries and had already become adept at church government within the apartheid church.

Northern, white missionaries who expected that freedmen and -women would be hungry for the Gospel could not escape the conclusion that black Virginians had already heard the message while enslaved—or were hearing it from other freedpeople. Quaker Lucy Chase, who traveled to Virginia to be a teacher in 1863 with funding from the Boston Educational Commission, expressed in letters home first disgust, then begrudging respect for black religion. Prepared by the abolitionist press to find heathens, she was quick to identify the freedmen's prayer meetings as irreligious affairs upon her arrival. "At one of their prayer-meetings," she reported a week following her arrival at Craney Island off the coast of Norfolk, "we saw a painful exhibition of their barbarism. Their religious feeling is purely emotional; void of principle, and of no practical utility." Over the next eight months, Chase's disdain gave way to a reluctant acknowledgment of the integrity of black spirituality. "We often hear the negroes singing this—'Jesus been here, been here, been here,—Dun bless my soul and gone,'" she wrote in September; "some of them show, unmistakably, that their souls are blessed." She continued to struggle with the enthusiasm expressed during African American worship but understood by July 1864 that African Americans were entirely capable of running their own churches. As a result, she explained to her supporters at home in Worcester, Massachusetts, "the congregations have manifested determined opposition to settling white preachers."[22]

African American Virginians did need, and did take advantage of, the access to education that northern missionaries such as Chase offered. Discovering the "natural religious bent" of the freedpeople, most northern whites attempting to do mission work among former slaves founded schools instead of churches.[23] The United Presbyterian Church sponsored schools in Norfolk, Chase City, and Blue Stone; black men and women in these communities typically attended Baptist churches but went to school with the Presbyterians. The black Baptist pastors in all three localities felt threatened enough by this situation to attempt to discourage school enrollment among their congregations, an enterprise that proved both futile and ultimately unnecessary; African Americans rarely shifted their denominational affiliation in order to attend classes.[24] In Charlottesville, Fairfax Taylor, a slave until his self-purchase in the years immediately preceding the Civil War, was only one of hundreds of Albemarle County African Americans who attended bureau schools (often staffed by Presbyterians) but gave his real allegiance to the Baptist Church.[25] In his 1867 report for the Freedman's Bureau, Tidball had praised Taylor, who would eventually become the head pastor of First Baptist Church: he described him as "an officer of the Baptist church. He has been attending the colored school in this place, and can not only read and write, but has some knowledge of grammar, which none of the others have."[26]

As whites delighted to point out and blacks were usually hesitant to acknowledge, Taylor, Gibbons, and most other leaders of these new churches had converted and learned the basic traditions of Christian ministry under the tutelage of southern whites.[27] Those slaves and freedmen who had submitted to white ecclesiastical authority before the war did not necessarily possess a more authentic faith or a more charismatic manner than did their family and friends in the invisible church, but they had more practice at managing the institutional affairs of the kingdom of God on earth. In the segregated antebellum church, African American evangelicals could both observe white church governance and exercise a significant amount of control over affairs pertaining exclusively to black members. Moreover, some black men had served as preachers before the war, notwithstanding the restrictions put in place after Nat Turner's insurrection. For many black men, assuming the pastorate of all-black churches was therefore an easy and long-awaited step.

African Americans in all-black congregations under the nominal supervision of white pastors were particularly well prepared to take control of their ecclesiastical affairs. Members of Culpeper's "African" church demonstrated their preparedness for more self-governance in August 1859 when they successfully petitioned their white codenominationalists for the right to hold meetings at a different time. Already semiautonomous by emancipation, they were ready in 1865 to acquire Bibles, find a meetinghouse, and designate their own pastor. By 1867, they had a new name, the Antioch Church, and a new building.[28] Methodists at Norfolk's giant Bute Street Church decided to affiliate with the AME Church in 1863 and reconstituted themselves as St. John's Church. The AME representative who came to visit them, Elder Alexander W. Wayman, found a leadership team already in place and promptly ordained R. H. Parker, James Tynes, Peter Sheppard, Americus Woodhouse, and Amos Wilson.[29] Dozens of members of Richmond's First African [Baptist] Church, including several members of the influential Deacon Board, became ministers following emancipation. Baptized a slave by Ryland in 1842 and ordained a deacon by him in 1856, James H. Holmes became pastor of the First African Baptist Church itself in 1867. He had trained in chains for a marvelously successful pastorate of one of the world's largest Protestant churches, one that lasted for thirty-three years.[30]

Both white and black Virginians knew that many postbellum ministers of African American churches had received their introduction to Christianity and ministerial training in proslavery, white-controlled churches, but they described black evangelicals' sojourn in biracial evangelicalism in different ways. The white and black biographers of John Jasper, the most famous minister of any race in postwar Virginia, exemplified the different modes of remembering antebellum evangelicalism. Jasper had preached before the war under the supervision of white evangelicals, and after the war he filled a series of pastorates in Virginia and North Carolina before taking a call to the new Sixth Mount Zion Baptist Church of Richmond in 1867. There, he earned a national reputation for his sermon "De Sun Do Move," in which he used a powerful combination of humor, folk wisdom, and biblical exegesis to argue that a literal reading of scripture should trump scientific observation.[31] He preached this sermon by invitation before the Virginia General Assembly and on speaking tours in cities in both the North and the South. Even European scientists debated Jasper's ideas publicly, which added considerably to his domestic celebrity.

Jasper's early-twentieth-century white biographer, William Hatcher, defended white evangelicals' antebellum conduct by emphasizing that Jasper had learned his eloquence under the watchful eyes of southern whites. "In picturing the condition of things which encompassed Jasper during the days of slavery," he reminded his readers, "it is worth while to let it be understood that it was during their bondage and under the Christian influence of Southern [white] people, that the negroes of the South were made a Christian people. It was the best piece of missionary work ever yet done upon the face of the earth."[32] Indeed, in every hamlet of the former Confederacy, whites pointed to the antebellum conversions of black southerners to prove that God had smiled upon slavery. White evangelicals censored clerics such as Georgia Methodist John H. Caldwell who dared to suggest that slavery may have been wrong and instead embellished stories of harmonious prewar relations between black and white believers.[33] The Methodists even published the recollections of white missionaries and of grateful slave converts, *The Gospel among the Slaves*. In one of the prized testimonials, Bishop Isaac Lane of the Colored Methodist Episcopal Church remembered, "I began to seek religion at the age of twelve years. My owners were pious and religious people. . . . I heard preaching from the time I can remember. The missionaries came regularly."[34] Instead of recognizing that their complicity in denying black men and women the right to read or to lead their own worship services had for generations hindered the maturation of the black church, whites during Reconstruction and afterward assembled evidence that slavery had, in fact, been a school for Christianization.

John Jasper's black biographer, E. A. Randolph, remembered slavery and the "contributions" of white Christians far less charitably. Instead of celebrating the compassion and extent of white evangelical outreach toward African American Virginians, he highlighted the obstacles that slaves had to overcome in order to exercise their preaching gifts within biracial churches. He criticized white evangelicals for preventing blacks from being formally ordained, for depriving bondmen of literacy, for not doing more to protect slave marriages, and for mandating white supervision of black worship meetings. Jasper and other black ministers, Randolph implied in his argument, flourished in spite of and not because of white intervention. Randolph, for instance, did not count the fact that Jasper's Richmond-based owner had allowed him to preach in Richmond's Third Baptist Church two Sundays a month as an example of white kindness, for the same man forbade Jasper to accept a full-time position at Jasper's favorite church in Petersburg. Randolph described how Jasper made do with slavery's inequalities, not how those inequalities prepared him for his postwar career. Of the Third Baptist Church, he explained that "while they were not allowed to hold their meetings unless some white person was present, Mr. Jasper was virtually the pastor of the church."[35]

Most, but not all, black evangelicals anticipated Randolph's condemnation of the proslavery antebellum church very soon after emancipation. Meeting near Richmond in Manchester on 7 August 1867, representatives from the churches comprising the all-black Shiloh Association warmly praised their new status of freedom and cursed the memory of the slave regime. They passed a resolution thanking the Fortieth Congress for inaugurating a new Reconstruction program, one better calculated to protect their persons and their right to vote. As a direct critique of the segregated prewar church, they passed an additional resolution in which they "recommend[ed] to our churches to strike out the name 'African,'" for the word evoked the separate and unequal status those congregations had suffered before emancipation. Even more sensationally than these bold public resolutions, the members of the association stood and cheered when a representative from Southampton County was introduced, because, in the words of Assistant Clerk H. Williams, his "church was located where Nat Turner first struck for freedom."[36] Thirty-six years after the rebellion, black evangelicals boldly proclaimed the justice of the slave preacher's cause and their desire to continue his work.

White evangelicals initially assumed that they would enjoy the same paternalist influence over men and women in independent black churches as they had over those in biracial congregations. They therefore reacted with hurt, suspicion, and—finally—anger toward men like those at the 1867 meeting of the Shiloh Baptist Association. At first, white evangelicals did not suspect how radically their relationship with their black brothers and sisters had changed. At the meeting of the General Association of Virginia Baptists in 1866, for example, whites advanced the argument that their presumed racial superiority would guarantee a continuation of the same paternalist relationship, even though slavery had ended. "The obligations lately existing, growing out of the relations of master and slave, having ceased," a special committee explained, "no longer is the master required to do justice to his slave, as such, nor the slave required to render obedience to the master; and yet, as members of one common family, there are mutual obligations devolving upon us. The white, being the more enlightened race, are bound to use their influence to instruct and elevate the other." Whites thus made explicit in the postwar period the demand that paternal kindness be linked to an acknowledgment of their racial superiority. Black Baptists recognized the white supremacist implications of accepting the educational aid that whites offered and cut short whites' attempt to "instruct and elevate" them after the war. Their resistance to white interference, combined with white churchgoers' unwillingness to fund their educational initiatives for African Americans, shut down this and every similar program across the South.[37]

By leaving white churches and setting up separate denominational structures, black Virginians communicated to white churchmen that they did not want the charity or missionary attention of whites. Instead of allying with white Virginians, they looked to the emerging national denominations of black Christians. In 1871, Virginia's black Baptists affiliated with the new National Baptist Convention, a nascent, interregional organization of African American Baptists. In 1870, those black Methodists who had tried to gain fair and equal treatment within the ME Church, South, finally abandoned the ill-fated attempt and formed the Colored Methodist Episcopal Church. These new, nationwide denominations took their places beside the AME Church, which grew from approximately 50,000 in 1866 to more than 300,000 in 1876, and the AME Zion Church, which increased from 4,600 in 1860 to 125,000 by 1870, and signaled the institutional arrival of the independent black churches.[38]

Some influential black leaders offered to stay in fellowship or return to fellowship with white evangelicals, but only on terms of equality. In 1871, the Virginia Baptist State Convention, composed of representatives from the state's black Baptist associations, wrote to the predominantly white General Association a letter full of Christian charity. "We are adherents to one faith, one Lord and one baptism, yea, to all the vital principles of the great Baptist family," they offered generously, "therefore, we respectfully ask correspondence with you in the laudable work of evangelizing this our State." Though decent enough to recognize that African American evangelicals also possessed "the right, which we claim for ourselves, of organizing and governing churches," white Baptists determined "that from considerations, which we need not specify and cannot control, we deem it inexpedient to enter into an exchange of corresponding messengers."[39] White evangelicals, as a pioneer historian of the Methodist Church said most poignantly, might have preferred to keep every black evangelical in their churches (where they could exercise some measure of control over him or her), "but they had no notion of giving him any different status than he had had as a slave."[40]

Without a literally captive audience, most white preachers found that they could not hold the attention of black auditors, and they lashed out at their former brethren. Following Williams's paean to Nat Turner at the Shiloh Association's meeting, a white contributor to Richmond's *Daily Dispatch* publicly yearned for bygone days in which black Christians submitted to white ecclesiastical authority. "The blacks will find out the shallowheartedness of the unscrupulous and selfish persons who are widening the breach between them and those whose prosperity is theirs and whose peace alone can give them repose," he prophesied, "and they will curse the day when they listened to the cunning and heartless stories of the hypocrites now misleading them."[41] Presbyterian Robert L. Dabney, former proponent of slave missions, bitterly articulated the feeling of betrayal and race hatred that white evangelicals cultivated after the war. When the Synod of Virginia on 9 November 1867 debated the possibility of ordaining black men to the ministry, Dabney poured his vitriol forth against the measure. Appalled at the specter of black ministers having authority over white congregations, he asked, "Who that knows the negro, does not know that his is a subservient race; that he is made to follow, and not to lead; and his temperament, idiosyncrasy, and social relation, make him untrustworthy as a depositary of power?" The leading Presbyterian then explicitly identified black flight into independent black churches as proof of blacks' inconsistent character. "Have they not done enough recently, to teach us how thoroughly they are untrustworthy?" he asked. "They have, in a body, deserted their true friends, and natural allies, and native land, to follow the beck of the most unmasked and unprincipled set of demagogues on earth, to the most atrocious ends."[42]

White Virginians, who for so long associated the "look and feel" of evangelism with biracial worship, with the physical proximity with black worshippers, set new racial boundaries for their communities of faith. In church and in the public sphere, they tried to eliminate close contact with a people whom they now regarded as deceitful usurpers.[43] Some white evangelicals even began to doubt fundamental biblical teachings about the unity of creation, so intense was their reaction against their former brethren. Presbyterian George H. Venable wrote to his mother in March 1868 that he had read a convincing book about polygenesis. "It is an ingenuous argument and quite conclusive as to the fact that the negro is not descended from Adam," he confidently reported. "It has become the prevalent belief that the flood was not universal, and I doubt whether the progenitor of the darkies be he beast or man ever was in the ark at all."[44] Freedom, and the choices that black Virginians had made with it, made all the difference. Ann Gordon, who taught a class of black Sunday school scholars before the war, believed that even the most faithful evangelical blacks were unsuited for their new condition. When one of her former slaves died, she reported in her diary in January 1866 that "since I wrote last death has visited us & claimed Uncle Nat (colored). He died Friday night after a brief illness & was laid in his last resting place yesterday eve. Mr. Wallace the Baptist minister attended the funeral. His *freedom* cost him his life!"[45]

A lack of ecclesiastical engagement between white and black evangelicals was a necessary precondition for this escalation of white race hatred. White evangelicals before the war expended their time and treasure to bring blacks into their churches, and they treated charitably those African American men and women who accepted subordinate positions in their congregations. White and black churchgoers, even when they met at separate times but in the same building, perceived themselves at some level to be a part of the same, great body of Christ on Earth. In other words, evangelicalism, as practiced by white and black southerners, was simultaneously proslavery and pro-community. Furthermore, black evangelicals tempered the proslavery arguments advanced by white evangelicals and forced them to add a measure of moral obligation to their defense of the institution. The fragmentation of spiritual community in the late 1860s removed the most significant check on white antagonism and left only the impulse for racial control. When spiritual supervision became an obsolete method of controlling the commonwealth's black residents, white evangelicals aligned with secular white supremacists to keep black men and women in subjugation by any means necessary.

White evangelical Virginians could no longer boast during Reconstruction of their solicitude for their black neighbors, but they continued to interpret the world around them through their belief in an omnipotent God. Former Confederates sought and found solace amid defeat in faith. Their attempts to make a separate political nation foiled, southern whites set about making a separate spiritual nation, with evangelical Protestantism at the center.[46] No longer did black southerners have any place in this vision, at least not as long as they insisted on spiritual equality. "The white race must rule," southern whites insisted, in both church and the statehouse.[47] Rather than call attention to their charitable works on behalf of enslaved Virginians, whites instead emphasized the evangelical character of their former Confederate leaders. John William Jones, a chaplain who served as a private in the Confederate army, assured southern readers of his 1887 *Christ in the Camp* that "Jesus *was* in our camps with wonderful power, and that no army in all history—not even Cromwell's 'Roundheads'—had in it as much of real, evangelical religion and devout piety as the Army of Northern Virginia."[48] When whites shifted their religious attitudes, from championing the mission to the slaves to championing the men who fought to preserve slavery, they unleashed a torrent of violence on the black men and women whom they no longer recognized as their neighbors.

APPENDIX A

Evangelical Virginians in 1790 and 1850, by Race and Denomination

Denominational statistics are never as accurate as historians would like for them to be, but they are the best available measure for how deeply evangelicalism penetrated into the cultural and intellectual life of the Old Dominion. Statistics from 1790 and 1850 reveal the remarkable rise to influence of white evangelicals, and the equally remarkable tripling—almost quadrupling—of black evangelical adherence from 1790 to 1850.

Table 1 in the Introduction does not include Presbyterians or Episcopalians, for two reasons. First, the records for the Baptists and Methodists are better, and the numbers are more reliable.[1] In the data below, I have extrapolated the number of Presbyterians and Episcopalians in 1790 from numbers of congregations, for no statewide membership lists survive.[2] Second, most Presbyterians and all Episcopalians would have resisted the label "evangelical" in 1790, so the comparison is asymmetrical from 1790 to 1850.

Table 3. Evangelical Virginians in 1790 and 1850, by Race and Denomination

	Church members	Henry Carroll's adherence ratios (number of adherents per member)	Estimated total of members and adherents	Members and adherents as a percentage of all Virginians (by race)
1790[a]				
Whites	29,883		112,247	25.4
Baptists	15,391	2.9	60,025	13.6
Methodists	12,992	2.5	45,472	10.3
Presbyterians	1,500	3.5	6,750	1.5
Episcopalians	3,000	4.6	16,800	3.8
Blacks	9,653		36,456	11.9
Baptists	5,926	2.9	23,111	7.6
Methodists	3,427	2.5	11,995	3.9
Presbyterians	300	3.5	1,350	0.4
Episcopalians	10	4.6	56	0.0
Total	37,736		140,603	18.8
1850[b]				
Whites	126,278		480,163	53.7
Baptists	42,377	2.9	165,271	18.5
Methodists	68,075	2.5	238,263	26.6
Presbyterians	10,905	3.5	49,073	5.5
Episcopalians	4,921	4.6	27,558	3.1
Blacks	55,239		211,816	40.2
Baptists	44,832	2.9	174,844	33.2
Methodists	9,963	2.5	34,871	6.6
Presbyterians	350	3.5	1,575	0.3
Episcopalians	94	4.6	526	0.1
Total	181,517		691,980	48.7

Sources: Carroll, *Religious Forces*, xxxv; Heyrman, *Southern Cross*, 261–66; U.S. Bureau of the Census, *First Census, 1790*, 48–50; *Seventh Census, 1850*, 242–57; Asplund, *Universal Register*, 50, 89; Gardner, "Virginia Baptists and Slavery," pt. 2, 1259; *Minutes of the Methodist Conferences*; 14 Sept. 1791, *Hanover Presbytery*, UTS; Brydon, *Virginia's Mother Church*, 2:478; Dashiell, *Digest*, 40–41; *Minutes of the Virginia*

Baptist Anniversaries (1849), 61; *Minutes of the Virginia Baptist Anniversaries* (1851), 66; *Minutes of the Accomac, Albemarle, Columbia, Concord, Dan River, Dover, Goshen, James River, Middle District, Portsmouth, Rappahannock, Roanoke, Salem Union, Shiloh, Strawberry Baptist Associations* (1850); *Minutes of the Columbia and Goshen Associations* (1853); *Minutes of the Annual Conferences of the Methodist Episcopal Church, South*, and *Minutes of the Annual Conferences of the Methodist Episcopal Church* (1850–51); *Minutes of the Synod of Virginia* (1850), 60.

Note: Presbyterians did not identify their members by race in the official tallies, but unofficial counts indicate that there were no more than 350 black communicants in the Presbyterian Church in Virginia. See "Colored Communicants," *Watchman and Observer*, 7 Sept. 1848, which gives the figure at 236 for 1847 and 188 for 1848 but claims rampant underreporting. See also McIlwaine, *Memories*, 178. By this point, it is safe to include all Presbyterians in the Virginia Synod in the ranks of evangelicals. See *Journal of the Convention* (1849), 52–67. There is no synopsis of Episcopal members in 1849, so the tally here is from the reports of individual parishes.

[a]Includes Baptists, Methodists, Presbyterians from the Hanover Presbytery only, and Episcopalians. Episcopalians are not included in the total number of white or black evangelicals for 1790.

[b]Includes Virginia Baptists affiliated with the SBC, Virginia Methodists affiliated with the ME Church, South, or ME Church, Episcopalians, and Old School Presbyterians, which were already dominant numerically in 1837 and became more so as the New School became more openly antislavery. All denominations below are included in the totals.

Distribution of Virginia Evangelicals in 1860, by Denomination and County

In 1860, the Bureau of the Census recorded the number and affiliation of churches within each county, as well as the estimated total accommodations and property values of those churches. The "number of chairs" that the Bureau of the Census counted does not enable the historian to calculate membership or adherence with any precision, but it does provide a good general estimate of numbers and a sense of proportion about which denominations were strongest in which counties. It is worth noting that the Baptist Church seems to have fewer chairs than the estimated number of adherents for that denomination would suggest, while the other denominations seem to have surplus capacity. This could suggest flaws in the way that historians calculate total adherents from members. But there are two factors that may partially explain this discrepancy. First, African American Virginians who attended a Baptist church sometimes met in the same building as the whites, but at a different time, effectively multiplying the use of a fixed number of seats. This was the case in Charlottesville, for example, when the black members first began to declare their ecclesiastical independence.[1] Second, the black church membership grew faster than some churches could hold, and there are accounts of black Baptists listening outside the churches during the services because there was not enough room for them inside. Horace Tonsler, who was only a child when the war came, remembered crowded churches. "When we git to de church, de white folks would go inside, an' de slaves would sit round under de trees outside. Den de preacher git de white folks to singin' an' shoutin, an' he start to walkin' up an' down de pulpit an' ev'y once in a while he lean out de winder an' shout somepin' out to us black folks. 'Twarn't no room inside fo' us."[2]

Table 4. Distribution of Virginia Evangelicals in 1860, by Denomination and County

County	Mainline Baptist accommodations[a]	Episcopal accommodations	Methodist accommodations	Presbyterian accommodations[b]	Total slave and free black population	Total population
Northwest						
Barbour	1,650	0	7,150	0	230	8,958
Braxton	No data available.				107	4,992
Brooke	300	0	2,800	400	69	5,494
Cabell	3,800	0	1,600	0	329	8,020
Calhoun	460	0	2,250	0	10	2,502
Clay	100	0	400	0	26	1,787
Doddridge	150	300	950	0	35	5,203
Gilmer	2,000	0	600	160	74	3,759
Hancock	0	0	1,730	2,000	3	4,445
Harrison	4,200	0	4,850	750	614	13,790
Jackson	0	350	3,900	400	66	8,306
Kanawha	2,400	650	3,700	950	2,365	16,150
Lewis	950	350	5,000	300	263	7,999
Marion	2,500	250	9,685	400	66	12,722
Marshall	200	150	3,080	1,400	86	12,997
Mason	900	0	6,500	4,000	423	9,173

County						
Monongalia	3,200	0	9,600	1,650	147	13,048
Nicholas	1,460	0	4,460	0	156	4,627
Ohio	300	1,000	4,000	2,800	226	22,422
Pleasants	150	250	1,200	200	20	2,945
Pocahontas	0	0	3,100	1,900	272	3,958
Preston	2,200	0	5,300	1,000	112	13,312
Putnam	No data available.				593	6,301
Randolph	200	0	1,900	1,550	197	4,990
Ritchie	975	0	3,575	250	38	6,847
Roane	1,980	0	2,520	0	74	5,381
Taylor	4,100	0	3,150	0	163	7,463
Tucker	0	0	1,400	0	36	1,428
Tyler	524	0	1,849	400	29	6,517
Upshur	0	0	5,900	600	228	7,292
Wayne	1,950	300	2,000	0	143	6,747
Webster	No data available.				3	1,555
Wetzel	300	300	2,300	0	12	6,703
Wirt	750	0	1,400	0	23	3,751
Wood	2,100	300	2,300	900	255	11,046
Median Northwest	825	0	2,940	350	107	6,703

Table 4 *Continued*

County	Mainline Baptist accommodations[a]	Episcopal accommodations	Methodist accommodations	Presbyterian accommodations[b]	Total slave and free black population	Total population
Piedmont						
Albemarle	7,280	2,050	5,250	1,400	14,522	26,625
Amelia	1,000	0	2,250	600	7,844	10,741
Amherst	1,400	800	2,800	24	6,575	13,742
Appomattox	4,800	0	2,750	1,200	4,771	8,889
Bedford	7,350	1,400	8,450	750	10,680	25,068
Brunswick	1,150	2,100	3,450	200	9,817	14,809
Buckingham	4,900	400	4,025	1,900	9,171	15,212
Campbell	2,250	1,250	5,200	3,600	12,609	26,197
Charlotte	1,750	500	1,600	1,800	9,490	14,471
Culpeper	6,400	1,500	1,200	500	7,104	12,063
Cumberland	300	600	1,250	900	7,015	9,961
Dinwiddie	3,800	2,400	9,200	1,900	16,520	30,198
Fauquier	4,200	1,575	4,050	1,025	11,276	21,706
Fluvanna	3,200	400	3,000	0	5,260	10,353
Franklin	6,550	0	4,800	500	6,456	20,098

Goochland	2,650	1,100	550	900	6,842	10,656
Greene	1,700	0	2,750	0	2,007	5,022
Halifax	7,500	1,050	3,400	1,100	15,460	26,520
Henry	4,095	175	1,300	0	5,332	12,105
Loudoun	3,550	800	5,075	650	6,753	21,774
Louisa	6,500	600	4,300	700	10,518	16,701
Lunenburg	600	300	1,800	480	7,562	11,983
Madison	2,800	350	2,700	400	4,494	8,854
Mecklenburg	4,050	2,050	8,000	3,000	13,318	20,096
Nelson	4,500	1,350	2,900	500	6,366	13,015
Nottoway	1,800	100	5,250	625	6,566	8,836
Orange	1,700	400	1,100	900	6,298	10,851
Patrick	1,700	0	1,690	0	2,201	9,359
Pittsylvania	9,300	450	4,900	1,100	14,999	32,104
Powhatan	2,650	850	1,200	800	5,812	8,392
Prince Edward	1,800	0	2,900	3,600	7,807	11,844
Rappahannock	4,100	500	1,350	250	3,832	8,850
Median Piedmont	3,375	550	2,900	725	7,060	12,560

Table 4 *Continued*

County	Mainline Baptist accommodations[a]	Episcopal accommodations	Methodist accommodations	Presbyterian accommodations[b]	Total slave and free black population	Total population
Southwest						
Boone	400	0	1,600	0	159	4,840
Buchanan	200	0	0	0	31	2,793
Carroll	1,250	0	1,800	500	293	8,012
Craig	300	0	250	600	450	3,553
Fayette	2,000	0	3,500	0	281	5,997
Floyd	2,125	0	675	350	491	8,236
Giles	200	0	2,950	300	845	6,883
Grayson	2,100	0	4,200	0	599	8,252
Greenbrier	1,800	0	7,650	3,850	1,711	12,211
Lee	2,500	250	5,200	300	837	11,032
Logan	150	0	150	0	149	4,938
McDowell	300	0	150	0	0	1,535
Mercer	1,800	0	3,025	0	391	6,819
Monroe	1,100	0	2,505	1,835	1,221	10,757
Montgomery	300	0	2,200	1,400	2,366	10,617
Pulaski	150	0	800	750	1,602	5,416

Raleigh		No data available.			76	3,367
Russell	2,700	0	2,390	0	1,150	10,280
Scott	1,350	0	2,325	0	542	12,072
Smyth	1,250	0	2,000	500	1,220	8,952
Tazewell	1,500	0	4,780	2,000	1,295	9,920
Washington	2,000	200	4,650	3,000	2,796	16,892
Wise	650	0	1,200	0	92	4,508
Wyoming	500	0	1,800	0	66	2,861
Wythe	0	400	7,650	3,400	2,319	12,305
Median Southwest	1,175	0	2,263	300	542	8,012
Tidewater						
Accomack	2,100	1,100	6,050	300	7,925	18,586
Arlington/Alexandria	900	1,600	2,200	1,000	2,801	12,652
Caroline	8,800	400	1,350	0	11,516	18,464
Charles City	875	575	1,000	0	3,803	5,609
Chesterfield	7,000	200	4,000	200	8,997	19,016
Elizabeth City	1,100	1,000	1,800	0	2,618	5,798
Essex	3,800	750	1,300	0	7,173	10,469
Fairfax	0	0	8,100	4,200	3,788	11,834
Gloucester	1,550	1,600	2,250	0	6,439	10,956
Greensville	630	400	1,450	0	4,400	6,374
Hanover	5,100	1,700	2,350	950	9,740	17,222

Table 4 *Continued*

County	Mainline Baptist accommodations[a]	Episcopal accommodations	Methodist accommodations	Presbyterian accommodations[b]	Total slave and free black population	Total population
Henrico	12,400	4,700	5,950	3,200	23,631	61,616
Isle of Wight	1,500	300	1,950	300	4,940	9,977
James City	1,200	600	780	0	3,631	5,798
King and Queen	4,000	0	1,200	0	6,522	10,328
King George	1,600	1,348	1,100	0	4,061	6,571
King William	2,800	300	300	0	5,941	8,530
Lancaster	1,400	700	850	0	3,170	5,151
Mathews	800	300	2,450	0	3,226	7,091
Middlesex	3,500	300	1,600	0	2,501	4,364
Nansemond	2,200	550	3,100	0	7,961	13,693
New Kent	1,200	600	1,650	300	3,738	5,884
Norfolk	5,625	2,500	12,050	1,500	11,807	36,227
Northampton	850	1,250	2,000	450	4,834	7,832
Northumberland	1,700	0	3,300	0	3,661	7,531
Prince George	750	700	1,355	0	5,512	8,411
Prince William	800	600	1,600	600	2,875	8,565
Princess Anne	1,700	550	3,150	0	3,381	7,714

Richmond	1,950	700	700	0	3,286	6,856
Southampton	3,150	0	5,450	0	7,202	12,915
Spotsylvania	11,050	1,450	2,950	500	8,360	16,076
Stafford	1,100	800	2,300	750	3,633	8,555
Surry	0	1,200	1,700	0	3,799	6,133
Sussex	2,300	0	3,450	1,400	7,057	10,175
Warwick	800	0	0	0	1,078	1,740
Westmoreland	800	1,200	1,550	0	4,895	8,282
York	1,900	0	1,400	300	2,607	4,949
Median Tidewater	1,600	600	1,800	0	4,400	8,530
Valley						
Alleghany	0	0	2,025	1,150	1,122	6,765
Augusta	450	1,150	5,525	5,800	6,202	27,749
Bath	0	300	400	1,200	1,024	3,676
Berkeley	525	725	1,390	1,355	1,936	12,525
Botetourt	650	450	2,000	750	3,075	11,516
Clarke	1,600	1,400	2,000	600	3,439	7,146
Frederick	1,250	750	8,485	2,300	3,467	16,546
Hampshire	1,075	1,150	5,350	3,100	1,435	13,913
Hardy	0	0	1,820	700	1,343	9,864
Highland	0	0	1,450	600	429	4,319

Table 4 *Continued*

County	Mainline Baptist accommodations[a]	Episcopal accommodations	Methodist accommodations	Presbyterian accommodations[b]	Total slave and free black population	Total population
Jefferson	300	1,500	3,100	1,400	4,471	14,535
Morgan	0	0	3,450	0	118	3,732
Page	2,500	0	1,500	0	1,234	8,109
Pendleton	0	0	1,900	300	294	6,164
Roanoke	1,450	0	400	500	2,798	8,048
Rockbridge	1,700	500	3,150	5,450	4,407	17,248
Rockingham	1,400	0	7,500	2,650	2,919	23,408
Shenandoah	200	0	2,500	1,100	1,069	13,896
Warren	2,250	500	2,325	500	1,859	6,442
Median Valley	525	300	2,025	1,100	1,859	9,864
Virginia totals[c]	298,029	68,498	436,044	117,504	548,902	1,596,318

Source: U.S. Bureau of the Census, *Eighth Census, 1860*, as accessed via Geospatial and Statistical Data Center, "Historical Census Browser" <http://fisher.lib.virginia.edu/collections/stats/histcensus/>. The Bureau of the Census omitted information on the churches in Braxton, Putnam, Webster, and Raleigh counties from their returns.

[a]Baptists affiliated with the General Baptist Association of Virginia only.

[b]Presbyterians only in Old or New School.

[c]Totals derived by adding numbers from individual counties; Historical Census Browser totals differ slightly.

Church Governance

Evangelicals in the Baptist, Methodist, Presbyterian, and Episcopal traditions shared a great deal in common by the mid-nineteenth century, but their church polities remained distinctive. This brief note on ecclesiology is not meant as a theological exposition of the various models of church governance practiced by these four denominations. Its aims are much more modest: to introduce the reader to the institutional frameworks in which Virginia's evangelicals operated. The brief organizational charts below neither cover every layer of church governance nor track every schism from each denomination nor bring the church polities up to the present. They nonetheless provide a solid foundation for understanding the relationship between the organizational units discussed in this book.[1]

Baptist

The fundamental unit of governance for Baptists is the congregation, which theoretically exercises final authority in all decisions affecting the local body of believers. In practice, the regional associations played an important role in governance by resolving difficult doctrinal issues, standardizing Baptist faith and practice, and representing the local congregations at state and national meetings. The Southern Baptist Convention brought more centralized control to the denomination than had the weak Triennial Convention.

Methodist

The Methodist Church balanced the intimacy of congregational governance with the maintenance of episcopal authority. Throughout most of the nineteenth century, itinerant ministers traveled a circuit, and they or their delegated assistants ran class meetings for small groups within congregations throughout the circuit. These same itinerants also met in conference at least quarterly to oversee the business of the church. Itinerant members of each conference, which was itself made up of several districts, met annually to take care of the year's business. A general conference of Methodists from across the nation still meets every four years, under the supervision of the church's bishops.

Presbyterian

Presbyterians, by definition, reject episcopal authority. On the local and the national levels, they instead govern by committee. On the local level, this shared governance takes the form of a session of members selected from the congregation. On the regional and then state levels, this takes the form of conferences of ministers (presbyters). The Presbyterian Church's national organization, the General Assembly, fragmented into several pieces in the decades before the war, making it exceptionally difficult to keep track of Virginia Presbyterians' national affiliations. The bulk of Presbyterians in Virginia stayed with the Old School in the schism of 1837 and finally broke off in 1861 to form the Presbyterian Church in the Confederate States of America.

Episcopal

The Episcopal Church's governance closely resembles that of its predecessor, the Anglican Church. Elected vestries govern each congregation, and their lay authority is in constructive tension with the ordained leadership of the church, including priests and bishops. At an annual convention for the faithful within a diocese, both ordained and lay members participate (on a state level for the period under examination here), and the bishop presides. Shared governance is also the ideal at the national conventions, which also have representative laymen and clerics.

Table 5. Church Governance

Congregation	Association	State organization	National or regional organization
The congregation is the most important level of Baptist polity.	e.g., Dover Association, Portsmouth Association	General Committee of Baptist Associations (1787–99) General Meeting of Correspondence (1800–1822) Baptist General Association of Virginia (1823–present)	General Missionary Convention of the Baptist Denomination in the United States of America for Foreign Missions, or "Triennial Convention" (1814–44) Southern Baptist Convention (1845–present)

METHODIST

Congregation	Circuit/District	Annual conference	General Conference
Each congregation could include multiple class meetings.	Early in the Methodist experience, itinerants presided over circuits that were the primary unit of organization. A district is a group of proximate circuits linked together for more efficient governance.	e.g., Baltimore Conference, Virginia Conference	Methodist Episcopal Church (1784–1844) Methodist Episcopal Church, South (1845–1939)

Table 5 *Continued*

Congregation	Presbytery	Synod	General Assembly
A session governs each congregation.	e.g., Hanover Presbytery, Lexington Presbytery	e.g., Synod of Virginia	General Assembly of the Presbyterian Church in the U.S.A. (1789–1837/1857/1861)
			Old School General Assembly of the Presbyterian Church in the U.S.A (1837–61)
			New School General Assembly (1837–57)

EPISCOPAL

Parish	Diocese (convention)	General convention	
A vestry governs each parish.	e.g., Diocese of Virginia	Protestant Episcopal Church (1789–present)	

NOTES

Abbreviations

DocSouth	University of North Carolina at Chapel Hill, "Documenting the American South." University Library, University of North Carolina at Chapel Hill, 2004. <http://docsouth.unc.edu/index>
Duke	Special Collections, Duke University, Durham, North Carolina
LVa	Library of Virginia, Richmond
SHC	Southern Historical Collection, Wilson Library, University of North Carolina, Chapel Hill
Tulane	Special Collections, Howard-Tilton Memorial Library, Tulane University, New Orleans, Louisiana
UTS	Union Theological Seminary, Richmond, Virginia
UVa	Albert and Shirley Smalls Special Collections Library, University of Virginia, Charlottesville
VBHS	Virginia Baptist Historical Society, Richmond
VHS	Virginia Historical Society, Richmond

Acknowledgments

1. Lumpkin, *Making of a Southerner*, 187–93.

Introduction

1. Birney, *American Churches* (1842), and Stearns, *Henry Box Brown*, DocSouth. For the best account of Brown and his struggles with the southern church, see Ruggles, *Unboxing*, 12–14, 21–22.

   Several scholars have charted southern evangelicals' involvement with slavery and corresponding divergence from northern churches in the late antebellum period. See esp. Smith, *In His Image, But*; Goen, *Broken Churches, Broken Nation*; Snay, *Gospel of Disunion*. Others have concentrated on the evangelicals' ideological contributions to proslavery, notably, Genovese and Fox-Genovese,

Mind of the Master Class, 473; Farmer, *Metaphysical Confederacy*; Tise, *Pro-slavery*; Daly, *When Slavery Was Called Freedom*. Furthermore, scholars have agreed that white evangelicals endorsed slavery and southern interests most vocally during the Civil War itself. See, for example, Silver, *Confederate Morale*; Faust, *Creation of Confederate Nationalism*; Rubin, *Shattered Nation*.

2. U.S. Bureau of the Census, *Seventh Census, 1850*, 285–96. This figure is based on accommodations for Baptists, Methodists, Presbyterians, and Episcopalians as a percentage of total accommodations in Virginia churches. Some within the larger families of Baptists and Presbyterians resisted identification as evangelicals, but their numbers were offset by evangelical members of the much smaller Christian and Union churches. Ten years later, the proportion of evangelicals among churchmen in Virginia, as measured by number of accommodations in the census, was roughly the same, 86 percent. This calculation excludes Reformed Presbyterians and splinter Baptist groups. See U.S. Bureau of the Census, *Eighth Census, 1860*, 485–88.

3. Sernett, *Black Religion*; Boles, *Masters and Slaves*; Sobel, *Trabelin' On*; Cornelius, *Slave Missions*.

4. Boles, "Evangelical Protestantism." But the classic statement of this journey remains Mathews, *Religion in the Old South*. See also Sparks, *Jordan's Stormy Banks*; Heyrman, *Southern Cross*; Schweiger, *Gospel Working Up*.

5. Here, I am responding to Mitchell Snay's observation: "While it has long been accepted that Southern Christians united around a scriptural justification of human bondage, the nature of this consensus remains unclear" ("Civil War Religion," 391). See also Young, *Proslavery and Sectional Thought*, 1, and Bailey, "Protestantism and Afro-Americans," for the observation that, at the very least, white evangelicals continued to wrestle with their relationship with black evangelicals throughout the antebellum period. On nonslaveholders, see Spangler, "Becoming Baptists," 246.

6. Huston, "Experiential Basis," 620; Ashworth, *Slavery, Capitalism, and Politics*, 5–13.

7. Goodman, *Of One Blood*; Newman, *Transformation of American Abolitionism*; Stauffer, *Black Hearts of Men*.

8. Albert, *House of Bondage*, DocSouth.

9. Noll, Bebbington, and Rawlyk, *Evangelicalism*. The fifteen essays on evangelicalism before 1900 in this volume stress the transatlantic roots of the movement and chart the shift of evangelicalism from a series of revivals within established churches to a theological worldview institutionalized in new denominations. Also see Mathews, *Religion in the Old South*, 13–22; Sparks, *Jordan's Stormy Banks*, 1–2; Johnson, *Redeeming America*, 5. On conflict within the Episcopal Church, see Butler, "Church and American Destiny."

10. U.S. Bureau of the Census, *Seventh Census, 1850*, 243, 257.

For a full discussion of denominational statistics, see Appendices A and B. On adherence ratios, see Carroll, *Religious Forces*, xxxv; Bonomi, *Cope of Heaven*,

88–92; Mathews, *Religion in the Old South*, 47; Goen, *Broken Churches, Broken Nation*, 55; Heyrman, *Southern Cross*, 265; Beeman and Isaac, "Cultural Conflict and Social Change," 535. It is worth emphasizing the extremely conservative nature of Carroll's numbers. Robert Baird, writing in 1844, calculated many more adherents per member. Whereas Baird estimated 4.7 Baptist adherents per member, for example, Carroll calculated 2.9. In fact, Baird's ratios were significantly higher than Carroll's for every denomination: 5.4 instead of 3.5 for Presbyterians, 3.2 instead of 2.5 for Methodists, and 6.9 instead of 4.6 for Episcopalians. As cited in "Religion in America," 497.

Statistics on the number of accommodations available in 1850 confirm the proportions resulting from the use of Carroll's ratios. There were enough seats in Virginia's Baptist, Methodist, Episcopal, and Presbyterian churches to seat 754,606 persons at one time, or 53 percent of all Virginia residents. See U.S. Bureau of the Census, *Seventh Census, 1850*, 285–96.

11. U.S. Bureau of the Census, *Seventh Census, 1850*, 247–48, 253, 256. For a much more pessimistic view of black conversion, see Johnson, " 'Delusive Clothing,' " and Fountain, "Christ in Chains." Johnson and Fountain cite several factors, such as the rural concentration of the slave population, which might have prevented enslaved men and women from attending church.

12. Raboteau, *Slave Religion*, 48–75, explained the relevance of African cultural survivals. There are many different explanations for divergences between black and white evangelicals, which are not mutually exclusive. For example, Smith, in "Slavery and Theology," has argued that the terrors of slavery introduced men and women of African descent to a deeper, more authentic understanding of Western Christianity; Thornton, in "Trail of Voodoo," has suggested that African Christian traditions, established before the transatlantic slave trade, shaped African American religious expression; Saillant, in "Lemuel Haynes," has argued that black divines in the American Revolution forged a liberating, new "Black Theology"; and Sensbach, in *Rebecca's Revival*, 50–68, using an Atlantic perspective, has demonstrated that early black converts to evangelicalism used the belief system to channel antagonism against their ostensible owners. On African American cosmology, see Sobel, *Trabelin' On*, 3–75.

13. Bratton, "Fields's Observations," DocSouth.

14. For a brilliant exception, see Noll, *Theological Crisis*.

15. Sobel, *Trabelin' On*. Sobel's concentration on the Baptist tradition is especially relevant for Virginia, for roughly five in six black Virginians who joined a church chose the Baptists.

16. Frey and Wood, *Come Shouting to Zion*, 115.

17. See Chapter 2 for demographic notes. On the role of Virginia, see Kulikoff, "Colonial Chesapeake"; Fischer and Kelly, *Bound Away*; Ayers, "Virginia History as Southern History."

18. More than anyone else, Berlin has shown the limitations of regionwide generalizations about slavery by showing significant variations in the practice of slave-

holding and the experiences of slaves according to time and to place; see Berlin, *Many Thousands Gone*. Berlin's work, especially in conjunction with Morgan's *Slave Counterpoint*, demands a revisitation of such monolithic accounts as Genovese's *Roll, Jordan, Roll*.

19. Williamson, *Rage for Order*, 24–25. Though he did not write specifically about religious arguments for slavery, Jenkins helped to establish this erroneous trend by describing a sudden, politically driven turn to proslavery after the Missouri Compromise; see Jenkins, *Pro-Slavery Thought*, 48, 65.

20. Loveland, *Southern Evangelicals*, 199; Goen, *Broken Churches, Broken Nation*, 183; Heyrman, *Southern Cross*, 251. On the endurance and preeminence of this view, see Sparks, "Religion in the Pre–Civil War South." For an excellent critique of the approach, see Tise, *Proslavery*, 3–11, 98–102.

21. Mathews, *Religion in the Old South*, 149, 185; Smith, *In His Image, But*, 130; Hill, "South's Two Cultures," 4; Eighmy, *Churches in Cultural Captivity*.

22. Boyden, *Epidemic*, 16. See Chapters 1 and 2 for a more thorough discussion of eighteenth-century antislavery and its limitations.

23. For a survey of the literature on the guilt thesis and a strong rejection of it, see Foster, "Guilt over Slavery."

24. Douglass, *Narrative*, DocSouth. For equally damning remarks, see the narratives of William Wells Brown and Henry Bibb, also on DocSouth.

25. Genovese and Fox-Genovese, "Divine Sanction," 215.

26. Genovese and Fox-Genovese, "Religious Ideals," 19; Genovese, *"Slavery Ordained of God."*

27. The promise is most clear in Genovese, *Roll, Jordan, Roll*, and Fox-Genovese, *Within the Plantation Household*, while the absence of black actors is most noticeable in Genovese and Fox-Genovese, *Mind of the Master Class*.

28. Link, *Roots of Secession*; Iaccarino, "Virginia and the National Contest." The idea that black southerners shaped the politics of slavery is now well established; see, for example, Mason, *Slavery and Politics*, 106–29; Berlin, "Who Freed the Slaves?"; Freehling, *South vs. the South*; Robinson, *Bitter Fruits of Bondage*, 37–57.

29. Scott, *Arts of Resistance*. Perhaps because historians of the American South "discovered" black agency with the Civil Rights Movement and observed the central role that black clerics played in that movement, they have ever since linked black resistance to slavery with black adherence to evangelical Protestantism. In 1972, Blassingame argued that slaves found in religious expression a basis for community solidarity, and Mullin identified appeal to evangelicalism as the sine qua non of successful slave rebellions; see Blassingame, *Slave Community*; Mullin, *Flight and Rebellion*. Genovese made this interpretation the orthodox one with *Roll, Jordan, Roll*, in which he argued that faith enabled slaves to resist white hegemony and therefore to shape the contours of plantation life. Other important paeans to slave agency in religion include Harding, "Religion and Resistance" and *There Is a River*; Sidbury, *Ploughshares into Swords*; and

Gomez, *Exchanging Our Country Marks*. On resistance as the great theme of African American history, see most recently Hahn, *Nation under Our Feet*. For an early refutation of this trend, see Marty's foreword to Sernett, *Black Religion*.

30. Williamson uses a dialectic paradigm in *Rage for Order*. See Sobel, *Trabelin' On* and *World They Made Together*; Frey and Wood, *Come Shouting to Zion*, xii; Harvey, *Redeeming the South* and *Freedom's Coming*; Burton, *In My Father's House*; and Clarke, *Dwelling Place*, for the best available models. Mathews affirms this approach in " 'We Have Left Undone,' " 318.

31. O'Brien, *Conjectures of Order*, 2:1098. See also Farmer, *Metaphysical Confederacy*; Genovese, *Consuming Fire*; Daly, *When Slavery Was Called Freedom*.

32. Genovese and Fox-Genovese, *Mind of the Master Class*, 526–27; Noll, *Theological Crisis*, 51–64, quotation from 56.

33. Levine, *Black Culture and Black Consciousness*.

34. Stroupe, *Religious Press*, 99–100, 157–59.

35. Raboteau et al., "Retelling Carter Woodson's Story."

Chapter 1

1. While the period of racial fluidity may not have been as egalitarian or as long as Breen and Innes, Vaughan, Berlin, or others have suggested, English colonial planners did initially hope for a society without slavery, and it was not until the early eighteenth century that white Virginians constructed a coherent apparatus of racial control. See Morgan, *American Slavery, American Freedom*; Breen and Innes, *"Myne Owne Ground"*; Vaughan, "Blacks in Virginia"; Berlin, *Many Thousands Gone*; Morgan, *Slave Counterpoint*, 1–13.

2. Jernegan, "Slavery and Conversion," 504. For the same sentiment without the ethnocentric context, see Morgan, *Slave Counterpoint*, 420.

3. James I in his 1621 "Instructions to Governor Wyatt," in Cushing, *Colony Laws*, 21. In the parish system, ministers were theoretically responsible for all of the souls within their geographic boundaries. For a clear discussion of parish responsibilities, see Nelson, *Blessed Company*, 259.

4. Berlin, *Many Thousands Gone* and "Creole to African"; Bond, *Damned Souls*, 196–203; Sluiter, "New Light on the '20' "; Billings, "Fernando and Elizabeth Key."

5. Thornton, "Trail of Voodoo"; Gomez, "Muslims in Early America."

6. Jordan, *White over Black*, esp. 20–24; Bond, *Damned Souls*, 200–202.

7. Kulikoff, " 'Prolifick' People," 393; Minchinton, King, and White, *Virginia Slave-Trade Statistics*, xv. The peak years were from 1732 to 1740, when imports averaged over 1,800 slaves per year. Other notable peaks were from 1749 to 1752 and from 1760 to 1763, when the volume averaged over 2,000 and 1,500 per year, respectively. For Africans as a proportion of the colonial population, see the similar estimates in Berlin, *Many Thousands Gone*, 369, and Greene, *Pursuits of Happiness*, 178–79.

8. Leviticus 25:44–46, KJV.

9. Haynes, *Noah's Curse*, 7–8. Haynes explains that some colonists were using the Curse of Ham by the 1670s, but that it did not become ubiquitous until the antebellum period.

10. Jernegan, "Slavery and Conversion," 521; Raboteau, *Slave Religion*, 100. Du Bois was one of the first to observe the self-interest at work in these protestations in "Slavery and Christianity," *Negro Church*, DocSouth.

11. Thornton, "Trail of Voodoo." It is true, however, that there were more available catechists for the Portuguese because of the conversion of King João I in 1491 and the subsequent surge of Kongolese Catholicism. See Blackburn, *New World Slavery*, 117.

12. For at least half a century, scholars have argued about how much of their religious heritage Africans were able to maintain upon entering chattel slavery. Herskovits in *Myth of the Negro Past* and Frazier in *Negro Church in America* famously framed the debate, Herskovits arguing for extensive "holdovers" and Frazier that the middle passage and horrors of slavery erased all religious bonds in African American life. Though there are still very vigorous proponents of each perspective (see, for example, Butler, *Sea of Faith*, 129–63, and Mitchell, *Black Church Beginnings*, 1–22), the current consensus, articulated most fully by Sobel in *World They Made Together*, is that African Americans were rarely able to reproduce complete communities in which they practiced an intact African religion, but that everywhere men and women of African origin retained enough of an African worldview to influence dramatically the development of the New World religious practices of European Americans. For particularly effective applications of this approach, see Frey and Wood, *Come Shouting to Zion*, 35–62, and Clarke, *Dwelling Place*, 152–66. For the argument that intact African religions may not have survived but that hybrid African-based religions remained dominant until the nineteenth century, see Rucker, *River Flows On*; Fountain, "Long on Religion," 114–44.

13. Brydon, *Virginia's Mother Church*, 1:52–59; Jones, "Established Virginia Church"; Brown, *Good Wives*, 42–45; Kupperman, *Indians & English*, 224. Note that this shift was more ideological than geographic. Indians did not "vanish" from Virginia, but Europeans defined them out of the commonwealth.

14. Stanwood, "Captives and Slaves," 439. White Virginians would conceive of African slavery in the same way more than a century later, though they did not recognize the precedent.

15. Bond, *Damned Souls*, 201.

16. Nelson, *Blessed Company*, 259.

17. Woolverton, *Colonial Anglicanism*, 16–20. For an early emphasis on the role that black Virginians played in the process, see Jones, "Established Virginia Church," 18: "If Virginia lacked a serious threat from dissenters before the middle of the eighteenth century, African infidels provided a dark challenge to the Establishment through their silent but anomalous presence."

18. Practically speaking, dissenters were non-Anglican Protestants. Technically, they were Christians who enjoyed liberty of conscience under the Act of Toleration (1689), which most Virginians believed to apply on both sides of the Atlantic.

19. Billings, "Fernando and Elizabeth Key," 467–68, 471. For the contradiction between enslavement and Christianity in the European tradition, see Blackburn, *New World Slavery*, 31–83; Davis, *Inhuman Bondage*, 48–76.

20. The full text appears in Brydon, *Virginia's Mother Church*, 1:470. The preamble reads, "Whereas some doubts have arisen whether children that are slaves by birth, and by the charity and piety of their owners made partakers of the blessed sacrament of baptisme, should by vertue of their baptisme be made ffree. . . ." This language suggests that the framers of the statute may have been targeting primarily slaves born in-country, a growing demographic.

21. Godwyn, *Negro's & Indians Advocate*. Background information from Woolverton, *Colonial Anglicanism*, 71–73, and Brydon, *Virginia's Mother Church*, 1:506–16.

22. Godwyn, *Negro's & Indians Advocate*, title page and 5.

23. Ibid., 139. For evidence of Godwyn's antislavery sentiment, see 143, where he laments that so few slaveholders consider it "a matter of *Conscience* to continue Christians in Servitude."

    Other scholars have noticed that men and women opposed in principle to slaveholding might inadvertently have strengthened the practice by conceding too much in their efforts to encourage the evangelization of the enslaved. By assuring their coreligionists that evangelization would create better slaves, in other words, ministers accidentally enabled their auditors to believe that slavery and Christianity were compatible. In general, scholars place the origins of this argument much too late. Boles dates it to the 1780s and 1790s; Clarke, to the 1830s. See Boles, "Southern Way of Religion," 241, and Clarke, *Dwelling Place*, 103–5.

24. Feight, "Good and the Just," 9.

25. Brydon, *Virginia's Mother Church*, 1:219.

26. Jordan, *White over Black*, 191. On evidence that Anglican laity in Virginia may have been more reluctant than Anglican clergy trained in England to accept this change, see Bond, *Damned Souls*, 196–203, and Wood, " 'Jesus Christ Has Got Thee,' " 1–7.

27. Jones, "Established Virginia Church," 13, and Stanwood, "Captives and Slaves," esp. 456–58.

28. Parent, *Foul Means*, 236–64. Parent describes how a minority of Anglican ministers in the 1720s urged a more active ministry to the slaves, citing a particularly interesting 1727 sermon by Peter Fontaine, a typescript of which is available at the Colonial Williamsburg Foundation. He interprets this interest in slave conversions almost exclusively as a strategy for social control, an interpretation with which I disagree.

29. Jernegan, "Slavery and Conversion," 521–22, and Brydon, *Virginia's Mother Church*, 1:370–91; the full text of the responses is on 392–93. Jernegan notes responses from twenty-nine churches, while Brydon reprints responses from only twenty-eight.

30. Parent, *Foul Means*, 159–62.

31. Tate, *Negro in Eighteenth-Century Williamsburg*, 202–8, and Jones, "Established Virginia Church," 18–19.

32. Both sources reprinted in Brydon, *Virginia's Mother Church*, 1:392–93, 396–405; Jones quotation, 400.

33. Kulikoff, "'Prolifick' People," esp. tab. 1, 393.

34. Morgan and Nicholls, "Slaves in Piedmont Virginia," 220.

35. Hening, *Statutes at Large*, 9:471–72.

36. Michael Gomez places the native-born percentage around 80 from 1780 to 1810. Gomez, however, uses this as a regionwide rate and does not account for the early date of natural increase for Virginia slaves. The Virginia percentage likely hovered closer to 90, reflecting an earlier shift to positive natural population growth and an earlier cessation of the Atlantic trade. See Gomez, *Exchanging Our Country Marks*, 20, 194. For additional evidence of the accelerated rate in Virginia, see also Chambers, "Historical Creolization."

37. The term "First Great Awakening" is not meaningful in a Virginia context. In Virginia, there were more than fifty years of relatively distinct revivals from 1740 to 1792, making the construct of a single event seem rather forced. See Gewehr, *Great Awakening in Virginia*, 46–165. To the extent that there was a First Great Awakening, Lambert suggests that it was a cluster of revivals in New England and the Middle Colonies (largely bypassing Virginia) surrounding the visits of George Whitefield and ranging from 1739 to 1746; see *Inventing the Great Awakening*, 24, 253–55.

38. The best introduction to Whitefield is Stout, *Divine Dramatist*.

39. Evangelicals' advocacy for the enslaved had more consequences in the South, but emphasis on bondmen as a way of communicating God's demand for a regenerate heart rather than for outward forms of piety was a strategy that northern evangelicals pursued as well. For the example of Jonathan Edwards, see Minkema, "Edwards on Slavery," 828–29. For a sustained look at the phenomenon in the South, see Essig, *Bonds of Wickedness*.

40. *Virginia Gazette*, 14 Dec. 1739.

41. Though the letter was published in Philadelphia, Whitefield actually wrote it from Savannah on 23 January 1740, just weeks after his stay in Virginia. See Whitefield, *Three Letters*, 13–16. For more on how Whitefield's understanding of evangelicalism did not require him to take an antislavery position, see Bellot, "Defense of Slavery," 22.

42. Jackson, "Hugh Bryan," esp. 606–8; Gallay, "Origins of Slaveholders' Paternalism," 380.

43. Whitefield, *Three Letters*, 15–16.

44. Anderson, "Presbyterians and Augusta Parish."

45. Unless otherwise noted, material on Samuel Davies and his ministry is from Davies, *Letters*; quotations from 3, 14. See also Richards, "Campaign for Slave Literacy"; Payne, "New Light in Hanover County"; Pilcher, *Samuel Davies*. For "moral one-upmanship" between dissenters and Anglicans, see Young, *Proslavery and Sectional Thought*, 19.

46. Jefferson, *Notes*, 140: "In music they are more generally gifted than the whites with accurate ears for tune and time, and they have been found capable of imagining a small catch."

47. Davies, *Letters*, particularly 13–22.

48. Ibid.; Todd, *Improvement of Psalmody*, 14; Southern, *Music of Black Americans*, 58–59. Also notable is the work of western (and less evangelical) Presbyterian John Craig, who around 1760 took in and nurtured an Algerian man named Selim, a fugitive from Spanish slavery; see Meade, *Old Churches*, 1:341–48.

49. Foote, *Sketches of Virginia*, 2nd ser., 49–52; Davies, *Letters*, 28–29.

50. Pilcher, *Samuel Davies*, 111.

51. Henry et al., "Letters," 280.

52. As quoted in Nelson, *Blessed Company*, 261.

53. The exact date of arrival of the Regular Baptists is contested. Even a rough contemporary, William Fristoe, had to guess that the first Regulars arrived "between 1750 and 1755." Their minute book in the Virginia Baptist Historical Society indicates that Regulars had organized Mill Creek Baptist Church by 1753. Ketocton Baptist Church was perhaps one or two years earlier. See Fristoe, *Ketocton Baptist Association*, 5. Most scholars agree on the 1754 date for the Separate Baptists, citing Shubal Stearns's visit in that year. For a concise overview of the different strands of Baptists merging in Virginia, including the General Baptists, see White, *Silhouettes of Baptist Life*.

54. Alley, *History of Baptists*, 41–42; Lindman, "World of Baptists," 99–100; Brekus, *Strangers and Pilgrims*, 62–63. Martha Stearns Marshall, the sister of Shubal Stearns, was the most well-known Separate woman gifted in exhortation.

55. As quoted in Gardner, "Virginia Baptists and Slavery," pt. 1, 1217.

56. 13 May, 10 June 1764, Broad Run Baptist Church, VBHS.

57. 20 Mar. 1779, Upper King and Queen Baptist Church, VBHS. Three were from the Pitt family; two others, from the Gresham family; one each, from the Major and Spencer families.

58. Wright, *Church Records of Rockingham*, 61–62.

59. Toler, *Faithful Minister's Work*, 37.

60. Gardner, "Virginia Baptists and Slavery," pt. 2, 1259.

61. Unlike Presbyterians, Baptists did not, in general, seek state permission to preach as dissenters. They believed state interference undermined the integrity of Christian worship and willingly faced legal sanction rather than submit their faith to civil authority. The standard account of the persecution that Baptists in Virginia faced for their civil disobedience is Little, *Imprisoned Preachers*.

62. Isaac, *Transformation of Virginia*, 218–22.

63. Thomas, *Virginian Baptist*, 58–59.

64. Gallay, "Origins of Slaveholders' Paternalism," 380; Bolton, *Southern Anglicanism*, 116–19; Morgan, *Slave Counterpoint*, 420.

65. As quoted in Nelson, *Blessed Company*, 266–68.

66. Tate, *Negro in Eighteenth-Century Williamsburg*, 46, 47, 137–55.

67. Brydon, *Virginia's Mother Church*, 2:39–40.

68. *Minutes of the Methodist Conferences*, 5–6.

69. Thomas Lyell Autobiography, Smedes Papers, SHC.

70. Lee, *History of the Methodists*, 35.

71. Jarratt's letter reprinted in Asbury, *Journal and Letters*, 1:221. See also Morgan, *Slave Counterpoint*, 428–29; Lambert, "I Saw the Book Talk," 194.

72. *Minutes of the Methodist Conferences*, 60, though I used the 1796 minutes to identify Virginia circuits. The aggregate statistic is typically given as 1,890 black Methodists and 18,791 white Methodists, though 1,000 of the black members are listed for Antigua and 510 of the whites from Nova Scotia.

73. While evangelicals exaggerated their claims of humble origins (see n. 74 below), they did present an outlook on Virginia society different from that of the Anglicans. See Isaac, *Transformation of Virginia*.

74. Many of the pioneering Baptists and Methodists claimed low social status. Robert Semple summarized the class-based arguments of John Waller and other early Baptists "that if the higher ranks in society did not countenance them it was no more than what befell their Master and His inspired Apostles; that rich men in every generation, with some few exceptions, were enemies to a pure Gospel; but that God had declared that He had chosen the poor of this world to be rich in faith" (*Rise and Progress*, 38). Thomas Lyell described early Methodists as "a poor and despised people in the eyes of men" (Autobiography, Smedes Papers, SHC).

   Twentieth-century historians have generally accepted these claims. The most notable example is Isaac, *Transformation of Virginia*, 163–66; see also Beeman and Isaac, "Cultural Conflict and Social Change," 546; Mathews, *Religion in the Old South*, 40–41; Heyrman, *Southern Cross*, 76; Boles, "Southern Way of Religion," 241. For another critique of this position, see Spangler, "Becoming Baptists."

75. Davies, *Duty of Masters*, 17; Spangler, "Proslavery Presbyterians"; Robson, "'Important Question Answered.'"

76. On the implosion of the Anglican Church, see Obrion, "'Mighty Fortress.'" For accounts of disestablishment, see Buckley, *Church and State*; Dreisbach, "Church-State Debate."

77. These petitions are available online courtesy of the Library of Congress and the Library of Virginia, <http://memory.loc.gov/ammem/collections/petitions/>. See Hening, *Statutes at Large*, 10:197–98, 288–89, and 11:62–63. Jefferson's bill passed the house on 17 December 1785, was reported with slight amend-

ments from the senate on 16 January 1786, and was signed by the speaker on 19 January 1786.

78. Historians for many years followed Thomas Jefferson's 1786 estimate of 30,000 fugitives; for the revised figure, see Pybus, "Jefferson's Faulty Math," 29. These new numbers suggest that one in thirty Virginia slaves escaped. See also Holton, *Forced Founders*, 133–63; Frey, "Between Slavery and Freedom" and *Water from the Rock*; Iaccarino, "Virginia and the National Contest," 35–37. For the estimated total number of slaves, see Morgan and Nicholls, "Slaves in Piedmont Virginia," 218.

79. Schama, *Rough Crossings*.

80. Hard numbers are not available until 1790, when there were already 12,866 free blacks in Virginia, or roughly 4 percent of the total black population. In 1810, the number was 30,570, or 7 percent of the total black population. See U.S. Bureau of the Census, *First Census, 1790*, 3, and *Third Census, 1810*, 1; Albert, "Protean Institution," 145; Wolf, *Race and Liberty*, 43–47. Wolf believes that the estimate of 2,000 for 1760 may be low.

   For an account of Carter's manumissions, see Levy, *First Emancipator*; for an extended longitudinal study of a community liberated under this statute, see Ely, *Israel on the Appomattox*. For more on white evangelicals and the statute, see Chapter 2.

81. Raboteau wrestles with this issue in *Slave Religion*, 43–75; Sobel, in *Trabelin' On*, 99–108.

82. Mathews, *Religion in the Old South*, 196; Clarke, *Dwelling Place*, 253.

83. 1 Oct. [1791], Buck Marsh Baptist Church, VBHS.

84. Simpson, "Henry Toler's Journal," 1651.

85. Jones, *Religious Instruction of the Negroes*, 48. For additional examples of black spiritual "virtuosity," see Heyrman, *Southern Cross*, 217–20.

86. Semple, *Rise and Progress*, 290–91.

87. Ibid., 170.

88. Backus, "Yankee Baptist," 71.

89. 13 June 1777, Mill Swamp Baptist Church, VBHS.

90. U.S. Bureau of the Census, *Heads of Families*, 9; Linville Creek resolution from 12 Nov. 1791, in Wright, *Church Records of Rockingham*, 65; 2 Oct. 1778, South Quay Baptist Church, VBHS. Lindman describes the constriction of black congregational privileges in "World of Baptists," esp. 200–202.

91. Lindman, "World of Baptists," 185; Frey and Wood, *Come Shouting to Zion*, 126.

92. Raboteau, *Slave Religion*, 134–35.

93. Aug. 1780, 4 Jan., 5 Apr., 5 July 1782, 5 May, 3 July 1786, 4 Oct. 1788, South Quay Baptist Church, VBHS.

94. For a specific example, see 13 Nov. 1791, *Mill Creek Baptist Church*, VBHS. See also Gardner, "Virginia Baptists and Slavery," pt. 2, 1266.

95. Dec. 1789, Buck Marsh Baptist Church, VBHS.

96. Sobel, *Trabelin' On*, 250; Jackson, "Religious Development of the Negro," 181–203. There were several churches in and around Gloucester, and it is unclear if Sobel is referring to the church that William Lemon pastored. If so, she would be incorrect in categorizing it as an all-black church, because Semple makes its biracial composition clear. See Semple, *Rise and Progress*, 169–70.

97. Slightly conflicting accounts of these black churches—especially Williamsburg—appear in Semple, *Rise and Progress*, 114–15, and Gardner, "Virginia Baptists and Slavery," pt. 2, 1260.

98. Morgan, *Slave Counterpoint*, 429.

99. On Charleson, see Bennett, *Memorials of Methodism*, 297; Bradley, "Development of African Churches"; Lyerly, *Methodism and the Southern Mind*, 59–60.

100. Lyerly, *Methodism and the Southern Mind*, 48.

101. As quoted in Wilson, "Religion of the American Negro Slave," 51.

102. Costa et al., "Geography of Slavery in Virginia." Costa and his team have gathered and transcribed more than 4,000 advertisements for fugitives, making them fully text searchable. Items quoted above, in order: *Virginia Gazette and General Advertiser*, 23 Mar. 1791; *Virginia Herald and Fredericksburg Advertiser*, 5 July 1792; *Virginia Chronicle and Norfolk and Portsmouth General Advertiser*, 26 Jan. 1793; *Virginia Herald and Fredericksburg Advertiser*, 13 June 1793, 18 Aug. 1795; *Virginia Chronicle and General Advertiser*, 6 Oct. 1794.

103. Frey and Wood, *Come Shouting to Zion*; for the Alley and Campbell account, 105. See also Turner, *Slaves and Missionaries*, 11.

104. Sensbach, *Rebecca's Revival*.

105. Raboteau, *Slave Religion*, 139–41. Bryan was a native of South Carolina, not Virginia.

106. Egerton, *Gabriel's Rebellion*, 167.

107. On Pamphlet, see Alderson, "Charleston's Rumored Slave Revolt," 93; Egerton, "Tricolor in Black and White," in *Rebels, Reformers, & Revolutionaries*, 169; Sidbury, *Ploughshares into Swords*, 38–47. On black sailors, see Scott, "Common Wind"; Bolster, *Black Jacks*. For more on Virginia-specific webs of communication among African Americans, see Kimball, *American City, Southern Place*.

108. Liele et al., "Letters," 73.

109. Jones, *Religious Instruction of the Negroes*, 47–49.

110. This statistic is from an early version (1789) of John Leland's "Virginia Chronicle," the original of which may be found in the John Carter Brown Library at Brown University, Providence, R.I. A photocopy exists in the University of Virginia's Special Collections Library. John Wylie, former University of Virginia head of special collections, thinks the edition is likely one published by T. Green in Fredericksburg, 1789. Subsequent editions (from 1790) do not have this claim.

111. Asplund, *Universal Register*, 50, 89. Using the ratio suggested by Carroll of 2.9

adherents per member. According to Gewehr, *Great Awakening in Virginia*, 135, the Great Revival made Baptists the most numerous sect in Virginia.

112. Gardner, "Virginia Baptists and Slavery," pt. 2, 1259. See Table 1.

113. Lee, *History of the Methodists*, 126–27; *Minutes of the Methodist Conferences*, 60; for a similar estimate, see Bennett, *Memorials of Methodism*, 233. For 1792 numbers, see Chapter 2, n. 3.

114. This conflict among evangelicals over slavery receives full treatment in Chapter 2.

115. 25 Sept. 1757, Hanover Presbytery, UTS; Pattillo, *Plain Planter's Assistant*, 49–50.

Chapter 2

1. Reuben Pickett to Isaac Backus, 27 Jan. 1797, Backus Correspondence, VBHS. This sentiment appears with remarkable consistency in evangelical correspondence of the 1790s, across denominations. Many commentators observed the widespread and interdenominational nature of the "wintry season." See also Devereux Jarratt to John Coleman, 28 Jan. 1796, in Jarratt, *Life of Jarratt*, 180.

2. For 1792, see Asplund, *Universal Register*, 50, 89. The 1810 estimate is from associational reports contained in Semple, *Rise and Progress*.

3. Calculating Methodist membership numbers by state is a difficult enterprise, despite that denomination's penchant for statistics. In the early period, only from 1796 through 1801 did the compilers of the minutes from the various annual conferences list the members by state. For years before this, when membership totals are given by circuit alone, I have used the 1796 *Minutes* as a basis to determine which circuits fell in the boundaries of Virginia and totaled those numbers. The results of this method are slightly lower than the totals that Sweet gives in *Virginia Methodism*, 134: 16,316 instead of 17,605 for 1794, and 13,211 instead of 13,935 for 1795.

For years after 1801, the process becomes considerably more complicated. From 1802, the circuits are organized into districts, and the districts into conferences. Most scholars simply use the membership information from the Virginia Conference to calculate the number of Methodists in Virginia—see, for example, the oft-cited Allen, "Great Revival in Virginia," 99. This is a clumsy guide, however, because many members of the Virginia Conference resided in North Carolina, and Virginians belonged to several other conferences as well.

I have attempted to correct this mistake and to count only Virginia residents as Virginia Methodists. I have derived my numbers from 1802 to 1807 by adding members in the Holston District (Western Conference), Norfolk and Richmond districts (Virginia Conference), and Alexandria and Greenbrier districts (Baltimore Conference). From this total, I have deducted known North Carolina circuits, viz., Franklin, Bertie, Camden, and Banks; known Tennessee circuits, viz., Nollichuckie, French-Broad, and Clinch; and known Maryland circuits, viz., Montgomery, Frederick, and Frederick Town. Changing circuit and district boundaries, the absence of reports for certain years and from certain circuits, and mistaken state boundaries undoubtedly render even this calculation imprecise; however, the effort helps to show the devastating effects of O'Kelly's rebellion. In 1805, there were 15,073 white Virginia Methodists and 3,313 African American Methodists. This total of 18,386 had climbed to 21,091 by 1807, by which date Methodists had safely contained O'Kelly's challenge. See *Minutes of the Methodist Conferences.*

4. My phraseology here intentionally echoes that of Dillon, *Slavery Attacked.* Dillon is attentive to this moment as one of possibility for interracial alliances, though most scholars treat the debate as one among whites only. An important exception, and one that has had a greater influence on this chapter than the notes below may indicate, is Najar, who has argued, "Together white and black evangelicals faced the contradictions between the equality of souls and the institution of slavery, and churches became the arenas in which southerners debated what slavery meant in an evangelical society and what religion meant in a slave society" ("Evangelizing the South," 197).

5. For a strong statement of the continuity of the defense of slavery as an "organic," hierarchical institution, see Young, *Proslavery and Sectional Thought,* 19–26.

6. Isaac, *Transformation of Virginia.* As noted in the Introduction, it is now the prevailing interpretation that evangelicals made some sort of a compact with the devil—or at least with slaveowning values—in order to attract more members in the early national period. For example, see Mathews, *Religion in the Old South,* 75–80; Heyrman, *Southern Cross,* 251; Boles, "Southern Way of Religion," 241. For a similar complaint about the historiography, see Feight, "Good and the Just," 14, and, for convincing rebuttals, Ambrose, "Of Stations and Relations," and Spangler, "Salvation Was Not Liberty."

7. On dissenters' attempts to exploit the Revolution for their own purposes, see Irons, "Believing in America" and "Spiritual Fruits of Revolution"; Ragosta, "Fighting for Freedom."

8. Identification with the War for Independence was a part of the ecclesiastical implementation of the egalitarian political ideas expressed during the Revolution, a phenomenon that crossed denominational lines. The best introduction to this story is in Hatch, *Democratization of American Christianity.*

9. Leland, "Virginia Chronicle," 112. The quotation is from the 1790 edition.

10. In Oct. 1776, George Shadford submitted to the General Assembly "in Behalf of the whole Body of the people Commonly called Methodists in Virginia, consisting of near If not altogether three thousand members," a petition in which they asked the legislators not to destroy the establishment, for they claimed that they were "not Dessenters, but a Religious Society in Communion with the Church of England" ("Methodist Petition," 143–44).

11. Account of the Broken-Back (Fluvanna County) conference from Lee, *History of*

the Methodists, 63; Stevens, *History of the Methodist Episcopal Church*, 2:56–66; Lupold, "Methodism in Virginia," 69–79.

The story of Methodists' move to ecclesiastical independence has been truncated here. In 1784, Methodists broke from the Anglican Church and refused to accept the overseers that John Wesley designated for them without first voting on them. The break became even more pronounced in 1787, when American Methodists deleted a minute obligating them to obey Wesley during his lifetime. See Tigert, *Constitutional History*, 151–220; *Minutes of the Methodist Conferences*; M'Tyeire, *History of Methodism*, 390–401. On the leading role that Virginians played in resisting Wesley (and an episcopacy in general), see Richey, "Methodism's Growing Pains" and *Methodist Conference in America*, 36; Lee, *History of the Methodists*, 124–25.

12. Sobel, *World They Made Together*, 197.

13. Juvenis, *Slavery of the Negroes*, 14–15. For an early example, see [Rush], *Address to the Inhabitants*.

14. Still, the best introduction to the Revolutionary movement against slavery may be found in Davis, *Problem of Slavery*. See also Zilversmit, *First Emancipation*.

15. Albert, "Protean Institution," 116–58; Iaccarino, "Virginia and the National Contest," 10–14; Wolf, *Race and Liberty*, 28–38.

16. Jefferson, *Notes*, 87. Myriad scholars have addressed Jefferson's apparently contradictory position on slavery. Useful starting points for this tremendous literature are Miller, *Wolf by the Ears*, and Freehling, "Founding Fathers and Slavery." But for exciting new directions, see esp. Helo and Onuf, "Problem of Slavery," and Onuf, "Every Generation." The research staff at Monticello has produced an excellent series on the enslaved community on Jefferson's mountain, including Stanton, *Slavery at Monticello*, *Free Some Day*, and "Other End of the Telescope."

17. Tucker, *Dissertation on Slavery*, 9. For an excellent treatment of the Tucker family and their evolving position on slavery, including information regarding the 1796 sale, see Hamilton, "Revolutionary Principles," 537.

18. The statewide figure is derived from Wells, "Household Size and Composition," 551, and Schwarz, "Virginia," 936. I multiplied Wells's estimate of 5.5 white persons per household and Schwarz's figure of 34,026 slaveholders, interpreting "slaveholders" for "slaveholding households." For the county figures, I used 1783 state enumerations, since the federal census data by household for that year burned in 1814. These are available in U.S. Bureau of the Census, *Heads of Families*, 58–59, 63–66.

19. Gardner, "Virginia Baptists and Slavery," pt. 1, 1218–19. Even in their piece asserting that Baptists were lower-class challengers to gentry authority, Beeman and Isaac conclude that Baptists in Lunenburg County in 1785 owned an average of 2.5 slaves; see "Cultural Conflict and Social Change," 547.

20. 24 Feb. 1788, Upper King and Queen Baptist Church, VBHS.

21. Daniel, "Southern Presbyterians and the Negro," 304.

22. O'Kelly, *Essay on Negro-Slavery*, 8.

23. Jordan's extraordinary discussion of the role of spiritual difference in facilitating the rise of African slavery in British North America remains the most compelling and was formative in this study. I find exception only to his depiction of black Americans as passive receptors of Christianization and his suggestion that the recognition of Africans' immortal souls was enough to make whites reconsider slavery. Africans and African Americans were the chief agents of their own Christianization, and the first evangelicals had little difficulty accommodating an immortal soul to temporal slavery. See Jordan, *White over Black*, esp. 179–215; Davis, *Inhuman Bondage* and *Problem of Slavery*.

24. Iaccarino, "Virginia and the National Contest," 15.

25. Coke's Journal reprinted in *Arminian Magazine*, July, Aug. 1789.

26. Anglicans did not entirely disappear from the United States; they made some attempt to reconstitute themselves as the Protestant Episcopal Church, the first bishop of which was ordained in 1784. James Madison became the first Virginia bishop in 1787 and presided over a church that was a shadow of its former self; rectors had charge of only fifty-six parishes when Madison took charge, a number that would decline further as Anglican influence waned. For a basic account, see Cleaveland et al., *Up from Independence*.

27. Moulton, *Journal and Essays of John Woolman*, 195–97.

28. Weeks, *Southern Quakers and Slavery*, 210–13, and Albert, "Protean Institution," 173–77.

29. Wolf, *Race and Liberty*, 239–41. Of the 62 manumitters whose religion she identified, 11 were Quakers (including 1 former Quaker), 6 Baptist, 11 Episcopal, 33 Methodist, and 1 Methodist/Episcopal.

30. Wolf argues that previous historians have overestimated the number of manumissions by failing to account for the natural increase of the free black population and by relying on very low estimates of the number of free blacks in 1780. Her estimate of 8,000 to 11,500 manumissions between 1782 and 1806 is significantly below the previous estimate of 15,000. See Wolf, *Race and Liberty*, 39–84, esp. 43, 59; Burin, *Peculiar Solution*, 35; Albert, "Protean Institution," chap. 7.

31. Also Mathews, *Religion in the Old South*, 72–73.

32. 22 Aug. 1782, Anselm Bailey for Aaron, Surry County Clerk Records, VHS. I would like to thank Lee Shepard for calling my attention to these documents.

33. The Methodists' 1785 petition, discussed below, is one possible source, but this seems very unlikely. Many manumissions predated the circulation of the petition, and the language of the deeds and the petition is not identical.

34. 26 Jan. 1790, George Gardner for Rachel, Moll, David, Margaret, Isam, Surry County Clerk Records, VHS. Deeds for Southampton, Sussex, Prince George, and Perquimans (N.C.) counties found their way into the Surry County file.

35. Noll, "American Revolution and Protestant Evangelicalism"; McCoy, *Last of the Fathers*, 5–6; Freeberg, "Why David Barrow Moved to Kentucky."

36. *Minutes of the Methodist Conferences*; U.S. Bureau of the Census, *First Census, 1790*, 49.

37. Essig, *Bonds of Wickedness*, 117; Najar, "Evangelizing the South," 198.

38. Col. 3:22, KJV.

39. Haynes, *Noah's Curse*, 7. For the text of many of these petitions, see Schmidt and Wilhelm, "Early Proslavery Petitions." The classic work, however, and one that supports the above assertion that slaveholders in the 1790s and early 1800s were not innovators of a new, proslavery argument, is Tise, *Proslavery*.

40. In "The Bible and Slavery," in Miller, Stout, and Wilson, *Religion and the American Civil War*, Noll first explained how evangelicals' literal hermeneutic kept many of them from the conviction that slaveholding was sinful. More recently, in *Theological Crisis*, chap. 4, he has used the writings of lesser-known nineteenth-century theologians to show that American slavery failed to pass the scriptural bar even according to that hermeneutic.

41. For biographical information on Jarratt, see Adair and Jarratt, "Autobiography," 346–51, and Jarratt, *Life of Jarratt*. All quotations from Jarratt to Edward Dromgoole Sr., 22 Mar. 1788, Dromgoole Papers, SHC.

42. Wolf, *Race and Liberty*, 97; McDaniel, "Elder John Alderson," 313.

43. Ryland, *Baptists of Virginia*, 150. The General Committee referred in 1791 to action taken by its antecedent group in 1785; see *Minutes of the Baptist General Committee* (1791), 5.

44. *Minutes of the Baptist General Committee* (1790), 5–7.

45. Ryland, *Baptists of Virginia*, 151. Essig posits that some of the frustration of Baptists was doctrinal, that many believed the General Committee had no power to suggest any particular stance on slavery; see "Very Wintry Season."

46. *Minutes of the Baptist General Committee* (1791), 5.

47. 14 Feb., 26 May, 25 Aug., 24 Nov. 1786, 23 Feb., 24 May, 23 June, July 1787, Black Creek Baptist Church, VBHS.

48. 26 May, 25, 26 Aug., 24 Nov. 1786, 23 Feb., 24 May 1787, ibid.

49. 25 Feb., 24 June, 26 Aug. 1791, 22 Nov. 1793, ibid.

50. 21 Feb. 1794, ibid.

51. *Minutes of the Baptist General Committee* (1792), 5; *Minutes of the Baptist General Committee* (1793), 4.

52. *Minutes of the Dover Baptist Association* (1797), 5.

53. On Baptists and the demand for a strict separation, see Buckley, *Church and State* and "Evangelicals Triumphant."

54. Jefferson to P. H. Wendover, 13 Mar. 1815, in Bergh, *Writings*, 279–83.

55. Methodists, it seems clear, have the most authentic claim to a strong antislavery tradition in the post-Revolutionary period, though it is an open question how deeply that feeling percolated into the Methodist membership, especially in Virginia. My own interpretation, that a majority of white Methodists never favored emancipation, should be clear below. The classic work is Mathews,

Slavery and Methodism, but see also Lyerly, *Methodism and the Southern Mind*, esp. chap. 6, and *Minutes of the Methodist Conferences*.

56. Lee, *History of the Methodists*, 97.

57. Lyerly, *Methodism and the Southern Mind*, 124–27; MacMaster, "Liberty or Property?"; Wolf, *Race and Liberty*, 88–96; Iaccarino, "Virginia and the National Contest," 21–24. On the counterpetitions, see Schmidt and Wilhelm, "Early Proslavery Petitions."

58. O'Kelly, *Essay on Negro-Slavery*, 34, 20.

59. Ibid., 24, 34; *Minutes of the Methodist Conferences*; MacClenny, *Life of Rev. James O'Kelly*, 21.

60. For O'Kelly's thoughts on episcopacy, see O'Kelly, *Vindication*, 30. In addition to the standard treatments of O'Kelly—including the plainly partisan but biographically rich MacClenny, *Life of Rev. James O'Kelly*, and the extended account in Bennett, *Memorials of Methodism*—see Richey, "Methodism's Growing Pains."

61. For these calculations, see *Minutes of the Methodist Conferences* and n. 3 above; Sweet, *Virginia Methodism*, 131.

62. Thompson, *Presbyterians in the South*, 1:325–27; Spangler, "Proslavery Presbyterians." For an example within the Hanover Presbytery, see 1 Aug., 29 Oct. 1791, 12 May, 30 July 1792, Hanover Presbytery, UTS.

63. Murray, *Presbyterians and the Negro*, 20–28. Bourne ultimately published *Condensed Anti-Slavery Bible Argument*, DocSouth.

64. Mathews, *Religion in the Old South*, 77; Boles, "Southern Way of Religion," 241.

65. Schwarz, *Migrants against Slavery*. An even more important work on these antislavery migrants is Feight, "Good and the Just," 248–444.

66. Allen, "David Barrow's Circular Letter," 445; Freeberg, "Why David Barrow Moved to Kentucky."

67. Feight, "Good and the Just," 187–89.

68. Philip Gatch to Edward Dromgoole Sr., 11 Feb. 1802; John Sale to Edward Dromgoole Sr., 20 Feb. 1807; Bennett Maney to Edward Dromgoole Sr., 27 July 1807, Dromgoole Papers, SHC.

69. Foote, *Sketches of Virginia*, 232–33.

70. It is important to remember the voluntary nature of black church membership. For particularly vivid examples of black believers choosing their own way in terms of church membership, see 27 Sept. 1800, Mill Creek Baptist Church, VBHS; 4 Aug. [1805], Register of the Baptists from Chappawamsic, VHS.

71. Morgan, *American Slavery, American Freedom*, 374–87; Goodman, *Of One Blood*, 5–22. Morgan suggests that white Virginians' initial affinity for republicanism was conditioned by slaveholding; Goodman argues that they later "whitewashed" the republican legacy of the war. In either case, by the 1790s, white Virginians understood the national experiment to be for whites only.

72. *Minutes of the Dover Baptist Association* (1793–1814); Rowe, "Biographical Sketch."

73. Jackson, "Religious Development of the Negro," 191; Brooks, "Evolution of the Negro Baptist Church," 16; *Minutes of the Dover Baptist Association* (1813, 1814).
74. Allen, "Great Revival in Virginia," 99.
75. Jackson, "Religious Development of the Negro," 203.
76. For examples of scholars who stress discipline as social control, see Cornelius, *Slave Missions*, 38–45; Spangler, " 'Salvation was Not Liberty,' " 230. Others, including Najar, "Citizens of the Church," 210–14; Mathews, *Religion in the Old South*, 225; Raboteau, *Slave Religion*, 180–87; Morgan, *Slave Counterpoint*, 431; and Sobel, *World They Made Together*, 190–97, stress the empowering effects of submitting to discipline. Sparks offers a sustained and particularly balanced treatment of this issue in *Jordan's Stormy Banks*, 146–73.
77. Gardner, "Virginia Baptists and Slavery," pt. 1, 1267.
78. Burton, *In My Father's House*, 157.
79. Frey and Wood, *Come Shouting to Zion*, 172–90.
80. 29 Oct. 1791, Hanover Presbytery, UTS.
81. 2 Mar., 6 Apr., 3 Aug. 1793, Buck Marsh Baptist Church, VBHS.
82. Good treatments of the evolution of evangelical approaches to slave marriage include Raboteau, *Slave Religion*, 183–87; Sobel, *Trabelin' On*, 173–80, but with insufficient attention to chronology; and, for the same issue revisited during the Civil War, Mohr, *Threshold of Freedom*, 255–59.
83. 1 Oct., 5 Nov., 4, 31 Dec. 1791, 4 Feb., 31 Mar. 1792, Buck Marsh Baptist Church, VBHS.
84. As quoted in Raboteau, *Slave Religion*, 183–84. The Middle District Association considered the same issue in 1789, though its resolution of the question is not recorded. See Backus, "Yankee Baptist," 75.
85. *Minutes of the Dover Baptist Association* (1793), 4.
86. 1 Aug. 1791, Hanover Presbytery, UTS, and, for a particularly good discussion of the paternalist underpinnings of this decision, Clarke, *Dwelling Place*, 211.
87. 24 Feb., 22 June 1792, Black Creek Baptist Church, VBHS.
88. As quoted in Lindman, "World of Baptists," 192. The Middle District Association also wondered in 1789 "whether a master or mistress had a right to correct servants who were members of the same church, for family disobedience," though the response to this query is not available. See Backus, "Yankee Baptist," 75.
89. *Minutes of the Dover Baptist Association* (1796), 3–5.
90. Genovese, *Roll, Jordan, Roll*, 5, 6. For the seeds of this interpretation, see Rose, "Domestication of Domestic Slavery."
91. Genovese's argument inspired many critics. Oakes, in *Ruling Race*, attacked the idea of paternalism, especially on the grounds that Genovese did not give adequate attention to the market relations or financial interests that shaped owner-slave relations. For a review of this debate and a conclusion apropos to this book's argument, see Ayers, "Review of *Slavery and Freedom*," 199. Frederickson, in

"Skeleton in the Closet," ventured a more capacious survey of the debate in 2002 and surveyed scholars who have followed Genovese's paternalist characterization of slavery and those who have emphasized instead the coercive physical power and financial interest that lay at the heart of the practice of slaveholding. He offers Johnson's *Soul by Soul* as a new approach, one that integrates commercial and paternalist models. In this vein, see also Deyle, *Carry Me Back*, 206–44.

The critique here is not of paternalism, per se, but of the undifferentiated way in which the Genoveses use paternalism to explain interracial interactions without sufficient variation according to time or place or without sufficient explanation of the ecclesiastical roots of the worldview.

92. Genovese, *Roll, Jordan, Roll*, 5.

93. Morgan and Nicholls, "Slaves in Piedmont Virginia," 220.

94. Kulikoff, "Origins of Afro-American Society," 253; Lee, "Problem of Slave Community"; Dunn, "Black Society."

95. For a still more thorough description of the emotional and practical changes in the practice of slaveholding as both slaveholders and slaves became evangelical Protestants at the turn of the century, see Rose, "Domestication of Domestic Slavery." For several helpful theoretical approaches to this process of negotiation within biracial churches, the best starting place is Boles, *Masters and Slaves*.

96. *Minutes of the Dover Baptist Association* (1797), 5. Daniel summarizes this substitution of paternalism for debate over emancipation in "Virginia Baptists and the Negro," 1.

97. Hamilton, "Revolutionary Principles," 549. Clarke, in *Dwelling Place*, gives an even more detailed account of this process, but set in a later period.

98. Feight, "Good and the Just," 173.

99. Whitefield, *Three Letters*, 14, 15.

100. For a thoughtful discussion of the continuity of slaveholder ethics and the conflict over whether or not slaveholding itself was a sin, see Feight, "Good and the Just," xiii–xxii.

101. *Minutes of the Dover Baptist Association* (1796), 7–12.

102. Robson, "Important Question Answered," 651. But see also 1 Cor. 7:20–24, Eph. 6:5–9, 1 Tim. 6:1–8, Titus 2:9–10, Philem. 1:10–19, and 1 Pet. 2:18–24, KJV.

103. 19, 30 Oct. 1793, Jeremiah Norman Diary, 1793–1801, Weeks Papers, SHC.

104. As quoted in Earnest, *Religious Development*, 70.

105. As quoted in Sobel, *World They Made Together*, 197–98.

106. Drew, *North-Side View*, DocSouth. Needless to say, Lucas's owner demonstrated an incomplete understanding of the parable from which he excerpted this expression. The reference is to Luke 12:47, KJV.

107. Randolph, *Sketches of Slave Life*, DocSouth.

108. Anderson, *Interesting Account*, DocSouth.

109. Drew, *North-Side View*, DocSouth. For the combination of loathing and empowerment, see also Ruggles, *Unboxing*, 22.

110. As quoted in McGill, *Sketches of History*, 110–12. For an example of how this principle played out on a local level, see McDaniel, "Elder John Alderson," 313.

111. 14 Jan. 1809, Register of the Baptists from Chappawamsic, VHS; 19 Mar. 1790, Mill Swamp Baptist Church, VBHS.

112. The two most important books on Gabriel's stillborn rebellion are Sidbury, *Ploughshares into Swords*, and Egerton, *Gabriel's Rebellion*. The authors disagree about the place of religion in the conspiracy, with Egerton placing more emphasis on the republican rhetoric employed by Prosser, and Sidbury stressing Prosser's leniency toward Methodists and his alliance with black religious leaders. For an earlier work culminating in an analysis of the religious content of Prosser's rebellion, see Mullin, *Flight and Rebellion*; Mullin concluded that Prosser did not exploit the insurrectionary potential of evangelical Protestantism as thoroughly as he might have. Rucker, in *River Flows On*, chap. 4, argues that Prosser organized using African, not evangelical, principles.

113. Sargent, *Grove Plantation*. See Chapter 1 for Caribbean connections that may have played a role in earlier plots, as well as Sidbury, "Saint Domingue in Virginia"; Scott, "Common Wind," 247–92, 326.

114. Shepherd, *Statutes at Large*, 2:300–301.

115. As quoted in Essig, *Bonds of Wickedness*, 121.

116. Shepherd, *Statutes at Large*, 3:108.

117. *Minutes of the Dover Baptist Association* (1804), 8, and (1808), 8.

118. Shepherd, *Statutes at Large*, 3:251; Wolf, *Race and Liberty*, 121–27.

119. As quoted in Egerton, *Gabriel's Rebellion*, 153.

Chapter 3

1. On the Missouri crisis, see Mason, *Slavery and Politics*, chap. 8; on evangelicalism as a unifying bond across the sections during this period, see Goen, *Broken Churches, Broken Nation*, chap. 1.

2. U.S. Bureau of the Census, *Fourth Census, 1820*, 107.

3. For an overview of these changes, see Sellers, *Market Revolution*, and, as the market revolution related to slavery, Rothman, *Slave Country*, chap. 5; Deyle, *Carry Me Back*, chap. 4.

4. Finney, "What a Revival of Religion Is," in Hollinger and Capper, *American Intellectual Tradition*, 198.

5. *Minutes of the Virginia Baptist General Meeting of Correspondence*, 4.

6. Luther Rice, who converted from Congregationalism to the Baptist persuasion while on a mission trip to Calcutta during the War of 1812, was the catalyst for this and many other mission groups. See Thompson, "Luther Rice's Early Travels"; Walters, *America's Reformers*, 3–76.

7. For the chronology of major Methodist benevolent initiatives, see Goss, *Statistical History*, 114–43.

8. Foster, *Errand of Mercy*. For more on the relationship of southerners to the

benevolent empire, see Kuykendall, *Southern Enterprize*; Faust, "Evangelicalism and the Meaning of the Proslavery Argument"; Butler, "Church and American Destiny"; Quist, "Slaveholding Operatives." Mason, *Slavery and Politics*, 164–71, suggests that the rise of benevolence institutions frightened southern slaveholders, who regarded them as "enthusiastic" enterprises emanating from England and New England that might ultimately threaten slavery. This chapter argues that most white evangelicals in the South actually accommodated benevolence work in a paternalist, proslavery worldview.

9. For a more thorough treatment of these critics (from the mainline perspective), see Alley, *History of Baptists*, chap. 11, and Ryland, *Baptists of Virginia*, chaps. 13 and 14, quotation from 246. Also see Taylor, *Formation of the Primitive Baptist Movement*.

10. *Journal of the Convention* (1845), 19. An excellent treatment of the process by which Moore, Meade, and a small cohort of evangelical clergy remade the Episcopal Church and embraced volunteerism and benevolence appears in Bond and Gunderson, "Episcopal Church in Virginia," 220–34.

11. As quoted in Maxwell, *John H. Rice*, 134. See also Rice to Rev. Archibald Alexander, 31 Dec. 1817, ibid., 132.

12. Rice, *Character & Conduct*, 38.

13. *Journal of the Convention* (1845), 11–20.

14. Staudenraus, *African Colonization Movement*.

15. See Dorsey, "Gendered History."

16. Costen, *African American Christian Worship*, 57–64. One does not need to go as far as Stuckey, who—in reference to baptism—asserts that "Christianity provided a protective exterior beneath which more complex, less familiar (to outsiders) religious principles and practices were operative," to recognize the African influence on the ritual; see Stuckey, *Slave Culture*, 35. Also see Sobel, *Trabelin' On*, 139–40; Raboteau, *Slave Religion*, 227–28.

17. Blake Touchstone, "Planters and Slave Religion in the Deep South," in Boles, *Masters and Slaves*, 123.

18. Harvey, "African American Spirituals," 141. I have followed Levine, *Black Culture and Black Consciousness*, 20–23; Southern, *Music of Black Americans*, 94–98; and Sobel, *Trabelin' On*, 153.

19. Davies, *Letters*, 12.

20. White, *African Preacher*, 21.

21. Sernett, *Black Religion*, 93–101; Clarke, *Dwelling Place*, 208.

22. Frey and Wood, *Come Shouting to Zion*, 168, 242 n. 93.

23. Fountain, "Long on Religion," 27–28. There are substantial methodological problems with Fountain's study, including his use of WPA narratives (recorded from 1936 to 1938) to gauge antebellum church membership among slaves and his failure to recognize the difference between adherence and membership. Notwithstanding these flaws and the minuscule size of his sample for the urban

Upper South (twenty-four persons), his observation that urban slaves were more likely to convert is likely accurate, and his ratios are provocative.

24. Sobel, *Trabelin' On*, 250–51; Jackson, "Religious Development of the Negro," 188. Kimball, in *American City, Southern Place*, documented the functioning of one of these church-based rural networks, that emanating from Richmond's First African Baptist.

25. Randall's story is recorded in an appendix of Wickham, *Lost Family Found*, DocSouth.

26. Gurley, *Jehudi Ashmun*, 148.

27. Randolph, *John Jasper*, 13.

28. Stearns, *Henry Box Brown*, DocSouth. This may or may not be the same as the "Uncle John," also a preacher in the invisible church, who appears in Brown's narrative.

29. As quoted in Wilson, "Religion of the American Negro Slave," 51.

30. Foote, *Sketches of Virginia*, 2nd ser., 302–3.

31. Albert, *House of Bondage*, DocSouth.

32. White, *African Preacher*, 61–66.

33. Allen did not make a complete break in 1787; he, Absalom Jones, and other black Methodists simply established a new Methodist community for people of color. As late as 1799, when none other than Francis Asbury ordained Allen a deacon in the Methodist Church, Allen was still nominally a Methodist. Full schism did not occur until 1816. See Campbell, *Songs of Zion*, 3–31.

34. Cornelius, *Slave Missions*, 27. For a discussion of "African-American virtuosos," see Heyrman, *Southern Cross*, 217–18.

35. Jackson, "Religious Development of the Negro," 203. See Table 1, Evangelical Baptists and Methodists in Virginia, 1790 and 1850. This figure correlates closely to Heyrman's calculation in *Southern Cross*, 265, that 28 percent of black southerners attended an evangelical church by 1835.

36. 4 May 1816, Register of the Baptists from Chappawamsic, VHS. This statistic includes number of cases, not number of persons involved in cases. There were several multiple offenders and several cases involving more than one person. In most cases, racially distinct membership rolls made determining the race of the defendant simple, but there were some individuals for whom the racial identity was inferred by the presence or lack of a last name.

37. Based on the chart of black members, ostensibly for 1800 to 1838, but only for 1800 to 1815. The clerk noted the disposition of each person who joined the church, whether their owners had "Removed" them from the bounds of fellowship, the church had "Dismissed" them to other congregations, the church had "Excluded" or "Excommunicated" them, or they had died.

38. 8 May 1819, Register of the Baptists from Chappawamsic, VHS.

39. Ferrill, *Biography*, DocSouth.

40. Anderson, *Life and Narrative*, DocSouth. For another example of ministering

before recognition by a white church, see Randolph, *Sketches of Slave Life*, DocSouth.

41. Shepard, "Records of Upper Goose Creek," 1998–99.
42. Anderson, *Interesting Account*, DocSouth.
43. Drew, *North-Side View*, 73–74, DocSouth.
44. On Sundays off, see Berlin, *Many Thousands Gone*, 134; Genovese, *Roll, Jordan, Roll*, 314–15.
45. *Minutes of the Dover Baptist Association* (1816), 7.
46. As quoted in Earnest, *Religious Development*, 68. Some whites did advocate giving slaves the Sabbath off for religious instruction at a very early date, even though the practice was quite rare actually to deliver that instruction. Henry Pattillo called for the Sabbath to be used more appropriately in 1787 but acknowledged that this was rarely the case. "From the manner of spending the sabbath, in these middle and southern States, children are lead to believe, that the command, *Remember the sabbath day, to keep it holy*, signifies, that people are to put on clean clothes; the children to play the day out; the Negroes to walk about idle, or go to work for themselves; and that their parents are obliged to go abroad, or to entertain their neighbors, and to talk on every subject but religion and their duty" (*Plain Planter's Assistant*, 19).
47. Smith, *Autobiography*, DocSouth.
48. Fedric, *Slave Life in Virginia and Kentucky*, DocSouth. Also, Albert, *House of Bondage*, DocSouth, and Davis, *Narrative of the Life*, DocSouth.
49. Davis, *Narrative of the Life*, DocSouth.
50. Randolph, *Sketches of Slave Life*, DocSouth.
51. Williams, *Self-Taught*, 19, 21; Cornelius, *When I Can Read My Title Clear*, 106–17.
52. Genovese, *Roll, Jordan, Roll*, 168.
53. Sidbury, *Ploughshares into Swords*; Frey and Wood, *Come Shouting to Zion*; Hinks, *To Awaken My Afflicted Brethren*. For an even stronger statement of evangelicalism as a binding force, see Harding, *There Is a River*. An important intermediate work is Sobel, *Trabelin' On*.
54. Both Rucker and Gomez agree that the process was well advanced by Nat Turner's rebellion in 1831, though Rucker sees Turner as a transitional figure between traditional African beliefs and Christianity, and Gomez sees 1830 as a very rapid pivot point, with strong African cultural currents before then. See Rucker, *River Flows On*, 188, and Gomez, *Exchanging Our Country Marks*, 5, 245–51.
55. It should be noted that there are scholars who reject this formulation entirely. See Johnson, "'Delusive Clothing,'" 303–7; Fountain, "Long on Religion," 127–43. Both argue that African systems were much more durable.
56. Sobel, *Trabelin' On*, 149–53; Fountain, "Christ in Chains," 95–98.
57. Fedric, *Slave Life in Virginia and Kentucky*, DocSouth, and Ruggles, *Unboxing*, 21–22.

58. From Dec. 1825 to Sept. 1827, Black Creek Baptist Church, VBHS, and Breen, "Nat Turner's Revolt," 284–85.

59. Egerton, "'Its Origin is Not a Little Curious,'" 479, and "Averting a Crisis," 143.

60. Onuf, "Every Generation"; Saillant, "American Enlightenment in Africa." Saillant cites the Jeffersonian origins of the movement but argues that colonization bridged to a more liberal (not enlightened) critique of slavery.

61. For racism, see Goodman, *Of One Blood*, 11–22; on security, see Sidbury, *Ploughshares into Swords*, 133–38.

62. A 1972 dissertation has been among the most important works supporting this perspective: Opper, "Mind of the White Participant," esp. 1.

63. The more comprehensive works, Staudenraus, *African Colonization Movement*, and Burin, *Peculiar Solution*, recognize the ideological complexity and multi-faceted origins of the ACS.

64. For a challenge to this view, see Freehling, "'Absurd' Issues and the Causes of the Civil War"; for a convincing rebuttal, see Burin, *Peculiar Solution*, 20–21.

65. See, for example, Portnoy, *Right to Speak*, 91–93; Mason, *Slavery and Politics*, 161; Iaccarino, "Virginia and the National Contest," 165–82; Harlow, "Neither Slavery nor Abolitionism" and "Robert J. Breckinridge." On the prominent role that white Virginia women played in promoting colonization as a means of compromise, see Varon, *We Mean to Be Counted*, 43–47.

66. Quotation from "[Review of] The Reports," *Christian Spectator*, 1 Sept. 1823; article continued 1 Oct. 1823. See also "Sixth Annual Report," *North American Review*, Jan. 1824, and, for one of several examples of national ecclesiastical support, see the Presbyterians in *Minutes of the General Assembly, 1818*, 693.

67. Virginians freed 2,214 slaves for Liberia and funded all or part of the journey for 1,230 free blacks, roughly one-third of the total number of emigrants. See Burin, *Peculiar Solution*, tabs. 4 and 5, though this count excludes the Maryland State Colonization Society's emigrants. The proportion of Virginians among emigrants was likely even higher for the earlier period. Excluding the 287 individuals captured at sea aboard slave-trading ships and deposited at Liberia, Shick, "Quantitative Analysis," 48, found that 38 percent of all migrants between 1820 and 1843 left from Virginia.

68. Slaughter, *Virginian History of African Colonization*, 11–13.

69. William Meade to [Strather] Jones, 26 May 1819, Andrews Papers, Duke.

70. See Tyler-McGraw, "Richmond Free Blacks."

71. "List of Emigrants ready to embark for Liberia," 7 Mar. 1824, Brand Papers, VHS; discussed also in Tyler-McGraw, "Richmond Free Blacks," 217–18. Tyler-McGraw discusses the unintended outcomes of the meeting, among which were a white backlash at a proposed tax on slaves and free blacks to fund colonization.

72. Burin, *Peculiar Solution*, 41.

73. Though most of Dorsey's evidence is from northern colonists, his argument in "Gendered History," 84–86, captures this dynamic well.

74. For Richmond whites' perspective on the African Baptist Missionary Society, see Tupper, *First Century*, 221–23.
75. Biographical information on Cary throughout from Fisher, "Colonizing Missionary"; Poe, "Lott Cary"; Gurley, *Jehudi Ashmun*; and Taylor, *Elder Lott Cary*, DocSouth. A full-length biography of this important figure is sorely needed.
76. Gurley, *Jehudi Ashmun*, 148–49.
77. Broadside excerpted from a newspaper and dated 28 Jan. 1825, Brand Papers, VHS.
78. Staudenraus, *African Colonization Movement*, 64–66.
79. Burin has calculated that 29 percent of the 1,670 emigrants who arrived between 1820 and 1830 died of disease; see *Peculiar Solution*, 17. See also Shick, "Quantitative Analysis," 51.
80. Staudenraus, *African Colonization Movement*, appendix: "Table of the Annual Receipts and Colonists." For the best treatment of the slow development of a feedback loop to Virginia black evangelicals, see Tyler-McGraw, "Richmond Free Blacks," 219–21.
81. Black willingness to experiment with colonization never completely evaporated, though the numbers of blacks willing to emigrate did dwindle considerably. In Chapters 4 and 5 there are examples of men and women in the 1840s and 1850s who sought colonization.
82. 24 Feb. 1817, reprinted in Garrison, *Thoughts on African Colonization*, pt. 2, 62–63. The Richmond group favored a domestic colony, perhaps on the Missouri River.
83. Smallwood, *Narrative*, DocSouth.
84. Williams and Goldie, *Sunshine and Shadow*, DocSouth.
85. Tyler-McGraw, "Richmond Free Blacks," 221. Hunt's 1859 biography, by a white author, finds this issue uncomfortable and invents frivolous reasons why Hunt did not endorse Liberia; see Barrett, *Gilbert Hunt*, DocSouth.
86. Berlin, *Generations of Captivity*; for the earliest stages of this movement, see Kulikoff, "Uprooted Peoples."

These numbers would seem modest compared with what the late antebellum period would bring: more than 100,000 in the 1830s and at least 60,000 per decade in the 1840s and 1850s. In all, in the half-century before the Civil War, whites separated more than 300,000 slaves from the state of Virginia and from their families. This figure, heart-wrenching as it is, actually understates the psychological effect of the slave trade in the nineteenth century, for it does not include those slaves sold, a number perhaps as high as 600,000, within the state.

Numbers of migrants are derived from Gibson and Jung, *Historical Census Statistics*. Records from Virginia and West Virginia are combined for totals for antebellum Virginia. The estimates of forced migrants are the numbers of slaves missing each decade, assuming a decennial growth rate of 18.1 percent for the black population (the average of the growth rate for the 1790s and for the first decade of the 1800s). Using the 1790s growth rate of 20.3 percent, the five-decade total is 353,263; using the 1800s growth rate of 15.9 percent, the five-decade total is 255,776. The number is in line with a recent estimate of the total interstate internal trade at 1 million persons between 1790 and 1860. See Deyle, *Carry Me Back*, 4. Deyle estimates that two-thirds of the victims were sent by sale and that one-third migrated with white families. Furthermore, he calculates that up to 2 million may have been traded locally.

87. On paternalism and the internal trade, see Deyle, *Carry Me Back*, 206–44, and Johnson, *Soul by Soul*, 107–12. For an example of a paternalist sale seen from a slave's perspective, see Elliott, *Story of Archer Alexander*, DocSouth.

88. Tazewell, *Virginia's Ninth President*, 27; Burrowes, "Black Christian Republicanism," 31.

89. From Ashmun's report, reprinted in Gurley, *Jehudi Ashmun*, 137.

90. Staudenraus, *African Colonization Movement*, 100–103.

91. "Conversion of a Native African," *African Repository and Colonial Journal*, July 1825.

92. "The Rev. Lott Cary," *African Repository and Colonial Journal*, Oct. 1825.

93. "Christian Conduct Towards Servants," ibid., Dec. 1825.

94. "Benefits of Religious Instruction to the People of Colour," ibid., Jan. 1826.

95. Mars Lucas to Townsend Heaton, 12 Mar. 1830. Letters online at "Loudoun Museum: Historic Leesburg, Virginia." For an analysis of the Lucas-Heaton letters, one that emphasizes republicanism rather than evangelicalism in the founding of Liberia, see Tyler-McGraw, "Loudoun County Family in Liberia." The conflict between evangelicalism and republicanism in this context is a false one; see Burrowes, "Black Christian Republicanism."

96. Lott Cary to Benjamin Brand, 11 June 1827, Brand Papers, VHS.

97. As quoted in Opper, "Mind of the White Participant," 88. Gray does not appear in Burin's ACS database. Burin graciously shared Virginia data used for *Peculiar Solution*.

98. Broadside, 17 June 1825, Brand Papers, VHS.

99. Brand to Lott Cary, Jan. 1826, ibid.

100. Crane, *Anti-slavery in Virginia*.

101. Thomas, " 'O That Slavery's Curse Might Cease,' " 56; deed for slaves, 28 Feb. 1833, Andrews Papers, Duke.

102. Cary, "Circular Addressed to the Colored Brethren." Also available in manuscript in the Brand Papers, VHS. Text here is Saillant's transcription.

103. As quoted in Freehling, *Drift Toward Dissolution*, 120. See also Egerton's essay, "Averting a Crisis." Some Virginia critics of colonization in the mid- to late 1820s were not frightened by black agency, per se, but by the threat that the federal government would acquire too much power through its role supporting the ACS and would ultimately take firmer steps against slavery. See Iaccarino, "Virginia and the National Contest," 183–84.

104. Fedric, *Slave Life in Virginia and Kentucky*, DocSouth.

105. Randolph, *Sketches of Slave Life*, DocSouth.

106. The exact date of the petition is unclear, and I have not located the original to resolve disagreements within the secondary sources. Earnest, *Religious Development*," 72–73, included a transcript of the entire petition and gave the date as 1823. In O'Brien, *From Bondage to Citizenship*, 34–35, it appears as 1821.

107. As quoted in Plumer, *Religious Instruction of the Negroes*, 20–21.

108. Hinks, *To Awaken My Afflicted Brethren*, 39, 134–37.

109. Gray, "Confessions," in Greenberg, *Confessions*, 47.

Chapter 4

1. Nat Turner's status as a slave preacher and the question of whether or not he preached on the morning of 21 August 1831 have been hotly debated. It seems fairly clear that no Baptist or Methodist church officially ordained him for the ministry, as several have asserted. He probably served the slave community as an exhorter, a speaker who, since not ordained, simply encouraged Christians in their daily lives, rather than teaching them doctrine. See *Minutes of the Portsmouth Baptist Association* (1832), 45; Aptheker, *Nat Turner's Slave Rebellion*, 37; Breen, "Nat Turner's Revolt," 23; Gray, "Confessions," in Greenberg, *Confessions*, 37–58, 46. More speculatively, see Drewry, *Southampton Insurrection*, 157, which indicates that Turner definitely preached at a revival meeting in Southampton County on 14 August 1831.

2. Warner, *Authentic and Impartial Narrative*, 10.

3. Basic chronology drawn from Tragle, *Southampton Slave Revolt*, xv–xviii, and Foner, *Nat Turner*, 11–12; Parker's Field, from Johnson, *Nat Turner Slave Insurrection*, 99–104.

4. Cromwell, "Aftermath of Nat Turner's Insurrection," 212; Warner, *Authentic and Impartial Narrative*, 15. An additional seventeen slaves and three free blacks—including Turner himself—were executed as a result of the legal proceedings. See Drewry, *Southampton Insurrection*, 96.

5. Eliza Meyers to Rachel Lazarus, 9 Oct. 1831, Mordecai Family Papers, SHC.

6. Helen Read to Louisa Cocke, 17 Sept. 1831, Papers of the Cocke Family, UVa; Martha Jefferson Randolph to Joseph Coolidge Jr., 27 Oct. 1831, in Coolidge Correspondence, UVa.

7. Mary McPhail to Mary C. Carrington, Carrington Family Papers, VHS.

8. "Nat Turner Certainly Taken!" *Norfolk Herald*, 4 Nov. 1831, in Greenberg, *Confessions*, 88–90; French, *Rebellious Slave*, 45–51.

9. Greenberg, *Confessions*, 44, 47–48; Mathews, *Religion in the Old South*, 231–36. For a more nuanced view of the baptism, see Breen, "Prophet in His Own Land," in Greenberg, *Nat Turner*, 112–13. Rucker, in *River Flows On*, 188, has taken this same evidence to link Turner more closely to African religious traditions, notwithstanding Turner's disavowal of conjure.

10. Fabricant, "Critical Look"; Allmendinger, "Construction of *The Confessions*," in Greenberg, *Nat Turner*. Quotation from Gray's letter to the public in Greenberg, *Confessions*, 40.
11. U.S. Bureau of the Census, *Fifth Census, 1830*, 18.
12. Quotation from 7 Sept. 1831, in Raper, "Walker's Appeal and Turner's Insurrection," 105–6.
13. The most forceful arguments for slavery as a positive good came from the political or scientific quarters (e.g., from John C. Calhoun, William Fitzhugh, Henry Hughes, and others); the religious argument was always more nuanced.
14. It is difficult to ascertain the percentage of evangelical legislators, notwithstanding the presence of vocal evangelicals such as William Henry Broadnax. Mississippi's 1860 secession convention is one of the few elected bodies in the South for which the ratio of evangelicals to statesmen is available, and the picture in that state likely approximated the ratio in Virginia. Of 100 representatives in Mississippi, 23 were Methodist, 16 Presbyterian, 16 Baptist, and 12 Episcopalian, for a total evangelical cohort of 67. Presbyterians and Episcopalians were typically overrepresented in such elite bodies, and Virginia probably also had a higher number of Presbyterian and Episcopal legislators in 1831 than there were Presbyterians and Episcopalians in the state as a whole. See Wooster, *Secession Conventions*, 30.
15. Genovese, *Roll, Jordan, Roll*, 186–90. There are several works on the missionary enterprises of individual denominations to convert slaves, but the best two books on the movement as a whole are Cornelius, *Slave Missions*, and Sernett, *Black Religion*. These works are particularly useful both because of their attempts at synthesis and because they recognize the interplay between black religious practice and changing white ideas about slaveholding.
16. Scholars long trusted the accounts of contemporary white authorities that told of an extensive conspiracy. Those white officials ordered 35 conspirators hanged and 43 deported and clearly believed that Vesey had concrete plans for armed revolt. See Robertson, *Denmark Vesey*, and Egerton, *He Shall Go Out Free*. Michael Johnson, following a much earlier suggestion by Richard Wade, has reexamined those sources and concluded that Vesey did not plan a conspiracy at all—that white authorities overreacted to the existence of a community of literate blacks (both slave and free) who publicly discussed the desirability of general emancipation. See Johnson, "Denmark Vesey and His Co-Conspirators."
17. Egerton, " 'Why They Did Not Preach Up This Thing,' " 305.
18. Cornelius, *Slave Missions*, 50–51, 74–75.
19. Hinks, *Walker's Appeal*, 14–15.
20. State of Virginia, *Acts Passed, 1830*, 107–8.
21. Raboteau, *Slave Religion*, 138.
22. *Constitutional Whig*, 29 Aug. 1831, in Greenberg, *Confessions*, 66.
23. *Richmond Enquirer*, 30 Aug. 1831, in ibid., 67. *Richmond Compiler*, 29 Aug. 1831, was reprinted in the *Enquirer*.

24. *Constitutional Whig*, 3 Sept. 1831.

25. Aptheker, *Nat Turner's Slave Rebellion*, 37–38.

26. Anonymous letter from Jerusalem, Virginia, dated 21 Sept. 1831, reprinted in Foner, *Nat Turner*, 29–30. Attributed to William C. Parker in Allmendinger, "Construction of *The Confessions*," in Greenberg, *Nat Turner*, 34–35.

27. Account from French, *Rebellious Slave*, 37–41, 61–64.

28. AL [Cornelia Jefferson Randolph] to Mrs. Joseph Coolidge Jr., 28 Aug. 1831, Coolidge Correspondence, UVa.

29. Martha Jefferson Randolph to Joseph Coolidge Jr., 27 Oct. 1831, ibid.

30. As quoted in Raper, "Walker's Appeal and Turner's Insurrection," 104.

31. From Lydia Maria Child's 1847–48 interviews with Charity Bowery, in Blassingame, *Slave Testimony*, 267.

32. William Campbell to Col. Baldwin, 4 Sept. 1831, Letter to Col. Baldwin, UVa.

33. Randolph Harrison Sr. to John Hartwell Cocke, Sept. 1831, Papers of the Cocke Family, UVa.

34. *Journal of the House of Delegates*, 9–14.

35. In Gomez's words, "Measures had to be taken to decouple Christianity from the just war" (*Exchanging Our Country Marks*, 257).

36. Ambler, *John Floyd*, 170.

37. Freehling, *Drift Toward Dissolution*, 269. The difference was even starker when considering only the trans-Allegheny counties, which contained 26.5 percent of the state's whites and 4.0 percent of the state's slaves.

38. Freehling, *Drift Toward Dissolution*, 54.

39. Charles A. Stuart to John Hartwell Cocke, 20 Oct. 1831, Papers of the Cocke Family, UVa.

40. Ibid. for the initial suggestion. For Cocke's follow-through, see Virginia Cary to John Hartwell Cocke, 11 Nov. 1831, Papers of the Cocke Family, UVa.

41. Charles A. Stuart to John Hartwell Cocke, 12 Nov. 1831, Papers of the Cocke Family, UVa. For an excellent discussion of the ways in which women framed petitions at this transitional moment in women's history, see Portnoy, *Right to Speak*.

42. Varon, *We Mean to Be Counted*, 48–57; quotation, 50. Of the three petitions Varon cites, one was unsent and one (from Fluvanna County) may have been a forgery along the lines of Charles Stuart's efforts.

43. For lists of petitions, see *Journal of the House of Delegates* and, for extended quotations from several of the petitions, Cromwell, "Aftermath of Nat Turner's Insurrection."

44. Freehling, *Drift Toward Dissolution*, 127–36.

45. Samuel McDowell Moore to [?], 5 Jan. 1832, Stuart-Baldwin Family Papers, UVa.

46. ALS Mary [Jefferson Randolph] to Mrs. Joseph Coolidge Jr., 25 Sept. 1831, Coolidge Correspondence, UVa. Antislavery legislators did win a small rhetori-

cal victory: the assembly agreed to a preamble suggested by Archibald Bryce Jr. in which they stated the desirability of taking more concrete steps to end slavery when public opinion permitted.

47. Tyler-McGraw, "Richmond Free Blacks," 217–18.
48. Schwarz, *Migrants against Slavery*, 72; Staudenraus, *African Colonization Movement*, 179–80.
49. M. F. Robertson to Louisa Cocke, 24 Sept. 1831, Papers of the Cocke Family, UVa.
50. Quotation from Slaughter, *Virginian History of African Colonization*, 61. On the politics of colonization, see Iaccarino, "Virginia and the National Contest," 189–90; Varon, *We Mean to Be Counted*, 46–47.
51. Slaughter, *Virginian History of African Colonization*, 67.
52. 30 Oct. 1831, Records of the Antioch Baptist Church (Raccoon Swamp), VBHS.
53. 12 Nov. 1831, ibid.
54. 30 Sept. 1831, Black Creek Baptist Church, VBHS.
55. *Religious Herald*, 7 Oct. 1831. For the best account of inter- and intraracial conflict within Southampton County churches, see Breen, in "Contested Communion," 692–702.
56. *Minutes of the Portsmouth Baptist Association* (1832), 45.
57. Raboteau, *Slave Religion*, 178, 196–97; *Minutes of the Dover Baptist Association* (1831), 5.
58. "Bertie Circuit, N.C., Extract of a Letter," *Christian Sentinel*, 31 Aug. 1832.
59. "Letter from John D. Holstead and James M. Boatright," *Christian Sentinel*, 18 Jan. 1833.
60. Historian Patrick Breen, in "Contested Communion," 699–701, elegantly traced the effects of this shift in Black Creek Baptist Church. Whites narrowly agreed not to expel black members but segregated communion so that whites would not have to endure the intimacy or "degradation" of serving blacks.
61. *Religious Herald*, 14 Oct. 1831.
62. As quoted in Earnest, *Religious Development*, 77.
63. Joyner, " 'Believer I Know,' " 23.
64. State of Virginia, *Acts Passed, 1832*, 20–22.
65. Ibid. There were antecedents to this provision in "An ACT to amend and explain an act further declaring what shall be deemed unlawful meetings of slaves," passed 4 Jan. 1805. Lawmakers in the 1805 act also made it clear that they did not want to prevent whites from bringing blacks to worship, but they did not add the clause about depriving owners of the right to hire white ministers for the purpose of missions to the slaves. See Shepherd, *Statutes at Large*, 3:124.
66. "Proceedings of the Twelfth Annual Meeting," *Religious Herald*, 8 May 1835.
67. *Religious Herald*, 14 Oct. 1831.
68. "False Rumors Corrected," *Religious Herald*, 23 Sept. 1831.
69. "Pastoral Letter of the Virginia Conference," *Christian Sentinel*, 15 June 1832.

70. Ryland, "First African Church," in Tupper, *First Century*, 245–72.
71. *Minutes of the Dover Baptist Association* (1834), 7–8.
72. *Minutes of the Portsmouth Baptist Association* (1833), 10.
73. White, *First Baptist Church*, 95.
74. Wickham, *Lost Family Found*, DocSouth.
75. Knight, "Notes on John Chavis," in Wills and Newman, *Black Apostles*, 29–30.
76. "Presbytery of Orange," *Southern Religious Telegraph*, 18 Dec. 1835.
77. Bratton, "Fields's Observations," DocSouth.
78. Jacobs, *Incidents in the Life*, 67.
79. Stearns, *Henry Box Brown*, DocSouth.
80. Wickham, *Lost Family Found*, DocSouth.
81. Johnson, *Africa for Christ*, DocSouth.
82. Smith, *Autobiography*, DocSouth.
83. Meade, *Old Virginia Family Servants*, 76.
84. Willis, "Slave Honor and Christianity," 38. The numbers in Fountain, "Long on Religion," 19, suggest a feminization of black Christianity as well. According to this study of WPA narratives with religious content, 43.8 percent of women but only 35.1 percent of men converted while enslaved.
85. *Journal of the Convention* (1833), 21.
86. Ibid. (1834), 16.
87. All quotations from ibid.
88. Meade, *Duty of Affording Religious Instruction*, 14, 4.
89. Precise numbers are difficult to come by. Of the 3,444 total emigrants from Virginia, most (1,807) left between 1817 and 1837. Approximately 920 of the remaining 1,637 left during one six-year period, 1847–53, mostly free blacks from the Shenandoah Valley. See Elsinger, "Rufus W. Bailey," 42, and Burin, *Peculiar Solution*, tabs. 4 and 5.
90. Meade, *Duty of Affording Religious Instruction*, 4.
91. John Hartwell Cocke to Sally F. Cocke, 4 Mar. 1832, Papers of the Cocke Family, UVa.
92. Burin, *Peculiar Solution*, 45–48.
93. These letters are republished with a thoughtful introduction in Miller, *"Dear Master."* The letters, and the theme of false assurance, appear in more detail in Chapter 5.
94. "Slavery and Colonization," *Christian Sentinel*, 15 Nov. 1833.
95. "Colored People of the United States," *Religious Herald*, 20 Jan. 1832.
96. Ibid.
97. "Domestic Missionary Society," *Southern Religious Telegraph*, 25 Apr. 1834.
98. Cornelius, *When I Can Read My Title Clear*, 33; Cromwell, "Aftermath of Nat Turner's Insurrection," 231–34.
99. Jones, *Religious Instruction of the Negroes*, 78.
100. Ibid., 73–74.

1. The defense of their regional honor became an additional incentive for the evan-gelization of slaves in the 1830s and 1840s. See Snay, *Gospel of Disunion*, 49, 95; Goen, *Broken Churches, Broken Nation*, 65. Indeed, Tise (*Proslavery*, 114) says that the characterization of slavery as "a missionary institution to civilize and Christianize Africans" was the single most common defense of slavery advanced by southerners between 1831 and 1861.

2. Early abolitionism took the form of a conflict between colonization and imme-diatism, and black men and women catalyzed the movement of some coloniza-tionists to immediatism. For the above, see Goodman, *Of One Blood*, 36–45, and Portnoy, *Right to Speak*, 161–86; also Newman, *Transformation of American Abolitionism*, and Stauffer, *Black Hearts of Men*.

3. John H. Cocke to Rev. R. R. Gurley, 23 Sept. 1831, Papers of the Cocke Family, UVa.

4. Wyatt-Brown, "Abolitionists' Postal Campaign," 227–30.

5. "Meeting of the Clergy," *Religious Herald*, 4 Sept. 1835.

6. "Presbytery of Winchester," *Southern Religious Telegraph*, 20 Nov. 1835.

7. *Religious Herald*, 28 Aug. 1835.

8. "Meeting of the Clergy," *Religious Herald*, 4 Sept. 1835.

9. "[Unreadable]," *Religious Herald*, 6 Aug. 1835. Antislavery colonizationists also had to adopt new strategies to avoid being labeled abolitionists. See Varon, *We Mean to Be Counted*, 60–61.

10. "To the Editors of the Whig," *Religious Herald*, 11 Sept. 1835.

11. From "Colored People of the United States," *Religious Herald*, 20 Jan. 1832. See Chapter 4, text at n. 95.

12. Snay, *Gospel of Disunion*, 95.

13. As quoted in Perdue, Barden, and Phillips, *Weevils in the Wheat*, 183; see also 100, 241; Johnson, *Africa for Christ*, DocSouth; Stearns, *Henry Box Brown*, DocSouth. Several historians, including Fountain, in "Christ in Chains," 95–97, and Johnson, in "'Delusive Clothing,'" 300–301, have taken this to be the core of Christian instruction.

14. To date the most balanced approach to these issues is Clarke, *Dwelling Place*, chap. 11.

15. "Highly Important," *Religious Herald*, 13 Feb. 1835.

16. For example, "Religious Instruction of Slaves," 20 Feb. 1835; "Instruction for Colored People—Cont.," 17 Apr. 1835; and "Religious Instruction for Colored Persons," 8 May 1835, all in *Religious Herald*; "Catechism for Colored Persons," *Southern Religious Telegraph*, 13 June 1834.

17. "Domestic Assistant," *Southern Churchman*, 20, 27 Feb. 1835, 4 Mar. 1837; "Stories for Servants," *Southern Churchman*, 31 Aug., 28 Sept. 1838. The "Sto-ries for Servants" had stopped by 1839.

18. "Instruction of Colored Members," *Religious Herald*, 13 Feb. 1835.
19. "Remarks on the Religious Instruction of Colored People," *Religious Herald*, 24 Apr. 1835.
20. Noll, *Theological Crisis*, 51–64.
21. Cornelius, *Slave Missions*, 88, 99; Snay, *Gospel of Disunion*, 96.
22. For a list of the most popular catechisms, see Sernett, *Black Religion*, 241–42, and, for a discussion of their content, 66–67. Jones also surveyed literature published on the topic through 1842 in *Religious Instruction of the Negroes*, 65–89.
23. M'Tyeire, *Duties of Christian Masters*, publication history in preface.
24. As quoted in Mathews, "Southern Evangelical Crusade," 301; see also Cornelius, *Slave Missions*, 77–85; Clarke, *Dwelling Place*, chap. 8. Clarke's biography of the Jones family is spectacular in its detailed accounts of the black and white families connected with the Jones plantations, and it includes an elegant account of how the mission to the slaves led C. C. Jones into proslavery, esp. on 355–56.
25. Jones, *Catechism of Scripture*, v.
26. Jones, *Religious Instruction of the Negroes*, 100.
27. John Hartwell Cocke to Charles Colcock Jones, 26 June 1844, Papers of the Cocke Family, UVa.
28. "Narrative of the State of Religion," *Watchman of the South*, 11 Nov. 1843.
29. Ryland, *Scriptural Catechism*, iii–iv, 139–41.
30. Based on Luther P. Jackson's tally of 54,000 black Virginia Baptists and the contemporaneous nationwide counts of Daniel Hundley and David Christy, as recorded in Cornelius, *Slave Missions*, 184 n. See also *National Era*, 4 Nov. 1858.
31. "Religious Instruction of Servants," *Central Presbyterian*, 25 Aug. 1860.
32. Membership Statistics of the Ballenger Creek Baptist Church, 1855, UVa.
33. "Domestic Missions in Virginia," *Watchman of the South*, 2 Nov. 1843.
34. Jones, *Religious Instruction of the Negroes*, 235–39; "Religious Instruction of Slaves," *Southern Religious Telegraph*, 24 Mar. 1837; "Domestic Missions in Virginia," 2 Nov. 1843, and "Pastoral Letter," 29 Feb. 1844, both in *Watchman of the South*; *Watchman and Observer*, 25 Sept. 1845.
35. Sernett, *Black Religion*, 41–42, 290; Hartzell, "Methodism and the Negro," 309.
36. For Huntington and Goodwin, see Huntington Papers and Goodwin Papers, VHS. See Meade, *Old Virginia Family Servants*, 93; see also 20, 52–55, 61, 73, 104, 108.
37. "Albemarle Association," *Religious Herald*, 8 Nov. 1833.
38. Jackson, "Religious Development of the Negro," 192–205.
39. State of Virginia, *Acts Passed, 1831*, 20–22.
40. Reed and Matheson, *Narrative of the Visit*, 1:151–55, 190–93.
41. Stevens, *Anthony Burns*, DocSouth.
42. Davis, *Narrative of the Life*, DocSouth.

43. See, for example, Drew, *North-Side View*, DocSouth; Williams and Goldie, *Sunshine and Shadow*, DocSouth.

44. 3 June 1843, Aug., Sept. 1852, Register of the Baptists from Chappawamsic, VHS.

45. Sobel, *Trabelin' On*, 433.

46. Sept. 1849, Mill Creek Baptist Church, VBHS.

47. White evangelicals' attempts to reform the legal foundations of slavery would not peak until the Civil War. See Genovese, *Consuming Fire*, 3–71; Mohr, *Threshold of Freedom*, 247–70.

48. Jeter, *Recollections of a Long Life*, 175.

49. Schweiger, *Gospel Working Up*, 72–73.

50. Cornelius, *When I Can Read My Title Clear*, 47; "Old African Church," *Daily Dispatch*, 16 Aug. 1876.

51. Williams, *Self-Taught*, 19.

52. "The Bible in the South," *National Era*, 1 July 1847; "Is the Bible Withheld," *National Era*, 6 Jan. 1848.

53. Jones, *Religious Instruction of the Negroes*, 274.

54. Schweiger, *Gospel Working Up*, viii, 51–52.

55. Jeter, *Recollections of a Long Life*, 209–13; Ryland, "First African Church," in Tupper, *First Century*, 245–72. Each of the Baptist ministers cited black preference for independent worship only indirectly, explaining that it was impossible for whites to meet the needs of black Christians in joint assembly. According to Jeter, "There were several reasons for organizing them into a separate and independent church. The space allotted for their use in the house of worship was utterly insufficient for their accommodation. The style of preaching demanded by the white congregation was not well adapted to the instruction of the colored people. Besides, it was quite impossible for the pastor, with a large white congregation under his care, to pay much attention to the necessities of the colored portion of his flock" (209). See also O'Brien, *From Bondage to Citizenship*, 34–35.

56. Jeter, *Recollections of a Long Life*, 213.

57. Irons, "And All These Things."

58. Takagi, *"Rearing Wolves,"* 17; *Minutes of the Dover Baptist Association* (1844).

59. Irons, "And All These Things," 35; Takagi, *"Rearing Wolves,"* 103–10; Ruggles, *Unboxing*, 12–13. The church only helped purchase those slaves who they felt could have profitable preaching careers. They contributed money to Thomas Allen of Richmond, Noah Davis of Madison County, and "Bro. Elliot" of Norfolk.

60. *Minutes of the Dover Baptist Association* (1844, 1846, 1855, 1860); for a discussion of black preference for these churches, see Cornelius, *Slave Missions*, 108–10.

61. "Colored Members in Baptist Churches," *Religious Herald*, 13 Oct. 1837.

62. "The Triennial Convention," *Religious Herald*, 23 May 1844.

63. "A Crazy Man's Idea," *Richmond Christian Advocate*, 11 June 1846.

64. "Duties of Masters," *Watchman of the South*, 28 Sept. 1843.

65. *Central Presbyterian*, 26 Jan. 1861.

66. "Abolitionists—Mr. Birney," *Religious Herald*, 3 July 1835; 25 July 1835, Register of the Baptists from Chappawamsic, VHS.

67. For this estimate, see "Colored Church Members," *Richmond Christian Advocate*, 26 Jan. 1854.

68. Mathews, *Religion in the Old South*, 149.

69. 19 Oct. 1845, 26 Apr. 1846, undated loose sheet, Goodwin Papers, VHS.

70. Scott, *Southern Lady*; Gimelli, "Louisa Maxwell Cocke," 53–54.

71. Paulina LeGrand to William Huntington, 8 Mar. 1838, Huntington Papers, VHS.

72. Ibid., 26 Sept. 1839.

73. 10 July 1844, Personal Diary, Papers of the Cocke Family, UVa.

74. Peyton Skipwith to John Hartwell Cocke, 29 Sept. 1844, Papers of the Cocke Family, UVa; see also Miller, *"Dear Master."* For a similar collection of letters for several families, see Wiley, *Slaves No More*.

75. Sarah Page Andrews to Charles Wesley Andrews, 3 July 1839, Andrews Papers, Duke. When the news from white evangelicals' trusted correspondents was bad, disturbed whites often sought second opinions, or assurances that their correspondents were malcontents. See Varon, *We Mean to Be Counted*, 63.

76. "Colonization Sketch" and "Sentiments on Colonization in Liberia," *Southern Churchman*, 28 Apr. 1837.

77. Taylor, *Elder Lott Cary*, 108.

78. As quoted in Slaughter, *Virginian History of African Colonization*, 92.

79. Elsinger, "Rufus W. Bailey."

80. For the material that follows, see esp. Goen, *Broken Churches, Broken Nation*; Snay, *Gospel of Disunion*; and Smith, *In His Image, But*.

81. Wood, *Old and New Theology*.

82. Thompson, *Presbyterians in the South*, 1:407. The terms of the alliance with northern conservatives seem to have involved a more or less explicit promise never to discuss slavery in the Old School General Assembly. See Smith, "Role of the South," 58.

83. Sussex resolutions reprinted in *Watchman of the South*, 21 Sept. 1837.

84. See also Baker, *Northern and Southern Baptists*.

85. John Ruff to John S. Martin, 25 Mar. 1840, Martin Papers, SHC.

86. See also Mathews, *Slavery and Methodism*, 212–82.

87. Both the New School and the Old School would split again—in 1857 and 1861, respectively—over the issue of slavery. This second round of splits followed more closely political divisions between slaveholding and nonslaveholding states. Quotation from "Our Methodist Brethren," *Watchman of the South*, 29 Aug. 1844. On the ecumenical effect of schism, see Loveland, *Southern Evangelicals*, 256, and Snay, *Gospel of Disunion*, 95–97.

88. "Religious Instruction of the Negroes," *Richmond Christian Advocate*, 12 Mar. 1846.

89. 5 June 1844, as quoted in Gross, *History of the Methodist Episcopal Church, South*, 29.

90. *Proceedings of the Meeting in Charleston*, 72; Clarke, *Dwelling Place*, 247–51.

91. *Journal of the Convention* (1845), 35.

92. "Winchester Presbytery," *Watchman and Observer*, 25 Sept. 1845; "Proceedings of the Synod," *Watchman and Observer*, 6 Nov. 1845.

93. *Proceedings of the Meeting in Charleston*, 5.

94. Harrison, *Gospel among the Slaves*, 194–95, 318–24, 326.

95. *Minutes of the Annual Conferences of the Methodist Episcopal Church* (1844–45); *Minutes of the Annual Conferences of the Methodist Episcopal Church, South* (1845–59).

96. *Minutes of the Dover Baptist Association* (1844–60).

97. Ibid. (1846), 8.

98. Ibid. (1847), 14–17.

99. By "catholic" I mean inclusive. Episcopal churches still retained some sense of the parish system from their Anglican heritage, in which the ideal remained that all inhabitants of a given area would attend the same church. The voluntarism of other evangelical churches cut against this sort of catholicity.

100. *Journal of the Convention* (1861).

101. Ibid. (1860), 31, 63–70; quotations, 31, 68.

102. For slave trade numbers, see Chapter 3, n. 86.

Jackson, "Religious Development of the Negro," 234, claims only 60,000 black church members. The number was probably closer to 70,000, based on Jackson's undercounting of black Methodists. There seems to be agreement on the 54,000 black Baptists; cf. Daniel, "Virginia Baptists and the Negro," 10–11. But see *Minutes of the Annual Conferences of the Methodist Episcopal Church, South* (1860) and *Annual Register of the Baltimore Conference* (1861). There were fewer than 1,000 black Presbyterians and Episcopalians, according to Thompson, *Presbyterians in the South*, 1:443, and *Journal of the Convention* (1861).

103. See Appendix A.

104. Perdue, Barden, and Phillips, *Weevils in the Wheat*, 178. Jones was interviewed in 1937 in Portsmouth, Virginia.

105. Stearns, *Henry Box Brown*, DocSouth.

106. Veney, *Narrative*, DocSouth.

107. Basil Manly Jr. to Charles Colcock Jones, 31 July 1852, Jones Papers, Tulane.

108. Plumer, *Religious Instruction of the Negroes*, 19.

109. All quotations in this paragraph and the next from Shaver, "Memorial," UVa. This document, which is undated, was once erroneously cataloged as dating from 1831–32, "protesting suppression of the African Baptist Church Following Nat Turner's rebellion." It has since been dated to 1853, which fits with the

multiplication of quasi-independent churches post-1845. For an earlier (1832) example of white evangelicals fighting among themselves about making the churches accessible to African Americans, see Breen, "Contested Communion," 702.

110. Nott and Gliddon, *Types of Mankind*. See Acts 17:26.

111. Holifield, *Gentlemen Theologians*, 72–109; Cabell, *Unity of Mankind*; the piece first appeared in the Jan. 1857 *Protestant Episcopal Review and Church Register*. See also Slaughter, *Virginian History of African Colonization*, xiv.

112. For a sustained discussion of white teaching and black reception, see Webber, *Deep Like the Rivers*.

113. Stevens, *Anthony Burns*, DocSouth.

114. Drew, *North-Side View*, DocSouth.

115. This article first appeared in the *Southern Churchman* and was reprinted as "Negro Piety," *Central Presbyterian*, 12 Mar. 1859.

116. Cf. Colossians 4:1 and Matthew 28:29–30, KJV.

Chapter 6

1. Link, *Roots of Secession*. Though black agents are conspicuously absent from this particular chapter and omnipresent in Link's book, the overarching thesis here, that enslaved Virginians influenced the way that evangelical whites felt and spoke about the all-important question of the day, slavery, strongly echoes Link's conclusions about Virginia politics.

2. Carmichael, *Last Generation*, 125–26. Carmichael's insight that the generation of white male Virginians who grew up with the sectional conflict had a distinct outlook is important. He acknowledges that these proslavery men were less willing to endorse secession after Lincoln's election than were their peers from the Deep South, though he suggests that the younger generation, at least, had moved to a secessionist position by late December 1860.

3. Influential recent examples include Daly, *When Slavery Was Called Freedom*, 74, and McCurry, *Masters of Small Worlds*, 150–58, 288–92.

4. Of the 490,877 slaves in Virginia in 1860, only 12,771 resided in the interior counties of the trans-Alleghenies—the future West Virginia. The best accounts of the economic and political conflict between eastern and western Virginia are Freehling, *Drift Toward Dissolution*, which traces the conflict from the 1829–30 constitutional convention, and Link, *Roots of Secession*, which picks it up in the 1850s.

5. For example, Genovese, *Consuming Fire*; O'Brien, *Conjectures of Order*; Farmer, *Metaphysical Confederacy*.

6. Crofts, "Late Antebellum Virginia"; Deyle, *Carry Me Back*, 46.

7. Crofts, *Reluctant Confederates*; Freehling, "Virginia's (Reluctant) Decision to Secede." Link does not focus on religious ideas about secession, but he empha-

sizes the distinction between support for slavery and support for secession; see *Roots of Secession*, 149.

8. Wyatt-Brown, *Shaping of Southern Culture*, 155.

9. Stringfellow, *Scriptural and Statistical Views*, 144; Faust, "Evangelicalism and the Meaning of the Proslavery Argument."

10. Stringfellow, *Brief Examination*, DocSouth.

11. Noll, *Theological Crisis*, 54. Genovese observed that the most thoughtful southern intellectuals noticed this inconsistency, though "proslavery protagonists proved so strong in their appeal to Scripture as to make comprehensible the readiness with which southern whites satisfied themselves that God sanctioned slavery" (see Genovese and Fox-Genovese, *Mind of the Master Class*, 505–26; quotation, 526).

12. Plumer, *Religious Instruction of the Negroes*, 1. For a very unfavorable description of Plumer, see Stearns, *Henry Box Brown*, DocSouth.

13. Smith, *Lectures on Slavery*, DocSouth.

14. See Chapters 4 and 5 for white evangelicals' changing understanding of colonization; Slaughter, *Virginian History of African Colonization*, iv, x, xii, 85. For biographical details, see Slaughter, "Reverend Philip Slaughter."

15. Rives, *Discourse on the Ethics of Christianity*, 22.

16. For the best discussion of Thornwell, see Farmer, *Metaphysical Confederacy*, in particular 59, 230.

17. Ibid., 264.

18. *Letter to the People of Georgia*, quoted in Wakelyn, *Southern Pamphlets on Secession*, 90–91.

19. 1 Dec. 1860, in Dumond, *Southern Editorials on Secession*, 284.

20. 9 Nov. 1860, in ibid., xviii.

21. Palmer, *The South*, 8–9, 11.

22. As quoted in Snay, *Gospel of Disunion*, 179; Haynes, *Noah's Curse*, 128–31.

23. "Speech of Hon. Wm. C. Rives," *Richmond Whig and Advertiser*, 6 May 1859.

24. Shade, *Democratizing the Old Dominion*, 178; Crofts, *Reluctant Confederates*, 130–38; Link, *Roots of Secession*, 220–22.

25. Botts, *Interesting and Important Correspondence*, 12.

26. See Gunderson, *Old Gentlemen's Convention*.

27. *Speech on the Proceedings of the Peace Conference*, in Wakelyn, *Southern Pamphlets on Secession*, 363, 368.

28. "Address, to the Clergy and Laity," *Central Presbyterian*, 26 Jan. 1861. Dabney had been less tactful in a letter to his mother on 28 December 1860, when he complained, "As for South Carolina, the little impudent vixen has gone beyond all patience. She is as great a pest as the Abolitionists" (Johnson, *Robert Lewis Dabney*, 215).

29. Wayne Wei-Siang Hsieh, "Christian Love and Martial Violence," in Wallenstein and Wyatt-Brown, *Virginia's Civil War*, 88–90.

30. Moses Drury Hoge, quoted in "Local Matters," *Daily Dispatch*, 5 Jan. 1861.

31. "A Liberal Regard for Private Opinions," *Richmond Christian Advocate*, 4 Apr. 1861.

32. For a clear statement of the compromise Unionist position, see Link, *Roots of Secession*, 229.

33. Jeter to J. A. Broadus, 11 Dec. 1860, in Robertson, *John Albert Broadus*, 179–80.

34. "Coercion," *The Review* (Charlottesville, Va.), 4 Jan. 1861, in Dumond, *Southern Editorials on Secession*, 387–90.

35. "Nathaniel Beverly Tucker," *Dictionary of American Biography*, 37–38; Nathaniel Beverley Tucker to Richard Cocke, 10 Jan. 1861, Letters and Documents, "The Ground Beneath Our Feet: Reconfiguring Virginia," <http://www.vahistory.org/reconfiguring/cockeo11061.html>.

36. [Lyons], *Four Essays*, 5, 11, 23.

37. Shanks, *Secession Movement in Virginia*, 153; Crofts, *Reluctant Confederates*, 140; Link, *Roots of Secession*, 227. Link estimates that as many as fifty of the representatives may have been secessionists.

38. Episcopalians, who did not make up a significant proportion of the state's evangelical population in terms of either numbers or influence until the late 1820s, never felt the necessity of making such a resolution, though they adhered to the same general principle.

39. As Sparks shows very well in his excellent treatment of evangelicalism in Mississippi, *Jordan's Stormy Banks*, there were some egalitarian rumblings in the Deep South before the cotton boom. The demographic tidal wave that swept over Mississippi and Alabama after the War of 1812, however, overwhelmed whatever remnants of this older evangelical tradition there may have been.

40. Berlin, *Slaves without Masters*, 137.

41. As quoted in Loveland, *Southern Evangelicals*, 202.

42. Botts, *Interesting and Important Correspondence*, 7.

43. Membership from *Minutes of the Annual Conferences of the Methodist Episcopal Church* (1850). The Baltimore, Philadelphia, Western Virginia, Pittsburgh, and Ohio conferences all contained Virginians (though the Ohio Conference contained only ninety-six Germans in a mission church in Wheeling).

44. Long, *Slavery in Church and State*, DocSouth. Francis A. Harding was expelled from the ministry in the Baltimore Conference when he inherited slaves by marriage. The rejection of his appeal at the 1844 General Conference was an additional reason—along with the conflict over Bishop James O. Andrew—for the schism. See Mathews, *Slavery and Methodism*, 252–55.

45. For information on the conference pre-1844, see Mathews, *Slavery and Methodism*, 33–37; Armstrong, *History of the Old Baltimore Conference*, 269.

46. *Annual Register of the Baltimore Conference* (1861), 38–43. The conference grew so quickly that in 1857 it spun off the East Baltimore Conference.

47. *Republican Vindicator*, 29 June 1860, Civil War–Era Newspapers, Churches/

Religious Activities, Valley of the Shadow, <http://www.vcdh.virginia.edu/xml_docs/valley_news/html/topics.html>.

48. *Annual Register of the Baltimore Conference* (1861), 46.

49. Ibid., 48.

50. Jeffus, "Invitation to a Carnival of Death," tab. 1, and *Annual Register of the Baltimore Conference* (1861), 38–43. Jeffus is a useful complement to Crofts and Shanks, for he included several useful appendices, including the results of nine critical roll-call votes of the convention.

51. Reese, *Virginia State Convention*, 1:792–94.

52. Wooster, *Secession Conventions*. Of the sixty-four delegations from counties or cities with less than 12.5 percent of the population enslaved, thirty-three voted Unionist, and the remainder split between moderate Unionist and Secessionist.

53. Reese, *Virginia State Convention*, 1:11; Link, *Roots of Secession*, 227–48.

54. *Journals and Papers of the State Convention*, 1:57, 63. Nolley's name first appears as pastor of Richmond's black Methodists in *Minutes of the Annual Conferences of the Methodist Episcopal Church, South* (1855–56).

55. *Journals and Papers of the State Convention*, 1:45–47. The other delegates to propose anticoercive resolutions were Jeremiah Morton (Greene and Orange), John. S. Carlile (Harrison), Walter D. Leake (Goochland), George W. Richardson (Hanover), and Thomas Flournoy (Halifax).

56. Jeffus, "Invitation to a Carnival of Death," 23, tab. 4.

57. Freehling, *Drift Toward Dissolution*, 263. Residents of western Virginia, as Freehling well documents, were not convinced even after Lincoln's call for troops.

58. Gunderson, *Old Gentlemen's Convention*, 60.

59. Edward C. Burks to Rowland [Buford], 24 Jan. 1861, in Walmsley, "Change of Secession Sentiment," 88. Also see Crofts, *Reluctant Confederates*, 208; Link, *Roots of Secession*, 336–37, n. 28. The Peace Conference concluded on 28 February 1861.

60. 12 Mar. 1861, Diaries of Overton and Jesse Bernard, SHC.

61. Reese, *Virginia State Convention*, 4:76–93; Dew, *Apostles of Disunion*, 59–73.

62. Reese, *Virginia State Convention*, 1:93.

63. Jeffus, "Invitation to a Carnival of Death," tab. 1.

64. Dunaway, *Life and Writings of Rev. Addison Hall*, 73. It is not clear if Hall actually cast a vote for secession at the convention, though his sympathies certainly lay with separation. Jeffus does not record a vote for Hall, whom I first learned about from Daniel, "Virginia Baptists, 1861–1865," 96.

65. Reese, *Virginia State Convention*, 4:22, 66.

66. Ibid., 24. Preston's role was symbolic on several levels. He was the moderate representative of an eleventh-hour delegation sent to Abraham Lincoln, and his swing therefore showed the swing of the moderates to secession. He had also proposed in the debates following Nat Turner's rebellion that it would be "expedient" for the Virginia General Assembly to legislate against slavery. See Link, *Roots of Secession*, 239–41; Wolf, *Race and Liberty*, 219–27.

67. Jeffus, "Invitation to a Carnival of Death," tab. 1.

68. McIlwaine, *Memories*, 184–85.

69. John B. Minor to Mary Berkeley Minor Blackford, 16 Apr. 1861, in Blackford, *Mine Eyes Have Seen the Glory*, 158–59.

70. J. M. Broadus to J. A. Broadus, 27 Apr. 1861, in Robertson, *John Albert Broadus*, 183.

71. *Journal of the Convention* (1861), 28.

72. James H. Otey to Edward C. Burks, 17 July 1861, in Walmsley, "Change of Secession Sentiment," 100.

73. Church statistics from *Minutes of the Annual Conferences of the Methodist Episcopal Church* (1850) and *Minutes of the Annual Conferences of the Methodist Episcopal Church, South* (1850); Jackson speech in Reese, *Virginia State Convention*, 4:30–31.

74. Willey to Harrison Hagans, 1 May 1862, in Willey, "Note on the Motives," 275.

75. William D. Cabell Journal, 1861 (Jan.–Nov.), Cabell Family Papers, UVa.

76. 20 Apr. 1861, Lynch Diary, VHS.

77. "Our New-Born Nation," *Central Presbyterian*, 13 July 1861.

78. See, for example, Schweiger, *Gospel Working Up*, esp. 91–107; Daly, *When Slavery Was Called Freedom*, 136; Farmer, *Metaphysical Confederacy*; Faust, *Creation of Confederate Nationalism*; Wight, "Churches and the Confederate Cause"; Silver, *Confederate Morale*.

79. *Journal of the Convention* (1861), 27.

80. *Minutes of the Baptist General Association* (1861, 1862, 1863), 16.

81. "The Sentiment of Virginia," *Richmond Christian Advocate*, 2 May 1861.

82. As quoted in Wight, "Churches and the Confederate Cause," 361.

83. As quoted in Silver, *Confederate Morale*, 48. For a more complete statement of Presbyterian reasons for endorsing the Confederacy—but which also fails to mention slavery—see *Minutes of the Synod of Virginia* (1861), 285.

84. Daniel, "Virginia Baptists, 1861–1865," 98–99.

85. "Sunday School," *Richmond Christian Advocate*, 4 Apr. 1861.

86. Harrison, *Gospel among the Slaves*, 323–24.

87. "Pastoral Letter," *Southern Churchman*, 2 Jan. 1863. For amelioration, see Genovese, *Consuming Fire*, 51–61.

88. Berends, "Wholesome Reading," in Miller, Stout, and Wilson, *Religion and the American Civil War*.

89. Jones, *Christ in the Camp*, 223.

90. Gross, *History of the Methodist Episcopal Church, South*, 74.

91. The strongest arguments against evangelicalism's role as a prop for Confederate morale were Linderman, *Embattled Courage*, and Beringer, Hattaway, Jones, and Still, *Why the South Lost the Civil War*. As consensus has emerged that evangelicalism was critical to the maintenance of Confederate morale, the precise reasons why it was so have multiplied. On emotional trauma, see Faust, "Christian Soldiers" and "Civil War Soldier," 22–28. On Providential intervention, see

Phillips, "Religious Belief and Troop Motivation," in Wallenstein and Wyatt-Brown, *Virginia's Civil War*. On identification with Christ, see Berends, "Confederate Sacrifice," in Schweiger and Mathews, *Religion in the American South*.

92. Wood, *Virginia Bishop*, 1, 43.

93. Dabney, *True Courage*, DocSouth. Much of Dabney's tribute fits Faust's description of a "good death"; see Faust, "Civil War Soldier."

94. McGuire, *Diary of a Southern Refugee*, 255–56.

95. 21 Apr. 1861, Lynch Diary, VHS.

96. "Preachers and War," *Richmond Christian Advocate*, 13 June 1861.

97. All quotations from Tucker, *Southern Church Justified*.

98. Minnigerode, *"He that believeth,"* 10.

99. Gallagher, *Confederate War*, 36. For a slightly different view, one that stresses the ultimate durability of evangelical support for the war but describes several distinct phases, see Stout and Grasso, "Civil War, Religion, and Communications," in Miller, Stout, and Wilson, *Religion and the American Civil War*.

100. As quoted in Wight, "Churches and the Confederate Cause," 373.

Epilogue

1. Hahn, *Nation under Our Feet*, 82, 499 n. 33. Of an estimated 475,000 total fugitives, at least 50,000 were from Virginia. Though the story of black flight appears in secondary works, it is best told through the documents published in Berlin et al., *Free at Last*, including the report mentioned here (9–11).

2. Wight, "Churches and the Confederate Cause," 369.

3. The Richmond, Charlottesville, Lynchburg, Farmville, and Petersburg districts recorded data for each year from 1860 through 1866. In these five districts, the numbers fell from 3,103 black members and 223 black probationary members in 1860 to 1,131 black members and no probationary members in 1866. The only year that did not record a decline was 1863, when the number of members and probationary members both increased, to 2,555 and 423, respectively. In contrast, the white membership in the same five districts rose in five of six years, from 24,601 in 1860 to 27,362 in 1866. See *Minutes of the Annual Conferences of the Methodist Episcopal Church, South* (1861–66).

4. Based on ibid. (1860, 1866). These figures include ME Church, South, members in slaveholding states outside the Confederacy (i.e., Kentucky, Missouri, Maryland, and the trans-Mississippi West) and treat probationary members as full members.

5. On White and Carter, see Ely, *Israel on the Appomattox*, 421–24; "Names of Colored Members Remaining," Register of the Baptists from Chappawamsic, VHS. For a more regional perspective on black church formation, see Stowell, *Rebuilding Zion*, 80–83. There is no good discussion of the black evangelicals who remained in biracial churches after the war, and even their approximate number remains somewhat mysterious.

6. Faust, "Evangelicalism and the Meaning of the Proslavery Argument," 15.

7. Previous generations of scholars mistakenly assumed that white Christians forced African Americans into racially separate churches in the same way that they segregated public spaces. Dvorak most systematically rejected this argument and explained the now widely accepted interpretation that blacks left white churches because they felt that they could better meet their own spiritual needs independently. See Dvorak, *African-American Exodus*; see also Montgomery, *Under Their Own Vine and Fig Tree*.

8. See Chapter 5, n. 102; U.S. Bureau of the Census, *Eighth Census, 1860*, 514–15, 518, and *Statistics Compiled from the Eighth Census, 1860*, 485.

9. Carroll, *Religious Forces*, lvi, and U.S. Bureau of the Census, *Eleventh Census, 1890*, 2:246. Carroll marveled, "The increase in the number of colored communicants since emancipation has been marvelous. . . . I know of no parallel to this development in the history of the Christian church, when all the denominations are considered" (*Religious Forces*, lvii). Lincoln and Mamiya estimated that the black Baptist membership in the states that comprised the Confederacy went from 150,000 in 1850 to 500,000 in 1870; see *Black Church*, 25. Fountain raises the legitimate possibility that it was not only the integration of the invisible church that increased numbers so dramatically, but the fact that the "Christian core" from within the slave community gained in emancipation proof that their message of liberation was true; see "Long on Religion," 90–106.

10. On the separation between white and black Baptists in Charlottesville, see Benfer, "History of First Baptist Church," UVa; McKinney, *Keeping the Faith*; First Baptist Church, *135th Anniversary Pamphlet*; Witmer, "Race, Religion, and Rebellion."

11. Stowell, *Rebuilding Zion*, 65.

12. Lewis Bayley quotation from 1864–65 notations in Church Register for the Albemarle Circuit, UVa. See also U.S. Bureau of the Census, *Eleventh Census, 1890*, 2:246.

13. McKinney, *Keeping the Faith*, 39–40.

14. Witmer, "Race, Religion, and Rebellion."

15. McKinney, *Keeping the Faith*, 41.

16. By selecting "Delevan Church" as their name, blacks in Charlottesville were rejecting white naming practices; whites typically named black churches in town "African," as in First African Baptist, African Methodist, etc.

17. As quoted in Montgomery, *Under Their Own Vine and Fig Tree*, 109.

18. There is some controversy regarding the establishment of Mount Zion. Congregants at Mount Zion insist that the founders of their church "came out of the white church and began meeting from house to house" in 1867. However, this seems quite unlikely, since virtually all blacks left that church at the same time and formed the Delevan Church. Furthermore, First Baptist just as firmly insists that it "planted" Mount Zion, and that it was, in fact, the "first" black Baptist

church in town. See Mount Zion Baptist Church, *Century of Christian Service*, and personal interview with Rev. Dr. Bruce A. Beard, First Baptist Church, 4 Dec. 1998.

19. Du Bois, *Souls of Black Folk*, 257–58.

20. The exact duration of Gibbons's pastorate is unclear. Memorialists of the First Baptist churches (white and black) in Charlottesville note that he began preaching at some time before his 1870 departure, but they do not speculate at what time he replaced Randolph, the last recorded white pastor, or whether there was an intervening pastor. From the Freedman's Bureau papers, it seems clear that Gibbons had taken an active ministerial role in the church by early 1867. See William Lewis Tidball to O. Lewis, 12 Mar. 1867, in Freedman's Bureau, "Reports on Prominent Whites and Freedmen."

21. See the example of Norfolk below; for AME and AME Zion initiatives, see Walker, *Rock in a Weary Land*.

22. Letters from Lucy Chase to "Dear Ones at Home," 15 Jan., 30 Sept. 1863, 1 July 1864, in Swint, *Dear Ones at Home*, 21, 91, 124–25. For the transformative experience of interracial cooperation between missionaries and freedmen, see Blum, *Reforging the White Republic*, chap. 2.

23. Butchart, *Northern Schools, Southern Blacks*.

24. McGranahan, *Freedmen's Missions*, 21, 64, 70.

25. Students in the University of Virginia's Architecture School reported in a research project on file in the Fiske Kimball Library that one such school temporarily met in the same building in which the black Baptists eventually worshipped, the Delevan building. See Liebman and McQuaid, "Study of Ten Black Baptist Churches," fig. 16.

26. William Lewis Tidball to O. Lewis, 12 Mar. 1867, in Freedman's Bureau, "Reports on Prominent Whites and Freedmen."

27. Cornelius, *Slave Missions*, 196–99.

28. Dudley and Taylor, "African and Antioch Baptist Churches," 301.

29. Butt, *African Methodism in Virginia*, DocSouth, and Wayman, *My Recollections of African Methodist Episcopal Ministers*, DocSouth.

30. On the size of the church, see *(Richmond) Daily Dispatch*. For records of Holmes's baptism and ordination as a deacon, see 14 Sept. 1842 and 26 Apr. 1856, First African Baptist Church, Minutes, 1841–1859, LVa, and O'Brien, *From Bondage to Citizenship*, 58.

31. On preaching prior to emancipation, see 2 Jan. 1858, First African Baptist Church, Minutes, 1841–1859, LVa. "De Sun Do Move" is reprinted in several places, including Hatcher, *John Jasper*, 133–49.

32. Hatcher, *John Jasper*, 44–45.

33. Stowell, " 'We Have Sinned.' "

34. Harrison, *Gospel among the Slaves*, 381–82.

35. Randolph, *John Jasper*, 19.

36. "The Colored Shiloh Regular Baptist Association of Virginia," *Richmond Daily Dispatch*, 9 Aug. 1867; Crofts, *Old Southampton*, 243–46; French, *Rebellious Slave*, 140–43.

37. Ryland, *Baptists of Virginia*, 247; Stowell, *Rebuilding Zion*, 46–48, 93–94; *Minutes of the Baptist General Association* (1866), 25–26.

38. See Harvey, *Redeeming the South*, chap. 2, for the growth of the National Baptist Convention, and Stowell, *Rebuilding Zion*, 94, 96, for black Methodist numbers.

39. Exchange recorded in Ryland, *Baptists of Virginia*, 314–16. Jeremiah Bell Jeter, the chair of the committee of the General Association that penned the response, later went on to explain that he feared the "intimate social discourse" that would result from an exchange of messengers.

40. Sweet, *Virginia Methodism*, 289.

41. "Nat Turner's Massacre," *Richmond Daily Dispatch*, 12 Aug. 1867.

42. Dabney, *Against the Ecclesiastical Equality*, 6.

43. Smith, *How Race Is Made*, 49–54.

44. George H. Venable to [?] Venable, 9 Mar. 1868, Venable Papers, VHS.

45. 15 Jan. 1866, Christian Diary, VHS.

46. Wilson, *Baptized in Blood*, remains the classic account, but see also the essays in Blum and Poole, *Vale of Tears*, esp. those in pt. 1, "Sanctifying Southern Violence and Segregation."

47. From the *Richmond Christian Advocate*, 31 Oct. 1867, as quoted in Farish, *Circuit Rider Dismounts*, 221.

48. Jones, *Christ in the Camp*, 20. See also Moore, "John William Jones."

Appendix A

1. This does not mean that it was easy to calculate the total membership, even for 1850, when records abound. For the Baptists, the challenge was deciding how many black and how many white members there were. Statistics that differentiated between white and black were only available for 72,348 of the total 87,209 recorded on rolls for churches in the Baptist General Association. For those individuals, the ratio of black to white was high: 40,983 blacks to 31,365 whites. I did not apply that high ratio to individuals whose race was not known, however, because most of those persons came from the western portion of the state, where there were few African Americans. For Greenbrier, Judson, Lebanon, Parkersburg, Teah's Valley, Union, and Valley associations, therefore, I assumed that 90 percent of the members were white. For Appomattox, Broad Run, and the catchall category of "Other Associations Having Churches in Virginia," I assumed that 50 percent of the members were white. Thus, the 1850 numbers for the Baptists, which show a black majority, are still quite conservative. There may have been an even higher number of black Baptists.

   For the Methodists, I tried to correct the common error of allowing the Virginia Conference to stand in for Methodists in the whole state by tracking Virginians in other conferences. This I did by identifying 1850 circuits on period maps and adding Virginians from other conferences while subtracting non-Virginians from the Virginia Conference. This method produced the following number of members (white/black) from the ME Church, South: Virginia Conference (28,452/4,721), Western Virginia Conference (2,998/54), Holston Conference (9,538/1,037), North Carolina Conference (1,834/316); and from the ME Church: Baltimore Conference (12,048/2,969), Philadelphia Conference (849/442), Western Virginia Conference (11,509/381), Pittsburgh Conference (751/43), and Ohio Conference (96/0).

2. I used the figure of 75 members per congregation. Like Heyrman, I initially thought this number was too high, but the Baptist congregations in Asplund's *Universal Register* for the same period indicate an average congregation size of approximately 100 members.

Appendix B

1. See McKinney, *Keeping the Faith*, 38–41.
2. Perdue, Barden, and Phillips, *Weevils in the Wheat*, 287. Tonsler also remembered the way that black adherents would entertain themselves when the service dragged on.

Appendix C

1. For additional guidance, see Mead and Hill, *Handbook of Denominations*.

BIBLIOGRAPHY

Primary Sources

Manuscripts

Louisiana
Special Collections, Howard-Tilton Memorial Library, Tulane University, New Orleans
  Charles Colcock Jones Papers

North Carolina
Southern Historical Collection, Wilson Library, University of North Carolina, Chapel Hill
  Diaries of Overton and Jesse Bernard
  Edward Dromgoole Papers
  John S. Martin Papers
  Mordecai Family Papers
  Aldert Smedes Papers
  Stephen B. Weeks Papers
Special Collections, Duke University, Durham
  Charles Wesley Andrews Papers

Virginia
Library of Virginia, Richmond
  First African Baptist Church, Minutes
Albert and Shirley Smalls Special Collections Library, University of Virginia, Charlottesville
  Neil A. Benfer, "Unpublished Manuscript of History of First Baptist Church"
  Cabell Family Papers
  Church Register for the Albemarle Circuit of the Virginia Methodist Conference
    [from the Albemarle Co. Historical Society]

Ellen Wayles Coolidge Correspondence
Letter to Col. Baldwin
Membership Statistics and 2 Minute Books of the Ballenger Creek Baptist Church
[from the Albemarle Co. Historical Society]
Papers of the Cocke Family
David Shaver, "Memorial to the Common Council of the City of Lynchburg, Va."
Stuart-Baldwin Family Papers
Union Theological Seminary, Richmond
Hanover Presbytery Minutes, 1755–1823, P 278-A.
Virginia Baptist Historical Society, Richmond
Antioch Baptist Church (Raccoon Swamp), Minute Books, 1772–1837
Isaac Backus Correspondence
Black Creek Baptist Church, Minute Books, 1774–1804, 1804–18, 1818–62
Buck Marsh (now Berryville) Baptist Church, 1786–1803
Minutes of the Broad Run Baptist Church (Fauquier Co.), 1762–1872
Minutes of the Mill Creek Baptist Church (Berkeley Co.), 1757–1928
Minutes of the Mill Swamp Baptist Church, 1774–90
Minutes of the South Quay Baptist Church, 1775–1827
Records of the Antioch Baptist Church (Raccoon Swamp), 1772–1837
Upper King and Queen Baptist Church Minutes, 1774–1815
Virginia Historical Society, Richmond
Benjamin Brand Papers
Carrington Family Papers
Ann Webster Gordon Christian Diary
Frederick Deane Goodwin Papers
William Huntington Papers
Mildred Gibson Lynch Diary
Register of the Baptists from Chappawamsic (Stafford Co.)
Surry County Clerk Records
George Henry Venable Papers

Denominational Sources

BAPTIST

Minutes of the Accomac Baptist Association, 1850.
Minutes of the Albemarle Baptist Association, 1850.
Minutes of the Baptist General Association of Virginia, 1861–66.
Minutes of the Baptist General Committee, 1790–93.
Minutes of the Columbia Baptist Association, 1850, 1853.
Minutes of the Concord Baptist Association, 1850.
Minutes of the Dan River Baptist Association, 1850.
Minutes of the Dover Baptist Association, 1790–1820, 1834, 1844–50, 1855, 1859–
60.

Minutes of the Goshen Baptist Association, 1850, 1853.

Minutes of the James River Baptist Association, 1850.

Minutes of the Middle District Baptist Association, 1850.

Minutes of the Portsmouth Baptist Association, 1832–33, 1850, 1860–61, 1866.

Minutes of the Rappahannock Baptist Association, 1849, 1850.

Minutes of the Roanoke Baptist Association, 1850.

Minutes of the Salem Union Baptist Association, 1850.

Minutes of the Shiloh Baptist Association, 1850.

Minutes of the Strawberry Baptist Association, 1850.

Minutes of the Virginia Baptist Anniversaries, 1849, 1851.

Minutes of the Virginia Baptist General Meeting of Correspondence, 1815.

EPISCOPAL

Dashiell, T. Grayson. *A Digest of the Proceedings of the Conventions and Councils in the Diocese of Virginia*. Richmond: Wm. Ellis Jones, 1883.

Journal of the Proceedings of the Convention of the Protestant Episcopal Church of the Diocese of Virginia, 1833–34, 1845, 1849, 1851, 1860–61.

METHODIST

Annual Register of the Baltimore Conference of the Methodist Episcopal Church, 1861.

Minutes of the Annual Conferences of the Methodist Episcopal Church, for the Years 1773–1828. Vol. 1. New York: T. Mason and G. Lane, 1840.

Minutes of the Annual Conferences of the Methodist Episcopal Church, for the Years 1829–1839. Vol. 2. New York: T. Mason and G. Lane, 1840.

Minutes of the Annual Conferences of the Methodist Episcopal Church, for the Years 1839–1845. Vol. 3. New York: T. Mason and G. Lane, [1846].

Minutes of the Annual Conferences of the Methodist Episcopal Church, for the Years 1846–1851. Vol. 4. New York: T. Mason and G. Lane, [1852].

Minutes of the Annual Conferences of the Methodist Episcopal Church, South, 1845–1866. Nashville: Southern Methodist Publishing House, 1845–66.

Minutes of the Methodist Conferences, Annually Held in America; From 1773 to 1813, Inclusive. Volume the First. New York: Daniel Hitt and Thomas Ware for the Methodist Connexion in the United States, 1813.

PRESBYTERIAN

Minutes of the General Assembly of the Presbyterian Church in the United States of America, From Its Organization A.D. 1789 to A.D. 1820 Inclusive. Philadelphia: Presbyterian Board of Publication, [1835].

Minutes of the Synod of Virginia, 1850, 1861.

State Papers

Cushing, John D., ed. *Colony Laws of Virginia, 1619–1640*. Wilmington, Del.: Michael Glazier, 1978.

Freedman's Bureau. "Reports on Prominent Whites and Freedmen." *Records of the Assistant Commissioner for the State of Virginia, Bureau of Refugees, Freedmen, and Abandoned Lands, 1865–1869.*

Gibson, Campbell, and Kay Jung. *Historical Census Statistics on Population Totals By Race, 1790 to 1990, and By Hispanic Origin, 1970 to 1990, For the United States, Regions, Divisions, and States.* U.S. Census Bureau, 2002.

Hening, William Waller, ed. *Statutes at Large*. 13 vols. Richmond: Samuel Pleasants, 1809–23.

Journal of the House of Delegates of the Commonwealth of Virginia, Begun and Held at the Capitol, in the City of Richmond, on Monday, the Fifth Day of December, One Thousand Eight Hundred and Thirty-One. Richmond: Thomas Ritchie, 1831.

Journals and Papers of the Virginia State Convention of 1861. 3 vols. Richmond: Virginia State Library, 1966.

Reese, George H., ed. *Proceedings of the Virginia State Convention of 1861: February 13–May 1*. 4 vols. Richmond: Virginia State Library, 1965.

Shepherd, Samuel. *The Statutes at Large of Virginia, From October Session 1792, to December Session 1806, Inclusive, In Three Volumes, (New Series,) Being a Continuation of Hening*. 3 vols. Richmond: Samuel Shepherd, 1835.

State of Virginia. *Acts Passed at a General Assembly of the Commonwealth of Virginia, begun and Held at the Capitol . . . on 6 December, 1830*. Richmond: Thomas Ritchie, 1831.

———. *Acts Passed at a General Assembly of the Commonwealth of Virginia, Begun and Held at the Capitol, in the City of Richmond . . . on the 5th of Dec, 1831*. Richmond: Thomas Ritchie, 1832.

U.S. Bureau of the Census. *First Census of the United States, 1790. Return of the Whole Number of Persons within the Several Districts of the United States*. 1791. London: J. Phillips, 1793.

———. *Heads of Families at the First Census of the United States Taken in the Year 1790: Records of the State Enumerations: 1782 to 1785. Virginia*. Washington, D.C.: Government Printing Office, 1908.

———. *Third Census of the United States, 1810*. Vol. 1. Washington, D.C., 1811.

———. *Fourth Census of the United States, 1820*. Washington, D.C.: Gales & Seaton, 1821.

———. *Abstract of the Returns of the Fifth Census, Showing the Number of Free People, the Number of Slaves . . . in the United States of America*. Washington, D.C.: Duff Green, 1832.

———. *Seventh Census of the United States, 1850*. Washington, D.C.: Robert Armstrong, Public Printer, 1853.

——. *Eighth Census of the United States, 1860.* Washington, D.C.: Government Printing Office, 1864.

——. *Statistics of the United States . . . Compiled from the Original Returns and being the Final Exhibit of the Eighth Census.* Washington, D.C.: Government Printing Office, 1866.

——. *Ninth Census of the United States, 1870.* Vol. 1, *Population and Social Statistics.* Washington, D.C.: Government Printing Office, 1872.

——. *Compendium of the Eleventh Census: 1890.* Pt. 2. Washington, D.C.: Government Printing Office, 1897.

Newspapers

African Repository and Colonial Journal (Washington, D.C.)
Arminian Magazine (Methodist) (Philadelphia, Pa.)
Central Presbyterian (Richmond, Va.)
Christian Sentinel (Methodist) (Richmond, Va.)
Christian Spectator (New Haven, Conn.)
Daily Dispatch (Richmond, Va.)
National Era (Washington, D.C.)
North American Review (Boston, Mass.)
Religious Herald (Baptist) (Richmond, Va.)
Richmond Christian Advocate (Methodist)
Richmond Whig and Advertiser
Southern Churchman (Episcopal) (Richmond, Va.)
Southern Religious Telegraph (Presbyterian) (Richmond, Va.)
Virginia Gazette (Williamsburg, Va.)
Watchman of the South (Richmond, Va.)

Books, Broadsides, and Articles

Adair, Douglas, and Devereux Jarratt. "The Autobiography of the Reverend Devereux Jarratt, 1732–1763." *William and Mary Quarterly*, 3rd ser., 9, no. 3 (1952): 346–93.

Albert, Octavia V. Rogers. *The House of Bondage, or, Charlotte Brooks and Other Slaves, Original and Life Like.* [1890]. Electronic ed., 2000. Available at <http://docsouth.unc.edu>.

Allen, Carlos R., Jr. "David Barrow's Circular Letter of 1798." *William and Mary Quarterly*, 3rd ser., 20, no. 3 (1963): 440–51.

Ambler, Charles H. *The Life and Diary of John Floyd: Governor of Virginia, an Apostle of Secession, and the Father of the Oregon Country.* Richmond: Richmond Press, 1918.

Anderson, Thomas. *Interesting Account of Thomas Anderson, a Slave, Taken from His Own Lips.* 1854. Electronic ed., 2000. Available at <http://docsouth.unc .edu>.

Anderson, William J. *Life and Narrative of William J. Anderson, Twenty-four Years a Slave.* [1857]. Electronic ed., 2000. Available at <http://docsouth.unc.edu>.

Asbury, Francis. *The Journal and Letters of Francis Asbury, in Three Volumes.* Edited by Elmer T. Clark, J. Manning Potts, and Jacob S. Payton. London: Epsworth and Abington Presses, 1958.

Asplund, John. *The Universal Register of the Baptist Denomination in North America, for the Years 1790, 1791, 1792, 1793, and part of 1794.* Boston: John W. Folsom, 1794.

Backus, Isaac. "An 18th Century Yankee Baptist Tours Virginia on Horseback." *Virginia Baptist Register* 2 (1963): 64–84.

Barrett, Philip. *Gilbert Hunt, the City Blacksmith.* 1859. Electronic ed., 1999. Available at <http://docsouth.unc.edu>.

Barrow, David. *Circular Letter. Southampton County, Virginia; February 14, 1798.* [Southampton Co.]: Witlet & Conner, Near the Market, 1798.

Bergh, Albert Ellery, ed. *The Writings of Thomas Jefferson.* Vol. 14 of 20. Washington, D.C.: Thomas Jefferson Memorial Association, 1905.

Berlin, Ira, et al. *Free at Last: A Documentary History of Slavery, Freedom, and the Civil War.* New York: New Press, 1991.

Bibb, Henry. *Narrative of the Life and Adventures of Henry Bibb, An American Slave, Written by Himself.* 1849. Electronic ed., 2000. Available at <http://docsouth.unc.edu>.

Birney, James G. *The American Churches the Bulwarks of American Slavery.* 1842. Reprint, New York: Arno Press & the New York Times, 1969.

Blassingame, John. *Slave Testimony.* Baton Rouge: Louisiana State University Press, 1977.

Botts, John Minor. *The Past, The Present, and the Future of Our Country. Interesting and Important Correspondence between Opposition Members of the Legislature of Virginia and Hon. John Minor Botts, January 17, 1860.* Washington, D.C.: Lemuel Towers, 1860.

Bourne, George. *A Condensed Anti-Slavery Bible Argument; By a Citizen of Virginia.* 1845. Electronic ed., 1999. Available at <http://docsouth.unc.edu>.

Boyden, E[benezer]. *The Epidemic of the Nineteenth Century.* Richmond: Chas. H. Wynne, 1860.

Bratton, Mary J., ed. "Fields's Observations: The Slave Narrative of a Nineteenth-Century Virginian." *Virginia Magazine of History and Biography* 88 (1980): 75–93. Electronic ed., 2004. Available at <http://docsouth.unc.edu>.

Brown, William Wells. *Narrative of William W. Brown, A Fugitive Slave. Written by Himself.* 1847. Electronic ed., 2001. Available at <http://docsouth.unc.edu>.

Butt, Israel L. *History of African Methodism in Virginia; or, Four Decades in the Old Dominion.* 1908. Electronic ed., 2000. Available at <http://docsouth.unc.edu>.

Cabell, James L. *The Testimony of Modern Science to the Unity of Mankind . . . .* New York: Robert Carter & Brothers, 1859.

Cary, Lott. "Circular Addressed to the Colored Brethren and Friends in America:

An Unpublished Essay by Lott Cary, Sent from Liberia to Virginia, 1827." Edited by John Saillant. *Virginia Magazine of History and Biography* 104, no. 4 (1996): 481–504.

Crane, William. *Anti-slavery in Virginia: Extracts from Thos. Jefferson, Gen. Washington and Others Relative to the "Blighting Curse of Slavery."* Baltimore: J. F. Weishampel, 1865.

Dabney, Robert L. *Speech of Rev. Robert L. Dabney in the Synod of Virginia, Nov. 9, 1867; Against the Ecclesiastical Equality of Negro Preachers in Our Church, and Their Right to Rule Over White Christians.* Richmond: Printed at the Office of the "Boys and Girls" Monthly, 1868.

——. *True Courage: A Discourage Commemorative of Lieut. General Thomas J. Jackson.* 1863. Electronic ed., 2000. Available at <http://docsouth.unc.edu>.

Davies, Samuel. *The Duty of Masters to Their Servants: in a Sermon, by the late Reverend, Pious, and Learned, Samuel Davies, of Hanover County, Virginia.* Lynchburg, Va.: William W. Gray, 1809.

——. *Letters from the Rev. Samuel Davies & c., Shewing the State of Religion in Virginia, particularly among the Negroes. Likewise An Extract of a Letter from a Gentleman in London to his Friend in the Country, Containing some Observations on the Same.* 2nd ed. London: R. Pardon, 1757.

Davis, Noah. *A Narrative of the Life of Rev. Noah Davis, A Colored Man. Written By Himself, at the Age of Fifty-Four.* [1859]. Electronic ed., 1999. Available at <http://docsouth.unc.edu>.

Douglass, Frederick. *Narrative of the Life of Frederick Douglass, an American Slave. Written by Himself.* 1845. Electronic ed., 1999. Available at <http://docsouth.unc.edu>.

Drew, Benjamin. *A North-Side View of Slavery. The Refugee: or the Narratives of Fugitive Slaves in Canada . . . .* 1856. Electronic ed., 2000. Available at <http://docsouth.unc.edu>.

Dumond, Dwight Lowell, ed. *Southern Editorials on Secession.* 1931. Reprint, Gloucester, Mass.: Peter Smith, 1964.

Dunaway, Thomas S. *Life and Writings of Rev. Addison Hall.* Introduction by Jeremiah B. Jeter. Philadelphia: Bible and Publication Society, 1872.

Elliott, William G. *The Story of Archer Alexander: From Slavery to Freedom.* 1885. Electronic ed., 1999. Available at <http://docsouth.unc.edu>.

Fedric, Francis. *Slave Life in Virginia and Kentucky; or, Fifty Years of Slavery in the Southern States of America.* 1863. Electronic ed., 1999. Available at <http://docsouth.unc.edu>.

Ferrill, London. *Biography of London Ferrill, Pastor of the First Baptist Church of Colored Persons, Lexington, KY.* 1854. Electronic ed., 2001. Available at <http://docsouth.unc.edu>.

Foote, William Henry. *Sketches of Virginia: Historical and Biographical.* 1850. Reprint, Richmond: John Knox Press, 1966.

——. *Sketches of Virginia.* 2nd series. Philadelphia: Lippincott, 1856.

Fristoe, William. *A Concise History of the Ketocton Baptist Association*. Staunton, Va.: William Gilman Lyford, 1808.

Garrison, William Lloyd. *Thoughts on African Colonization*. 1832. Reprint. New York: Arno Press and the New York Times, 1968.

Godwyn, Morgan. *The Negro's & Indians Advocate, Suing for their Admission into the Church: or a Persuasive to the Instructing and Baptizing of the Negro's and Indians in our Plantations*. London: J. D. and [Co.], 1680.

Goss, C. C. *Statistical History of the First Century of American Methodism: with a Summary of the Origin and Present Operations of Other Denominations*. New York: Carlton & Porter, 1866.

Greenberg, Kenneth S., ed. *The Confessions of Nat Turner and Related Documents*. Boston: Bedford Books, 1996.

Gurley, Ralph R. *Life of Jehudi Ashmun: Late Colonial Agent in Liberia. With an Appendix, Containing Extracts from His Journal and Other Writings, with a Brief Sketch of the Life of the Rev. Lott Cary*. Washington, D.C.: James C. Dunn, 1835.

Harrison, William P. *The Gospel among the Slaves: A Short Account of Missionary Operations among the African Slaves of the Southern States*. Nashville: M. E. Church, South, 1893.

Henry, Patrick, Sr., Samuel Davies, James Maury, Edwin Conway, and George Trask. "Letters of Patrick Henry, Sr., Samuel Davies, James Maury, Edwin Conway, and George Trask." *William and Mary College Quarterly Historical Magazine*, 2nd ser., 1, no. 4 (1921): 261–81.

Hinks, Peter, ed. *David Walker's Appeal to the Colored Citizens of the World*. University Park: Pennsylvania State University Press, 2000.

Hollinger, David A., and Charles Capper, eds. *The American Intellectual Tradition: A Sourcebook*. Vol. 1, *1630–1865*. New York: Oxford University Press, 1993.

Jacobs, Harriet. *Incidents in the Life of a Slave Girl: Written by Herself*. 1861. Edited with an introduction by Jean Fagan Yellin. Cambridge: Harvard University Press, 1987.

Jarratt, Devereux. *The Life of the Reverend Devereux Jarratt*. 1806. Reprint, New York: Arno Press, 1969.

Jefferson, Thomas. *Notes on the State of Virginia*. Edited by William Peden. 1785. Reprint, New York: Norton, 1982.

Jeter, Jeremiah Bell. *Recollections of a Long Life*. Edited with an introduction by J. L. M. Curry. Richmond: Religious Herald Co., 1891.

Johnson, Thomas Cary. *The Life and Letters of Robert Lewis Dabney*. Richmond: Presbyterian Committee of Publication, 1903.

Johnson, Thomas Lewis. *Africa for Christ: Twenty-Eight Years a Slave*. [1892]. Electronic ed., 2001. Available at <http://docsouth.unc.edu>.

Jones, Charles C. *Catechism of Scripture Doctrine and Practice for Families and Sabbath-Schools Designed Also, for the Oral Instruction of Colored Persons*. 2nd ed. Savannah: T. Purse Co., 1837.

——. *The Religious Instruction of the Negroes in the United States.* 1842. Reprint, New York: Negro Universities Press, 1969.

Jones, J. William. *Christ in the Camp: Or Religion in Lee's Army.* Richmond: B. F. Johnson & Co., 1887.

Juvenis. *Observations on the Slavery of the Negroes, in the Southern States, Particularly Intended for the Citizens of Virginia.* New York: W. Ross, 1785.

Lee, Jesse. *A Short History of the Methodists, in the United States of America; Beginning in 1766, and Continued till 1809. To which is Prefixed a Brief Account of their Rise in England, in the Year 1729, & c.* Baltimore: Magill and Clime, 1810.

Leland, John. *The Virginia Chronicle.* [Fredericksburg: T. Green, 1789].

——. "The Virginia Chronicle." In *The Writings of the Late Elder John Leland, Including Some Events in His Life, Written by Himself, with Additional Sketches, & c. by Miss L. F. Greene.* New York: G. W. Wood, 1845.

Liele, George, Stephen Cooke, Abraham Marshall, Jonathan Clarke, and Thomas Nichols Swigle. "Letters Showing the Rise and Progress of the Early Negro Churches of Georgia and the West Indies." *Journal of Negro History* 1, no. 1 (1916): 69–92.

Long, John Dixon. *Pictures of Slavery in Church and State; Including Personal Reminiscences, Biographical Sketches, Anecdotes, etc.* 1857. Electronic ed., 2000. Available at <http://docsouth.unc.edu>.

[Lyons, James.] *Four Essays on the Right and Propriety of Secession by Southern States by a Member of the Bar of Richmond.* Richmond: Ritchie & Dunnavant, 1861.

Maxwell, William. *A Memoir of the Rev. John H. Rice, D.D.* Philadelphia: J. Whetham and R. I. Smith, 1835.

McGill, J. D. *Sketches of History of the Baptist Churches within the Limits of the Rappahannock Association in Virginia.* Richmond: Harrold & Murray, 1850.

McGuire, Judith W. *Diary of a Southern Refugee During the War, by a Lady of Virginia.* 1867. Reprint, Lincoln: University of Nebraska Press, 1995.

McIlwaine, Richard. *Memories of Three Score Years and Ten.* New York: Neale Publishing Co., 1908.

Meade, William. *Old Churches, Ministers, and Families of Virginia.* 2 vols. 1857. Reprint, Baltimore: Genealogical Publishing Co., 1966.

——. *Pastoral Letter of the Right Rev. William Meade, Assistant Bishop of Virginia, to the Ministers, Members, and Friends, of the Protestant Episcopal Church in the Diocese of Virginia, on the Duty of Affording Religious Instruction to Those in Bondage.* Alexandria: Printed at the Gazette Office, 1834.

——. *Sermons Addressed to Masters and Servants, and Published in the Year 1743 by the Rev. Thomas Bacon. Now Republished with Other Tracts and Dialogues on the Same Subject, and Recommended to All Masters and Mistresses to be Used in their Families.* Winchester, Va.: John Heiskell, 1813.

——. *Sketches of Old Virginia Family Servants.* Philadelphia: Isaac Ashmead, 1847.

"Methodist Petition, Oct. 28, 1776." *Virginia Magazine of History and Biography* 18 (1910): 143–44.

Miller, Randall M., ed. *"Dear Master": Letters of a Slave Family*. Ithaca: Cornell University Press, 1978.

Minnigerode, Charles. *"He that believeth shall not make haste": A Sermon Preached on the First of January, 1865, in St. Paul's Church, Richmond*. Richmond: Charles H. Wynne, 1865.

Moulton, Philips P., ed. *The Journal and Major Essays of John Woolman*. New York: Oxford University Press, 1971.

M'Tyeire, Holland N. *Duties of Christian Masters*. Nashville: Southern Methodist Publishing House, 1859.

———. *A History of Methodism* . . . . Nashville: Southern Methodist Publishing House, 1884.

Nott, J. C., and George R. Gliddon. *Types of Mankind, or Ethnological Researches*. Philadelphia: Lippincott, Grambo, & Co., 1854.

O'Kelly, James. *Essay on Negro-Slavery*. Philadelphia: Prichard & Hall, 1789.

———. *A Vindication of the Author's Apology, with Reflections on the Reply, and a Few Remarks on Bishop Asbury's Annotations on His Book of Discipline*. Raleigh: Joseph Gale, 1801.

Palmer, Benjamin M. *The South; Her Peril and Her Duty. A Discourse, Delivered in the First Presbyterian Church, New Orleans, On Thursday, November 29, 1860*. New Orleans: Office of True Witness & Sentinel, 1860.

Pattillo, Henry. *The Plain Planter's Assistant; Containing an Address to Husbands and Wives, Children and Servants; With some Helps for Instruction by Catechisms; and Examples of Devotion for Families: With a brief Paraphrase on the Lord's Prayer*. Wilmington, N.C.: James Adams, 1787.

Perdue, Charles L., Jr., Thomas E. Barden, and Robert K. Phillips, eds. *Weevils in the Wheat: Interviews with Virginia Ex-Slaves*. Charlottesville: University Press of Virginia, 1976.

Plumer, William S. *Thoughts on the Religious Instruction of the Negroes of This Country*. Princeton: John T. Robinson, 1848.

Proceedings of the Meeting in Charleston, S.C., May 13–15, 1845, on the Religious Instruction of the Negroes, Together with the Report of the Committee, and the Address to the Public. Charleston: B. Jenkins, 1845.

Randolph, E. A. *The Life of Rev. John Jasper, Pastor of Sixth Mt. Zion Baptist Church, Richmond, VA. From his Birth to the Present Time, with His Theory on the Rotation of the Sun*. Richmond: R. T. Hill & Co., 1884.

Randolph, Peter. *Sketches of Slave Life: Or, Illustrations of the "Peculiar Institution."* 1855. Electronic ed., 2000. Available at <http://docsouth.unc.edu>.

Reed, Andrew, and James Matheson. *A Narrative of the Visit to the American Churches by the Deputation from the Congregational Union of England and Wales*. 2 vols. New York: Harper and Brothers, 1835.

"Religion in America." *Methodist Quarterly Review*, 3rd ser., 27, no. 5 (1845): 485–503.

Rice, John H. *An Illustration of the Character & Conduct of the Presbyterian Church in Virginia*. Richmond: Duval & Burke, 1816.

Rives, William C. *Discourse before the Young Men's Christian Association of Richmond, on the Ethics of Christianity*. Richmond: John Nowlan, 1855.

Robertson, Archibald Thomas. *Life and Letters of John Albert Broadus*. Philadelphia: American Baptist Publication Society, 1901.

[Rush, Benjamin.] *An Address to the Inhabitants of the British Settlements in America upon Slave-Keeping*. New York: Hodge and Shober, 1773.

Ryland, Robert. *The Scriptural Catechism, for Coloured People*. Richmond: Harrold & Murray, 1848.

Sargent, Gov. Winthrop. *The Grove Plantation, M[ississipi]. T[erritory]. November 16, 1800*. Early American Imprints, 1st series, n. 37974. [Natchez, Miss.?: n.p., 1800].

Semple, Robert B. *A History of the Rise and Progress of the Baptists in Virginia*. Revised and extended by Rev. George William Beale. 1810. Richmond: Witt & Dickinson, 1894.

Shepard, E. Lee. "Records of Upper Goose Creek Baptist Church, 1801–1859." *Virginia Baptist Register* 40 (2001): 1988–2018.

Simpson, William S., ed. "Henry Toler's Journal." *Virginia Baptist Register*, 31 and 32 (1992 and 1993): 1566–95, 1628–58.

Slaughter, Philip. *The Virginian History of African Colonization*. Richmond: Mac-Farlane & Ferguson, 1855.

Smallwood, Thomas. *A Narrative of Thomas Smallwood, (Coloured Man:) Giving an Account of His Birth—The Period He Was Held in Slavery—His Release—and Removal to Canada, etc. Together With an Account of the Underground Railroad. Written by Himself*. 1851. Electronic ed., 2001. Available at <http://docsouth.unc.edu>.

Smith, James L. *Autobiography of James L. Smith, Including, Also, Reminiscences of Slave Life, Recollections of the War, Education of Freedmen, Causes of the Exodus, etc*. 1881. Electronic ed., 2000. Available at <http://docsouth.unc.edu>.

Smith, William A. *Lectures on the Philosophy and Practice of Slavery . . . .* 1856. Electronic ed., 2000. Available at <http://docsouth.unc.edu>.

Stearns, Charles. *Narrative of Henry Box Brown, Who Escaped from Slavery Enclosed in a Box 3 Feet Long and 2 Wide*. 1849. Electronic ed., 2001. Available at <http://docsouth.unc.edu>.

Stevens, Charles Emery. *Anthony Burns: A History*. 1856. Electronic ed., 1999. Available at <http://docsouth.unc.edu>.

Stringfellow, Thornton. *A Brief Examination of Scripture Testimony on the Institution of Slavery . . . .* 1850. Electronic ed., 2000. Available at <http://docsouth.unc.edu>.

———. *Scriptural and Statistical Views in Favor of Slavery*. Richmond: J. W. Randolph, 1856.

Swint, Henry L., ed. *Dear Ones at Home: Letters from Contraband Camps*. Nashville: Vanderbilt University Press, 1966.

Taylor, James B. *Biography of Elder Lott Cary, Late Missionary to Africa, with an Appendix on the Subject of Colonization, by J. H. B. Latrobe*. 1837. Electronic ed., 2001. Available at <http://docsouth.unc.edu>.

Thomas, David. *The Virginian Baptist: or A View and Defence of the Christian Religion, as It is Professed by the Baptists of Virginia . . . .* Baltimore: Enoch Story, [1774].

Todd, John. *An Humble Attempt towards the Improvement of Psalmody: The Propriety, Necessity and Use of Evangelical Psalms, in Christian Worship*. Philadelphia: Andrew Steuart, 1763.

Toler, Henry. *The Faithful Minister's Work and Course Pursued and Finished: Being the Substance of Two Sermons, Occasioned by the Death of Elder Lewis Lunsford . . . .* Philadelphia: Omrod & Conrad, 1795.

Tragle, Henry Irving, ed. *The Southampton Slave Revolt of 1831: A Compilation of Source Material*. Amherst: University of Massachusetts Press, 1971.

Tucker, John Randolph. *The Southern Church Justified in its Support of the South in the Present War: A Lecture, Delivered before the Young Men's Christian Association, of Richmond, on the 21st May, 1863*. Richmond: William H. Clemmitt, 1863.

Tucker, St. George. *A Dissertation on Slavery, with a Proposal for the Gradual Abolition of it, in the State of Virginia*. Philadelphia: Mathew Carey, 1796.

Veney, Bethany. *The Narrative of Bethany Veney, A Slave Woman*. 1889. Electronic ed., 1997. Available at <http://docsouth.unc.edu>.

Wakelyn, Jon L., ed. *Southern Pamphlets on Secession, November 1860–April 1861*. Chapel Hill: University of North Carolina Press, 1996.

Walmsley, James E., ed. "The Change of Secessionist Sentiment in Virginia in 1861." *American Historical Review* 31, no. 1 (1925): 82–101.

Warner, Samuel. *Authentic and Impartial Narrative of the Tragical Scene Which Was Witnessed in Southampton County (Virginia) on Monday the 22d of August Last . . . .* [New York]: Warner & West, 1831.

Wayman, Alexander W. *My Recollections of African Methodist Episcopal Ministers, or Forty Years' Experience in the African Methodist Episcopal Church*. 1881. Electronic ed., 2000. Available at <http://docsouth.unc.edu>.

White, William S. *The African Preacher: An Authentic Narrative*. 1849. Reprint, Freeport, N.Y.: Books for Libraries Press, 1972.

Whitefield, George. *Three Letters from the Reverend Mr. G. Whitefield*. Philadelphia: B. Franklin, 1740.

Wickham, Elizabeth Merwin. *A Lost Family Found: An Authentic Narrative of Cyrus Branch and His Family, Alias John White*. [1869]. Electronic ed., 2000. Available at <http://docsouth.unc.edu>.

Wiley, Bell I., ed. *Slaves No More: Letters from Liberia, 1833–1869.* Lexington: University Press of Kentucky, 1980.

Willey, W. T., Chester D. Hubbard, Wa Wheeling, and Richard O. Curry. "A Note on the Motives of Three Radical Republicans." *Journal of Negro History* 47, no. 4 (1962): 273–77.

Williams, Isaac D., and William Ferguson Goldie. *Sunshine and Shadow of Slave Life. Reminiscences As Told by Isaac D. Williams to "Tege."* 1885. Electronic ed., 2003. Available at <http://docsouth.unc.edu>.

Wood, James. *Old and New Theology: Or, the Doctrinal Differences which have Agitated and Divided the Presbyterian Church.* 1838. Reprint, Philadelphia: Presbyterian Board of Publication, 1853.

Wright, F. Edward, ed. *Early Church Records of Rockingham County, Virginia.* Westminster, Md.: Willow Bend Books, 2000.

Secondary Sources

Books and Pamphlets

Alley, Reuben E. *A History of Baptists in Virginia.* Richmond: Virginia Baptist General Board, [1973].

Aptheker, Herbert. *Nat Turner's Slave Rebellion.* New York: Humanities Press, 1966.

Armstrong, James E. *History of the Old Baltimore Conference from the Planting of Methodism in 1773 to the Division of the Conference in 1857.* Baltimore: by the author, 1907.

Ashworth, John. *Slavery, Capitalism, and Politics in the American Republic.* Vol. 1, *Commerce and Compromise, 1820–1850.* Cambridge: Cambridge University Press, 1995.

Baker, Robert Andrew. *Relations between Northern and Southern Baptists.* 1954. Reprint, New York: Arno Press, 1980.

Baptist, Edward E. *Creating an Old South: Middle Florida's Plantation Frontier before the Civil War.* Chapel Hill: University of North Carolina Press, 2002.

Bennett, William W. *Memorials of Methodism in Virginia, From Its Introduction into the State, in the Year 1772, to the Year 1829.* Richmond: by the Author, 1871.

Beringer, Richard, Herman Hattaway, Archer Jones, and William N. Still Jr. *Why the South Lost the Civil War.* Athens: University of Georgia Press, 1986.

Berlin, Ira. *Generations of Captivity: A History of African-American Slaves.* Cambridge: Belknap Press of Harvard University Press, 2003.

———. *Many Thousands Gone: The First Two Centuries of Slavery in North America.* Cambridge: Belknap Press of Harvard University Press, 1998.

———. *Slaves without Masters: The Free Negro in the Antebellum South.* New York: Pantheon Books, 1974.

Blackburn, Robin. *The Making of New World Slavery: From the Baroque to the Modern, 1492–1800.* London: Verso, 1997.

Blackford, L. Minor. *Mine Eyes Have Seen the Glory: The Story of a Virginia Lady Mary Berkeley Minor Blackford (1802–1896) Who taught her sons to hate Slavery and to love the Union.* Cambridge: Harvard University Press, 1954.

Blassingame, John. *The Slave Community: Plantation Life in the Antebellum South.* New York: Oxford University Press, 1972.

Blum, Edward J. *Reforging the White Republic: Race, Religion, and American Nationalism.* Baton Rouge: Louisiana State University Press, 2005.

Blum, Edward J., and W. Scott Poole, eds. *Vale of Tears: New Essays on Religion and Reconstruction.* Macon, Ga.: Mercer University Press, 2005.

Boles, John B., ed. *Masters and Slaves in the House of the Lord: Race and Religion in the American South, 1740–1870.* Lexington: University Press of Kentucky, 1988.

Bolster, W. Jeffrey. *Black Jacks: African-American Seamen in the Age of Sail.* Cambridge: Harvard University Press, 1997.

Bolton, S. Charles. *Southern Anglicanism: The Church of England in Colonial South Carolina.* Westport, Conn.: Greenwood Press, 1982.

Bond, Edward L. *Damned Souls in a Tobacco Colony: Religion in Seventeenth-Century Virginia.* Macon, Ga.: Mercer University Press, 2000.

Bonomi, Patricia U. *Under the Cope of Heaven: Religion, Society, and Politics in Colonial America.* New York: Oxford University Press, 1986.

Breen, T. H., and Stephen Innes. *"Myne Owne Ground": Race & Freedom on Virginia's Eastern Shore, 1640–1676.* New York: Oxford University Press, 1980.

Brekus, Catherine A. *Strangers and Pilgrims: Female Preaching in America, 1740–1845.* Chapel Hill: University of North Carolina Press, 1998.

Brimm, Henry M., and William M. E. Rachal, eds. *Yesterday and Tomorrow in the Synod of Virginia.* Richmond: Synod of Virginia, 1962.

Brooks, Walter H. "The Evolution of the Negro Baptist Church." *Journal of Negro History* 7, no. 1 (1922): 11–22.

Brown, Kathleen M. *Good Wives, Nasty Wenches, and Anxious Patriarchs: Gender, Race, and Power in Colonial Virginia.* Chapel Hill: University of North Carolina Press, 1996.

Brydon, George MacLaren. *Virginia's Mother Church and the Political Conditions under Which It Grew.* 2 vols. Richmond: Virginia Historical Society and Church Historical Society, 1947–52.

Buckley, Thomas E. *Church and State in Revolutionary Virginia, 1776–1787.* Charlottesville: University Press of Virginia, 1977.

Burin, Eric. *Slavery and the Peculiar Solution: A History of the African Colonization Society.* Gainesville: University Press of Florida, 2005.

Burton, Orville Vernon. *In My Father's House Are Many Mansions: Family and Community in Edgefield, South Carolina.* Chapel Hill: University of North Carolina Press, 1985.

Butchart, Ronald E. *Northern Schools, Southern Blacks, and Reconstruction: Freedmen's Education, 1862–1875*. Westport, Conn.: Greenwood Press, 1980.

Butler, Jon. *Awash in a Sea of Faith: Christianizing the American People*. Cambridge: Harvard University Press, 1990.

Campbell, James T. *Songs of Zion: The African Methodist Episcopal Church in the United States and South Africa*. Chapel Hill: University of North Carolina Press, 1998.

Carmichael, Peter S. *The Last Generation: Young Virginians in Peace, War, and Reunion*. Chapel Hill: University of North Carolina Press, 2005.

Carroll, Henry K. *The Religious Forces of the United States: Enumerated, Classified, and Described on the Basis of the Government Census of 1890, With an Introduction on the Condition and Character of American Christianity*. New York: Christian Literature Co., 1893.

Clarke, Erskine. *Dwelling Place: A Plantation Epic*. New Haven: Yale University Press, 2006.

Cleaveland, George J., et al., eds. *Up from Independence: The Episcopal Church in Virginia*. Orange, Va.: Interdiocesan Bicentennial Committee of the Virginias, 1976.

Cornelius, Janet Duitsman. *Slave Missions and the Black Church in the Antebellum South*. Columbia: University of South Carolina Press, 1999.

———. *When I Can Read My Title Clear: Literacy, Slavery, and Religion in the Antebellum South*. Columbia: University of South Carolina Press, 1991.

Costen, Melva Wilson. *African American Christian Worship*. Nashville: Abingdon Press, 1993.

Crofts, Daniel W. *Old Southampton: Politics and Society in a Virginia County, 1834–1869*. Charlottesville: University Press of Virginia, 1992.

———. *Reluctant Confederates: Upper South Unionists in the Secession Crisis*. Chapel Hill: University of North Carolina Press, 1988.

Daly, John Patrick. *When Slavery Was Called Freedom: Evangelicalism, Proslavery, and the Causes of the Civil War*. Lexington: University Press of Kentucky, 2002.

Davis, David Brion. *Inhuman Bondage: The Rise and Fall of Slavery in the New World*. New York: Oxford University Press, 2006.

———. *The Problem of Slavery in the Age of Revolution, 1770–1823*. Ithaca: Cornell University Press, 1975.

Dew, Charles B. *Apostles of Disunion: Southern Secession Commissioners and the Causes of the Civil War*. Charlottesville: University Press of Virginia, 2001.

Deyle, Steven. *Carry Me Back: The Domestic Slave Trade in American Life*. New York: Oxford University Press, 2005.

Drewry, William S. *The Southampton Insurrection*. Washington, D.C.: Neale Company, 1900.

Dillon, Merton. *Slavery Attacked: Southern Slaves and their Allies, 1619–1865*. Baton Rouge: Louisiana State University Press, 1990.

Du Bois, W. E. B. *The Negro Church. Report of a Social Study Made under the Direction of Atlanta University; Together with the Proceedings of the Eighth Conference for the Study of the Negro Problems, held at Atlanta University, May 26th, 1903.* 1903. Electronic ed., 2001. Available at <http://docsouth.unc.edu>.

———. *The Souls of Black Folk.* 1903. New York: Penguin, 1996.

Dvorak, Katharine. *An African-American Exodus: The Segregation of Southern Churches.* Brooklyn, N.Y.: Carlson Publishing, 1991.

Earnest, Joseph B., Jr. *The Religious Development of the Negro in Virginia.* Charlottesville: Michie Co., 1914.

Egerton, Douglas R. *Gabriel's Rebellion: The Virginia Slave Conspiracies of 1800 and 1802.* Chapel Hill: University of North Carolina Press, 1993.

———. *He Shall Go Out Free: The Lives of Denmark Vesey.* Madison, Wisc.: Madison House, 1999.

———. *Rebels, Reformers, & Revolutionaries: Collected Essays and Second Thoughts.* New York, Routledge, 2002.

Eighmy, John Lee. *Churches in Cultural Captivity: A History of the Social Attitudes of Southern Baptists.* Knoxville: University of Tennessee Press, 1972.

Ely, Melvin Patrick. *Israel on the Appomattox: A Southern Experiment in Black Freedom from the 1790s through the Civil War.* New York: Knopf, 2004.

Essig, James David. *The Bonds of Wickedness: American Evangelicals against Slavery, 1770–1808.* Philadelphia: Temple University Press, 1982.

Farish, Hunter Dickinson. *The Circuit Rider Dismounts: A Social History of Southern Methodism, 1865–1900.* Richmond: Dietz Press, 1938.

Farmer, James Oscar. *The Metaphysical Confederacy: James Henry Thornwell and the Synthesis of Southern Values.* Macon, Ga.: Mercer University Press, 1986.

Faust, Drew Gilpin. *The Creation of Confederate Nationalism: Ideology and Identity in the Civil War South.* Baton Rouge: Louisiana State University Press, 1988.

Finke, Roger, and Rodney Stark. *The Churching of America, 1776–1990: Winners and Losers in Our Religious Economy.* New Brunswick, N.J.: Rutgers University Press, 1992.

First Baptist Church [Charlottesville, Va.]. *135th Anniversary Pamphlet.* Charlottesville: First Baptist Church, 1998.

Fischer, David Hackett, and James C. Kelly. *Bound Away: Virginia and the Westward Movement.* Charlottesville: University Press of Virginia, 2000.

Foner, Eric, ed. *Great Lives Observed: Nat Turner.* Englewood Cliffs, N.J.: Prentice Hall, 1971.

Foster, Charles I. *An Errand of Mercy: The Evangelical United Front, 1790–1837.* Chapel Hill: University of North Carolina Press, 1960.

Fox-Genovese, Elizabeth. *Within the Plantation Household: Black and White Women of the Old South.* Chapel Hill: University of North Carolina Press, 1988.

Frazier, E. Franklin. *The Negro Church in America.* New York: Schocken Books, 1963.

Freehling, Alison Goodyear. *Drift Toward Dissolution: The Virginia Slavery Debate of 1831–1832*. Baton Rouge: Louisiana State University Press, 1982.

Freehling, William W. *The South vs. the South: How Anti-Confederate Southerners Shaped the Course of the Civil War*. Oxford: Oxford University Press, 2001.

French, Scot. *The Rebellious Slave: Nat Turner in American Memory*. Boston: Houghton Mifflin, 2004.

Frey, Sylvia R. *Water from the Rock: Black Resistance in a Revolutionary Age*. Princeton: Princeton University Press, 1991.

Frey, Sylvia R., and Betty Wood. *Come Shouting to Zion: African American Protestantism in the American South and British Caribbean to 1830*. Chapel Hill: University of North Carolina Press, 1998.

Gallagher, Gary. *The Confederate War: How Popular Will, Nationalism, and Military Strategy Could Not Stave Off Defeat*. Cambridge: Harvard University Press, 1997.

Gaustad, Edwin Scott, and Philip L. Barlow. *New Historical Atlas of Religion in America*. Oxford: Oxford University Press, 2001.

Genovese, Eugene D. *A Consuming Fire: The Fall of the Confederacy in the Mind of the White Christian South*. Athens: University of Georgia Press, 1998.

——. *Roll, Jordan, Roll: The World the Slaves Made*. 1972. Reprint, New York: Vintage Books, 1976.

——. *"Slavery Ordained of God": The Southern Slaveholders' View of Biblical History and Modern Politics*. 24th Annual Fortenbaugh Memorial Lecture. Gettysburg: Gettysburg College, 1985.

Genovese, Eugene D., and Elizabeth Fox-Genovese. *The Mind of the Master Class: History and Faith in the Southern Slaveholders' Worldview*. New York: Cambridge University Press, 2005.

Gewehr, Wesley M. *The Great Awakening in Virginia, 1740–1790*. Durham: Duke University Press, 1930.

Goen, C. C. *Broken Churches, Broken Nation: Denominational Schisms and the Coming of the American Civil War*. Macon, Ga.: Mercer University Press, 1985.

Gomez, Michael A. *Exchanging Our Country Marks: The Transformation of African Identities in the Colonial and Antebellum South*. Chapel Hill: University of North Carolina Press, 1998.

Goodman, Paul. *Of One Blood: Abolitionism and the Origins of Racial Equality*. Berkeley: University of California Press, 1998.

Greenberg, Kenneth S. *Nat Turner: A Slave Rebellion in History and Memory*. Oxford: Oxford University Press, 2003.

Greene, Jack P. *Pursuits of Happiness: The Social Development of Early Modern British Colonies and the Formation of American Culture*. Chapel Hill: University of North Carolina Press, 1988.

Gross, Alexander. *A History of the Methodist Episcopal Church, South*. American Church History Series, vol. 11. New York: Charles Scribner's Sons, 1904.

Gunderson, Robert Gray. *Old Gentlemen's Convention: The Washington Peace Conference of 1861*. Madison: University of Wisconsin Press, 1961.

Hahn, Steven. *A Nation under Our Feet: Black Political Struggles in the Rural South from Slavery to the Great Migration*. Cambridge: Belknap Press of Harvard University Press, 2003.

Harding, Vincent. *There Is a River: The Black Struggle for Freedom in America*. New York: Harcourt Brace, 1981.

Hatch, Nathan O. *The Democratization of American Christianity*. New Haven: Yale University Press, 1989.

Hatcher, William E. *John Jasper: The Unmatched Negro Philosopher and Preacher*. New York: Fleming H. Revel Co., [1908].

Harvey, Paul. *Freedom's Coming: Religious Culture and the Shaping of the South from the Civil War through the Civil Rights Era*. Chapel Hill: University of North Carolina Press, 2005.

———. *Redeeming the South: Religious Culture and Racial Identities among Southern Baptists, 1865–1925*. Chapel Hill: University of North Carolina Press, 1997.

Haynes, Stephen R. *Noah's Curse: The Biblical Justification of American Slavery*. Oxford: Oxford University Press, 2002.

Herskovits, Melville J. *The Myth of the Negro Past*. Boston: Beacon Presbyterian, 1958.

Heyrman, Christine Leigh. *Southern Cross: The Beginnings of the Bible Belt*. New York: Knopf, 1997.

Hinks, Peter. *To Awaken My Afflicted Brethren: David Walker and the Problem of Antebellum Slave Resistance*. University Park: Pennsylvania State University Press, 1997.

Holifield, E. Brooks. *The Gentlemen Theologians: American Theology in Southern Culture, 1795–1860*. Durham: Duke University Press, 1978.

Holton, Woody. *Forced Founders: Indians, Debtors, Slaves, and the Making of the American Revolution in Virginia*. Chapel Hill: University of North Carolina Press, 1999.

Isaac, Rhys. *The Transformation of Virginia, 1740–1790*. Chapel Hill: University of North Carolina Press, 1982.

Jenkins, William Sumner. *Pro-Slavery Thought in the Old South*. 1935. Reprint, Gloucester, Mass.: Peter Smith, 1960.

Johnson, Curtis D. *Redeeming America: Evangelicals and the Road to Civil War*. Chicago: Ivan R. Dee, 1993.

Johnson, Frank Roy. *The Nat Turner Slave Insurrection*. Murfreesboro, N.C.: Johnson Publishing Co., 1966.

Johnson, Walter. *Soul by Soul: Life inside the Antebellum Slave Market*. Cambridge: Harvard University Press, 1999.

Jordan, Winthrop D. *White over Black: American Attitudes Toward the Negro, 1550–1812*. Chapel Hill: University of North Carolina Press, 1968.

Kimball, Gregg D. *American City, Southern Place: A Cultural History of Antebellum Richmond*. Athens: University of Georgia Press, 2000.

Kupperman, Karen Ordhal. *Indians & English: Facing Off in Early America*. Ithaca: Cornell University Press, 2000.

Kuykendall, John W. *Southern Enterprize: The Work of National Evangelical Societies in the Antebellum South*. Westport, Conn.: Greenwood Press, 1982.

Lambert, Frank. *Inventing the Great Awakening*. Princeton: Princeton University Press, 1999.

Levine, Lawrence W. *Black Culture and Black Consciousness: Afro-American Folk Thought from Slavery to Freedom*. New York: Oxford University Press, 1977.

Levy, Andrew. *The First Emancipator: The Forgotten Story of Robert Carter, the Founding Father Who Freed His Slaves*. New York: Random House, 2005.

Lincoln, C. Eric, and Lawrence H. Mamiya. *The Black Church in the African American Experience*. Durham: Duke University Press, 1990.

Linderman, Gerald P. *Embattled Courage: The Experience of Combat in the American Civil War*. New York: Free Press, 1987.

Link, William A. *Roots of Secession: Slavery and Politics in Antebellum Virginia*. Chapel Hill: University of North Carolina Press, 2003.

Little, Lewis Peyton. *Imprisoned Preachers and Religious Liberty in Virginia . . . .* Lynchburg, Va.: J. P. Bell Co., 1938.

Loveland, Anne C. *Southern Evangelicals and the Social Order, 1800–1860*. Baton Rouge: Louisiana State University Press, 1980.

Lumpkin, Katharine Du Pre. *The Making of a Southerner*. 1946. Reprint, Athens: University of Georgia Press, 1991.

Lyerly, Cynthia Lynn. *Methodism and the Southern Mind, 1770–1810*. New York: Oxford University Press, 1998.

MacClenny, William E. *The Life of Rev. James O'Kelly and the Early History of the Christian Church in the South*. Raleigh: Edwards & Broughton Printing Co., 1910.

Mason, Matthew. *Slavery and Politics in the Early American Republic*. Chapel Hill: University of North Carolina Press, 2006.

Mathews, Donald G. *Religion in the Old South*. Chicago: University of Chicago Press, 1977.

——. *Slavery and Methodism: A Chapter in American Morality, 1780–1845*. Princeton: Princeton University Press, 1965.

Mayer, Henry. *All On Fire: William Lloyd Garrison and the Abolition of Slavery*. New York: St. Martin's Press, 1998.

McCoy, Drew R. *The Last of the Fathers: James Madison & the Republican Legacy*. Cambridge: Cambridge University Press, 1989.

McCurry, Stephanie. *Masters of Small Worlds: Yeoman Households, Gender Relations, & the Political Culture of the Antebellum South Carolina Low Country*. New York: Oxford University Press, 1995.

McGranahan, Ralph W. *Historical Sketch of the Freedmen's Missions of the United Presbyterian Church, 1862–1904*. Knoxville: Printing Dept., Knoxville College, 1904.

McKinney, Richard I. *Keeping the Faith: A History of the First [African] Baptist Church, 1863–1980, in Light of Its Times*. Charlottesville: First Baptist Church, 1981.

McKivigan, John R. *The War against Proslavery Religion: Abolitionism and the Northern Churches, 1830–1865*. Ithaca: Cornell University Press, 1984.

Mead, Frank S., and Samuel S. Hill. *Handbook of Denominations in the United States*. 11th ed. Revised by Craig D. Atwood. Nashville: Abingdon Press, 2001.

Miller, John Chester. *The Wolf by the Ears: Thomas Jefferson and Slavery*. New York: Free Press, 1977.

Miller, Randall M., Harry S. Stout, and Charles Reagan Wilson, eds. *Religion and the American Civil War*. New York: Oxford University Press, 1998.

Minchinton, Walter, Celia King, and Peter White, eds. *Virginia Slave-Trade Statistics, 1698–1775*. Richmond: Virginia State Library, 1984.

Mitchell, Henry H. *Black Church Beginnings: The Long-Hidden Realities of the First Years*. Grand Rapids, Mich.: Eerdmans, 2004.

Mohr, Clarence L. *On the Threshold of Freedom: Masters and Slaves in Civil War Georgia*. Athens: University of Georgia Press, 1986.

Montgomery, William E. *Under Their Own Vine and Fig Tree: The African-American Church in the South, 1865–1900*. Baton Rouge: Louisiana State University Press, 1993.

Morgan, Edmund. *American Slavery, American Freedom: The Ordeal of Colonial Virginia*. New York: Norton, 1975.

Morgan, Philip D. *Slave Counterpoint: Black Culture in the Eighteenth-Century Chesapeake and Lowcountry*. Chapel Hill: University of North Carolina Press, 1998.

Mount Zion Baptist Church [Charlottesville, Va.]. *A Century of Christian Service: 1867–1967*. Charlottesville: Mount Zion Baptist Church, 1967.

Mullin, Gerald P. *Flight and Rebellion: Slave Resistance in Eighteenth-Century Virginia*. New York: Oxford University Press, 1972.

Murray, Andrew E. *Presbyterians and the Negro—A History*. Philadelphia: Presbyterian Historical Society, 1966.

Nelson, John K. *A Blessed Company: Parishes, Parsons, and Parishioners in Anglican Virginia, 1690–1776*. Chapel Hill: University of North Carolina Press, 2002.

Newman, Richard S. *The Transformation of American Abolitionism: Fighting Slavery in the Early Republic*. Chapel Hill: University of North Carolina Press, 2002.

Noe, Kenneth. *Southwest Virginia's Railroad: Modernization and the Sectional Crisis*. Urbana: University of Illinois Press, 1994.

Noll, Mark A. *The Civil War as a Theological Crisis*. Chapel Hill: University of North Carolina Press, 2006.

Noll, Mark A., David W. Bebbington, and George A. Rawlyk, eds. *Evangelicalism:*

Comparative Studies of Popular Protestantism in North America, the British Isles, and Beyond, 1700–1990. New York: Oxford University Press, 1994.

Oakes, James. *The Ruling Race: A History of American Slaveholders.* New York: Vintage, 1983.

O'Brien, John Thomas, Jr. *From Bondage to Citizenship: The Richmond Black Community, 1865–67.* New York: Garland Publishing, 1990.

O'Brien, Michael. *Conjectures of Order: Intellectual Life and the American South, 1810–1860.* 2 vols. Chapel Hill: University of North Carolina Press, 2004.

Parent, Anthony S., Jr. *Foul Means: The Formation of a Slave Society in Virginia, 1660–1740.* Chapel Hill: University of North Carolina Press, 2003.

Phillips, Ulrich B. *American Negro Slavery: A Survey of the Supply, Employment and Control of Negro Labor As Determined by the Plantation Regime.* 1918. Reprint, Baton Rouge: Louisiana State University Press, 1966.

Pilcher, George William. *Samuel Davies: Apostle of Dissent in Colonial Virginia.* Knoxville: University of Tennessee Press, [1971].

Portnoy, Alisse. *Their Right to Speak: Women's Activism in the Indian and Slave Debates.* Cambridge: Harvard University Press, 2005.

Raboteau, Albert J. *Slave Religion: The "Invisible Institution" in the Antebellum South.* Oxford: Oxford University Press, 1978.

Richey, Russell E. *The Methodist Conference in America: A History.* Nashville: Kingswood Books, 1996.

Robertson, David. *Denmark Vesey: The Buried History of America's Largest Slave Rebellion and the Man Who Led It.* New York: Knopf, 1999.

Robinson, Armstead L. *Bitter Fruits of Bondage: The Demise of Slavery and the Collapse of the Confederacy, 1861–1865.* Charlottesville: University of Virginia Press, 2005.

Rothman, Adam. *Slave Country: American Expansion and the Origins of the Deep South.* Cambridge: Harvard University Press, 2005.

Rountree, Helen C. *Pocahontas's People: The Powhatans of Virginia through Four Centuries.* Norman: University of Oklahoma Press, 1990.

Rubin, Anne Sarah. *A Shattered Nation: The Rise and Fall of the Confederacy, 1861–1868.* Chapel Hill: University of North Carolina Press, 2005.

Rucker, Walter C. *The River Flows On: Black Resistance, Culture, and Identity Formation in Early America.* Baton Rouge: Louisiana State University Press, 2006.

Ruggles, Jeffrey. *The Unboxing of Henry Box Brown.* Richmond: Library of Virginia, 2003.

Ryland, Garnett. *The Baptists of Virginia, 1699–1926.* Richmond: Virginia Baptist Board of Missions and Education, 1955.

Schama, Simon. *Rough Crossings: Britain, the Slaves and the American Revolution.* New York: Harper Collins, 2006.

Schwarz, Philip J. *Migrants against Slavery: Virginians and the Nation.* Charlottesville: University Press of Virginia, 2001.

Schweiger, Beth Barton. *The Gospel Working Up: Progress and the Pulpit in Nineteenth-Century Virginia*. New York: Oxford University Press, 2000.

Schweiger, Beth Barton, and Donald G. Mathews, eds. *Religion in the American South: Protestants and Others in History and Culture*. Chapel Hill: University of North Carolina Press, 2004.

Scott, Anne Firor. *The Southern Lady: From Pedestal to Politics, 1830–1930*. Chicago: University of Chicago Press, 1970.

Scott, James C. *Domination and the Arts of Resistance: Hidden Transcripts*. New Haven: Yale University Press, 1990.

Sellers, Charles G. *The Market Revolution: Jacksonian America, 1815–1846*. New York: Oxford University Press, 1991.

Sensbach, Jon F. *Rebecca's Revival: Creating Black Christianity in the Atlantic World*. Cambridge: Harvard University Press, 2005.

Sernett, Milton C. *Black Religion and American Evangelicalism: White Protestants, Plantation Missions, and the Flowering of Negro Christianity, 1787–1865*. Metuchen, N.J.: Scarecrow Press, 1975.

Shade, William G. *Democratizing the Old Dominion: Virginia and the Second Party System, 1824–1861*. Charlottesville: University Press of Virginia, 1996.

Shanks, Henry T. *The Secession Movement in Virginia, 1847–1861*. 1934. Reprint, New York: AMS Press, 1971.

Sidbury, James. *Ploughshares into Swords: Race, Rebellion, and Identity in Gabriel's Virginia, 1730–1810*. Cambridge: Cambridge University Press, 1997.

Silver, James W. *Confederate Morale and Church Propaganda*. 1957. Reprint, New York: Norton, 1967.

Smith, H. Shelton. *In His Image, But . . . Racism in Southern Religion, 1780–1910*. Durham: Duke University Press, 1972.

Smith, Mark M. *How Race Is Made: Slavery, Segregation, and the Senses*. Chapel Hill: University of North Carolina Press, 2006.

Snay, Mitchell. *Gospel of Disunion: Religion and Separatism in the Antebellum South*. New York: Cambridge University Press, 1993.

Sobel, Mechal. *Trabelin' On: The Slave Journey to an Afro-Baptist Faith*. Westport, Conn.: Greenwood Press, 1979.

——. *The World They Made Together: Black and White Values in Eighteenth-Century Virginia*. Princeton: Princeton University Press, 1987.

Southern, Eileen. *The Music of Black Americans: A History*. New York: Norton, 1971.

Sparks, Randy J. *On Jordan's Stormy Banks: Evangelicalism in Mississippi, 1773–1876*. Athens: University of Georgia Press, 1994.

Stanton, Lucia. *Free Some Day: The African American Families of Monticello*. Charlottesville: Thomas Jefferson Foundation, 2000.

——. *Slavery at Monticello*. Charlottesville: Thomas Jefferson Memorial Foundation, 1996.

Staudenraus, P. J. *The African Colonization Movement, 1816–1865*. 1961. Reprint, New York: Octagon Books, 1980.

Stauffer, John. *The Black Hearts of Men: Radical Abolitionists and the Transformation of Race*. Cambridge: Harvard University Press, 2002.

Stevens, Abel. *History of the Methodist Episcopal Church in the United States of America*. Vol. 2, *The Planting and Training of American Methodism*. New York: Carlton & Porter, 1867.

Stout, Harry S. *The Divine Dramatist: George Whitefield and the Rise of Modern Evangelicalism*. Grand Rapids, Mich.: Eerdmans, 1991.

———. *Upon the Altar of the Nation: A Moral History of the Civil War*. Viking: New York, 2006.

Stowell, Daniel W. *Rebuilding Zion: The Religious Reconstruction of the South, 1863–1877*. New York: Oxford University Press, 1998.

Stroupe, Henry Smith. *The Religious Press in the South Atlantic States, 1802–1865*. Durham: Duke University Press, 1956.

Stuckey, Sterling. *Slave Culture: Nationalist Theory and the Foundations of Black America*. New York: Oxford University Press, 1987.

Sweet, William Warren. *Virginia Methodism: A History*. Richmond: Whittet and Shepperson, 1955.

Takagi, Midori. *"Rearing Wolves to Our Own Destruction": Slavery in Richmond, Virginia, 1782–1865*. Charlottesville: University Press of Virginia, 1999.

Tate, Thad W., Jr. *The Negro in Eighteenth-Century Williamsburg*. Charlottesville: University Press of Virginia, 1965.

Taylor, Jeffrey Wayne. *The Formation of the Primitive Baptist Movement*. Kitchener, Ont.: Pandora Press, 2004.

Tazewell, C. W., ed. *Virginia's Ninth President: Joseph Jenkins Roberts*. Virginia Beach: W. S. Dawson Co., 1991.

Thompson, Ernest Trice. *Presbyterians in the South*. 3 vols. Richmond: John Knox Press, 1973.

Tigert, Jonathan J. *A Constitutional History of American Episcopal Methodism*. Nashville: Publishing House of the M.E. Church, South, 1894.

Tise, Larry. *Proslavery: A History of the Defense of Slavery in America, 1701–1840*. Athens: University of Georgia Press, 1987.

Tupper, H. A. *The First Century of the First Baptist Church of Richmond, Virginia*. Richmond: Carlton McCarthy, 1880.

Turner, Mary. *Slaves and Missionaries: The Disintegration of Jamaican Slave Society, 1787–1834*. Urbana: University of Illinois Press, 1982.

Varon, Elizabeth R. *We Mean to Be Counted: White Women and Politics in Antebellum Virginia*. Chapel Hill: University of North Carolina Press, 1998.

Walker, Clarence E. *A Rock in a Weary Land: The African Methodist Episcopal Church during the Civil War and Reconstruction*. Baton Rouge: Louisiana State University Press, 1982.

Wallenstein, Peter, and Bertram Wyatt-Brown, eds. *Virginia's Civil War*. Charlottesville: University of Virginia Press, 2005.

Walters, Ronald G. *America's Reformers, 1815–1860*. New York: Hill and Wang, 1978.

Webber, Thomas L. *Deep Like the Rivers: Education in the Slave Quarter Community, 1831–1865*. New York: Norton, 1978.

Weeks, Stephen B. *Southern Quakers and Slavery: A Study in Institutional History*. 1896. Reprint, New York: Bergman Publishers, 1968.

White, Blanche Sydnor, ed. *First Baptist Church, Richmond, 1780–1955*. Richmond: Whittet and Shepperson, 1955.

———. *Silhouettes of Baptist Life in Virginia*. Richmond: Women's Missionary Union of Virginia, 1965.

Willey, Waitman T. *An Inside View of the Formation of the State of West Virginia, with Character Sketches of the Pioneers in that Movement*. Wheeling: News Publishing Co., 1901.

Williams, Heather A. *Self-Taught: African American Education in Slavery and Freedom*. Chapel Hill: University of North Carolina Press, 2005.

Williamson, Joel. *A Rage for Order: Black/White Relations in the American South since Emancipation*. New York: Oxford University Press, 1986.

Wills, David W., and Richard Newman, eds. *Black Apostles at Home and Abroad: Afro-Americans and the Christian Mission from the Revolution to Reconstruction*. Boston: G. K. Hall, 1982.

Wilson, Charles Reagan. *Baptized in Blood: The Religion of the Lost Cause, 1865–1920*. Athens: University of Georgia Press, 1980.

Wolf, Eva Sheppard. *Race and Liberty in the New Nation: Emancipation in Virginia from the Revolution to Nat Turner's Rebellion*. Baton Rouge: Louisiana State University Press, 2006.

Wood, John Summer. *The Virginia Bishop: A Yankee Hero of the Confederacy*. Richmond: Garrett & Massie, 1961.

Woolverton, John Frederick. *Colonial Anglicanism in North America*. Detroit: Wayne State University Press, 1984.

Wooster, Ralph A. *The Secession Conventions of the South*. Westport, Conn.: Greenwood Press, 1962.

Wyatt-Brown, Bertram. *The Shaping of Southern Culture: Honor, Grace, and War, 1760–1880s*. Chapel Hill: University of North Carolina Press, 2001.

Young, Jeffrey Robert. *Domesticating Slavery: The Master Class in Georgia and South Carolina, 1670–1837*. Chapel Hill: University of North Carolina Press, 1999.

———, ed. *Proslavery and Sectional Thought in the Early South, 1740–1829*. Columbia: University of South Carolina Press, 2006.

Zilversmit, Arthur. *The First Emancipation: The Abolition of Slavery in the North*. Chicago: University of Chicago Press, 1967.

Alderson, Robert. "Charleston's Rumored Slave Revolt of 1793." In *The Impact of the Haitian Revolution in the Atlantic World*, edited by David P. Geggus, 93–111. Columbia: University of South Carolina Press, 2001.

Ambrose, Douglas. "Of Stations and Relations: Proslavery Christianity in Early National Virginia." In *Religion and the Antebellum Debate over Slavery*, edited by John R. McKivigan and Mitchell Snay, 35–67. Athens: University of Georgia Press, 1998.

Ayers, Edward L. Review of *Slavery and Freedom: An Interpretation of the Old South*, by James Oakes. *Reviews in American History* 19, no. 2 (1991): 194–99.

——. "Virginia History as Southern History: The Nineteenth Century." *Virginia Magazine of History and Biography* 104, no. 1 (1996): 129–36.

Bailey, Kenneth K. "Protestantism and Afro-Americans in the Old South: Another Look." *Journal of Southern History* 41, no. 4 (1975): 451–72.

Beeman, Richard R., and Rhys Isaac. "Cultural Conflict and Social Change in the Revolutionary South: Lunenburg County, Virginia." *Journal of Southern History* 46, no. 4 (1980): 525–50.

Bellot, Leland J. "Evangelicals and the Defense of Slavery in Britain's Old Colonial Empire." *Journal of Southern History* 37, no. 1 (1971): 19–40.

Berlin, Ira. "From Creole to African: Atlantic Creoles and the Origins of African-American Society in Mainland North America." *William and Mary Quarterly*, 3rd ser., 53, no. 2 (1996): 252–88.

——. "Who Freed the Slaves? Emancipation and Its Meaning." In *Union and Emancipation: Essays on Politics and Race in the Civil War Era*, edited by David Blight and Brooks D. Simpson, 105–21. Kent, Ohio: Kent State University Press, 1997.

Billings, Warren M. "The Cases of Fernando and Elizabeth Key: A Note on the Status of Blacks in Seventeenth-Century Virginia." *William and Mary Quarterly*, 3rd ser., 30, no. 3 (1973): 467–74.

Boles, John B. "Evangelical Protestantism in the Old South: From Religious Dissent to Cultural Dominance." In *Religion in the South*, edited by Charles R. Wilson, 13–34. Jackson: University Press of Mississippi, 1985.

——. "The Southern Way of Religion." *Virginia Quarterly Review* 75, no. 2 (1999): 226–47.

Bond, Edward L., and Joan R. Gunderson. "The Episcopal Church in Virginia, 1607–2007." *Virginia Magazine of History and Biography* 115, no. 2 (2007): 163–344.

Bonomi, Patricia U., and Peter R. Eisenstadt. "Church Adherence in the Eighteenth-Century British American Colonies." *William and Mary Quarterly*, 3rd ser., 39, no. 2 (1982): 245–86.

Bradley, David H. "Francis Asbury and the Development of African Churches in America." *Methodist History* 10, no. 1 (1971): 3–29.

Breen, Patrick H. "Contested Communion: The Limits of White Solidarity in Nat Turner's Virginia." *Journal of the Early Republic* 27, no. 4 (2007): 685–703.

Buckley, Thomas E. "Evangelicals Triumphant: The Baptists' Assault on the Virginia Glebes, 1786–1801." *William and Mary Quarterly*, 3rd ser., 45, no. 1 (1988): 33–69.

Burrowes, Carl Patrick. "Black Christian Republicanism: A Southern Ideology in Early Liberia, 1822 to 1847." *Journal of Negro History* 86, no. 1 (2001): 30–44.

Butler, Diana Hochstedt. "The Church and American Destiny: Evangelical Episcopalians and Voluntary Societies in Antebellum America." *Religion and American Culture* 4, no. 2 (1994): 193–219.

Carroll, Kenneth. "Religious Influences on the Manumission of Slaves in Caroline, Dorchester, and Talbot Counties." *Maryland Historical Magazine* 56, no. 2 (1961): 176–97.

Chambers, Douglas B. " 'He is an African But Speaks Plain': Historical Creolization in Eighteenth-Century Virginia." In *The African Diaspora*, edited by Joseph E. Harris, Alusine Jalloh, and Stephen E. Maizlish, 100–133. Austin: Texas A&M University Press, 1996.

Crofts, Daniel W. "Late Antebellum Virginia Reconsidered." *Virginia Magazine of History and Biography* 107, no. 3 (1999): 253–86.

Cromwell, John W. "The Aftermath of Nat Turner's Insurrection." *Journal of Negro History* 5, no. 2 (1920): 208–34.

Daniel, W. Harrison. "Southern Presbyterians and the Negro in the Early National Period." *Journal of Negro History* 58, no. 3 (1973): 291–312.

——. "Virginia Baptists, 1861–1865." *Virginia Magazine of History and Biography* 72 (1964): 94–114.

——. "Virginia Baptists and the Negro in the Antebellum Era." *Journal of Negro History* 56, no. 1 (1971): 1–16.

Dorsey, Bruce. "A Gendered History of African Colonization in the United States." *Journal of Social History* 41, no. 1 (2000): 77–103.

Dreisbach, Daniel L. "Church-State Debate in the Virginia Legislature: From the Declaration of Rights to the Statute for Establishing Religious Freedom." In *Religion and Political Culture in Jefferson's Virginia*, edited by Garrett Ward Sheldon and Daniel L. Dreisbach, 135–65. New York: Rowan & Littlefield, 2001.

Dudley, Virginia, and Rosa Taylor. "History of African and Antioch Baptist Churches." In *Early Churches of Culpeper County, Virginia: Colonial and Antebellum Congregations*, edited by Arthur Dicken Thomas and Angus McDonald Green, 301–4. Culpeper, Va.: Culpeper Historical Society, 1987.

Dunn, Richard S. "Black Society in the Chesapeake, 1776–1810." In *Slavery and Freedom in the Age of the American Revolution*, edited by Ira Berlin and Ronald Hoffman, 49–82. Charlottesville: University Press of Virginia, 1983.

Egerton, Douglas R. "Averting a Crisis: The Proslavery Critique of the American Colonization Society." *Civil War History* 43, no. 2 (1997): 142–56.

——. "'Its Origin is Not a Little Curious': A New Look at the American Colonization Society." *Journal of the Early Republic* 5, no. 4 (1985): 463–80.

——. "'Why They Did Not Preach Up This Thing': Denmark Vesey and Revolutionary Theology." *South Carolina Historical Magazine* 100, no. 4 (1999): 298–317.

Elsinger, Ellen. "The Brief Career of Rufus W. Bailey, American Colonization Society Agent in Virginia." *Journal of Southern History* 71, no. 1 (2005): 39–74.

Essig, James David. "A Very Wintry Season, Virginia Baptists and Slavery, 1785–1797." *Virginia Magazine of History and Biography* 88, no. 2 (1980): 170–85.

Fabricant, Daniel. "Thomas R. Gray and William Styron: Finally, a Critical Look at the 1831 Confessions of Nat Turner." *American Journal of Legal History* 37, no. 3 (1993): 332–61.

Faust, Drew Gilpin. "Christian Soldiers: The Meaning of Revivalism in the Confederate Army." *Journal of Southern History* 53, no. 1 (1987): 63–90.

——. "The Civil War Soldier and the Art of Dying." *Journal of Southern History* 67, no. 1 (2001): 3–38.

——. "Evangelicalism and the Meaning of the Proslavery Argument: The Reverend Thornton Stringfellow of Virginia." *Virginia Magazine of History and Biography* 85, no. 1 (1977): 3–17.

Fisher, Miles Mark. "Lott Cary, the Colonizing Missionary." *Journal of Negro History* 7, no. 4 (1922): 380–418.

Foster, Gaines M. "Guilt over Slavery: A Historiographical Analysis." *Journal of Southern History* 56, no. 4 (1990): 665–94.

Fountain, Daniel L. "Christ in Chains: Slavery's Negative Impact on the Conversion of African American Slaves." In *Affect and Power: Essays on Sex, Slavery, Race, and Religion in Appreciation of Winthrop D. Jordan*, edited by David J. Libby, Paul Spickard, and Susan Ditto, 84–104. Jackson: University Press of Mississippi, 2005.

Frederickson, George M. "The Skeleton in the Closet." *New York Times Review of Books*, 2 Nov. 2002, 61–66.

Freeberg, Ernest A., III. "Why David Barrow Moved to Kentucky." *Virginia Baptist Register* 32 (1993): 1617–27.

Freehling, William W. "'Absurd' Issues and the Causes of the Civil War: Colonization as a Test Case." In *The Reintegration of American History: Slavery and the Civil War*, 138–57. New York: Oxford University Press, 1994.

——. "The Founding Fathers and Slavery." *American Historical Review* 77, no. 1 (1972): 81–93.

——. "Virginia's (Reluctant) Decision to Secede: Slavery or States Rights or ?" Douglass Southall Freeman and Southern Intellectual History Conferences. 21 Feb. 2002.

Frey, Sylvia R. "Between Slavery and Freedom: Virginia Blacks in the American Revolution." *Journal of Southern History* 49, no. 3 (1983): 375–98.

Gallay, Allan. "The Origins of Slaveholders' Paternalism: George Whitefield, the Bryan Family, and the Second Great Awakening in the South." *Journal of Southern History* 53, no. 3 (1987): 369–94.

Gardner, Robert G. "Virginia Baptists and Slavery, 1759–1790," pt. 1. *Virginia Baptist Register* 24 (1985): 1212–20.

——. "Virginia Baptists and Slavery, 1759–1790," pt. 2. *Virginia Baptist Register* 25 (1986): 1257–74.

Genovese, Eugene D., and Elizabeth Fox-Genovese. "The Divine Sanction of Social Order: Religious Foundations of the Southern Slaveholders' World View." *Journal of the American Academy of Religion* 55 (Summer 1987): 211–33.

——. "The Religious Ideals of Southern Slave Society." In *The Evolution of Southern Culture*, edited by Numan V. Bartley, 14–27. Athens: University of Georgia Press, 1988.

Gimelli, Louis B. "Louisa Maxwell Cocke: An Evangelical Plantation Mistress in the Antebellum South." *Journal of the Early Republic* 9, no. 1 (1989): 53–71.

Gomez, Michael A. "Muslims in Early America." *Journal of Southern History* 60, no. 4 (1994): 671–710.

Hamilton, Philip. "Revolutionary Principles and Family Loyalties: Slavery's Transformation in the St. George Tucker Household of Early National Virginia." *William and Mary Quarterly*, 3rd ser., 55, no. 4 (1998): 531–56.

Harding, Vincent. "Religion and Resistance among Antebellum Slaves, 1800–1860." In *African-American Religion: Interpretive Essays in History and Culture*, edited by Timothy E. Fulop and Albert J. Raboteau, 107–30. New York: Routledge, 1997.

Harlow, Luke E. "Neither Slavery nor Abolitionism: James M. Pendleton and the Problem of Christian Conservative Antislavery in 1840s Kentucky." *Slavery and Abolition* 27, no. 3 (2006): 367–89.

——. "Religion, Race, and Robert J. Breckinridge: The Ideology of an Antislavery Slaveholder, 1830–1860." *Ohio Valley History* 6, no. 3 (2006): 1–24.

Hartzell, Joseph C. "Methodism and the Negro in the United States." *Journal of Negro History* 8, no. 3 (1923): 301–15.

Harvey, Paul. "African American Spirituals." In *Religions of the United States in Practice*, vol. 1, edited by Colleen McDannell, 138–49. Princeton: Princeton University Press, 2001.

Helo, Ari, and Peter Onuf. "Jefferson, Morality, and the Problem of Slavery." *William and Mary Quarterly*, 3rd ser., 60, no. 3 (2003): 583–614.

Hill, Samuel, Jr. "The South's Two Cultures." In *Religion and the Solid South*, edited by Hill, 24–56. Nashville: Abingdon Press, 1972.

Huston, James L. "The Experiential Basis of the Northern Antislavery Impulse." *Journal of Southern History* 56, no. 4 (1990): 609–40.

Irons, Charles. "And All These Things Shall be Added unto You: The First African Baptist Church, Richmond, 1841–1865." *Virginia Cavalcade* 47, no. 1 (1998): 26–35.

——. "Believing in America: Faith and Politics in Early National Virginia." *American Baptist Quarterly* 21, no. 4 (2002): 396–412.

——. "The Spiritual Fruits of Revolution: Disestablishment and the Rise of the Virginia Baptists." *Virginia Magazine of History and Biography* 109, no. 2 (2001): 159–86.

Jackson, Harvey H. "Hugh Bryan and the Evangelical Movement in Colonial South Carolina." *William and Mary Quarterly*, 3rd ser., 43, no. 4 (1986): 594–614.

Jackson, Luther P. "The Religious Development of the Negro in Virginia from 1760 to 1860." *Journal of Negro History* 16, no. 2 (1931): 168–239.

Jernegan, Marcus W. "Slavery and Conversion in the American Colonies." *American Historical Review* 21, no. 3 (1916): 504–27.

Johnson, Michael P. "Denmark Vesey and His Co-Conspirators." *William and Mary Quarterly*, 3rd ser., 53, no. 4 (2001): 915–76.

Johnson, William Courtland. " 'A Delusive Clothing': Christian Conversion in the Antebellum Slave Community." *Journal of Negro History* 82, no. 3 (1997): 295–311.

Jones, Jerome W. "The Established Virginia Church and the Conversion of Negroes and Indians, 1620–1760." *Journal of Negro History* 46, no. 1 (1961): 12–23.

Joyner, Charles. " 'Believer I Know': The Emergence of African-American Christianity." In *African-American Christianity*, edited by Paul E. Johnson, 18–46. Berkeley: University of California Press, 1994.

Kroll-Smith, Stephen J. "Transmitting a Revival Culture: The Organizational Dynamic of the Baptist Movement in Colonial Virginia, 1760–1777." *Journal of Southern History* 50, no. 4 (1984): 551–68.

Kulikoff, Alan. "The Colonial Chesapeake: Seedbed of Antebellum Southern Culture?" *Journal of Southern History* 45, no. 4 (1979): 513–40.

——. "The Origins of Afro-American Society in Tidewater Maryland and Virginia, 1700–1790." *William and Mary Quarterly*, 3rd ser., 35, no. 2 (1978): 226–59.

——. "A 'Prolifick' People: Black Population Growth in the Chesapeake Colonies, 1700–1790." *Southern Studies: An Interdisciplinary Journal of the South* 16, no. 4 (1977): 391–428.

——. "Uprooted Peoples: Black Migrants in the Age of the American Revolution, 1790–1820." In *Slavery and Freedom in the Age of the American Revolution*, edited by Ira Berlin and Ronald Hoffman, 143–71. Charlottesville: University Press of Virginia, 1983.

Lambert, Frank. " 'I Saw the Book Talk': Slave Readings of the First Great Awakening." *Journal of Negro History* 77, no. 4 (1992): 185–98.

Lee, Jean Butenhoff. "The Problem of Slave Community in the Eighteenth-Century Chesapeake." *William and Mary Quarterly*, 3rd ser., 43, no. 3 (1986): 333–61.

MacMaster, Richard K. "Liberty or Property? The Methodists Petition for Emancipation in Virginia, 1785." *Methodist History* 10 (1971): 44–55.

Mathews, Donald G. "Charles Colcock Jones and the Southern Evangelical Crusade to Form a Biracial Community." *Journal of Southern History* 41, no. 3 (1975): 299–320.

——. " 'We Have Left Undone Those Things Which We Ought to Have Done': Southern Religious History in Retrospect and Prospect." *Church History* 67, no. 2 (1998): 305–25.

Matthews, Albert. "Notes on the Proposed Abolition of Slavery in Virginia in 1785." *Publications of the Colonial Society of Massachusetts* 6 (1899, 1900): 370–80.

McDaniel, Ralph C. "Elder John Alderson, Jr., and the Greenbrier Church." *Virginia Baptist Register* 7 (1968): 307–19.

Menard, Russell. "From Servants to Slaves: The Transformation of the Chesapeake Labor System." *Southern Studies: An Interdisciplinary Journal of the South* 16, no. 4 (1977): 355–90.

Minkema, Kenneth P. "Jonathan Edwards on Slavery and the Slave Trade." *William and Mary Quarterly*, 3rd ser., 54, no. 4 (1997): 823–34.

Moore, John S. "John William Jones (1836–1909): Historian of the Confederacy." *Virginia Baptist Register* 31 (1992): 1596–1611.

Morgan, Philip D., and Michael L. Nicholls. "Slaves in Piedmont Virginia, 1720–1790." *William and Mary Quarterly*, 3rd ser., 46, no. 2 (1989): 211–51.

Najar, Monica. "Citizens of the Church: Baptist Churches and the Construction of Civil Order in the Upper South, 1765–1815." *American Baptist Quarterly* 16, no. 3 (1997): 206–18.

Noll, Mark A. "The American Revolution and Protestant Evangelicalism." *Journal of Interdisciplinary History* 23, no. 3 (1993): 615–38.

Onuf, Peter S. "Every Generation Is an 'Independent Nation': Colonization, Miscegenation, and the Fate of Jefferson's Children." *William and Mary Quarterly*, 3rd ser., 57, no. 1 (2000): 153–70.

Payne, Rodger M. "New Light in Hanover County: Evangelical Dissent in Piedmont, Virginia, 1740–1755." *Journal of Southern History* 61, no. 4 (1995): 665–94.

Poe, William A. "Lott Cary: Man of Purchased Freedom." *Church History* 39, no. 1 (1970): 49–61.

Pybus, Cassandra. "Jefferson's Faulty Math: The Question of Slave Defections in the American Revolution." *William and Mary Quarterly*, 3rd ser., 62, no. 2 (2005): 243–64.

Quist, John W. "Slaveholding Operatives of the Benevolent Empire: Bible, Tract, and Sunday School Societies in Antebellum Tuscaloosa, Alabama." *Journal of Southern History* 62, no. 3 (1996): 481–526.

Raboteau, Albert J., and David W. Wills, with Randall K. Burkett, Will B. Gravely, and James Melvin Washington. "Retelling Carter Woodson's Story: Archival Sources for Afro-American Church History." *Journal of American History* 77, no. 1 (1990): 183–99.

Ragosta, John. "Fighting for Freedom: Virginia Religious Dissenters' Fight for Religious Liberty during the American Revolution." *Virginia Magazine of History and Biography* (forthcoming).

Richards, Jeffrey H. "Samuel Davies and the Transatlantic Campaign for Slave Literacy in Virginia." *Virginia Magazine of History and Biography* 111, no. 4 (2003): 333–78.

Richey, Russell E. "Francis Asbury, James O'Kelly, and Methodism's Growing Pains." *Virginia United Methodist Heritage: Bulletin of the Virginia Conference Historical Society* 27, no. 2 (2001): 24–40.

Robson, David W. "'An Important Question Answered': William Graham's Defense of Slavery in Post-Revolutionary Virginia." *William and Mary Quarterly*, 3rd ser., 37, no. 4 (1980): 644–52.

Rose, Willie Lee. "The Domestication of Domestic Slavery." In *Slavery and Freedom*, edited by William Freehling, 18–36. New York: Oxford University Press, 1982.

Saillant, John. "The American Enlightenment in Africa: Jefferson's Colonizationism and Black Virginians' Migration to Liberia, 1776–1840." *Eighteenth-Century Studies* 31, no. 3 (1998): 261–82.

———. "Lemuel Haynes and the Revolutionary Origins of Black Theology, 1776–1801." *Religion and American Culture* 2, no. 1 (1992): 79–102.

Schmidt, Fredrika Teute, and Barbara Ripel Wilhelm. "Early Proslavery Petitions in Virginia." *William and Mary Quarterly*, 3rd ser., 30, no. 1 (1973): 133–46.

Schwarz, Philip J. "Virginia." In *Macmillan Encyclopedia of World Slavery*, vol. 2, edited by Paul Finkelman and Joseph Miller, 935–37. New York: Simon & Schuster Macmillan, 1998.

Schweninger, Loren. "Prosperous Blacks in the South, 1790–1880." *American Historical Review* 95, no. 1 (1990): 31–56.

Shick, Tom W. "A Quantitative Analysis of Liberian Colonization from 1820 to 1843 with Special Reference to Mortality." *Journal of African History* 12, no. 1 (1971): 45–59.

Sidbury, James. "Saint Domingue in Virginia: Ideology, Local Meanings, and Resistance to Slavery, 1790–1800." *Journal of Southern History* 63, no. 3 (1997): 531–52.

Slaughter, Jane Chapman. "Reverend Philip Slaughter: A Sketch." *William and Mary College Quarterly Historical Magazine*, 2nd ser., 16, no. 3 (1936): 435–56.

Sluiter, Engel. "New Light on the '20. and Odd Negroes' Arriving in Virginia, August 1619." *William and Mary Quarterly*, 3rd ser., 54, no. 2 (1997): 395–98.

Smith, Elwyn A. "The Role of the South in the Presbyterian Schism of 1837–38." *Church History* 29, no. 1 (1960): 44–63.

Smith, Timothy L. "Slavery and Theology: The Emergence of Black Christian Consciousness in Nineteenth-Century America." *Church History* 41, no. 4 (1972): 497–512.

Snay, Mitchell. "Review Essay: Civil War Religion—Needs and Opportunities." *Civil War History* 49, no. 4 (2003): 388–94.

Spangler, Jewel L. "Becoming Baptists: Conversion in Colonial and Early National Virginia." *Journal of Southern History* 67, no. 2 (2001): 243–86.

——. "Proslavery Presbyterians: Virginia's Conservative Dissenters in the Age of Revolution." *Journal of Presbyterian History* 78, no. 2 (2000): 111–24.

——. "Salvation Was Not Liberty: Baptists and Slavery in Revolutionary Virginia." *American Baptist Quarterly* 13, no. 3 (1994): 221–36.

Sparks, Randy J. "Religion in the Pre–Civil War South." In *A Companion to the American South*, edited by John B. Boles, 156–75. Malden, Mass.: Blackwell, 2002.

Stanton, Lucia. "The Other End of the Telescope: Jefferson through the Eyes of His Slaves." *William and Mary Quarterly*, 3rd ser., 57, no. 1 (2000): 139–52.

Stanwood, Owen. "Captives and Slaves: Indian Labor, Cultural Conversion, and the Plantation Revolution in Virginia." *Virginia Magazine of History and Biography* 114, no. 4 (2006): 434–63.

Stowell, Daniel W. " 'We Have Sinned, and God Has Smittten Us!': John H. Caldwell and the Religious Meaning of Confederate Defeat." *Georgia Historical Quarterly* 78, no. 1 (1994): 1–38.

Thomas, Arthur Dicken, Jr. " 'O That Slavery's Curse Might Cease,' Ann Randolph Meade Page: The Struggle of a Plantation Mistress to Become an Emancipator." *Virginia Seminary Journal* 45, no. 5 (1993): 56–61.

Thompson, Evelyn Wingo. "Luther Rice's Early Travels in Virginia." *Virginia Baptist Register* 19 (1980): 893–909.

Thornton, John. "On the Trail of Voodoo: African Christianity in Africa and the Americas." *The Americas* 44 (1988): 261–78.

Tyler-McGraw, Marie. "Richmond Free Blacks and African Colonization, 1816–1832." *Journal of American Studies* 21, no. 2 (1987): 207–24.

——. " 'The Prize I Mean Is the Prize of Liberty': A Loudoun County Family in Liberia." *Virginia Magazine of History and Biography* 97, no. 3 (1989): 355–74.

Vaughan, Alden T. "Blacks in Virginia: A Note on the First Decade." *William and Mary Quarterly*, 3rd ser., 29, no. 3 (1972): 469–78.

Wells, Robert V. "Household Size and Composition in the British Colonies in America, 1675–1775." *Journal of Interdisciplinary History* 4, no. 4 (1975): 43–570.

Wight, Willard E. "The Churches and the Confederate Cause." *Civil War History* 6, no. 4 (1960): 361–73.

Willis, John C. "From the Dictates of Pride to the Paths of Righteousness: Slave Honor and Christianity in Antebellum Virginia." In *The Edge of the South: Life in Nineteenth-Century Virginia*, edited by Edward L. Ayers and John C. Willis, 37–55. Charlottesville: University Press of Virginia, 1991.

Wilson, G. R. "The Religion of the American Negro Slave: His Attitude toward Life and Death." *Journal of Negro History* 8, no. 1 (1923): 41–71.

Witmer, Andrew. "Race, Religion, and Rebellion: Black and White Baptists in Albemarle County, Virginia, during the Civil War." In *Crucible of the Civil War: Virginia from Secession to Commemoration*, edited by Edward L. Ayers, Gary W. Gallagher, and Andrew J. Torget, 136–64. Charlottesville: University of Virginia Press, 2006.

Wood, Peter. "'Jesus Christ Has Got Thee at Last': Afro-American Conversion as a Forgotten Chapter in Eighteenth-Century Southern Intellectual History." *Bulletin of the Center for the Study of Southern Culture and Religion* 3, no. 3 (1979): 1–7.

Wyatt-Brown, Bertram. "The Abolitionists' Postal Campaign of 1835." *Journal of Negro History* 50, no. 4 (1965): 227–38.

Theses and Dissertations

Albert, Peter Joseph. "The Protean Institution: The Geography, Economy, and Ideology of Slavery in Post-Revolutionary Virginia." Ph.D. diss., University of Maryland, 1976.

Allen, Carlos Richard. "The Great Revival in Virginia, 1783–1812." M.A. thesis, University of Virginia, 1984.

Anderson, John Logan. "The Presbyterians and Augusta Parish, 1738–1757: A Political and Social Analysis." M.A. thesis, University of Virginia, 1985.

Breen, Patrick H. "Nat Turner's Revolt: Rebellion and Response in Southampton County, Virginia." Ph.D. diss., University of Georgia, 2005.

Feight, Andrew Lee. "The Good and the Just: Slavery and the Development of Evangelical Protestantism in the American South, 1700–1830." Ph.D. diss., University of Kentucky, 2001.

Fountain, Daniel. "Long on Religion, Short on Christianity: Slave Religion, 1830–1870." Ph.D. diss., University of Mississippi, 1999.

French, Scot. "Remembering Nat Turner: The Southampton Slave Uprising in Social Memory, 1831 to the Present." Ph.D. diss., University of Virginia, 1999.

Iaccarino, Anthony. "Virginia and the National Contest over Slavery in the Early Republic, 1780–1833." Ph.D. diss., University of California, Los Angeles, 1999.

Jeffus, David Bret. "Invitation to a Carnival of Death: The Virginia State Convention of 1861." M.A. thesis, University of Virginia, 1994.

Liebman, Rosanna, and Matilda McQuaid. "A Study of Ten Black Baptist Churches in Albemarle County." For Professor Edward Lay, University of Virginia School of Architecture, n.d.

Lindman, Janet Moore. "A World of Baptists: Gender, Race, and Religious Community in Pennsylvania and Virginia, 1689–1825." Ph.D. diss., University of Minnesota, 1994.

Lupold, Dorothy M. "Methodism in Virginia from 1772–1784." M.A. thesis, University of Virginia, 1949.

Najar, Monica. "Evangelizing the South: Gender, Race, and Politics in the Early Evangelical South, 1765–1815." Ph.D. diss., University of Wisconsin, Madison, 2000.

Obrion, Catherine Greer. "'A Mighty Fortress Is Our God': Building a Community of Faith in the Virginia Tidewater, 1772–1845." Ph.D. diss., University of Virginia, 1997.

Opper, Peter Kent. "The Mind of the White Participant in the African Colonization

Movement, 1816–1840." Ph.D. diss., University of North Carolina, Chapel Hill, 1972.

Raper, Derris Lea. "The Effects of David Walker's Appeal and Nat Turner's Insurrection on North Carolina." M.A. thesis, University of North Carolina, Chapel Hill, 1969.

Scott, Julius Sherrard, III. "The Common Wind: Currents of Afro-American Communication in the Era of the Haitian Revolution." Ph.D. diss., Duke University, 1986.

Digital Resources

Costa, Tom, et al. "The Geography of Slavery in Virginia." Tom Costa and the Rector and Visitors of the University of Virginia, 2003. <http://www.vcdh.vir ginia.edu/gos/index.html>.

"The Ground Beneath Our Feet: Reconfiguring Virginia." George H. Gilliam and William G. Thomas, 1998. <http://www.vahistory.org/reconfiguring/index .html>.

Library of Congress and the Library of Virginia. "Early Virginia Religious Petitions." American Memory Project. <http://memory.loc.gov/ammem/collections/ petitions/>.

"Loudoun Museum: Historic Leesburg, Virginia." <http://www.loudounmuseum .org/home.html>.

Rowe, Linda H. "A Biographical Sketch of Gowan Pamphlet." Colonial Williamsburg Foundation, 2006–7. <http://research.history.org/Historical_Research/ Research_Themes/ThemeReligion/Gowan.cfm>.

University of North Carolina at Chapel Hill. "Documenting the American South." University Library, University of North Carolina at Chapel Hill, 2004. <http:// docsouth.unc.edu/index>.

University of Virginia, Geospatial and Statistical Data Center. "Historical Census Browser." Rector and Visitors of the University of Virginia, 2004. <http://fisher .lib.virginia.edu/collections/stats/histcensus/>.

Virginia Center for Digital History. "The Valley of the Shadow: Two Communities in the American Civil War." Rector and Visitors of the University of Virginia, 2006. <http://valley.vcdh.virginia.edu/>.

INDEX

Black ministers, 45–52, 81–82, 104–9, 252–56; and fear of insurrection, 51, 143–44, 145–56; and opposition to restrictions, 158–60, 184–86

Black Presbyterian churches, 38, 46, 52, 107

Blair, James, 32, 34

Branch, Cyrus, 158–59

Brand, Benjamin, 118, 127, 128–30, 165

Broaddus, Andrew, 173–75

Broadnax, William Henry, 149, 151

Broad Run Baptist Church, 39

Brooks, Charlotte, 2, 108

Brown, Henry Box, 1, 107, 159, 205

Buck Marsh Baptist Church, 46, 48, 84–85

Burns, Anthony, 185, 208

Cabell, William D., 237

Campbell (slave), 108

Capers, William, 142, 168, 177, 181–82, 198

Caribbean, 50–52

Carmichael, Peter, 217

Cary, Lott, 17, 98, 106–7, 120–30, 194

Cassells, Samuel, 179, 191

Catechisms, 12, 54, 107, 176, 177, 179–80, 187

Catholicism, 3, 24

Chappawamsic Baptist Church, 93, 109–11, 186, 191, 248

Charleston convention, 199–200

Charlottesville, 250–54

Chavis, John, 106, 158–59

Chesapeake Rebellion of 1730, 31–32

Church discipline, 47–48, 70–71, 83–87, 93, 109

Church membership: estimated state totals, 1–2, 3–5, 83, 109, 204, 249, 261, 265, 280 (n. 2), 315 (n. 102); 322 (n. 9), 324 (n. 1); and adherence, 4, 280 (n. 10); Baptists, 40, 52–53, 55, 180, 202; Methodists, 42, 53, 55, 75–

76, 82, 156, 201, 227–28, 236, 240, 248, 291 (n. 3); individual churches, 180, 189, 201, 250–51; Presbyterians, 196; Episcopalians, 203; AME and AME Zion, 258

Class, 42–43, 288 (n. 74)

Cocke, John Hartwell, 128, 148, 161, 164–65, 171, 179, 193

Coercion, 222–24, 230–34, 237

Coke, Thomas, 62–63, 74

Colonization, 12, 19, 116–30; antiblack nature of post–Nat Turner, 139, 150–51, 164–65, 193–95. *See also* American Colonization Society; Cary, Lott; Liberia

Committee of Correspondence, 172–73

"Confessions" of Nat Turner, 136–38

Conversion: and slavery, 19, 24–25, 27–32, 39; first black converts, 42, 52–53, 61–62

Crane, William, 121, 128–29

Curse of Ham, 25, 65

Dabney, Robert L., 213, 222, 242, 259

Davies, Samuel, 10, 35–39, 43; legacy of, 57, 90, 107

Davis, Noah, 114, 185, 313 (n. 59)

Debate. *See* Ban

Denominational schisms, 12, 20, 195–98, 314 (n. 87)

Dissenters, 23, 35–40, 44, 55, 285 (n. 18)

Dover Association, 72, 85, 86, 88, 89, 95, 99, 113, 157; black members of, 81–82, 92–93, 183, 202

Dromgoole, Edward, 67–68, 80

Ecclesiastical Autonomy, 45, 66, 74–76, 110–12, 296 (n. 70)

Ecumenism. *See* Interdenominational cooperation

Elam Baptist Church, 82, 183

Slave trade, 11; Atlantic, 24, 33, 283 (n. 7); internal, 99, 108, 124–25, 304 (n. 86)

Smith, James L., 113, 160

Smith, William A., 177, 198, 214–17, 228

Sobel, Mechal, 11, 15, 48, 58

Society for Promoting Religious Knowledge, 37

Society for the Propagation of the Gospel, 30

South Carolina: Whitefield visits, 34–35; black evangelicals in, 45, 51–52, 104, 109, 132, 141–42; and mission to the slaves, 167, 177, 199–201; secession of, 222, 233

Southampton County, Va. *See* Black Creek Baptist Church; Raccoon Swamp Baptist Church; Southampton Insurrection; Turner, Nat

Southampton Insurrection, 19, 133–38, 139–68 passim; published reactions to, 143–44, 153–54; private reactions to, 144–46; African American reactions to, 159–60. *See also* Turner, Nat

Southern nationalism, 10, 211, 219–20, 223, 279 (n. 1); and support for Confederacy, 234–46, 260

South Quay Baptist Church, 47–48

Stringfellow, Thornton, 214–15, 217, 249

Surry County, Va., 64–65, 75–77

Sussex County, Va., 144

Synod of Virginia, 79, 179, 200; black ministers in, 106, 259

Taylor, Fairfax, 254

Teague, Collin, 120–25

Thornwell, James Henley, 16, 196, 213, 218

Todd, John, 35, 36

Tucker, John Randolph, 243–46

Tucker, Nathaniel Beverly, 223–24

Tucker, St. George, 60–61, 88

Turner, Nat, 12, 19, 132, 133–69 passim; revolt of, 133–38; memory of, 158, 160, 257. *See also* Southampton Insurrection

Uncle Jack (slave), 47, 104–5, 108

Unionism, 211–14, 218–30

Upper King and Queen Baptist Church, 39, 61

Vesey, Denmark, 98, 141–42

Virginia Colonization Society, 151

Virginia Conference, 82, 156–57, 201, 248

Walker, David, 132, 145, 171

Western Virginia (divergent interests of), 5, 60–61, 146–48, 230, 235–36

Whitefield, George, 2, 33–35, 57, 89

William and Mary (college), 30, 41, 60, 163

Williamsburg, 34, 41. *See also* William and Mary; Williamsburg African Church

Williamsburg African Church: founding of, 48–49, 51; interactions of with whites, 81–82, 143; shut down after Southampton Insurrection, 152, 183; reorganization of, 202

Wolf, Eva, 45, 64

Women: free, 39, 92–93, 148–49, 192, 242–43; enslaved, 50, 110, 113–14